FAMILY LAW IN AMERICA

Family Law in America

SANFORD N. KATZ

OXFORD
UNIVERSITY PRESS

OXFORD
UNIVERSITY PRESS

Great Clarendon Street, Oxford OX2 6DP

Oxford University Press is a department of the University of Oxford.
It furthers the University's objective of excellence in research, scholarship,
and education by publishing worldwide in

Oxford New York

Auckland Bangkok Buenos Aires
Cape Town Chennai Dar es Salaam Delhi Hong Kong Istanbul
Karachi Kolkata Kuala Lumpur Madrid Melbourne Mexico City Mumbai
Nairobi São Paulo Shanghai Tokyo Toronto

Oxford is a registered trade mark of Oxford University Press
in the UK and in certain other countries

Published in the United States
by Oxford University Press Inc., New York

British Library Cataloguing in Publication Data
Data available

Library of Congress Cataloging in Publication Data
Data available

ISBN 0-19-926434-1

1 3 5 7 9 10 8 6 4 2

Typeset by Newgen Imaging Systems (P) Ltd., Chennai, India
Printed in Great Britain
on acid-free paper by
T. J. International Ltd. Padstow, Cornwall

To
My Family

Acknowledgments

From time to time colleagues at the International Society of Family Law would ask me to suggest a book on family law in the United States. I invariably recommended Professor Homer H. Clark's textbook, *Domestic Relations in the United States*, because it is a classic. However, they wanted a book that covered the basic principles of contemporary family law but was less encyclopedic, and one that bridged the gap between scholarship and practice. One friend suggested that because my career has from time to time taken me into both these worlds, I should be the one to write the book. This is it.

I began this book while I was on leave from Boston College Law School during two different years, first while I was a Visiting Fellow at All Souls College, Oxford and later as a Visiting Fellow at Pembroke College, Oxford. I wish to thank the Warden and Fellows of All Souls College and the Master and Fellows at Pembroke College for the opportunity they gave me to spend my complete time working on this book. In England I have been extremely fortunate in learning a great deal about English family law from Dame Elizabeth Butler-Sloss, Dame Ruth L. Deech, Stephen M. Cretney, and John M. Eekelaar. I am grateful to all of them for their friendship and for their many kindnesses to me. For making my leaves possible, I wish to thank Rev. William B. Neenan, S.J., Vice President of Boston College, who has been extraordinarily supportive of my research.

The Deans of Boston College Law School, beginning with Rev. Robert F. Drinan, S.J., followed by Richard G. Huber, Daniel R. Coquillette, Aviam Soifer, and John H. Garvey have been enthusiastic in their support of my scholarship through the years, and I wish to thank them. In addition I would like to thank Mr. and Mrs. Darald Libby for their generous support. It is an honor to hold the chair that bears their name.

I should like to thank specially my colleagues and friends, Mark S. Brodin, Mary Sarah Bilder, and Thomas C. Kohler for commenting on various parts of this book and making helpful suggestions with the text. For providing me with references and responding to my questions on areas of their specialization, I particularly would like to thank other colleagues at Boston College Law School: Reginald Alleyne, Hugh J. Ault, Charles H. Baron, Robert Bloom, Sharon Beckman, Alfred Brophy (now at the University of Alabama Law School), George Brown, Michael Cassidy, Scott FitzGibbon, Phyllis Goldfarb, Kent Greenfield, Frank Herrmann, S.J., Ruth-Arlene W. Howe, Joseph Liu, Ray Madoff, Zygmunt Plater, James R. Repetti, Aviam Soifer, Mark Spiegel, Judith Tracy, and Herbert Wilkins. For library assistance I would like to thank Karen Beck, Joan Shear, and Mark Sullivan. I also wish to thank Helen Drinan, Donna McDermott, and Paul Marzagalli for their help. For providing me with assistance in many ways since becoming my secretary, I want to express my profound gratitude to Alice Lyons, who worked beyond the call of duty in preparing this manuscript for publication.

Through the years I have been fortunate in having Boston College Law School students assist me in research, some of which has found its way into this book. For all their efforts, I wish to acknowledge the help of Tara L. Blackman, Dennis E. Baden, John M. Creedon, Brian R. Patterson, Brendan W. Piper-Smyer, Sophocles M. Sophocles, and Carla A. Salvucci. I also wish to thank Christopher McCain for his work on the editing process. Special thanks are owed to James P. Dowden who was of great assistance in reading and editing earlier drafts of some chapters.

I have benefited from the work of family law scholars, particularly that of Carol Bruch, Homer H. Clark, Jr., Ira Mark Ellman, Mary Ann Glendon, Charles P. Kindregan, Jr., Frances Olsen, Linda Silberman, J. Eric Smithburn, Walter Wadlington, Lynn Wardle, and Barbara Bennett Woodhouse. While a Fellow at Yale Law School, I was fortunate in studying with Joseph Goldstein, Jay Katz, and Anna Freud, who later invited me to the Hampstead Clinic in London where I deepened my understanding of the child development issues that affect child custody. The influence of Goldstein, Katz, and Freud can be seen throughout this book. Of all the family law scholars, however, it is my collaborator, Walter O. Weyrauch, to whom I owe a special debt of gratitude. For close to forty years I have benefited not only from Walter's friendship but also from his original perspectives on family law and jurisprudence. I also wish to thank my friend of over fifty years, Jerome A. Barron, for his support and for sharing with me his special insights on the impact of constitutional law on domestic relations. I wish to acknowledge others who have shared their particular views on their specialties with me: my good friends David J. Barron on local government law; Julie Ginsburg on adoption; Edward M. Ginsburg on judicial and court matters; Monroe L. Inker on the practice of family law; Barbara Okun on the psychological aspects of child custody; Elbert L. Robertson on the economics of the assignment of marital property; my son, Daniel R. Katz, on appellate practice in the field of child protection; and my wife, Joan R. Katz, on the psychological issues relating to divorce and child protection.

For over twenty years I have been a member of the seminar faculty of the Council of Juvenile and Family Court Judges in Reno, Nevada. Mrs. Virginia H. Cain was instrumental in introducing me to the Council. My experience in teaching judges at seminars and workshops for the Council has enriched my own scholarship. Through my association with the Council I have gained special insight into the various levels of judicial decision-making and how courts really work. For association with the Council, I wish to thank Virginia, now retired, and Joy Ashton, who invited me to help shape the educational curriculum. Dean James Toner of the Council has been my friend for many years, and I wish to thank him for all his support.

Some of the material in this book has appeared elsewhere but it has been substantially revised and rewritten. I wish to thank the JOURNAL OF CONTEMPORARY HEALTH LAW & POLICY for their permission to reproduce material from '*That They May Thrive' Goal of Child Custody: Reflections on the Apparent Erosion of the Tender Years Presumption and the Emergence of the Primary Caretaker Presumption*, in Vol. 8, Spring 1992. Material from *Historical Perspective and Current Trends in the Legal Process of Divorce*, in Vol. 4, No. 1, Spring 1994 of THE FUTURE OF CHILDREN is adapted and revised with the permission of The David and Lucile Packard Foundation. I would like to thank John Wiley & Sons for permission to use some material from *The Judge and Child Custody Decision-Making in the United States*, in FRONTIERS OF FAMILY LAW (Part II, 2d ed, 1995), edited by David Pearl and Ros Pickford. I am grateful to the Hart Publishing Company for permission regarding *Parental Rights and Social Responsibility in American Child Protection Law*, in THE CHANGING FAMILY— FAMILY FORMS & FAMILY LAW (1998), edited by John Eekelaar and Thandabantu Nhlapo. Thanks to the American Bar Association for permission to reprint *Prologue to the Millennium Issue*, Vol. 33, No. 3, Fall 1999 of the FAMILY LAW QUARTERLY; and to Oxford University Press for its permission regarding, *Dual Systems of Adoption in the United States* and *Individual Rights and Family Relationships* that appeared in CROSS CURRENTS—FAMILY LAW AND POLICY IN THE UNITED STATES AND ENGLAND (2000), edited by Sanford N. Katz, John Eekelaar, and Mavis Maclean.

I also wish to thank the National Conference of Commissioners on Uniform State Laws, which has granted me permission to reprint the Uniform Child Custody Jurisdiction Act, the Uniform Child Custody Jurisdiction and Enforcement Act, the Uniform Marriage and Divorce Act, the Uniform Pre-Marital Agreement Act, the Uniform Putative and Unknown Fathers Act, and the Uniform Parentage Act presented in the Appendix.

My first book was dedicated to my wife, Joan and my two sons, Daniel and Andrew. In the ensuing thirty years, my family has grown to include two daughters-in-law, Denise and Meg, and a granddaughter, Lucia. This book is affectionately dedicated to all of them and to my two sisters, Eleanor and Beverly, as well as to the memory of my mother and father, Rebecca and Jacob Katz. Each in her and his own way has made my journey through life a wonderfully enriching experience. And it is, as T. S. Eliot has said, 'the journey not the arrival matters'.

Sanford N. Katz
Darald and Juliet Libby Professor of Law

Boston College Law School

Contents

Table of Cases   xv

Introduction   1

1. FRIENDSHIP, MARRIAGE-LIKE RELATIONSHIPS,
   AND INFORMAL MARRIAGE   10
   Introduction   10
   Contract Cohabitation   11
   Registered Domestic Partnership   17
   Informal Marriage   23
     Common Law Marriage and De Facto Marriage   23
     Procedural Marriage and Other Informal Marriages
     for Limited Purposes   27
     Putative Marriage and Marriage by Estoppel   29
   Prenuptial Agreements   30

2. MARRIAGE   35
   Introduction   35
   The State's Role in Establishing the Marriage Relationship   37
   Freedom to Marry as a Fundamental Human Right   38
   The State's Efforts to Limit Marriage   40
     Annulment   42
     Age   45
     Prisoner's Marriage   46
     Mental Competence   47
     Incestuous Marriage   48
     Sex   52
       Transsexualism   52
       Same Sex   53
     Number (Bigamy)   58
   Maintaining the Marriage Relationship: From Inequality
   to Equality in Marriage   60
   Property Ownership and Control   62
   Regulating the Marriage through Private Contracts:
   Postnuptial Agreements   65
     Interspousal Immunity   65
     Personal Safety   67
     Privacy, Equality, and Autonomy: Sexual Intimacy in
       Marriage   69

　　　　Sexual Intimacy Outside of Marriage   72
　　　　Individual Rights and Equality in Marriage   75

3. DIVORCE   76
　　Introduction   76
　　Divorce Procedure   78
　　　　Fault   78
　　　　Residency   80
　　　　No-Fault Divorce   82
　　　　Distribution of Economic Resources   86
　　　　Property Distribution   87
　　　　Alimony   94
　　　　Child Support   99
　　Child Custody   102
　　　　Judicial Discretion and Codification   102
　　　　The Primary Caretaker Preference   104
　　　　The Best Interests of the Child   106
　　　　The Lawyer for the Child and the Guardian ad Litem 108
　　　　A Child-Focused Inquiry   109
　　　　Alternative Custodial Dispositions   111
　　　　Joint or Shared Custody   111
　　　　Continuity of a Relationship with Both Parents: Relocation   113
　　　　Unilateral Removal of the Child from the Jurisdiction   117
　　　　Continuity of a Relationship with Others   118
　　Divorce and Decision-Making   123
　　　　Summary Dissolution   123
　　　　Summary Process and Divorce by Registration   124
　　　　Mediation   125
　　The Future of Divorce   128

4. CHILD PROTECTION   131
　　Introduction   131
　　The Concept of Punishment   133
　　The Definition of Child Abuse   137
　　The Role of the Federal Government   139
　　Model Mandatory Child Abuse Reporting Statute   140
　　Other Model Acts   143
　　Child Abuse Prevention and Treatment Act of 1974   144
　　The Adoption Assistance and Child Welfare Act of 1980 145
　　Adoption and Safe Families Act of 1997   146
　　Child Protection Process   147
　　DeShaney *v.* Winnebago County Department of Social Services   149
　　Following *DeShaney*   151

5. ADOPTION   153

Introduction   153
Voluntary System   157
  The Role of Personal Autonomy   157
  Independent and Agency Adoptions   158
  Surrogacy   161
  Open Adoption: Visitation Rights for Birth Parents 167
  Open Adoption: Access to Adoption Records   168
  Placement   171
  Step-parent and Second Parent Adoptions   174
Involuntary System   176
The Role of the Federal Government and the
Absence of Personal Autonomy   176
  Placement   179
  Open Adoption   180
The Future of Adoption   181
Appendix   183
  Uniform Marriage and Divorce Act   185
  Uniform Pre-Marital Agreement Act   201
  Uniform Parentage Act   204
  Uniform Putative and Unknown Fathers Act   225
  Uniform Child Custody Jurisdiction Act   230
  Uniform Child Custody Jurisdiction and Enforcement Act 240
  Parental Kidnapping Prevention Act   258

Index   261

Table of Cases

Adams v. Howerton, 486 F. Supp. 1119 (D. Cal. 1980) 57
Adoption of B.L.V.B. & E.L.V.B., 628 A.2d 1271 (Vt. 1993) 17, 175
Adoption of Child by D.M.H., Matter of, 641 A.2d 235 (N.J. 1994) .. 166
Adoption of Gomez, In re, 424 S.W.2d 656 (Tex. Civ. App. 1967) 39
Adoption of K.L.P., In re, 735 N.E.2d 1071 (Ill. App. 2000) 148
Adoption of Tammy, In re, 619 N.E.2d 315 (Mass. 1993) 17, 175
ALMA Society Inc. v. Mellon, 601 F.2d 1238 (2d Cir.) 169
Arnold v. Arnold, 553 S.W.2d 255 (Ark. 1977) 32
Avitzur v. Avitzur, 446 N.E.2d 136 (N.Y. 1983) 99
Baby M, Matter of, 537 A.2d 1227 (N. J. 1988) 165–7
Baehr v. Lewin, 852 P.2d 44 (Haw. 1993) 20, 38, 53, 176
Baehr v. Miike, 950 P.2d 1234 (Haw. 1997) 20, 54, 55
Baker v. Nelson, 191 N.W.2d 185 (Minn. 1971) 53
Baker v. State of Vermont, 744 A.2d 880 (Vt. 1999) 20, 55–6, 57, 176
Ball v. Ball, 36 So. 2d 172 (Fla. 1948) 34
Barker v. Baker, 499 S.E.2d 503 (S.C. Ct. App. 1998) 24
Beagle v. Beagle, 678 So. 2d 1271 (Fla. 1996) 175
Bilowit v. Dolitsky, 304 A.2d 774 (N.J. Super. 1973) 44
Bivians' Estate, In re, 652 P.2d at 753 (N.M. App. 1982) 24
Blixt v. Blixt, 774 N.E.2d 1052 (Mass. 2002) 122–3
Bowers v. Hardwick, 478 U.S. 186 (1986) 53, 73–4
Bronfman v. Bronfman, 229 A.D.2d 314 (N.Y.A.D. 1996) 65
Brooks v. Parkerson, 454 S.E.2d 769 (Ga. 1995) 175
Burns v. Burns, 560 S.E.2d 47 (Ga. Ct. App. 2002) 22
Burr v. Board of County Comm'rs, 491 N.E.2d 1101 (Ohio 1986) 160
Buttrick, In re, 597 A.2d 74 (N.H. 1991) 26
Caban v. Mohammed, 441 U.S. 380 (1979) 154
Carrafa, In re, 77 Cal. App. 3d 788 (Cal.App. 1978) 46
Carbetta v. Carbetta, 438 A.2d 109 (Conn. 1980) 44
Catalano v. Catalano, 170 A.2d 726 (Conn. 1961) 51
Clark v. Clark, 202 P.2d 990 (Okla. 1949) 31
Cleveland Bd. of Educ. v. LaFleur, 414 U.S. 632 (1974) 72
Coates v. Watts, 622 A.2d 25 (D. C. 1993) 24
Commonwealth of Mass. v. Stowell, 449 N.E.2d 357 (Mass. 1983) 57
Conklin v. MacMillan Oil Co., 557 N.W.2d 102 (Iowa Ct. App. 1996) . 24
Cornnell v. Francisco, 898 P.2d 831 (Wash. 1995) 15
Currier v. Doran, 23 F. Supp. 2d 1277 (1998) 151
Curtis v. Curtis, 71 Mass. (5 Gray) 535 (1856) 157
Dakin v. Dakin, 384 P.2d 639 (Wash.1963) 96

Dalip Singh Bir's Estate, In re, 188 P.2d 499 (Cal. App. 1948) 59–60
DeMatteo v. *DeMatteo*, 762 N.E.2d 797 (Mass. 2002) 31–2
De Santo v. *Barnsley*, 476 A.2d 952 (Pa. Super. 1984) 53
DeShaney v. *Winnebago County Dept. of*
  Social Services, 489 U.S. 189 (1989) 132, 149–50, 151, 152
Dean v. *D.C.*, 653 A.2d 307 (D.C. 1995) 57
Doe v. *Sundquist*, 106 F.3d 702 (6th Cir. 1997) 170
Doe v. *Sundquist*, 1997 W.L. 354786 (Tenn. Cir. Ct. May 2, 1997) . . . 170
Doe v. *Sundquist*, 2 S.W.3d 919 (Tenn. 1999) 170
Downs v. *Downs*, 574 A.2d 156 (Vt. 1990) 91
Eisenstadt v. *Baird*, 405 U.S. 438 (1972) 72
Elden v. *Sheldon*, 758 P.2d 582 (Cal. 1988) 16
Elkus v. *Elkus*, 572 N.Y.S.2d 901 (A.D. 1 Dept. 1991) 89, 115
Estate of Alcorn, Matter of, 868 P.2d 629 (Mont. 1994) 24
Estate of Bivians, In re, 652 P.2d 744 (N.M. 1982) 24–5
Estate of Carroll, Matter of, 749 P.2d 571 (Okla. Ct. App. 1987) 24
Estate of Hall, In re, 588 N.E.2d 203 (Ohio Ct. App. 1990) 25
Everett v. *Everett*, 660 So. 2d 599 (Ala. Civ. App. 1995) 114
F. A. Marriage License, 4 Pa. D. & C.2d 1(1955) 40–1
Fadgen v. *Lenkner*, 365 A.2d 147 (Pa. 1976) 72–3
Ford v. *Johnson*, 899 F. Supp. 227 (1995) 151
Frambach v. *Dunihue*, 419 So. 2d 1115 (Fla. Dist. Ct. App. 1982) 60
Fung Dai Kim Ah Leong v. *Lau Ah Leong*, 27 F.2d 582 (9th Cir. 1928) . 28
Gault, In re, 387 U.S. 1 (1967) 108
Goldin v. *Goldin*, 426 A.2d 410 (Md. App. 1981) 26
Goldman, In re, 121 N.E.2d 843 (Mass. 1954) 171
Goldman v. *Goldman*, 554 N.E.2d 1016 (Ill. App. 1990) 99
Goodridge v. *Dept. of Pub. Health*, 2002 WL.1299135
  (Mass. Super. 2002) 21, 56, 57, 58
Gottsegen v. *Gottsegen*, 492 N.E.2d 1133 (Mass. 1986) 97–8
Griswold v. *Connecticut*, 381 U.S. 479 (1965) 70, 72
Hawk v. *Hawk*, 855 S.W.2d 573 (Tenn. 1993) 175
Herndon v. *Tuhey*, 857 S.W.2d 203 (Mo. 1993) 175
Hewitt v. *Hewitt*, 394 N.E.2d 1204 (Ill. 1979) 13
Holder v. *Polanski*, 544 A.2d 852 (N. J. 1988) 114
Hudson v. *Hudson*, 350 P.2d 596 (Okla. 1960) 31
Inhabitants of Milford v. *Inhabitants of Worcester*, 7 Mass.
  (1 Tyng) 48 56–7
Israel v. *Allen*, 577 P.2d 762 (Colo. 1978) 49
Jarrett v. *Jarrett*, 400 N.E.2d 421 (Ill. 1979) 13, 80
Jarrett v. *Jarrett*, 449 U.S. 927(1980) 80, 110
Jones v. *Callahan*, 501 S.W.2d 588 (Ky. Ct. App. 1973) 53
Jones v. *Daly*, 176 Cal. Rptr.130 (Cal. Ct. App. 1981) 15
Juvenile Appeal, In re, 189 Conn. 276 (1983) 148

Kennedy v. *Damron*, 268 S.W.2d 22 (Ky. 1954) 26

K.H. Through Murphy v. *Morgan*, 914 F.2d 846 (1990) 151

King v. *King*, 828 S.W.2d 630 (Ky. 1992) 175

Lalli v. *Lalli*, 430 U.S. 762 (1977) 19

Langan v. *St. Vincent's Hospital*, N.Y. Sup. Ct., Nassau Cty.,
   No. 11618/02, 29 Fam. L. Rep. (BNA) 1267 (April 22, 2003) . . . 16, 22

Larson v. *Larson*, 192 N.E.2d 594 (Ill. App. 1963) 47–8

Lehr v. *Robertson*, 463 U.S. 248 (1983) 154

Lovato v. *Evans*, 1 Fam. L. Rep. 2848 (1975) 45

Loving v. *Virginia*, 388 U.S. 1 (1987) 36, 38–9, 46

Lutz v. *Schneider*, 563 N.W.2d 90 (N.D. 1997) 32

M.T. v. *J.T.*, 355 A.2d 204 (N.J.Super 1976) 52–3

MacGregor v. *Unemployment Ins. Appeals Bd.*, 689 P.2d 453
   (Cal. 1984) 16

Mahoney v. *Mahoney*, 453 A.2d 527 (N.J. 1982) 91

Marriage of Cargill, In re, 843 P.2d 1335 (Colo. 1993) 24

Marriage of Francis, In re, 919 P.2d 776 (Colo. 1996) 172

Marriage of Greenwald, In re, 454 N.W.2d 34
   (Wis. Ct. App. 1990) 31

Marriage of Grubb, In re, 745 P.2d 661 (Colo. 1987) 89

Marriage of Lindsey, 678 P.2d 328 (Wash. 1984) 15

Maxwell, In re, 151 N.E.2d 484 (N.Y. 1958) 171

Marvin v. *Marvin*, 557 Pd 106 (Cal. 1976) 13–14, 29, 31

Marvin v. *Marvin*, 176 Cal. Reptr. 555 (Cal. Ct. App.1981) 14

May's Estate, In re, 114 N.E.2d 4 (N.Y. 1953) 51

May v. *Anderson*, 345 U.S. 528 (1953) 82

Maynard v. *Hill*, 125 U.S. 190 (1888) 35, 36, 39, 58

McClelland v. *McClelland*, 318 So. 2d 160 (Fla. Dist. Ct. App. 1975) . . . 83

McKee-Johnson v. *Johnson*, 444 N.W.2d 259 (Minn. 1989) 31

Medley v. *Strong*, 558 N.E.2d 244 (Ill. App.Ct. 1990) 16

MEW v. *MLB*, 4 Pa. D. & C 3d 51 (1977) 49–50

Meyer v. *Nebraska*, 262 U.S. 390 (1923) 119

Michael H. v. *Gerald D*, 491 U.S. 110 (1989) 166

Michaud v. *Wawruck*, 551 A.2d 738 (Conn. 1988) 181

M.L.B. v. *S.L.J.*, 519 U.S. 102 (1996) 39

Morgan v. *Morgan*, 81 Misc. 2d 616 (N.Y. Sup. 1975) 96

Newburgh v. *Arrigo*, 443 A.2d 1031 (N.J. 1982) 29–30

Norman v. *Unemployment Insurance Appeals Board*, 663 P.2d 904
   (Cal. 1983) 16

O'Brien v. *O'Brien*, 489 N.E.2d 712 (N.Y. 1985) 90

Orr v. *Orr*, 440 U.S. 268 (1979) 94

Pacelli v. *Pacelli*, 725 A.2d 565 (N.J. 1999) 65

Palmore v. *Sidoti*, 466 U.S. 429 (1984) 110

Parham v. *J. R.*, 442 U.S. 584 (1979) 119

Parkinson v. J. & S. Tool Co., 313 A.2d 609 (N.J. 1974) 27–8

Peck v. Peck, 30 N.E. 74 (Mass. 1892) 12

Peirce v. Peirce, 994 P.2d 193 (Utah 2000) 65

Pence v. Cole, 205 P. 172 (Okla. 1922) 30

Perez v. Lippold, 198 P.2d 17 (Cal. 1948) 39

Peters v. Peters, 103 P. 219 (Cal. 1909) 66

Petrarca v. Castrovillari, 448 A.2d 1286 (R.I. 1982) 24

Pickens v. Pickens, 490 So. 2d 872 (Miss. 1986) 15

Pierce v. Society of Sisters, 268 U.S. 510 (1925) 65, 119

Pikula v. Pikula, 374 N.W.2d 705 (Minn. 1985) 104, 106

Planned Parenthood v. Casey, 505 U.S. 833 (1992) 71

Ponder v. Graham, 4 Fla. 23 (1851) 35, 36

Posik v. Layton, 695 So. 2d 759 (Fla. Dist. Ct. App. 1997) 15

Posner v. Posner, 233 So. 2d 381 (Fla. 1970) 30–1

Powell v. Rogers, 496 F.2d 1248 (9th Cir. 1974) 28

Powell v. State, 510 S.E.2d 18 (Ga. 1998) 73

Prince v. Massachusetts, 321 U.S. 158 (1944) 119

Quilloin v. Walcott, 434 U.S. 246 (1978) 154

Quinn v. Quinn, 512 A.2d 848 (R.I. 1986) 88

Rayburn ex rel. Rayburn v. Hogue, 241 F.3d 1341 (2001) 151

R.R. v. M.H., 426 Mass. 501 (1998) 162

Reynolds v. Reynolds, 85 Mass. 605 (1862) 43–4

Reynolds v. U.S., 98 U.S. 145 (1878) 59

Roe v. Wade, 410 U.S. 113 (1973) 70–2

Romer v. Evans, 517 U.S. 620 (1996) 73

Russell v. Russell, 865 S.W.2d 929 (Tex. 1993) 24

Santi v. Santi, 633 N.W.2d 312 (Iowa 2001) 121–2

Santosky v. Kramer, 455 U.S. 745 (1982) 119

Secretary of the Comm. v. City Clerk of Lowell, 366 N.E.2d 717
  (Mass. 1977) 64

Sees v. Baber, 377 A.2d 628 (N.J. 1977) 166

Self v. Self, 376 P.2d 65 (Cal. 1962) 66

Seymour v. Seymour, 433 A.2d 1005 (Conn. 1980) 108

Shapiro v. Thompson, 394 U.S. 618 (1969) 169

Short v. Hotaling, 225 N.Y.S.2d 53 (N.Y. Sup. Ct. 1962) 46

Shuraleff v. Donnelly, 817 P.2d 764 (Or. Ct. App. 1991) 15

Simeone v. Simeone, 581 A.2d 162 (Pa. 1990) 31

Singer v. Hara, 522 P.2d 1187 (Wash App. 1974) 53, 57

Smith v. Lewis, 530 P.2d 589 (Cal. 1975) 87, 127

So. Carolina Dept. of Soc. Serv. v. Father & Mother, 366 S.E.2d 40
  (S.C.1988) 135

Stanley v. Illinois, 405 U.S. 645 (1972) 153–4

Stanton v. Stanton, 421 U.S. 7 (1975) 45

State v. Jones, 95 N.C. 588 (1886) 133

State v. Rhodes, 61 N.C. (Phil. Law) 349 (1868) 134

Stringer v. Stringer 689 So.2d 194 (Ala. Civ. App. 1997) 24

Staudenmayer v. Staudenmayer, 714 A.2d 1016 (Pa. 1998) 25–6

Stuart v. Board of Sup'rs of Elections for Howard County, 295
A.2d 223 (Md. Ct. App.1972) 63–4

Suter v. Artist M., 503 U.S. 347 (1992) 178

Sydney v. Pingree, 564 F. Supp. 412 (S.D. Fla. 1982) 65

Talley v. Harris, 182 P.2d 765 (Okla. 1947) 31

Taylor By and Through Walker v. Ledbetter, 818 F.2d 791
(11th Cir. 1987) 151

Thompson v. Thompson, 642 A.2d 1160 (R.I. 1994) 89

Tropea v. Tropea, 665 N.E.2d 145 (N.Y. 1996) 115–6

Troxel v. Granville, 530 U.S. 57 (2000) 119–23, 175

Turner v. Safley, 482 U.S. 78 (1987) 46–7

U.S. v. Morrison 529 U.S. at 617–18 (1740) 67

Vanderbilt v. Vanderbilt, 354 U.S. 416 (1957) 82

Vandever v. Industrial Commission, 714 P.2d 866
(Ariz. Ct. App. 1985) 26

Von Eff v. Azicri, 720 So. 2d 510 (Fla. 1998) 175

Walker v. Hildenbrand, 410 P.2d 244 (Or. 1966) 26

Warner v. Warner, 283 P.2d 931 (Idaho 1955) 68

Warren v. State, 336 S.E.2d 221 (Ga. 1985) 68

Washington v. Clucksberg, 521 U.S. 702 (1997) 119

Watt v. Watt, 971 P.2d 608 (Wyo. 1999) 114

Webster v. Reproductive Health Services, 492 U.S. 490 (1989) 71

Weller v. Dept. of Social Services for City of Baltimore,
901 F.2d 387 (1990) 151

West v. Barton-Malow Company, 230 N.W.2d 545 (Mich. 1975) 28

Whyte v. Blair, 885 P.2d 791 (Utah 1994) 24

Wilbur v. DeLapp, 850 P.2d 1151 (Or. Ct. App. 1993) 15

Wilcox v. Trautz, 693 N.E.2d 141 (Mass. 1998) 15

Wilkins v. Zelichowski, 140 A.2d 65 (N.J. 1958) 45

Williams v. State of N. C., 325 U.S. 226 (1945) 82

Williams v. Witt, 235 A.2d 902 (N.J. Super. 1967) 44

Wisconsin v. Yoder, 406 U.S. 205 (1972) 119

Zablocki v. Redhail, 434 U.S. 374 (1978) 40

Introduction

Family law came of age during the last half of the twentieth century. Earlier, in practice, scholarship, and legal education, it was given little attention or respect. Perhaps the reason for the low status of family law practice, defined narrowly as domestic relations and almost exclusively concerned with divorce, was that it dealt with human conflicts and real people in distress, not legal abstractions. It should also be remembered that divorce in the United States, opposed by some religions, was a taboo subject, and the status of a divorced person carried with it a social stigma. Therefore, it was natural that the reputation of divorce lawyers would suffer. Major law firms rarely accepted divorce cases, leaving them to be handled by lawyers in small firms or single practitioners.

Even though family law was almost exclusively statutory, in court it had the reputation of being essentially discretionary law. Interpretations of phrases like 'in the best interests of the child' or 'cruel and abusive conduct' were thought to be more dependent on the mood of the judge than on case law. A negative criticism of judicial decisions in family law cases was that they were fact-driven—as if decisions in other kinds of cases were not. Appeals in family law cases were infrequent so that the trial judge was basically the final decision-maker. It was rare for the U.S. Supreme Court to hear a family law case.

In mid-century family law was stagnant. Little law reform occurred in the 1940s. For one thing, few legislators were thinking about family law during World War II and immediately afterwards. In 1945 the country was concerned with rebuilding its economy and providing opportunities for veterans to enter colleges and return to their jobs.

During the decades of the 1940s and early 1950s, law schools were not educating students to practice family law. Indeed, if a course in family law was offered at all, it was a basic course, often taught by a part-time lecturer. The major textbook that covered most areas of family law was Professor J. Warren Madden's *Handbook of the Law of Persons and Domestic Relations* published in 1931. The casebook that dominated the field was the 1952 edition of *Cases and Other Materials on Domestic Relations*, edited by Albert C. Jacobs, President of Trinity College and Julius Goebel, Jr., Professor of Law at Columbia University Law School. Unlike the law faculties at British and European universities, which had renowned family law scholars, and where family law was considered a serious intellectual study, American law schools had very few major family law professors. Mostly they were senior scholars educated in Europe like Max Rheinstein of the University of Chicago Law School, or with strong European ties, like Karl Llewellyn, first at Columbia and later at the University of Chicago Law School. Both of these scholars had interests in other disciplines, like sociology and anthropology, which they related to family law.

The period of major changes in family law began in the late 1950s and early 1960s. The latter decade and the one following might be considered the most important era in the last half of the twentieth century for family law practice and scholarship. The American Bar Association recognized family law as a specialty in 1958 and established the Family Law Section. Judge Paul W. Alexander of Ohio, the father of therapeutic divorce, was its first chairman.

Although it is hard to discern any consistent national family policy, during the late 1950s and 1960s in both state capitals and in Washington, D.C. there seemed to have been a willingness to look at the family in realistic terms and to address issues that had been dormant for years. The civil rights movement left its imprint on family law with respect to law reform and in raising consciousness about the protection of individual rights. At the same time through the efforts of governmental programs and private foundations, people of limited income were given access to legal services, which provided lawyers for family law cases in court as well as for representation at federal and state administrative hearings. A number of cases that have made major changes in family law were the result of the work of legal services lawyers.

The legislative movement to recodify state family law, particularly divorce law, began in mid-century. For example, attempts to change the divorce law in New York can be traced back to 1945. New York's recognition of adultery as the sole ground for divorce prompted lawyers to engage in deceptive practices. In response to the reform efforts of leaders of the New York Bar, the New York State Legislature broadened the grounds for divorce in 1966, thus bringing New York into line with other enlightened jurisdictions.

In 1969 California became the first state to enact a divorce law without fault-based grounds. As state after state began to enact no-fault divorce laws, the emphasis in divorce litigation shifted from proving grounds for a fault-based divorce to rethinking the purpose of alimony, and determining who should be awarded what property, and who should be the custodian of the children. The concept of rehabilitative alimony grew out of the discretionary powers of the judge in the 1970s and was adopted by courts, which began to award alimony as a temporary device to aid the dependent spouse (usually the wife) in becoming self-supporting. This was a major change in alimony, which was a method of spousal support after divorce, frequently for the wife's life, based on her needs and the husband's ability to pay. During that same decade, states began to examine their residency requirements for divorce jurisdiction, and slowly these requirements were shortened bringing some uniformity in the country and lessening the need for a couple to leave their home state to seek a divorce elsewhere.

An important influence on divorce reform was the efforts of the Commissioners on Uniform State Laws. That private agency was established in 1891 to bring uniformity to certain areas of law. Through the years it has drafted a number of uniform laws dealing with family law issues including marriage, divorce, adoption, premarital agreements, child custody jurisdiction, and parentage in cases of illegitimacy. I have included those referred to in the text in the Appendix. Even though not all states have followed the Commissioners' lead, the Acts nonetheless provide useful guides in determining the direction of the law or what lawyers, judges, and scholars think the law ought to be.

The Commissioners had been working on divorce law for seventy-five years before the Uniform Marriage and Divorce Act was promulgated in 1970. It was adopted in part only by eight states, yet it succeeded in alerting lawyers, legislators, and judges that the time had come to replace the old order with new ideas about marriage, divorce, and child custody. Some state bar associations responded by backing changes in their divorce laws and using the Uniform Marriage and Divorce Act as a model.

The Act introduced the concepts of irretrievable breakdown as a ground for no-fault divorce and equitable division of property, and it enumerated factors for determining both. Although it can be said that listing factors that judges must consider in assigning property in divorce or in any other area of family law decision-making is a legislative attempt to limit a judge's discretion and in a way to control judicial power, there are advantages both for lawyers and judges. Factors are enormously helpful to lawyers in organizing the amorphous amount of material in child custody and matrimonial property litigation. Also, they can provide a judge with a checklist for monitoring the presentation of evidence during trial as well as for writing findings of fact.

The hesitation of some lawyers to advocate the adoption of the Act may well have been based on their belief that it would end the kind of divorce practice to which they had become accustomed and basically complicate what was to them a simple process. After all, under the title theory of property subscribed to in many states, he who held property got it. What was simpler than that? With equitable division of property, lawyers would have to ask the following questions in preparing a divorce case for settlement or litigation: What is separate and what is marital property? What factors should be used to determine the characterization? What is its value? When should it be valued? Little did lawyers realize when equitable distribution was first introduced how complex it would be, and that they would need help from other professions like accountants, pension and actuarial experts, and real estate, business, and other valuators.

In child custody also, the Act brought clarity. The best interests of the child, which had been and continues to be the basis for determining custody decisions in any number of legal contexts was often criticized for being vague. The Act did more than just state that a decision should be in the best interests of the child. It provided factors that judges were to consider in awarding custody. This meant that judges were required to focus on, among other matters, the environment in which the child was raised, the child's relationship with his or her parents, friends, and others, as well as inquiring into the child's own wishes and the mental and physical health of those involved in the child's life. Just as experts in other fields were important in marital property issues, they were also necessary in child custody. Thus, psychiatrists, social workers, psychologists, educators, and pediatricians were consultants in child custody cases, both to lawyers in preparation of their cases and to judges in reaching decisions.

At the time some states were reviewing their divorce laws and procedure, they were also considering court reform. Humanizing the divorce process by utilizing alternatives to the adversarial system in an informal setting became a goal. Judge Paul W. Alexander had accomplished such procedural and court reforms in Toledo, Ohio in the 1950s, but that has long been forgotten. In a way, Judge Alexander was ahead of his time. Today we speak of negotiation, arbitration, and mediation as if they were entirely new concepts. Lawyers educated in rules of procedure and evidence and trained to argue find it difficult to think of alternative methods of dispute resolution in family matters. But as litigation becomes extremely expensive, as it is today in major metropolitan areas, middle-class divorcing couples may be forced to choose mediation for purely economic considerations and failing that, to represent themselves in court, now seen more and more.

The Bar's reluctance to promote the establishment of family courts known for their informality and often providing social services to litigants may be based on lawyers' belief that to do so would be retrogressive. To some, it would represent a return to the days of lax procedure, and perhaps turn courts into social service agencies. In addition, the Bar may believe that divorce practice, especially with regard to marital property, is so complex that only the techniques derived from the formal adversary process are appropriate. Yet, the Bar has been more receptive to the establishment of juvenile courts perhaps, because their jurisdiction deals with the behavior of children, not with economic matters.

In 1960s and 1970s, through the efforts of child welfare specialists at the Children's Bureau of the then U.S. Department of Health, Education, & Welfare, the federal government focused on the condition of children. In the early 1960s, that agency set up a working group to study the findings of a Denver, Colorado pediatrician, Dr. C. Henry Kempe, and those of the Los Angeles Police Department dealing with children who had been physically abused. The product of that group's deliberations was the Model Mandatory Child Abuse Reporting Act.

Looking back, it is hard to imagine that developing a child abuse reporting act would be controversial, but it was. Family privacy was deeply rooted in American life and law. To invade it was thought to be an infringement on fundamental parental rights. Requiring certain professional people like pediatricians and nurses to report abuse would be a breach of confidential relationships. Little thought then was given to mandating priests, rabbis, or ministers to report abuse under any circumstances. Every aspect of the Act was criticized, from who was to report, what was to be reported, and the penalties for not reporting. It took time for the concept of reporting child abuse to an appropriate state agency to be accepted, but eventually it was. The national concern for the protection of children in their homes in the 1960s raised the issue of the safety of others in the family. The reporting laws, greatly expanded from the original model law, and now found in all jurisdictions, may have laid the foundation for family violence laws that were to follow.

A curious paradox may have resulted from the enactment of laws meant to protect children. Mandated reporting of child abuse caused a significant increase in the foster care rolls, a disproportionate number of whom were Black children. Was this just the result of overzealous child welfare workers whose first response was removal? Or, had abuse been occurring, but just had not been detected? For whatever reason, the impact of state intervention on the family during the decade of the 1960s was the most disruptive for poor urban Black families. It has been said that their economic status made these families, forced to use public rather than private facilities, more highly visible, and thus more vulnerable. All the major problems of the poor, especially the lack of employment and educational opportunities, inadequate housing and health care, were stressors on urban Black families. But these families suffered the additional burden of racial and social prejudices within their communities and in the child protection system.

During the 1970s and 1980s, the federal government began to suggest solutions to the problem of foster care drift. At that time the idea of 'permanency planning' was first promoted and ultimately later became part of child protection practice and law. The Children's Bureau supported development of two model acts, the Model Act to Free Children for Permanent Placement and the Subsidized Adoption Act. They were designed to overcome barriers identified as preventing children from being adopted and to encourage suitable couples, especially foster parents, to adopt 'hard to place' children. During these decades, the plethora of negative social and economic conditions in many urban Black communities worsened. But there was no comprehensive national family policy that acknowledged the depth of the problems and need for long-range planning to solve them. The piecemeal approach was, and is, essentially applying small bandages to a major social wound.

The federal government made more attempts to deal with child protection during the mid-1970s, 1980s, and 1990s. To that end it undertook a number of initiatives by proposing laws for Congress to enact which had the effect of basically taking control of state child protection systems through federal financing. The Acts reflected a policy of encouraging state agencies to try to prevent intervention and removal of children from their parents, but if removal occurred to make reasonable efforts to reunite families by providing social and other services to parents in need of a range of services. It promulgated regulations for foster care, to which states had to adhere if they wished to secure funding for their foster care and adoption programs. In addition it introduced the concept of child support guidelines for states to adopt in order to bring some sense of uniformity and fairness to the system, once again using economic incentives as a method of encouraging the use of the guidelines and at the same time reducing the number of children dependent on public funds. State legislatures did enact laws that set down child support guidelines and a number of alternative methods of collecting support, usually from delinquent fathers.

During the 1960s and 1970s the law school world began to realize the importance of family law issues. Professor Homer H. Clark, Jr. completed his first edition of *The Law of Domestic Relations in the United States* in 1968, a brilliant textbook, which was national in scope and analytical in approach. That work and the second edition, published in 1987, have greatly stimulated family law scholarship and have been widely cited in appellate opinions. Casebooks for law school courses appeared, mostly influenced by Jacobs and Goebel, at least in the order of the presentation of cases and materials. A book that broke new ground, *The Family and the Law*, written by Professor Joseph Goldstein and Dr. Jay Katz, a law professor and psychoanalyst of Yale Law School, was published in 1965. Their twelve-hundred page volume departed from the traditional family law casebook in providing an overall theoretical framework in which they asked fundamental questions about substantive family law and the legal process that handles family law issues. Influenced by the approach of Yale law professor Harold Lasswell and the language of bankruptcy, they divided the family law process into questions dealing with the establishment, administration, and reorganization of family law relationships. In addition, Professor Goldstein and Dr. Katz brought Freudian psychology to bear on family law. The seeds of *Beyond the Best Interests of the Child*, written by Professor Joseph Goldstein, Dr. Albert Solnit, and Anna Freud in 1973 were planted in *The Family and the Law* eight years earlier.

A non-legal work that has had an influence on child custody judicial decision-making is *Beyond the Best Interests of the Child*, which applied Anna Freud's theory of child development to decisions about child placement. The authors' focus was on a child's physical and emotional well-being rather than on other values or on parental rights. Based on years of clinical experience, they concluded that a child needs continuity of care with an adult who wants the child and can provide him or her with affection, stimulation, nurturing, and an assurance of safety and protection. In a divorce case where the parents cannot resolve their child's custody, Goldstein, Solnit, and Freud wrote that the judge's job is to determine who, among the claimants for custody, can fulfill those needs. They introduced new terms like 'psychological parent' and 'least detrimental alternative', which have become part of the legal lexicon. Their emphasis on continuity of care has been thought to be the basis for the primary caretaker doctrine, which has found support in some jurisdictions. The idea of minimizing modifications in child custody cases is reflected in the Uniform Child Custody Jurisdiction Act.

By 1970 the complexities of family law were becoming even more visible. During the decades of the 1960s and 1970s, the number of U.S. Supreme Court cases that dealt with family relationships and children in the judicial process was impressive. They dealt with the extent to which family members received due process of law and equal protection of the law in matters dealing with illegitimate children and their rights of inheritance and support from their father, the rights of putative fathers to the custody of their illegitimate children and the right to notice and an opportunity to participate in cases dealing with their children's custody and in some adoption cases, the rights of husbands to receive alimony, the rights of parents to decide the kind of education their children should receive, the rights of parents and their minor daughters in abortion matters, and reproductive rights of women. With their decisions in the field of family law, the U.S. Supreme Court was not just setting down guiding principles, it was changing a culture.

At the same time, on the state supreme court level, family law issues that were previously well settled were litigated with surprising results. On the question of whether the law should recognize committed adult relationships other than informal or formal marriage, like contract cohabitation, the California Supreme Court responded in the affirmative. Whether a couple about to be married can set the terms by which their property will be divided upon divorce, a Florida court, breaking with tradition, responded affirmatively.

A decade later, it became clear that family law could no longer be studied separate from constitutional law, contracts, torts, property, business associations, trusts, and tax. Because family law practice had become so complex, it was not possible for lawyers to keep current in every aspect of family law. As a result, sub-specialties developed. To be an effective divorce lawyer one had to have a sophisticated knowledge about the latest developments in tax and marital property, the latter having been influenced by Professor Charles Reich's concept of 'the new property'. Child protection lawyers needed to learn about the child welfare system including the latest congressional enactments regulating certain aspects of foster care and adoption. Knowledge about international conventions being developed by the International Conference at The Hague, and the ability to work with foreign law materials were essential for international family law practice.

In the past twenty-five years, major social and political movements and advancements in reproductive technology have had a direct impact on family law. The social and political movements have not necessarily been successful in making changes in the law, although some have, but they have forced legislators, judges, lawyers, and scholars to rethink the bases for laws relating to family life.

The legal landscape of today has been shaped by many factors: the movement for racial equality, children's rights, women's rights, gay and lesbian rights, and the social and legal agenda of certain religious groups. Marriage, for example, has undergone fundamental changes because of its being considered a special kind of partnership, which a couple can almost define themselves by a prenuptial agreement. No longer does marriage mean that a wife's identity—her name and her domicile, for example—is totally linked to her husband's. Nor does marriage give a husband license to violate his wife's bodily integrity. With these and other changes, one can begin to see a movement to reduce what was clearly state-imposed inequality and dependency in marriage.

The institution of adoption is no longer monolithic. The traditional model of adoption involves termination of a birth parent's parental rights. The process is clothed in secrecy, and both adoption agency and court records are sealed. A second model being developed by adult adopted persons, some birth parents, and lawyers is called 'open adoption' and has two meanings: open adoption records and post-adoption visitation rights for birth parents.

With a new century, established principles in family law are increasingly being challenged. For example, the definition of heir, ordinarily easily determined by the identity of the parent and date of birth, is being re-examined in light of new reproductive technologies. Who is a male and who is a female, again thought to be easily determined by anatomy, is also being re-examined in light of discoveries about genetics. The historic definition of marriage as a union of a man and a woman is now seriously questioned. While litigation in a few states has resulted in affirming the conventional definition of marriage as a heterosexual relationship, a change could occur in the next few decades. Whether an American state using its discretionary powers under the doctrine of comity will recognize a same-sex marriage entered into in a foreign country that has legalized the union remains to be seen. Recent legislation has been enacted in three states establishing two types of marriages, one Covenant Marriage and the other conventional marriage, the choice being determined by the kind of divorce a couple agrees to in advance. Whether other states will follow may depend on the reception this special kind of marriage receives and the extent to which it is chosen. An effort is now under way to make marriage-like relationships the legal equivalent of marriage. No-fault divorce is being reconsidered, and a return to fault-based divorce is seriously being proposed in some state legislatures.

The American Law Institute, one of the most prestigious law groups in the United States, which produced the Restatement of Law series, undertook the job of drafting principles of family law, which reflect the most current thinking in the field. The American Law Institute's Principles of Family Dissolution, published in 2002, and to which I refer from time to time, represents an enormous amount of research to support its recommended principles regulating the economic consequences of divorce including child support, spousal maintenance and the assignment of property, contract cohabitation, domestic partnerships, and child custody decision-making. Whether state legislatures will adopt the Principles remains to be seen, but they certainly will have an impact on state supreme court justices when they are faced with new issues for which there is neither legislative guidance nor judicial precedent.

The family is being continuously redefined. Who will define it, individuals themselves, legislators, or the courts? What legal consequences will flow from being designated a member of a family? What should the role of the state be in establishing family relationships, in protecting family members, and terminating membership in the family? Will the movement toward legislative codification in family law continue with the result that judicial discretion will decrease considerably? Will existing models of marriage, divorce, or adoption, for example, be expanded or reshaped by either legislatures or judges, if they have the power, to include new fact patterns or will new models be established by legislatures? For example, we have already seen that the conventional model of adoption has been expanded, both by way of judicial discretion and by legislatures, and relabeled 'open adoption' to include visitations by biological parents. Will legislatures enact laws that will allow the conventional model of marriage as a monogamous relationship between a man and a woman be expanded to include same-sex couples or will they establish a new model for a committed adult relationship?

It is hoped that this book will provide information for responding to those general questions. Each chapter has been written separately and can be read without reference to others. Therefore, if there is any redundancy, that is the reason. I have tried to describe the models in family law, like marriage, divorce, and adoption, that legislatures and courts have developed over time, with an emphasis on the past fifty years, and how these models are either being enlarged or joined by new models. In the main, I have adopted the approach of an observer. But, from time to time I have made my own suggestions as to what I believe to be a sensible approach. These may be found both in the text and in the narrative footnotes.

In adopting a structure for this book, I have been influenced by the work of the late Professor Joseph Goldstein and Dr. Jay Katz with whom I studied and worked at Yale Law School while they were defining the family law process. I have found their perception of the cycle of state and family interaction in terms of three basic problems for decision: establishment, administration or maintenance, and termination or reorganization to be extremely useful and I have somewhat modified the framework. In Chapter 1, I discuss issues of establishing adult relationships, including friendship and informal marriage, and how individuals have attempted to regulate their upcoming marriage by entering into prenuptial agreements. In Chapter 2, I discuss the establishment of formal marriage and the legal issues involved in maintaining that relationship. In Chapter 3, I discuss divorce, both as a termination of a marriage and the reorganization of new relationships between the divorcing spouses and their children. In Chapter 4, I examine the parent–child relationship through the lens of child protection laws with emphasis on the issues of state intervention into that relationship. In Chapter 5, I discuss the establishment of a new parent–child relationship through adoption.

After teaching and writing in family law for the past forty years, I am astounded as to the changes that have occurred. If those years are any prologue for the decades ahead, the next generation of lawyers, judges, legislators, and family law scholars is in for a future that I believe is neither predictable nor imaginable.

1

Friendship, Marriage-Like Relationships, and Informal Marriage

INTRODUCTION

Family law in America reflects basic paradigms from which legal rules derive. These models relate to what the state has defined as family relationships: the relationship of one adult to another and the relationship of parent to child. The conventional model for establishing a family has been through the adult relationship called 'marriage', which the states through their legislatures regulate by setting rules for its establishment, maintenance, termination, and reorganization. Legislatures tended not to be concerned with nor did they regulate committed adult relationships short of marriage. Those kinds of relationships were not considered 'family' relationships, but friendships.

The law generally has not established any rules regulating friendship. In contract law, for example, informal social engagements between friends are not accorded any recognition. It has often been stated that these kinds of arrangements are best regulated by the parties themselves, not by courts. No matter how close, long lasting, affectionate, trusting, and loyal the friendship may be, laws of evidence do not accord friends any privileges nor provide any protection for shared confidences. Injury to a friend does not normally provide the other friend with a tort action. The death of a friend leaves the surviving friend unprotected by intestacy laws. The irony in all this is that friends may share more values and have closer ties with each other than family members. Yet, unless the friends themselves choose to enter a legally recognized relationship or structure their relationship by using a formal legal device like a contract or a will, that relationship will have no legal consequences.

The road to marriage has historically consisted of romantic friendship, courtship, engagement, and then formal marriage. It is during the formal or informal engagement period that a couple may think of entering into a prenuptial agreement. This behavior pattern has changed dramatically in the past fifty years. There may no longer be defined periods. And marriage may not be the final relationship. Couples may live together as a temporary and flexible arrangement allowing for the preservation of individual interests, as a prelude to marriage, as a trial marriage, or they may live together permanently either informally or with a formal agreement.[1] In the past same-sex couples could choose a formal or informal model, short of marriage, for a living arrangement. In a limited number of jurisdictions they may now enter into a formal arrangement generally called domestic partnership or civil union.

Whatever the arrangement, the questions for the law are what relationships should be labeled 'family'; who should be authorized to make such a designation, the state or the parties themselves; and should the state regulate them? At the present time, two kinds of adult relationships that are not formally recognized by the state as marriage are contract cohabitation and domestic partnership.

CONTRACT COHABITATION

Contract cohabitation is a relationship that is established when two adults live together without being either formally or informally married, without a desire

---

[1] Professor Morrison has written:

[C]ritical to an assessment of the centrality of marriage is the extent to which Americans are involved in non-marital unions, perhaps in lieu of marriage or remarriage. A dramatic rise in the prevalence of cohabitation over the past twenty-five years makes it clear that non-marital unions have become an increasingly acceptable: 1. alternative to marriage; 2. step in the progress toward first marriage (by giving couples the opportunity to size each other up as potential spouses); as well as 3. a substitute for marriage after separation and divorce. Moreover, the widespread acceptance of cohabitation, in turn, diminishes the 'imperative' of marriage. Lynn Casper and her colleagues at the US Census Bureau estimate a steep and nearly linear increase in unrelated couple households from 1 million in 1977 to more than 4 million in 1997, a figure that is even higher when other data sets are used for the estimates. Thus, despite a significant postponement in marriage, the prevalence of cohabitation makes contemporary young adults nearly as likely to be sharing a household with a partner as those in previous decades.

The rise in cohabitation is of course facilitated by the . . . loosening social mores about non-marital sex, contraception, and abortion, and changes in the importance placed on the institution of marriage, but also by the wariness on the part of young people whose own parents have divorced to enter more permanent unions. In addition, the oft-cited emphasis of contemporary Americans on self-fulfilment contributes to the prevalence of cohabitation. Cohabitation is a way to have some of the benefits of marriage, without the legally binding aspects. Cohabiting couples can stay together so long as it proves personally rewarding, but the door is implicitly always open if either party becomes dissatisfied.

Using data from the National Survey of Families and Households (NSFH), to examine cohabitation trends across American cohorts, Larry Bumpass and James Sweet found that the share of persons who lived in a non-marital union before first marriage increased fourfold from the 1965–74 marriage cohort (11 per cent) to the 1980–4 marriage cohort (44 per cent). They estimate that well over half of more recently formed marriages were preceded by cohabitation. When comparing successive birth cohorts from 1940–4 and 1960–4, they showed an increase from 3 to 37 per cent of females who had cohabited before

to be married or because they are of the same-sex, unable to marry in a legally recognized civil ceremony. Yet through their formal or informal expressions or conduct these adults wish to be legally recognized as a couple. The fact that contract cohabitants do not hold themselves out as married differentiates them from a couple who live in one model of marriage: common law marriage relationship. In fact, a cohabitation contract may even begin with a clause specifically denying a marriage relationship. For example, in the nineteenth-century case of *Peck v. Peck*,[2] a libel (petition) for divorce was filed in Massachusetts. The couple signed a written contract in 1877, which included the following provision:

We, the undersigned, hereby enter into a copartnership on the basis of the true marriage relation. Recognizing love as the only law which should govern the sexual relationship, we agree to continue this partnership so long as mutual affection shall exist, and to dissolve it when the union becomes disagreeable or undesirable to either party. We also agree that all property that shall be acquired by mutual effort shall be equally divided on the dissolution of said copartnership. Should any children result from this union, we pledge ourselves to be mutually held and bound to provide them support whether the union continues or is dissolved.

The Supreme Judicial Court of Massachusetts was unwilling to consider the relationship a marriage, and therefore affirmed the lower court's dismissal of the libel, since no state in which the couple had lived, including Massachusetts,

age 25. Comparing data from the late 1980s to the early 1990s, cohabitation increased in every age category, particularly among the youngest women. For example, while 17 per cent of single women ages 25 to 29 years cohabited in the first wave of the survey, 23 per cent did so by the second wave. Strikingly, almost one-quarter of unmarried 25 to 29-year-olds, 30 to 34-year-olds, and 35 to 39-year-olds were currently cohabiting in 1992–4. Blacks are more likely than whites to live with a non-married partner, but this is largely attributable to distinctive demographic characteristics such as low education, family background, and timing of marriage.

Available evidence makes it clear that cohabiting unions and marriages are not equivalent. Both the characteristics of those who choose to live together as well as the character of the unions themselves are distinctive. For example, those who live together outside of marriage have traits more in common with single persons than with married persons. Cohabiting unions are generally briefer and less stable than marriages. Specifically, it is estimated that 60 per cent of cohabiting unions dissolve within the first two years.

For some, cohabitation is a step in the courtship process. Larry Bumpass and his colleagues report that slightly less than half of cohabiting couples (who had not previously married) in the NSFH stated that they had definite plans to marry and 74 per cent of the couples either had definite plans or thought that they would marry their partners.

See Donna Ruane Morrison, *A Century of the American Family, in* CROSS CURRENTS: FAMILY LAW AND POLICY IN THE UNITED STATES AND ENGLAND 67–69 (Sanford N. Katz, John Eekelaar & Mavis Maclean eds., 2000) [hereinafter CROSS CURRENTS].

  [2] 30 N.E. 74 (Mass. 1892).

recognized a private contract of marriage. The case illustrates that over a hundred years ago, couples were attempting to define their relationship, in that case by flouting nineteenth-century conventions. The contract has a surprisingly modern tone to it, and although the agreement alone would still not meet the statutory requirements of a formal marriage, its terms might very well be enforceable if the couple signed the agreement before going through a proper ceremony. It could also serve as a cohabitation contract in a state sympathetic to such agreements.

Adults living together in an intimate relationship without being formally married were and in some states still may be considered to be living in an immoral relationship. Such a characterization can serve as the basis for modifying a custody decree. For example, in *Jarrett v. Jarrett*,[3] the Supreme Court of Illinois decided that a change in custody from a mother to a father 'whose conduct did not contravene the standards established by [the Illinois legislature] and earlier judicial decisions' was justified because of the mother's living in an open and continuous cohabitation with a man to whom she was not married but with whom she intended to continue to live. To that court such conduct had a negative impact on the children's emotional health as well as on their moral development.

In some states non-marital cohabitation is illegal because persons who enter into such relationships by definition do so without being married, and if they engage in intimate sexual conduct they would be violating fornication statutes.[4] In addition, cohabitation contracts have been criticized as promoting the inequality of women.[5]

The case that gave legitimacy to cohabitation arrangements by providing remedies for the couple was the California case of *Marvin v. Marvin*.[6] In 1964, while still married to another woman, the well-known actor Lee Marvin began living with his girlfriend, Michelle, who gave up her musical career to become Mr. Marvin's companion. The couple continued to live in that relationship after Mr. Marvin divorced his wife. The total amount of time the two lived together like a husband and wife without a written agreement was six years. Each contributed to the relationship in his or her own way, with Mr. Marvin providing the economic support for the relationship through his work in films and Michelle assuming the role of a companion and housekeeper. In fact, Michelle had changed her last name to Marvin, an act that would normally be strong evidence of a common law marriage, a relationship not recognized in California.

The relationship ended and after Mr. Marvin forced Michelle to leave the household, she sought the court's assistance in determining her contractual and

---

[3] 400 N.E.2d 421 (Ill. 1979).

[4] For a discussion of the policy underlying the non-enforcement of cohabitation contracts, see *Hewitt v. Hewitt*, 394 N.E.2d 1204 (1979).

[5] *See* Ruth Deech, *The Case against Legal Recognition of Cohabitation, in* CONTRACT COHABITATION 300 (John M. Eekelaar & Sanford N. Katz eds., 1980).

[6] 557 P.2d 106 (Cal. 1976).

property rights by way of declaratory relief. In her complaint for relief, Michelle alleged that the couple had had an oral agreement in which they promised to hold themselves out as married and to share their resources. Specifically, Michelle requested the court to impose a constructive trust upon half of the property acquired during the years the couple lived together. The trial court denied Michelle the relief she sought, and she appealed that decision to the Supreme Court of California.

The Supreme Court of California reversed the trial court, and held that Michelle Marvin did have a cause of action for breach of an express contract of cohabitation, and remanded the case to the trial court where the couple could establish facts necessary to support a cause of action. Two footnotes in the Supreme Court's opinion provided alternative remedies to contract if the case had the appropriate facts. These two footnotes read:

> 25. Our opinion does not preclude the evolution of additional remedies to protect the expectations of the parties to a nonmarital relationship in cases in which existing remedies prove inadequate; the suitability of such remedies may be determined in later cases in light of the factual setting in which they arise.
>
> 26. We do not pass upon the question whether, in the absence of an express or implied contractual obligation, a party to a nonmarital relationship is entitled to support payments from the other party after the relationship terminates.[7]

The availability of equitable remedies broadened Michelle's legal possibilities. And it was equity, not contract, to which the Superior Court of California reached to provide Michelle with an amount of money to educate herself so that she could be gainfully employed again. To the Superior Court, Michelle's lawyer had not built a strong enough case for proving through writings or conduct the existence of either an express or implied contract between the couple. Mr. Marvin appealed that decision to the California Court of Appeals, which reversed the Superior Court's monetary award stating that the award was not based on any recognized legal or equitable obligation.[8] To the Appeals Court, the Superior Court did not have the power to create a new substantive right to award what looked like a modern form of 'rehabilitative alimony' under the guise of 'doing equity'. But any kind of financial support would have presupposed a marriage, a status that did not exist. Thus, after years of litigation and the creation of new family law doctrine, Michelle Marvin was left with nothing.

What is startling about *Marvin v. Marvin* is that California, a state that did not recognize common law marriage, gave its judicial imprimatur on the legality of two persons living together in what appeared to be an informal marriage. In fact, by recognizing legal rights in the Marvin relationship, the California court was willing to move beyond traditional restrictions on common law marriage by recognizing a relationship that began meretriciously, that is, while Mr. Marvin was already married to another woman.

---

[7] *Id.* at 123.   [8] 176 Cal. Rptr. 555 (Cal. Ct. App. 1981).

Basically, *Marvin v. Marvin* stands for the proposition that two people may live together without being formally or informally married and set their own terms for the relationship so long as they do not contract for sexual services.[9] In addition, if a couple has not set their own terms through mutual promises, but if certain conduct is found to exist, a court may superimpose upon the parties liabilities under trust law or equitable theories including quasi-contract.

A major question is whether cohabitation contracts should be the secular or functional equivalent of traditional marriage. Certainly if in a formal document a couple defines their relationship to mirror the rights and obligations of marriage, it would seem that except for the matter of the legitimacy and custody of children, in an action for breach of contract, a court would enforce the contract. This is not to say that two parties to a cohabitation agreement can bind third parties or create rights that are limited by statute.

The more difficult question is whether courts should use the divorce model to divide assets and order support after the termination of a judicially determined, not privately negotiated, cohabitation contract. Footnote 26 in the California Supreme Court's decision in *Marvin* made it clear that the court was not deciding the support issue. At least three states apply marital property concepts to the distribution of cohabitants' property upon the termination of the relationship.[10] The Supreme Judicial Court of Massachusetts, however, would not extend the same rights to property upon the termination of a cohabitation contract as it would in a marriage case. That court rejected 'equitable remedies that might have the effect of dividing property between unmarried parties'.[11] Elsewhere I have said that 'applying the divorce model of equitable distribution of property to a cohabiting couple does make sense where property has been acquired jointly with the expectation that it would be jointly enjoyed'.[12] That such an expectation existed would be the result of a judicial finding of fact based on evidence drawn from formal declarations and the conduct of the parties.

Whether cohabiting adults enjoy the same benefits of a married couple depends on the issue and the state. California, for example, has an inconsistent record with regard to the rights of cohabiting adults. In that state, cohabitants

---

[9] The *Marvin* case dealt with a heterosexual couple, although nowhere in the opinion does the court limit its holding to a man and a woman. In *Posik v. Layton*, 695 So. 2d 759 (Fla. Dist. Ct. App. 1997), a Florida Appeals court upheld a cohabitation agreement between gay partners. But a California Appeals Court was unwilling to enforce a cohabitation contract between two gay men that included a promise to render services as a lover in addition to acting as a homemaker, companion, and housekeeper. *See* Jones v. Daly, 176 Cal. Rptr. 130 (Cal. Ct. App. 1981).

[10] *See* Cornnell v. Francisco, 898 P.2d 831 (Wash. 1995); Marriage of Lindsey, 678 P.2d 328 (Wash. 1984); Shuraleff v. Donnelly, 817 P.2d 764 (Or. Ct. App. 1991); Wilbur v. DeLapp, 850 P.2d 1151 (Or. Ct. App. 1993); *Pickens v. Pickens*, 490 So. 2d 872 (Miss. 1986).   [11] *See* Wilcox v. Trautz, 693 N.E.2d 141, 145 (Mass. 1998).

[12] *See* Sanford N. Katz, *Marriage as Partnership*, 73 NOTRE DAME L. REV. 1251, 1267 (1998).

do not enjoy the evidentiary protection given to a married couple even if the couple had promised to be loyal and to keep confidences. Nor does that state allow consortium claims for injury to live-in cohabitants, nor claims for negligent infliction of emotional distress.[13] The California Supreme Court was reluctant to provide a cohabiting couple with the same rights as marital couples in an unemployment compensation case where a woman sought unemployment compensation benefits because she was forced to move to another state with her boyfriend. To that court, such a move, which did not result in a marriage, was not a 'good cause'.[14] Yet in *MacGregor v. Unemployment Ins. Appeals Bd.*,[15] the same court did allow a woman to obtain unemployment benefits because her relocation to New York was based on her desire to 'maintain and preserve' her family, which included her fiancé and their child.

Persons living together in a formal or informal cohabitation contract must be particularly mindful of matters dealing with incapacity and death. Ordinarily, family members are considered 'next of kin', and are turned to by medical professionals to obtain consent for medical matters. Unless the cohabiting partners have formally signed documents giving each other the power to make decisions about their lives, like health-care proxies, physicians and hospital administrators turn to family members. Even where cohabiting couples do sign power of attorney documents, wills, or insurance policies, in which they name each other as beneficiary, such documents might be subject to attack by family members who may not have approved of the cohabitation contract.[16]

If a state requires a special family relationship for holding property in joint tenancy, contract cohabitants would have to be tenants in common. All the presumptions that attach to marriage, like the legitimacy of children and the presumption of gifts between the couple, do not attach to non-marital partners. Unless a state had a social policy favoring a cohabitation relationship or a statute authorized it, a cohabitant could not bring an action for wrongful death against his or her partner unless dependency was the criterion, as in some workmen's compensation statutes.[17]

Children born to a cohabiting couple present special problems both for the children and the parents. For the children, the major problem is support and

---

[13] *See* Elden v. Sheldon, 758 P.2d 582 (Cal. 1988). *See* also *Medley v. Strong*, 558 N.E.2d 244 (Ill. App. Ct. 1990), where the Appellate Court of Illinois affirmed the dismissal of a woman's claim against the doctors and hospitals for the negligent injury to her companion that resulted in the amputation of his penis. The Illinois court held that the plaintiff lacked legal standing to maintain the action.

[14] Norman v. Unemployment Ins. Appeals Bd., 663 P.2d 904 (Cal. 1983).

[15] 689 P.2d 453 (Cal. 1984).

[16] *See* Ray D. Madoff, *Unmasking Undue Influence*, 81 MINN. L. REV. 571 (1997).

[17] *But see Langan v. St. Vincent's Hospital*, N.Y. Sup. Ct., Nassau Cty., No. 11618/02, 29 Fam. L. Rep. (BNA) 1267 (April 22, 2003), where a New York trial court did allow a member of a same-sex civil union entered into and recognized in Vermont to collect under the New York Wrongful Death Statute, *infra* note 42 and accompanying text.

the possibility of the insecurity of their relationship with their parents.[18] For the father, the major problem from a legal perspective is the ambiguity of his relationship with his children. So long as the couple is not married to each other, and the state has no statute making all children legitimate,[19] the children are illegitimate. If a child is born to a heterosexual couple and the male would like to secure his relationship with his child, he must establish his parenthood by a DNA test and seek the appropriate remedy for acknowledgment before petitioning for co-guardianship or adoption. In a same-sex relationship of two women, one of whom has borne the child, the non-biological parent can either petition for co-guardianship or adoption.[20] In the same-sex relationship of two men, either co-guardianship or adoption is appropriate if a state will allow same-sex adoption. Adoption provides the more secure relationship because a guardianship not only does not involve statutory inheritance rights but ordinarily terminates when a child reaches majority. Adoption provides a child with inheritance rights and the security of a life-long relationship with his or her parents.

REGISTERED DOMESTIC PARTNERSHIP

The status of registered domestic partnership is the natural outgrowth of the law of contract cohabitation. In a certain sense it is the ultimate formalization of contract cohabitation with the added feature of its being highly regulated

[18] Professor Morrison has written:

Significantly, a growing number of cohabiting unions involve children. In 1960, of the 439,000 unmarried-couple households, 197,000 contained children under 15 years of age. By 1998, the number of unmarried-couple households had grown to over 4 million (4,236,000) with over 1.5 million of those (1,520,000) containing children. Because these data have not been collected at the national level until very recently, we know very little about how non-married and remarried partners share their incomes and assets, which has important implications for the economic standing of children in these unions. One possibility is that cohabiting couples do not pool their financial resources as much as married couples do, but income-sharing may be more common in relationships of longer duration or when the relationship has produced children. Alternatively, mothers rely exclusively on their own incomes in short-term cohabiting relationships. This makes cohabitation a risky enterprise for children in terms of economic standing and stability. Moreover, children whose mothers cohabit are also at risk of behavioral and emotional difficulties owing to the instability of these arrangements and the ambiguous parental role of non-marital partners.

See CROSS CURRENTS, *supra* note 1, at 69.

[19] *See, e.g.*, ARIZ. REV. STAT. ANN. § 8–601 (West 2003), which states 'Every child is the legitimate child of its natural parents and is entitled to support and education as if, born a lawful wedlock.' *Also see* the Uniform Parentage Act § 202 in the Appendix.

[20] *See In re Adoption of Tammy*, 619 N.E.2d 315 (Mass. 1993); Adoption of B.L.V.B. & E.L.V.B., 628 A.2d 1271 (Vt. 1993), where the highest courts in Massachusetts and Vermont allowed the adoption of the child of the birth mother's partner.

with specific requirements including those for establishing the relationship, maintaining it, for example by mutual support obligations and the sharing of a common residence, and for terminating the relationship. To a limited extent, cohabitation contracts are also regulated in those states that require the agreements to be in writing and comply with its statute of frauds.[21] But no state mandates cohabitation contracts to have the kind of requirements and documentation found in registered domestic partnerships. The importance of registration is that it provides the tangible evidence of a relationship without regard to that relationship's having to be proven. Therefore, a registered domestic partnership is to contract cohabitation what formal ceremonial marriage is to common law marriage. Formal marriage is presumed legal once documentation is presented; common law marriage has to be proven by a variety of evidentiary matters including documents, like bank accounts, and the testimony of third parties.

Generally speaking, the purpose of registered domestic partnerships is to provide legal recognition and a legal framework for a couple who either do not wish to marry or who do not qualify for a marriage license because of the heterosexual requirement, but who have committed themselves to living together and sharing their lives both economically and socially. Registered domestic partnerships in the United States began in an unconventional way. They first appeared in cities and were limited to city employees who lived with a partner of the same sex. Their purpose was to provide these employees with the same kind of social and economic benefits such as health insurance, institutional visitation rights, sick leave, and bereavement leave, as were available to married couples. In other words, the definition of 'family member' included registered domestic partners. What made this status unusual was that in the United States, as a general rule only, states, not cities, have the power to regulate the establishment of family relationships. And, in order for city governments to legislate in this area of the law, again as a general rule, they must obtain authority from their state legislatures under what is called 'home rule'.

Under the Tenth Amendment to the U.S. Constitution, there are certain legislative powers that have been reserved by the individual states. Most of these reserved authorities are within the realms of education, law enforcement, and domestic relations. Technically speaking, since local governments are the creation of the states and derive all of their authority from the state, the areas in which a city can act free from state government intervention are very limited. Throughout the latter half of this century, however, many states have recognized the need for local governments to have more autonomy. States have, therefore, amended their constitutions with home rule provisions that allow local governments to expand their realm of legislative authority.[22] While the

---

[21] *See, e.g.*, Minn. Stat. §§ 513.075–.076 (West 2003) (originally enacted in 1980); Tex. Bus. & Com. Code Ann. § 26.01(b)(3) (Vernon 1987).

[22] *See* Vada Berger, *Domestic Partnership Initiatives*, 40 DePaul L. Rev. 417, 437 (1991) (quoting Note, *Conflicts between State Statutes and Municipal Ordinances*, 72 Harv. L. Rev. 737, 739 (1959)).

amount of autonomous power the state gives to local governments varies widely, generally a city is given either specifically enumerated powers or broad 'police powers'.[23] Challenges to local domestic partnership ordinances have focused on whether the local government has the authority to act based on the powers that the state has granted to it by its specific home rule ordinance or whether the ordinance is beyond the power granted to the city and is contrary to a general state policy.[24] For example, in *Lilly v. City of Minneapolis*,[25] the Minnesota Court of Appeals held that the City of Minneapolis domestic partnership ordinance was invalid. The court reasoned, in part, that the ordinance was intended to address discrimination, which was an area of statewide concern, therefore the city exceeded its legislative authority.

Two major issues with registered domestic partnership is whether the status should be completely limited by the statute that created it or whether, like marriage, it should have benefits beyond its statutory basis like those embedded in the common law. For example, if a registered domestic partnership statute does not provide for mutual support obligations, could those obligations be implied? Those who argue for equality between registered domestic partnerships and marriage would respond by saying that the new status should mirror marriage. Equating a domestic partner with a spouse in all legal matters would require a total revision of state laws so that wherever the word 'spouse' is stated, the phrase 'or domestic partner' is added. The second issue is whether couples who anticipate registering their partnership can limit their statutory responsibilities by way of a pre-domestic partnership contract.[26]

Four American jurisdictions, California, the District of Columbia, Hawaii, and Vermont, have enacted some form of registered domestic partnership statute. Each one is different. Other jurisdictions have pending legislation dealing with establishing, terminating, or limiting the status.[27] The statutes in California and the District of Columbia are relatively restrictive. California's

[23] For an extensive analysis of the tensions between state authority and autonomous local authority, see Richard Briffault, *Our Localism: Part I—The Structure of Local Government Law*, 90 COLUM. L. REV. 1 (1990); Note, *Conflicts between State Statutes and Municipal Ordinances*, 72 HARV. L. REV. 737, 739 (1959); Gerald E. Frug, *The City as a Legal Concept*, 93 HARV. L. REV. 1059 (1980).

[24] For a discussion of these challenges, see Vada Berger, *Domestic Partnership Initiatives*, 40 DEPAUL L. REV. 417, 435–41 (1991); David C. Weigel, Note, *Proposal for Domestic Partnership in the City of Detroit: Challenges under the Law*, 74 DETROIT MERCY L. REV., 825, 835–44 (1997) (citing *City of Atlanta v. McKinney*, 454 S.E.2d 517 (Ga. 1995) (upholding in part the City of Atlanta's domestic partnership ordinance because it did not establish rights that would exceed the city's legislative authority). *See also* David J. Barron, *Reclaiming Home Rule*, 116 HARV. L. REV. 2255, 2355–56 (2003).

[25] 527 N.W.2d 107 (Minn. Ct. App. 1995).

[26] The American Law Institute takes the position that couples should be allowed to set their own terms within certain limits. *See* PRINCIPLES OF THE LAW OF FAMILY DISSOLUTION: ANALYSIS AND RECOMMENDATIONS, ch. 7, § 7.02 (Amer. Law Inst. 2000).

[27] These states are: Arkansas, Maine, Massachusetts, New York, Oregon, Rhode Island, and Washington.

Domestic Partnership Registration Law[28] is limited to two categories: same-sex couples who are not blood relatives and who agree to be jointly responsible for each other's basic living expenses incurred during the domestic partnership, and heterosexual couples, one or both of whom are over the age of 62. The law was described by the California governor as one 'which would enable domestic partners to make medical decisions for incapacitated loved ones, adopt their partner's child, use sick leave to care for their partner, recover damages for wrongful death, and allow the right to be named a conservator of a will'.[29] In addition, the California Domestic Partnership Law allows a domestic partner to recover for negligent infliction of emotional distress and also gives the partner spousal rights in probate and decedents estate matters. The District of Columbia's law[30] is limited to the employees of the District and the private sector and concerns work-related benefits.

The laws in Hawaii and Vermont were the result of two court cases that tested the right of same-sex couples to marry under each state's constitution. In the 1993 case of *Baehr v. Lewin*,[31] the Hawaii Supreme Court held that its marriage law that limited marriage to heterosexual couples was discriminatory. The case, in which the plaintiffs sought injunctive and declaratory relief, was remanded to a lower court so that it could apply the 'strict scrutiny' standard to the statute. The lower court was not convinced by the state's major argument that heterosexual marriage provided the best environment for raising children and held in 1996 in *Baehr v. Miike*[32] that the marriage law was unconstitutional as applied in violation of the equal protection clause of the state's constitution. The injunction was stayed pending an appeal to the Hawaii Supreme Court, which ultimately affirmed the decision without opinion.[33] In the mean time, the Hawaii legislature enacted its Reciprocal Beneficiary Law,[34] which provided same-sex couples with certain economic benefits. The following year, the citizens of Hawaii voted to amend its state constitution to limit marriage to heterosexual couples.[35]

In *Baker v. State of Vermont*,[36] the Vermont Supreme Court held that limiting marriage to heterosexual couples violated its state's Common Benefits Clause, which reads 'That government is, or ought to be, instituted for the common benefit, protection, and security of the people, nation, or community and not for the particular emolument or advantage of any single person, family, or set of persons, who are a part only of that community . . . '[37] However, the

---

[28] *See* CAL. FAM. CODE §§ 297–99.6 (West 2001).

[29] *See* Bill Ainsworth, *Governor Signs Measure Giving New Rights to Domestic Partners*, SAN DIEGO UNION TRIB., Oct. 15, 2001, at A1.

[30] *See* D.C. CODE 32–701, 702, 704, 705, 706 (2001).

[31] 852 P.2d 44 (Haw. 1993).

[32] *See* Baehr v. Miike, 1996 WL 694235 (Haw. Cir. Ct. 1996).

[33] *See* Baehr v. Miike, 950 P.2d 1234 (Haw. 1997).

[34] *See* HAW. REV. STAT. ch. 572C-1 to -7 (Michie Supp. 1998).

[35] *See* HAW. CONST. art. 1, § 23.   [36] 744 A.2d 864 (Vt. 1999).

[37] VT. CONST. ch. 1, art. 7.

court then went on to state that it was the function of the legislature to provide a remedy, not the courts.[38] Thus, the legislature was given the opportunity to make one of two changes in Vermont law: modify the marriage law and remove the restriction of marriage to heterosexual couples or create an alternative to marriage that would provide a same-sex couple with benefits equal to marriage. Rather than changing its legislation by expanding the definition of marriage, the legislature broke new ground and created a model for a committed adult relationship with its own definitions and its own requirements exclusively designed to meet the needs of same-sex couples.[39] Civil union was thus born free from the negative historical associations that marriage carries. Civil union partners are now free to develop how they wish to order their lives without the stereotype or conventional roles identified with marriage. The civil union model is more readily adaptable to the modern-day same-sex couple's wishes and expectations.

Thus, in both Hawaii and Vermont the same-sex couples who sought relief from the courts under each state's constitution convinced each court of the merits of their claim of discrimination.[40] While they were unsuccessful in obtaining an order for the issuance of a marriage license, they were, however, successful in obtaining legislative action by way of the enactment of domestic partnership laws, a new paradigm for adult relationships.

Hawaii chose to call its domestic partnership law 'Reciprocal Beneficiary Law', giving persons who met the requirements of the law certain rights and benefits that attach to the status of marriage. According to the law, the status is restricted to individuals over 18 years of age, unmarried or not committed to another reciprocal beneficiary. In order to meet the requirements of the law, the individuals must be under a legal disability to marry each other and voluntarily and formally consent to the establishment of the relationship. The unique nature of the law is that the disability to marry would include persons who are related to each other, like a widowed mother and her unmarried son. For purposes of inheritance, Hawaii chose to equate the status of reciprocal beneficiary with spouse throughout its probate code.

Unlike the Hawaii Reciprocal Beneficiary Law, the Vermont Civil Union Statute is not based on economic dependency, regardless of the family relationship and of the sex of the parties, but rather a desire to really provide a secular alternative to marriage for same-sex couples. The most important provision of the law is entitled 'Benefits, protections and responsibilities of parties to a civil

---

[38] A Massachusetts Superior Court made the same suggestion in *Hillary Goodridge and Julie Goodridge, et al. v. Department of Public Health, et al.*, Suffolk Superior Court, C.A. No. 01-1647-A (May 2002).

[39] *See* discussion of the Vermont Civil Unions Act, Pub. Act. 91. H. 847 below.

[40] Professor Barron points out that although the Vermont and Hawaii cases were decided under state constitutional law, federal constitutional law laid the predicate for the reasoning upon which the judgment was based. *See* Jerome A. Barron, *The Constitutionalization of American Family Law: The Case of the Right to Marry, in* CROSS CURRENTS, *supra* note 1, at 257.

union'. According to that provision, individuals who formally establish a civil union in Vermont are to be treated as if they were married in Vermont.

What neither Hawaii nor Vermont would provide the same-sex couples with was the remedy they sought: they wanted the label 'marriage' on their legal document; they wanted to be considered 'married', and they wanted the social recognition and respect that accompanies the status. For those goals, they shall have to wait for another day.

The Vermont Civil Union statute provides a model for other jurisdictions that seek to provide same-sex couples with the closest alternative to marriage without assigning the word 'married' to the couple. By expressly stating that couples who establish a civil union in Vermont can claim all benefits and protections given to married couples, whether the benefits and protections are based on a statute, regulation, or common law, the Vermont legislature has managed to reach a compromise with those who want to reserve the label 'marriage' to heterosexual couples and those who want to provide same-sex couples with equal rights and benefits under law.

The first state to explore the extraterritorial recognition of the Vermont Civil Union statute was Georgia. In *Burns v. Burns*,[41] the Court of Appeals of Georgia was asked to decide whether a former wife had violated a court visitation order by cohabiting with another adult with whom she was not married. The former wife's defense was that she had entered into a civil union with a woman in Vermont, and the two were thus married in Vermont. She argued that Georgia should give full faith and credit to the Vermont law. In addition, she argued that her right to privacy included a right to define for herself who was her family without Georgia's placing any limitation on that right. The Georgia court held that the wife was not married in Vermont because a civil union was not marriage under Vermont law. The court went on to say that even if the wife had entered into a marriage with another woman, Georgia would not recognize the status because of that's state's definition of marriage as a union 'only of man and woman'.

A year after Georgia decided that it would not recognize a Vermont civil union as a marriage, the New York Supreme Court (a trial court) held that it would recognize a Vermont civil union for purposes of conferring a right of the surviving member of the union to sue as a spouse for the wrongful death of his partner.[42] The court stated that had the case arisen in 1993, years before the enactment of the Vermont Civil Union Statute, the surviving partner would not have been considered a 'spouse' under the New York Estates, Powers, and Trust Law, which governs wrongful death suits. However, since then the judges stated that New York has manifested a public policy that would recognize the Vermont status. This manifestation has taken the form of New York laws that would consider a same-sex partner as a 'family member' under rent control

---

[41] 560 S.E.2d 47 (Ga. Ct. App. 2002).
[42] *See* Langan v. St. Vincent's Hospital, *supra* note 17.

laws. He would also be eligible to receive city or state employment benefits had his partner been killed in the September 11th attack; he would be able to adopt his partner's biological child, and he and his partner would be free from discrimination based on sexual orientation. In addition, the New York judge noted that New York had not enacted a 'mini-Defense of Marriage Act', based on the federal model and therefore the state was free to recognize a civil union between a same-sex couple. To the judge a couple in a civil union should be treated as spouses and should receive the same benefits as spouses in a heterosexual marriage.

INFORMAL MARRIAGE

Informal marriage is often misunderstood because of the widely held belief that unless a couple goes through a formal ceremony, no matter how simple, with documentation, they are not really married. There is a further assumption, which is clearly wrong, that there are no requirements for the establishment of an informal marriage, but that individuals have complete autonomy. In fact, informal marriage does have requirements and, if properly established, results in the creation of the exact same rights and obligations that attach to a formal ceremonial marriage. The important fact in all informal marriages is a couple's holding out to the community that they are married. In a way, this is an application of the old equity adage that if a couple behaves as if they are married, the law treats them as such. The 'as if' concept manifests a social policy of advancing legal or right conduct. Stated another way—the law assumes that a couple who acts as if they were married (not just living together) are married because to assume otherwise would be to assume illegal conduct.

Informal marriages can be divided into two major categories: substance—common law marriage and de facto marriage; and procedure—procedural marriage, which includes putative marriage and marriage by estoppel.

Common Law Marriage and De Facto Marriage

Common law marriage is basically a matter of substantive law. It is an informal marriage in which a man and a woman who fulfill the requirements of marriage, except for a ceremony and formal documentation, agree to live together openly as wife and husband and have the reputation in the community that they are married. This definition is subject to qualifications depending on the jurisdiction (whether it supports the status or is hostile toward it) and the context in which the claim is made (probate, workman's compensation, wrongful death, etc.) for common law marriage status.[43] The twelve American jurisdictions

---

[43] I have gleaned this definition from the cases, although I agree with Professor Weyrauch that there are 'infinite qualifications'. Professor Weyrauch has written the

(without any discernable pattern) that allow for the establishment of common law marriages are: Alabama, Colorado, District of Columbia, Iowa, Kansas, Montana, Oklahoma, Pennsylvania, Rhode Island, South Carolina, Texas, and Utah.[44] However, other states may recognize common law marriage under conflict of laws rules, assuming that common law marriage is not offensive to the public policy of those states, or recognize the relationship if it was entered into the state while the status was valid.[45] The more difficult question is one concerning domicile. If a couple, legally domiciled in one state where common law marriage was not recognized, lived in another state where common law marriage was recognized as husband and wife, and then moved back to their legal domicile, would the domiciliary state recognize the marriage? If the couple can prove that they have fulfilled the requirements using the standard of proof in the sister state, the answer should be 'yes'.[46] Common law marriages result in a legal marriage in which children are legitimate and termination of that marriage is accomplished through divorce.

The major problem with common law marriage is that of proof. So often the issue is raised years after the couple established the relationship. Frequently that occurs within the context of a decedent's estate contest where one party is challenging the claim of a widow or of a child as an heir. It is often suggested that in a dispute where there is an allegation of a common law marriage, unless there

---

classic article on common law marriage, and I have relied on his conclusions in that article and in personal conversations with him in my discussion. *See* Walter O. Weyrauch, *Informal and Formal Marriage*, 28 U. CHI. L. REV. 88, 91 (1960). A rich source of cases and materials on informal and common law marriages can be found in HOMER H. CLARK, JR. & ANN LAQUER ESTIN, DOMESTIC RELATIONS—CASES AND PROBLEMS 108–23 (6th ed. 2000); IRA MARK ELLMAN, PAUL M. KURTZ & ELIZABETH M. SCOTT, FAMILY LAW—CASES, TEXT, PROBLEMS 60–75 (3rd ed. 1998); WALTER O. WEYRAUCH, SANFORD N. KATZ & FRANCES OLSEN, CASES AND MATERIALS ON FAMILY LAW—LEGAL CONCEPTS AND CHANGING HUMAN RELATIONSHIPS 157–213 (1994).

[44] *See* (Alabama) Stringer v. Stringer, 689 So. 2d 194 (Ala. Civ. App. 1997); (Colorado) In re Marriage of Cargill, 843 P.2d 1335 (Co. 1993); (District of Columbia) Coates v. Watts, 622 A.2d 25 (D.C. 1993); (Iowa) Conklin v. MacMillan Oil Co., 557 N.W.2d 102 (Iowa Ct. App. 1996); (Kansas) Dixon v. Certain Teed Corp. 915 F. Supp. 1158 (D. Kan. 1996); (Montana) Matter of Estate of Alcorn, 868 P.2d 629 (Mont. 1994); (Oklahoma) Matter of Estate of Carroll, 749 P.2d 571 (Okla. Ct. App. 1987); (Rhode Island) Petrarca v. Castrovillari, 448 A.2d 1286 (R.I. 1982); (South Carolina) Barker v. Baker, 499 S.E. 2d 503 (S.C. Ct. App. 1998); (Texas) Russell v. Russell, 865 S.W.2d 929 (Tex. 1993); (Utah) Whyte v. Blair, 885 P.2d 791 (Utah 1994).

[45] The Georgia statute allows for recognition of common law marriage if the status existed before 1997. Georgia abolished common law marriage in 1996. *See* GA. ST. 19-3-1.1 (1996).

[46] *See In re Estate of Bivians*, 652 P.2d 744 (N.M. 1982), where the New Mexico Supreme Court held that even though the New Mexico couple had lived in Texas and Colorado where common law marriage is valid, they failed to present evidence to fulfill the requirement of a present agreement to be married in each state. The fact that the wife testified that the couple intended to be married wherever they were was insufficient to support a common law marriage even though the couple lived together in those states.

is some written evidence, there is the possibility of fraud and perjury.[47] Without an official marriage certificate or any other written documentation, convincing an official or a judge of the existence of a marriage requires other supporting written evidence, like bank accounts, tax forms, title to real property, medical records, employment applications, or insurance policies as well as the testimony of family members, neighbors, and friends. The evidentiary burden of proof of the relationship is either clear and convincing evidence, or a preponderance of the evidence. By requiring the higher standard of proof, and weighing the evidence in light of that standard, a court is basically making it more difficult to prove the existence of a marriage.[48] And it is through the rules of evidence that a court may manifest its position on common law marriage. In addition, if one were to request that a court take judicial notice of the law of a state that allows common law marriage, a legal memorandum of the state of that law would be required.

The New Mexico court looked to Colorado and Texas to determine the standard of proof in those states. The court wrote,

> Although New Mexico courts determine the quantum of proof here, we note the standard of proof applied by the courts in Colorado to prove a common law marriage is higher than that of Texas. To establish a presumption of marriage by cohabitation and repute, the marriage contract must be proven by clear, consistent and convincing and positive evidence. . . .

The court went on to state that there was not sufficient evidence to support the requirement of a present intention to become married in Colorado. *Id.* at 753.

[47] In *Staudenmayer v. Staudenmayer*, 714 A.2d 1016 (Pa. 1998), Justice Newman wrote:

> Because claims for the existence of a marriage in the absence of a certified ceremonial marriage present a 'fruitful source of perjury and fraud,' Pennsylvania courts have long viewed such claims with hostility. . . . Common law marriages are tolerated, but not encouraged. While we do not today abolish common law marriages in Pennsylvania, we reaffirm that claims for this type of marriage are disfavored.
>
> . . .
>
> The burden to prove the marriage is on the party alleging a marriage, and we have described this as a 'heavy' burden where there is an allegation of a common law marriage. When an attempt is made to establish a marriage without the usual formalities, the claim must be reviewed with 'great scrutiny.'

With those words as a prelude, the Supreme Court of Pennsylvania held that Linda Staudenmayer did not meet her burden of proof in establishing that she and Theodore had uttered words 'we are husband and wife'—*verba in praesent*—a requirement in Pennsylvania. Absent that sentence, the fact of their constant cohabitation and their reputation as being husband and wife was not sufficient evidence to establish a common law marriage.

[48] A case that illustrates this point is *In re Estate of Hall*, 588 N.E.2d 203 (Ohio Ct. App. 1990). In that case a man and a woman lived together from 1986 until 1988. Twenty-two witnesses testified and forty-nine documentary exhibits were presented at a decedent's estates hearing. Evidence elicited during the hearing brought out the fact that while the couple had worked and lived together and shared expenses, they each had separate checking accounts and filed separate income tax returns stating that each was 'single'. The decedent did not list the woman as his beneficiary on his life insurance policy

A common misunderstanding regarding common law marriage is that the status requires that the parties live together for a certain number of years. While fact patterns in individual cases may show that a couple cohabited for seven years, that number may not be a general requirement. New Hampshire, a state that does not generally recognize common law marriage, does have a three-year requirement of cohabitation (before death of one of the parties) to be considered de facto married.[49] Generally, evidence of sustained and open cohabitation is necessary for the establishment of a common law marriage. Merely registering in a motel for a night or passing through a jurisdiction that recognizes common law marriage would, under that requirement, be insufficient evidence.[50]

Through the years states have abolished common law marriage, the latest being Georgia in 1996.[51] The reasons given have mostly moral overtones, which may reflect an unconscious class bias. In addition, there seems to be an inordinate concern for respect for formality and a feeling that somehow the dignity and stability of a marriage is diminished by allowing a court to decide whether a couple was married rather than having a simple document speak for itself. That sentiment was reflected in Justice Nigor's concluding paragraph in his concurring opinion in *Staudenmayer v. Staudenmayer*: 'Thus, as marriage is necessarily an affirmative act, and ancient impediments no longer pertain, I would advocate the abolishment of common law marriage in Pennsylvania so that official records, not the courts, may determine if and when the parties were married.'[52] The emphasis on official records may be equally important as religious or moral concerns in the movement towards abolition of common law marriage. Bureaucrats, whether in government or private industry, who must decide questions of marital status for economic reasons (like determining who among claimants is the widow or legitimate child for obtaining insurance proceeds) seek clarity, which written documentation, if available, can provide.

(although the woman did list the man as her beneficiary under her policy). However, the couple had intermingled their finances, jointly purchased property and stock, and had a joint tombstone on which the decedent listed the woman as his wife. The Ohio appellate court noted that while that state did not 'favor' common law marriage, it did recognize the status if the couple fulfilled certain requirements: the mutual consent of both parties to join together as man and wife, manifested either expressly in conduct or in words, and a holding out to and a recognition by the community that the couple was married. The court affirmed the lower court's decision to deny the removal of an administrator of the estate and appoint the woman as the administratrix, since she was the common law widow.

[49] *See* In re Buttrick, 597 A.2d 74 (N.H. 1991).

[50] *See* Vandever v. Industrial Commission, 714 P.2d 866 (Ariz. Ct. App. 1985); Kennedy v. Damron, 268 S.W.2d 22 (Ky. 1954); Goldin v. Goldin, 426 A.2d 410 (Md. App. 1981); Walker v. Hildenbrand, 410 P.2d 244 (Or. 1966).

[51] *See* GA. ST. 19-3-1.1 (1996). In *Staudenmayer*, 714 A.2d at 1023, Justice Nigro wrote a concurring opinion in which he wrote, 'I would . . . advocate the abolition of common law marriage in this Commonwealth thereby joining the majority of jurisdictions which have recognized the inappropriateness of such an ancient convention in modern times.'   [52] *Staudenmayer*, 714 A.2d 1023.

Procedural Marriage and Other Informal Marriages for Limited Purposes

Even with a ceremonial marriage that has been documented, the written evidence may be lost or unavailable for a variety of reasons. It is unusual in daily life that one has to produce a marriage certificate. Yet couples, family members, and friends assume that if a couple has claimed to be married, they are in fact married. To assume otherwise would have dire consequences. In decedents' estates matters alone, the result would be catastrophic, creating no widow and making children illegitimate. In other words, there would be no legitimate heirs based on marriage.

To avoid such a result, the law has created procedural devices like certain presumptions, which reflect popular beliefs and are based on the idea, perhaps even the ideal, that persons act in an honorable and legal way. In addition, presumptions aid in the judicial process and facilitate reaching a decision. For example, there is the presumption, which may be rebutted with evidence, of the validity of the most recent of serial marriages. That presumption, based on the principle of monogamy, assumes that the absent spouse terminated the marriage by obtaining a divorce. The presumption of the validity of a marriage also presumes that the persons who married had the capacity to marry and were married by a person with the authority to marry. There is also the presumption that children born during a marriage are the legitimate children of that marriage. If that presumption did not exist, the result would be chaotic. The application of presumptions results in the establishment of a de facto marriage, which resembles a common law marriage.

There are a number of interesting cases that illustrate in certain contexts, like workman's compensation or the termination of a long-standing relationship, the extent to which courts will protect a spouse who believes she is married, when she has not gone through a formal ceremonial marriage and does not live in a state that recognizes common law marriage. In *Parkinson v. J & S. Tool Company*,[53] Ruth Parkinson attempted to collect compensation for the death of her husband under the New Jersey Workman's Compensation Law. She had been denied recovery from a lower tribunal and sought relief in the Supreme Court of New Jersey. Ruth Parkinson had married Richard Parkinson in a Roman Catholic ceremony in 1927. The couple had two children. In 1939 Ruth obtained a divorce from her husband, but eleven years later the couple reunited. They wanted to be remarried in the Catholic Church, and when they requested that a priest marry them, the priest replied that they were 'already married in the eyes of God'. Consequently, the couple did not remarry, either in a religious or civil ceremony. Assuming they were still married, they lived together with their children for over twenty years when Richard Parkinson was killed.

The Compensation Tribunal found that Ruth Parkinson did not fulfill the requirements for marriage in New Jersey, which does not recognize common law

---

[53] 313 A.2d 609 (N.J. 1974).

marriage,[54] and denied her death benefits. Ruth Parkinson's lawyers argued that even though she was not the legal widow, she should be considered the de facto widow who was dependent on the decedent. And, since dependency was a requirement under the workman's compensation statute,[55] Ruth Parkinson met the requirement.

The Supreme Court of New Jersey held that Ruth Parkinson, a person of limited education who relied on the advice of a priest, should receive the dependent's compensation as the de facto spouse of Richard Parkinson. The court made a major point of underscoring Ruth Parkinson's innocence both in her life experience and in the sense that she was under the mistaken belief that she was married. The dissenting justice took a narrow view, stating that one was either married—having fulfilled the state's requirement, or not married—failing to fulfill the state's requirement. Unlike other courts that are willing to carve out a status of de facto spouse based on dependency in the workman's compensation cases,[56] he was not.

In *Fung Dai Kimn Ah Leong v. Lau Ah Leong*,[57] a Chinese couple was married in Hawaii according to Chinese customs, but without a marriage license from civil authorities. They had thirteen children. The wife not only acted as mother by caring for the children and the house, but also participated in the husband's successful business. After living together as a family for thirty-five years, the husband ceased to recognize the mother of his children as his wife and denied her any interest in his property. The U.S. Court of Appeals held that principles of equity should protect the woman who lived in a de facto marriage with her husband, and provide her some equitable relief. The court stated:

We conclude that plaintiff is entitled to a measure of relief. Upon the question of what standard should be applied in determining the amount and character thereof, . . . no specific general rule can be formulated. Each case must be adjudged in the light of its own peculiar facts and the local laws. Here, we think, it will be proper for the court in further proceedings to take into consideration the relative contributions of property, and of personal service in point of value, made by the two parties in the accumulation of the

---

[54] N.J. STAT. ANN. 37:1-10 (1939) reads in part:

All common law marriages entered into after December 1, 1939 are invalid . . . and failure in any case to comply with both prerequisites (license and marriage performed by one authorized to solemnize marriages) which shall always be construed as mandatory and not merely directory, shall render the purported marriage absolutely void.

[55] N.J. STAT. ANN. 34:15-13(f) reads:

The term 'dependents' shall apply to and include any or all of the following who are dependent upon the deceased at the time of accident or the occurrence of occupational disease, or at the time of death, namely: . . . wife. . . .

[56] In Workman's Compensation cases, courts have tended to protect dependent de facto wives. *See, e.g.*, West v. Barton-Malow Company, 230 N.W.2d 545 (Mich. 1975) and Powell v. Rogers, 496 F.2d 1248 (9th Cir. 1974).

[57]   27 F.2d 582 (9th Cir. 1928).

property standing in the defendant's name, the amount and value of such property at the time their *de facto marital relation* ceased, and the amount of property accumulated by plaintiff during the same period and standing in her name, the local statutes affecting the *marital relation* and divorce, and alimony and dower, or other pecuniary interests of the wife, whether absolute or contingent, present or in expectancy.[58] (emphasis added)

What is so interesting about this 1928 case is that it is treated as a de facto marriage yet the suggested remedies sound like a modern version of a termination of a cohabitation contract. In a way, it is a precursor to *Marvin v. Marvin.*[59]

Putative Marriage and Marriage by Estoppel

A good faith belief in one's being married is the major factor in the putative marriage. Based on the civil law tradition and incorporated in the Uniform Marriage and Divorce Act,[60] the putative marriage is designed to protect parties, mostly women, who enter into a marriage without knowledge that either or both of the parties are under a disability. The putative marriage is thus a voidable marriage. Marriage by estoppel is designed to prevent a spouse from denying the validity of a marriage after he has accepted its benefits.

A case that illustrates the application of the putative marriage in the context of a decedent's estates contest and marriage by estoppel is *Newburgh v. Arrigo.*[61] In that case a stepson and his stepmother were in a dispute as to who should receive the proceeds from a settlement of a claim for the wrongful death of the stepson's father. The decedent had married his wife, Joan, in New Jersey in 1973, after Joan had been allegedly divorced in New Jersey two months prior. The stepson's allegation was that Joan's first divorce, which occurred in Mexico in 1962, was defective, and consequently her second marriage was invalid, as well as her third marriage to his father. After evaluating the evidence, the court held that the stepson had not met the burden of proving with clear and convincing evidence the invalidity of the Mexican divorce or the invalidity of his stepmother's prior marriages.

During the course of the opinion, the court discussed estoppel. The judge wrote that 'one who enters into and accepts the benefits of a marriage may be equitably estopped from denying the validity of that marriage. For example, a husband who participates in obtaining his wife's prior foreign divorce may be estopped to deny the validity of that divorce.'[62] Applying that principle to the case at hand, the court went on to write that marriage by estoppel would not be applicable because Joan's husband had not helped her to procure her Mexican divorce, in fact there was no evidence that her husband knew of her divorce. Further, the court went on to say that estoppel could not be imputed to Steven, the stepson.

---

[58] *See* WEYRAUCH, ET AL., *supra* note 43, at 179.   [59] 18 Cal. 3d 660 (1976).
[60] Uniform Marriage and Divorce Act § 209. See Appendix.
[61] 443 A.2d 1031 (N.J. 1982).   [62] *Id.* at 1036.

One can see how the application of estoppel, can in fact create marriage by estoppel, although in *Newburgh*, the husband was dead. The difference between marriage by presumption and marriage by estoppel is that in the former the law recognizes a marriage that may in fact be valid. However, in marriage by estoppel the law recognizes that the marriage may not be valid but that a spouse acted as if it was and must accept the consequences of that action.

A question that is raised about these procedural marriages is: How can one avoid the negative consequences? The answer is that once a spouse discovers a defect in the marriage, the spouse must take some action to either affirm or disaffirm the marriage. Otherwise, the good faith requirement of benefiting from the defective marriage may be lost. For example, in *Mason v. Mason*,[63] Lucy Mason had married Weary Mason in 1922. The marriage was not validly dissolved. Yet in 1962, Weary Mason married Sally Mason. Lucy Mason, knowing about the second marriage, never asserted her rights as Weary's wife. Thus, when Weary Mason died in 1962, by virtue of her knowledge and inaction, she was estopped from denying the invalidity of Weary's second marriage and taking title to his property as his widow just as Weary would have been estopped from denying the validity of his second marriage.

PRENUPTIAL AGREEMENTS

The history of prenuptial agreements in the United States illustrates the tension between the state regulation of marriage, on the one hand, and private ordering, on the other. Historically, prenuptial agreements were entered into by wealthy people who wanted to preserve their personal assets or their estate plan, which had been drafted before their marriage. Or prenuptial agreements were used by older people, usually after they had already married at least once, who wanted an agreement that would protect the financial interests of children from a previous marriage.

Indeed, until 1960, individuals entering into marriage could only contract away certain inheritance rights. Contract provisions about divorce, especially its economic consequences, were considered beyond the legal powers of individual parties. The permanence of marriage was such a fundamental legal principle that even mentioning divorce in a prenuptial agreement had the effect of invalidating the provision dealing with divorce or possibly the entire agreement. Judges felt that the divorce provision might encourage the termination of the marriage, an action that would be contrary to the strong public policy encouraging the lifetime character of marriage.

The 1970 Florida Supreme Court decision in *Posner v. Posner*[64] is the case most often cited for breaking new ground and establishing the validity of

---

[63] 174 So. 2d 629 (Fla. Dist. Ct. App. 1965).

[64] 233 So. 2d 381 (Fla. 1970). There are, however, earlier Oklahoma cases that have upheld prenuptial contracts that were just and reasonable. *See, e.g.*, Pence v. Cole,

a premarital agreement. The Florida court, referring to the changes in society and the prevalence of divorce, held that divorce could indeed be an event about which the marrying couple could contract. The couple could establish their own formula for the distribution of assets upon divorce. This was a major decision, handed down during the same decade as *Marvin v. Marvin*,[65] another decision about adult relationships that opened up a whole new area of law called contract cohabitation.

The major issue concerning prenuptial agreements is whether they really are formal contracts governed by conventional contract law doctrine including the requirement of consideration and other formalities,[66] or whether they are a special kind of contract peculiar to family law and governed by special rules.[67] Special kinds of contracts with their own set of rules are not unknown or unusual in the contract world. Not all contracts are 'bargained-for exchanges'. For example, contracts of adhesion, like those that dominate the insurance industry, are by definition not negotiated and not bargained for. They are basically 'take it or leave it' contracts. Yet they are contracts whose provisions are interpreted by different rules and standards compared with ordinary commercial contracts that are the result of negotiation.

Prenuptial agreements will be enforced if both the process by which they were negotiated was fair and the terms are fair. Generally, the 'fairness' of both the process and terms are evaluated at the time of execution, although fairness may be a standard at the time of enforcement (namely at the death of one of the parties or at the time of divorce) or both.[68] Unlike the pre-contractual period in ordinary contract negotiation where arm's length dealing may be common, that same time-frame in prenuptial agreements is one in which the couple stands, as one state supreme court stated, 'in a confidential relationship with each other'.[69]

205 P. 172 (Okla. 1922); Talley v. Harris, 182 P.2d 765 (Okla. 1947); Clark v. Clark, 202 P.2d 990 (Okla. 1949); and Hudson v. Hudson, 350 P.2d 596 (Okla. 1960).

[65] 557 P.2d 106 (Cal. 1976).

[66] Some states require prenuptial agreements to satisfy the state's statute of frauds and to be in writing. *See, e.g.*, MASS. GEN. L. ch. 209, §§ 25, 26 and Uniform Pre-Marital Agreement Act § 4. *See also* § 7.04(1) of the PRINCIPLES OF THE LAW OF FAMILY DISSOLUTION (Amer. Law Inst. 2002) (requiring that premarital agreement be in writing).

[67] Two cases decided in 1990 by different jurisdictions illustrate the tension between treating prenuptial agreements as ordinary contracts and treating them differently. In *Simeone v. Simeone*, 581 A.2d 162 (1990), after acknowledging the fact that husbands and wives have been treated unequally in the law, the Pennsylvania Supreme Court stated that the law has advanced to treat spouses equally. It then enforced the prenuptial agreement in the case using standard contract analysis. In the Wisconsin case of *In re Marriage of Greenwald*, 454 N.W.2d 34 (Wis. Ct. App. 1990), the Wisconsin Court of Appeal upheld a prenuptial agreement that it found to be fair at the time of divorce.

[68] *See* McKee-Johnson v. Johnson, 444 N.W.2d 259, 267–68 (Minn. 1989).

[69] In *DeMatteo v. DeMatteo*, 762 N.E.2d 797, 802 (Mass. 2002), the Supreme Judicial Court of Massachusetts stated, 'Full and fair disclosure of each party's financial circumstances is a significant aspect of the parties' obligation to deal with each other "fairly and understandingly" because they stand in a confidential relationship with each other.'

Courts have set the following conditions as manifesting a fair process: full disclosure of each person's assets, actual consultation with legal counsel or the opportunity for such consultation,[70] and a certain period time that must elapse between the signing of the prenuptial and the wedding.[71] If one or more of those conditions are not met, courts have questioned whether the process was fair. If an individual waives a condition, the waiver, if made with knowledge, will be enforced. If the enforcement of a prenuptial agreement would result in a noticeable disproportion of assets, at least one state utilizes a presumption of non-disclosure.[72] Unconscionability has also been used as a defense to the enforcement of a prenuptial contract when the result of enforcement would leave the parties in an extraordinarily unequal position, especially where there has been a provision for the wife to receive no support payments.[73]

[70] *See, e.g., Lutz v. Schneider*, 563 N.W.2d 90 (N.D. 1997), where the North Dakota Supreme Court held a premarital agreement unenforceable because one of the parties was not adequately advised to obtain independent counsel before executing the agreement.

[71] In *DeMatteo v. DeMatteo, supra* note 69, the Supreme Judicial Court of Massachusetts was asked to decide whether a prenuptial agreement in which there was a vast disparity between the man and woman was enforceable. At the time of execution, the wife's assets totaled $5,000 plus some personal property of no major consequence. The husband's assets totaled between $108 million and $133 million. The major term of the agreement provided that in the event of divorce, the wife was to receive $35,000 adjusted annually for increases in the cost of living. The wife's lawyer argued that both the process and the terms were unfair, losing on both claims. The court discussed the process in great detail, noting that the wife had had time to think about the terms of the agreement, knew about her prospective husband's financial worth, and had the assistance of counsel who explained the consequences of signing the agreement. To assure fairness, the court pointed out that a video camera was used to film the signing. *See also* §§ 7.05 and 7.07 of the PRINCIPLES OF THE LAW OF FAMILY DISSOLUTION, *supra* note 66, which set out the procedural and substantive requirements of a prenuptial agreement. With regard to the time-frame, the Principles require at least a 30-day period before marriage for the execution of the agreement.

[72] *See* Arnold v. Arnold, 553 S.W.2d 255 (Ark. 1977).

[73] *See* Uniform Premarital Agreement § 6. That section reads as follows:

Section 6. Enforcement.
(a) A premarital agreement is not enforceable if the party against whom enforcement is sought proves that:
   (1) that party did not execute the agreement voluntarily; or
   (2) the agreement was unconscionable when it was executed and, before the execution of the agreement, that party:
      (i) was not provided a fair and reasonable disclosure of the property or financial obligations of the other party;
      (ii) did not voluntarily and expressly waive, in writing, any right to disclosure of the property or financial obligations of the other party beyond the disclosure provided; and
      (iii) did not have, or reasonably could not have had, an adequate knowledge of the property or financial obligations of the other party.
(b) If a provision of a premarital agreement modifies or eliminates spousal support and that modification or elimination causes one party to the agreement to be eligible for support under a program of public assistance at the time of separation or marital

Premarital contracts have been attacked as having the potential of perpetuating the unequal economic status of women in marriage. Professor Brod has written:

Premarital agreements have a disparate impact on women—and thereby discriminate against them. Thus, the enforcement of premarital agreements implicates public policy concerns related to the eradication of gender discrimination, as well as concerns with individual autonomy and 'freedom of contract' principles.

Premarital agreements should be greeted with skepticism, not embraced with enthusiasm. In addition to strengthening the 'freedom of contract' principle and supporting individual autonomy, the law governing the enforcement of premarital agreements should be fashioned to effectuate other public policies: the eradication of gender discrimination and the attainment of economic justice for the economically vulnerable spouse at the end of a marriage. The tension between these policies and the 'freedom of contract' principle can be reconciled by the adoption of a regime that enforces a premarital agreement only if the agreement attains economic justice for the economically vulnerable spouse or, failing that, if the bargaining process culminating in execution of the agreement was demonstrably fair. In determining whether a premarital agreement should be enforced, the law may presume that an economically unjust agreement is the result of an unfair bargaining process and an economically just agreement is the result of a fair process. . . . By enforcing agreements only if there are guarantees of substantive or procedural fairness, the law will mitigate the disparate impact of premarital agreements on women as a class, while avoiding paternalism and respecting the rights of women (and men) to contract in their own interests.[74]

The point has been made that women are more economically vulnerable than men, and enforcing a premarital contract that leaves the wife in a less economically secure position than the man supports the inequality. Even if the assumption that women who enter into a prenuptial agreement are more economically vulnerable than men is true, the question is whether the present safeguards are sufficient to protect women. If those process safeguards are in place and the defense of unconscionability for substantive issues, like the amount of the division of assets, do not satisfy those who question the fairness of these agreements, the alternative is not to enforce prenuptial agreements at all. This would be unfortunate because of the great amount of judicial discretion in assigning property in the states that have adopted equitable distribution as a method of dividing assets upon divorce and community property states that adhere to a statutory share. Prenuptial agreements provide a vehicle for couples to arrange their own affairs and avoid a judicial or statutory imposed result.

Prenuptial agreements may include provisions concerning personal relationships, which may not be legally enforceable, but are formal understandings.

dissolution, a court, notwithstanding the terms of the agreement, may require the other party to provide support to the extent necessary to avoid that eligibility.
(c) An issue of unconscionability of a premarital agreement shall be decided by the court as a matter of law.

[74] Gail Frommer Brod, *Premarital Agreements and Gender Justice*, 6 YALE J.L. & FEMINISM 229, 294–95 (1994).

The subject matter of these provisions, like loyalty, the keeping of confidences, visitation of relatives, or the conduct of the couple's social life, may more appropriately be discussed in a counseling session with a psychologist or social worker, but may be also be found in an agreement.[75]

For the most part, parties are allowed to contract over almost all aspects of their married life. The exception relates to the religious upbringing of children and their care and treatment. Courts have generally been reluctant to enforce promises to raise a child in a particular faith whether in an intact family or one in which the parents are divorcing. One articulated reason relates to the American principle of separation of church and state, which translates into a judge not wanting to order anyone to perform a religious act or attend religious services. Another reason is based on the ambiguity of the promise, which does not specify the precise acts that the parent must carry out, like cooperating in religious rites, which might include baptism and confirmation as well as religious schooling. A third reason, and perhaps the most important, is the general refusal of probate judges, even with their general equity powers, to order anyone to specifically perform a positive act, which cannot be supervised. Other matters dealing with children of divorce such as the allocation of parental responsibilities, with whom the children should live, where and how they should be educated are usually subject to judicial determination as to whether the ultimate outcome will serve the child's best interests.

---

[75] The prenuptial agreement in the case of *Ball v. Ball*, 36 So.2d 172 (Fla. 1948) is reproduced in WEYRAUCH, ET AL., *supra* note 43, at 41–44. That agreement included the following provisions:

First: It is agreed by and between the parties hereto to be faithful and loyal, each to the other, in thought, speech and action, at all times and under all circumstances.

Second: It is agreed by and between the parties hereto that each will maintain and exhibit toward the other a courteous and considerate attitude in all relationships and under all circumstances.

. . .

Fifth: It is agreed by and between the parties hereto that when both of the parties hereto enjoy good health, we shall set aside three nights a week to entertain our friends and acquaintances, or to call on our friends and acquaintances, or to seek each other recreation as may be desirable. On the other four nights of each week we shall remain quietly at home, seeking such recreation and genuine happiness as is only to be found outside of the frivolities and ostentations of our present day social life.

. . .

Tenth: It is agreed by and between the parties hereto that each shall make a confidant of the other and that neither party hereto shall have any other confidant, and that on all occasions and under all circumstances each party hereto shall reveal in the frankest and fullest detail any and all matters affecting either of the parties hereto.

2
Marriage

Whether formal or informal, marriage in American law has ordinarily been thought of as a status entered into for life, regulated by the state through its legislature, and the basis for establishing a family. The American legal source of the status concept of marriage is the nineteenth-century U.S. Supreme Court case of *Maynard v. Hill*,[1] where the Court held that the legislative assembly of the territory of Oregon had the authority to dissolve the 'bonds of matrimony' between David Maynard and his wife, Lydia. It was in that case that Mr. Justice Field wrote what has perhaps become the most famous quotation about marriage in American appellate court opinions:

Marriage, as creating the most important relation in life, as having more to do with the morals and civilization of a people than any other institution, has always been subject to the control of the legislature. The body prescribes the age at which parties may contract to marry, the procedure or form essential to constitute marriage, the duties and obligations it creates, its effects upon the property rights of both, present and prospective and the acts which may constitute grounds for its dissolution.[2]

Thirty-seven years before *Maynard* was decided, the Supreme Court of Florida stated in *Ponder v. Graham*[3] that marriage was a contract. That concept was, of course, not new, having its roots in common law, incorporated in colonial practice and consistent with what has been described as a 'displacement of patriarchalism by contractualism' in the nineteenth century.[4] However,

---

[1] 125 U.S. 190 (1888).   [2] *Id.* at 205.   [3] 4 Fla. 23 (1851).
[4] Professor Michael Grossberg's excellent work on the law and the family in nineteenth-century America discusses this point. He has written that in the post-revolutionary era:

the law continued to portray marriage as a civil contract, in a vital transition the accent shifted from the first word to the second. The new emphasis was on the consensual nature of marriage. It also reflected the broader use of contract as the central metaphor for social and economic relations in early nineteenth-century America. . . . Contractualism gained strength from the same forces that were eroding the hierarchical conception of society. Rather than viewing the body politic as an amalgam of interdependent, status-defined groups, contract ideology stemmed from a world view whose lode star was the untrammeled autonomy of the individual will. Relations of all kinds were to be governed by the intentions, not the ascribed status, of their makers. The English philosopher Sir Henry Maine characterized this transition as the 'movement from status to contract.'

the Florida court's labeling of marriage as a contract in the context of the case was not designed to be interpreted as giving parties the power to set their own terms. Rather, it was that the Florida legislature had no power to dissolve a marriage contract for by so doing it would be impairing the right to contract guaranteed under the U.S. Constitution. Yet Justice Semmes's words help to define marriage as contract. He wrote, 'I know of no reason why the word contract, as used in the Constitution, should be restricted to those of pecuniary nature, and not embrace that of marriage, involving, as it does, considerations of the most interesting character and vital importance to society; to government, and the contracting parties.'[5] The two concepts of marriage, that of status and that of a special kind of contract, seemingly contradictory, have coexisted throughout the nineteenth century and are still not only referred to today but have taken on special importance.[6]

In contemporary times, however, it is difficult to fit marriage neatly into the legal construct called contract.[7] Normally, contract law assumes freedom of contract, party autonomy, and equal bargaining power. The marriage contract is not totally free of governmental regulation and therefore parties have limited freedom of choice. Party autonomy and equal bargaining power may not be present in the marriage contract. And, because of that, even though the modern marriage contract is not based on a printed form, it has some of the elements of a contract of adhesion (a one-sided contract often referred to as 'a take it or leave it' agreement) in the sense that some marital duties are imposed by law.[8] Perhaps the most that can be said is that while in the past the marital relationship was wholly defined by the state, now certain aspects of the relationship can be negotiated by

The concept of marriage as partnership could also be found in eighteenth-century America. Professor Grossberg quotes from the 1792 *Lady's Magazine*:

> A self-described 'Matrimonial Republican' defined the new perception. . . . She objected to the word 'obey in the marriage service because it is a general word, without limitations or definitions.' Instead, the writer insisted that the 'obedience between man and wife, I conceive, is, or ought to be, mutual. Marriage ought never to be considered as a contract between a superior and inferior, but a reciprocal union of interests, an implied partnership of interests, where all differences are accommodated by conference; and decision admits of no retrospect.

MICHAEL GROSSBERG, GOVERNING THE HEARTH 19 (1985).

[5] 4 Fla. at 45.

[6] *See, e.g., Loving v. Virginia*, 388 U.S. 1 (1987), where *Maynard v. Hill* was cited for the proposition that 'marriage is a social relation subject to the State's police power'. *Also see Ryan v. Ryan*, 277 So. 2d 266 (Fla. 1973), where the Supreme Court of Florida held that Florida's no-fault divorce law was constitutional. It cited *Ponder v. Graham* for the proposition that 'marriage is a contract'.

[7] Professor Ira Mark Ellman has made this point in *The Theory of Alimony*, 77 CAL. L. REV. 1, 10–11 (1989). *See also* Ira Mark Ellman & Sharon Lohr, *Marriage as Contract, Opportunistic Violence, and Other Bad Arguments for Fault Divorce*, 1997 ILL. L. REV. 719, 747.

[8] *See* WALTER O. WEYRAUCH & SANFORD N. KATZ, AMERICAN FAMILY LAW IN TRANSITION 2 (1983).

the parties, which may result in a more egalitarian relationship.[9] Also, by including the marriage within the world of contract, one effect is to move the status away from its religious roots and aspects and toward its being a secular relationship. In addition, labeling marriage as a contract has brought about a change in the attitudes of married couples and the courts. Further, the concept of marriage as a contractual relationship between two people replaces the old adage, no longer viable, of 'marriage being one' and that one is the husband. Presumptions that actions within marriage are motivated by a donative intent that have dominated family law have been abandoned giving rise to allowing spouses to sue each other. Vocabulary changes from words of intimacy, like love, to the language of commerce (e.g. profit and investment) and self-interest. Spouses become parties, participation becomes contribution, and divorce becomes dissolution.

The positive aspects of treating marriage as a special kind of partnership contract, emphasizes the individual nature of the relationship and downplays its community aspects. Indeed, the modern marriage is more like an association, in some situations a business association, of two adults who have preserved their individual rights, which have received constitutional protection.

THE STATE'S ROLE IN ESTABLISHING THE MARRIAGE RELATIONSHIP

What is the state's role in regulating marriage? The question of state intervention is often thought of narrowly, primarily in terms of the criminal law or laws dealing with child abuse and neglect. In child abuse and neglect, for example, the question posed is: under what circumstances and for what reasons should the state intervene or intrude into the parent–child relationship and make some adjustment in that relationship when allegations have been made of abuse or neglect? However, state intervention (control) is also present in subtle ways, for example, in defining the relationships that constitute a marriage and a family. It can also be seen in laws dealing with the formal requirements for marriage (like license and signatures on a marriage certificate), for obtaining a divorce, inheriting property when spouses have not made their own wishes known through wills and so forth. Even in cases of contract cohabitation or common law marriage, the jurisdictions that recognize them have controlled them by establishing certain requirements.[10]

Until the 1990s, the state's involvement in the formation of the marriage relationship appeared to be declining. That is to say, there had been more recognition of the power of individuals and couples to define their relationship or decide when to terminate it. However, at the beginning of the twenty-first century, that decline may be somewhat reversing. The current trend appears to represent a slight shift to more governmental control in the definition of marriage, but less control over divorce.

[9] *Id.*   [10] *See* Chapter 1.

FREEDOM TO MARRY AS A FUNDAMENTAL HUMAN RIGHT

Before the serious debate and flurry of legal activity about the legality of same-
sex marriages began in 1993 with the decision of *Baehr v. Lewin*[11] and the
legislative activity about recognition of same-sex marriages that occurred in
1996 and years following,[12] *Loving v. Virginia*,[13] the U.S. Supreme Court case

---

[11] 852 P.2d 44 (Haw. 1993).

[12] The Defense of Marriage Act passed by Congress (H.R. 3396) and signed by
President Clinton on September 21, 1996 reads in pertinent part as follows:

. . .

Sec. 2. POWERS RESERVED TO THE STATES
   (a) IN GENERAL—Chapter 115 of title 28, United States
Code, is amended by adding after section 1738B the following:
'Sec. 1738C. Certain acts, records, and proceedings and the effect thereof
   'No State, territory, or possession of the United States, or Indian tribe, shall
be required to give effect to any public act, record, or judicial proceeding of any
other State, territory, possession, or tribe respecting a relationship between
persons of the same sex that is treated as a marriage under the laws of such other
State, territory, possession, or tribe, or a right or claim arising from such
relationship.'
   (b) CLERICAL AMENDMENT—The table of sections at the beginning of
chapter 115 of title 28, United States Code, is amended by inserting after the
item relating to section 1738B the following new item:
   '1738C. Certain acts, records, and proceedings and the effect thereof.'
Sec. 3. DEFINITION OF MARRIAGE
   (a) IN GENERAL—Chapter 1 of title 1, United States
Code, is amended by adding at the end the following:
'Sec. 7. Definition of 'marriage' and 'spouse'
   'In determining the meaning of any Act of Congress, or any ruling, regulation,
or interpretation of the various administrative bureaus and agencies of the
United States, the word 'marriage' means only a legal union between one man
and one woman as husband and wife, and the word 'spouse' refers only to a
person of the opposite sex who is a husband or a wife.'
   (b) CLERICAL AMENDMENT—The table of sections at the beginning of
Chapter 1 of title 1, United States Code, is amended by inserting after the item
relating to section 6 the following new item:
'7. Definition of 'marriage' and 'spouse'.'

In his attack on the constitutionality of the Act, Professor Lawrence Tribe wrote:

The Full Faith and Credit Clause cannot be read as fount of authority for
Congress to set asunder the states that this clause so solemnly brought together.
Such a reading would mean, for example, that Congress could decree that any
state was free to disregard any Hawaii marriage, any California divorce,
any Kansas default judgment, any punitive damage award against a lawyer—or
any of a potentially endless list of official acts that a Congressional majority
might wish to denigrate. This would convert the Constitution's most vital
unifying clause into a license for balkanization and disunity.

Lawrence H. Tribe, *Toward a Less Perfect Union*, N.Y. TIMES, May 26, 1996, at 11E.
[13] 388 U.S. 1 (1967).

that decided the right to marry was a protected constitutional right, was considered of historical interest only. In *Loving*, the Court held that a statutory scheme that restricted a man and a woman from marrying on the basis of their race was unconstitutional as a violation of both the Equal Protection and Due Process Clauses of the Fourteen Amendment guarantees under the Federal Constitution. The Virginia miscegenation statute conformed to the Racial Integrity Act of 1924. Actually, miscegenation statutes in America date back to the nineteenth century. In the early part of the twentieth century, miscegenation laws were strengthened and the number of states with such legislation grew. By 1916 twenty-eight states and territories had some form of ban on interracial marriages.[14] The *Loving* Court's decision affected the miscegenation statutes on the books in sixteen states. The *Loving* decision should not have been a surprising outcome given the Supreme Court of California's decision almost twenty years earlier in *Perez v. Sharp*,[15] in which the California Supreme Court held that its miscegenation statute violated the Equal Protection Clause of the Federal Constitution.

From the viewpoint of precedent, *Loving* has lost its racial aspects. It has been cited most often for the concept of equality[16] or the general principle that the right to marry is a fundamental constitutional right, or for all or part of Chief Justice Warren's statement:

The freedom to marry has long been recognized as one of the vital personal rights essential to the orderly pursuit of happiness by free men.

Marriage is one of the 'basic civil rights of man,' fundamental to our very existence and survival.[17]

Indeed in the 1996 U.S. Supreme Court case of *M.L.B. v. S.L.J.*,[18] in which the Court decided that Mississippi may not deny a mother appellate review of a termination of parental rights case because of her inability to pay certain court fees, Justice Ginsburg cited *Loving* after the statement: '[c]hoices about marriage, family life, and the upbringing of children are among associational rights this Court has ranked as "of basic importance in our society".'[19] Further, citation to *Loving* is grouped with other U.S. Supreme Court cases to uphold the principle of either pro-state regulation of marriage or anti-regulation, regardless of the outcome of the case.[20]

---

[14] *See* GROSSBERG, *supra* note 4, at 136–40.   [15] 198 P.2d 17 (Cal. 1948).

[16] In the same year that the Court struck down Virginia's miscegenation statute, the Texas Court of Civil Appeals decided *In re Adoption of Gomez*, 424 S.W.2d 656 (Tex. Civ. App. 1967). In that case the court struck down the states' barrier to interracial adoption as unconstitutional under the Texas and the U.S. Constitution. The court's reference to *Loving* did not concern the application of the Fourteenth Amendment to the U.S. Constitution to interracial marriage, but to Chief Justice Warren's statement about equality, which the petitioner had cited.   [17] Loving, *supra* note 13, at 12.

[18] 519 U.S. 102 (1996).   [19] *Id.* at 116.   [20] It is cited with *Maynard v. Hill*.

Chief Justice Warren's now famous statement about the fundamental right to marry is quoted in *Zablocki v. Rehail*.[21] The case was brought to challenge the constitutionality of a Wisconsin statute that required a judicial proceeding to determine whether a divorced husband, who had an outstanding child support obligation, could remarry. The proceeding was meant to furnish fathers an opportunity to be counseled about their obligations and to protect their children. Such a requirement would test the extent to which a state can interfere with a man's fundamental right to marry. The case must be read in the context of the national 1970s problem of the public (federal and state) funding of child welfare economic support programs. From a practical perspective, the purpose of the Wisconsin statute was to reduce public expenditures by requiring divorced husbands to support their children. The Court found the statute to be unconstitutional under the Equal Protection Clause of the Fourteenth Amendment to the U.S. Constitution. Justice Marshall stated that insufficient state interests existed in this context to justify such a restriction on the fundamental right to remarry. To him, there were other, less drastic, ways of handling the problem of non-support.

THE STATE'S EFFORTS TO LIMIT MARRIAGE

How does the state limit marriage formation, something states have done since the founding of the country? State limitation can be illustrated in eight ways: the requirements for licensing (form); for avoiding a marriage (annulment); for entering marriage (age); for marrying while in confinement (prisoner's marriage); for marrying while suffering some kind of mental or emotional disorder (mental competency); for marrying with a family member (incestuous marriage); for marrying someone of the same sex (sex); and for marrying while being married to someone else (bigamous marriage). These restrictions, sometimes single and sometimes combined with others, will be illustrated with one or two leading cases.

Formal requirements for getting married existed in colonial America. At that time a marriage license along with the publication of banns was required.[22] The legal remedy for a person denied a marriage license by a clerk was and is the writ of mandamus: an order commanding an official to perform his or her ministerial duty. This was illustrated in the Pennsylvania District Court case of *F. A. Marriage License*,[23] where a clerk denied a marriage license to a woman because she had suffered from a mental illness within five years of applying for the license, a restriction imposed by the Pennsylvania marriage statute. Her application for the writ was granted after a judicial proceeding declared that the

---

[21] 434 U.S. 374 (1978).   [22] *See* GROSSBERG, *supra* note 4.
[23] 4 Pa. D. & C.2d 1 (1955).

woman had been successfully treated for her particular mental illness, had revealed her condition to her prospective husband, and that children born of the marriage would not be predisposed to the illness.

The case is interesting for a variety of reasons: the requirement of a license, its treatment of the remedy, and its discussion of the impact of mental illness on marriage. The latter raises the issue of the health requirements for a marriage license. If any trend is discernible regarding health requirements, it seems to be the abolishment of such requirements, except for blood tests in some states, for the granting of marriage licenses. The State of Florida, for example, used to require blood tests but even those were abolished perhaps because the danger of syphilis was perceived to be less harmful than it had been. AIDS testing was required for a short while before a marriage license could be issued in Illinois and Louisiana, but the statutes were repealed perhaps because they proved to be practically unenforceable.[24] People who wanted to get married but did not want to be tested went to other states to get married.

Labeling a person as mentally ill for purposes of getting married is too broad a characterization and makes little sense at the present time. In marriage, the fact that someone suffers from a defined mental illness like certain kinds of depression, or a bi-polar illness, may be unimportant unless the illness has a direct bearing on the marital relationship. A clinically depressed person may be unable to function as a spouse and that may be the basis for a divorce on the fault ground of cruelty or the no-fault basis of incompatibility of temperament. With so many methods of therapy including psychopharmaceutical, persons suffering from various forms of mental illness may be able to function in a marital relationship. Thus, denying a marriage license because someone was hospitalized for mental illness, illustrated by *F. A. Marriage License*, appears to be extremely dated.

The judge in *F. A. Marriage License* took a realistic approach to restricting marriage license requirements. He concluded his opinion with the resigned realization that, whatever the state's goal in setting marriage requirements, the parties cannot be prevented from living together without marriage or from getting married in another state and returning to Pennsylvania.

Even in cases of persons who are developmentally disabled, restrictions on their entering marriage may also be dated. If the fear for issuing a marriage

---

[24] What is the effect on a marriage if either party has AIDS? Utah declared such a marriage as void. UTAH CODE ANN. § 30-1-2 (1989). But that provision was held unenforceable in 1993 because it violated the Americans with Disabilities Act. California, Illinois, Indiana, Michigan, Rhode Island, Texas, and West Virginia require a state official to disseminate AIDS information and places for AIDS testing to couples applying for a marriage license. Would failure to disclose the existence of AIDS be grounds for annulment by the non-AIDS infected spouse? One would think that if a person failed to disclose that he or she was infected with the AIDS virus or was HIV positive, the major question asked in an annulment suit—does the condition go to the 'essentials' of the marriage—would be answered in the affirmative.

license is that the married couple might produce a developmentally disabled child, the origin of the parent's disability is important. If the source of the disability is genetic, then there could be a problem of children inheriting the defect. If the source is an injury during the birth process, there might be little concern for children being born with the same or a similar defect. A statute that would try to delve into such an area would be hopelessly complicated and unworkable. The tremendous advances in the education of persons with a developmental disability preclude making broad and definitive judgments. The important consideration should be whether these people understand the nature of marriage and whether they can function in it. A Florida statute, for example, states that persons who are developmentally disabled 'may be provided with instruction in sex education, marriage, and family planning'.[25] The assumption made by the Florida statute is that marriage is assumed to be valid. Both New York and Nebraska list mental retardation at the time of marriage as a condition that would allow for an annulment.[26]

Annulment

Annulment is a remedy for voiding a marriage. Indirectly, however, it can provide a definition of marriage as well as an understanding of what social values and societal goals the state wishes to promote through marriage. In addition, it can serve as a manifestation of the state's preference for what a married couple should look like.

The definition of marriage found in annulment cases, the focus of this discussion here, however, is retroactive because it comes after the fact of the establishment of the relationship. First, it must be said that the grounds for annulment are normally not statutory, but reflective of the common law bases for rescinding a contract. In contract law, if the process for entering into the contract is defective because of fraud, misrepresentation, duress, coercion, and some kinds of mistake, a contract can be avoided.[27] The conduct of the offending party must have an impact on material terms of the contract.

Ordinarily grounds for annulment are: fraud, misrepresentation, duress, incapacity, or existence of a prior marriage. Unlike grounds for divorce, which relate to events that occur after the marriage, these impediments or defects occur before the marriage and can prevent the marriage from being valid. In some instances the effect of the annulment ground is to avoid the marriage,

---

[25] *See* FLA. STAT. § 394.4459(7) (1989).

[26] *See* N.Y. COM. REL. LAW § 140 (Consol. 1996); NEB. REV. STAT. § 42-374 (1995).

[27] It should be noted, however, that unless a mistake as to the identity of a party to a contract is material, the contract will not be invalidated. This is consistent with the law of annulment. For a discussion of mistake as to identity of the contracting parties in contracts, see ARTHUR LINTON CORBIN, 1 CORBIN ON CONTRACTS §§ 601, 603 (1952).

meaning the marriage is invalid from its inception, like an incestuous marriage. In other instances, the marriage is voidable, meaning the marriage can be validated once the impediment is removed. For example, if an under-age person marries a person of a lawful age to marry, the marriage is voidable. However, if the couple continues to live together as husband and wife after the under-age person comes of marital age, the marriage is valid.

The most important difference between contract law and marriage law concerns the duty to disclose. As we have seen in ante-nuptial contracts, there is more of a duty to disclose information before marriage than before entering into a commercial contract. Indeed, the relationship before marriage is seen more like a period of trust than of arm's length dealing. The element of trust in the premarital context is reflected in the law's requirement that if certain facts about an individual that are thought to be material to a sound, honest, trusting, and compatible relationship are not revealed, the failure to disclose the facts may be used to support a spouse's allegation of fraud or misrepresentation, grounds for annulment. What is a material fact may change over time depending on the state's cultural (including ethnic and religious) make-up and the availability of an alternative remedy, like divorce.

The leading annulment case is *Reynolds v. Reynolds*,[28] where the Supreme Judicial Court of Massachusetts, in 1862, voided a marriage between a 17-year-old man and a 30-year-old woman. The woman had deceived the man by claiming to be 'a chaste and virtuous woman', but who in fact was pregnant by another man. The court's statement about what constitutes fraud for purposes of avoiding a marriage, written a hundred and forty years ago, defined the essential elements in marriage in nineteenth-century Massachusetts.

While, however, marriage by our law is regarded as a purely civil contract, which may well be avoided and set aside on the ground of fraud, it is not to be supposed that every error or mistake into which a person may fall concerning the character or qualities of a wife or husband, although occasioned by disingenuous or even false statements or practices, will afford sufficient reason for annulling an executed contract of marriage. . . . In the absence of force or duress, and where there is no mistake as to the identity of the person, any error or misapprehension as to personal traits or attributes, or concerning the position or circumstances in life of a party, is deemed wholly immaterial, and furnishes no good cause for divorce. Therefore no misconception as to the character, fortune, health or temper, however brought about, will support an allegation of fraud on which a dissolution of the marriage contract, when once executed, can be obtained in a court of justice. These are accidental qualities, which do not constitute the essential and material elements on which the marriage relation rests. The law, in the exercise of a wise and sound policy, seeks to render the contract of marriage, when once executed, as far as possible indissoluble. The great object of marriage in a civilized and Christian community is to secure the existence and permanence of the family relation, and to insure the legitimacy of offspring.[29]

[28] 85 Mass. 605 (1862).   [29] *Id.* at 607.

The court went on to state that the woman's false representation about being 'chaste and virtuous' later found to be untrue because of a pregnancy by another man was a ground for annulment. False statements about an individual's desires to have or not to have children have been held to be a ground for annulment even today because of the procreative goal of marriage.[30]

What is interesting about *Reynolds* is that the court implies that a certain kind of misrepresentation before marriage is excusable. Perhaps, even in the nineteenth century, it was thought that individuals may try to be attractive during courtship and engage in braggadocio, e.g. about wealth or social status, neither being judicially labeled as 'essential' to the marital relationship. In another sense, courts may take the position that an individual marries the person with whom he or she has established a relationship 'for better or for worse'.

What is 'essential'? An argument can be made that the standard for annulment should be subjective because marriages are entered into for 'love', an essentially subjective concept. The subjective test was persuasive in *Bilowit v. Dolitsky*,[31] where the New Jersey court allowed a wife to annul her marriage because of her strongly felt belief in Orthodox Judaism. In that case, the husband had misrepresented his orthodoxy, which was sufficient to avoid the marriage.

In annulment cases, a court's characterizing the revelation as 'essential' to marriage or not, or labeling the misrepresentation as relating to 'character, fortune or temper' will determine the outcome of the case. The former can result in an annulment; the latter ordinarily will not.

The majority of marriage licensing statutes in the United States are usually only 'directory' (directed to the official who issues a license) and not 'mandatory' (requiring strict compliance with licensing requirements). Thus, where the marriage licensing statute is directory, a marriage entered into without a proper license or officiated by a person without statutory authority may well be valid, although the clerk who issued the license may be subject to disciplinary action or punishment.[32] Where the statute is mandatory, the result of non-compliance with statutory requirements may lead to an invalid marriage.[33] This distinction

[30] *See Williams v. Witt*, 98 N.J. Super. 1, 235 A.2d 902 (1967), where a New Jersey Superior Court annulled a marriage because a man concealed from his wife his desire not to have children.

[31] 304 A.2d 774 (N.J. Super. 1973).

[32] *See, e.g.*, M.G.L.A. c. 207, § 48. That Massachusetts law provides a penalty for solemnizing a marriage without authority. However, such a marriage is not necessarily void. *See* CHARLES P. KINDREGAN, JR. & MONROE L. INKER, FAMILY LAW & PRACTICE 443–44 (1990).

[33] For a discussion of directory and mandatory licensing statutes, see *Carbetta v. Carbetta*, 438 A.2d 109 (Conn. 1980). In that case, Justice Peters wrote: 'In the majority of states, unless the licensing statute plainly makes an unlicensed marriage invalid, "the cases find the policy favoring valid marriages sufficiently strong to justify upholding the unlicensed ceremony . . ." ' (citation omitted). *Id.* at 112–13.

is not only important for determining the validity of a marriage in the state in which the marriage took place, but also has implications for the recognition of marriages beyond that state. Cases dealing with under-age couples who marry illustrate this point.

Age

In *Wilkins v. Zelichowski*,[34] the Supreme Court of New Jersey reversed the decisions of both the Chancery Court and the Appellate Division, which would not annul an under-age marriage entered into in another state. In that case, a 16-year-old young woman and her boyfriend eloped to Indiana to marry because the bride-to-be was too young to marry in their home state of New Jersey. After the Indiana wedding ceremony, the couple returned to New Jersey and lived together in their own household. Ten months later the young woman gave birth to a baby, fathered by her husband. Two months after the birth of the child, the child's father was convicted of certain crimes and confined to a reformatory where he was at the time of the annulment proceedings.

According to New Jersey law, the minimum age for a female to marry is 18 years old. In eloping to Indiana, the couple evaded the laws of New Jersey. Even though the young woman sought an annulment during her minority and had a child from her husband, and even though an annulment would be in the best interests of the child, the Chancery Court would not annul the marriage. It based its decision on the conflict of laws rule that a marriage valid where celebrated should be recognized everywhere. The Appellate Division affirmed that decision.

The Supreme Court of New Jersey, however, decided that its state's strong public policy against under-age marriages should be respected, and it reversed the decision of the Appellate Division. Ordinarily an annulment would treat a child born of an annulled marriage to be illegitimate, however, New Jersey's statute provides otherwise.[35]

It is interesting to note that the under-age party in most of the marriages where age is a problem is a young woman. The common law age limits for marriage are 12 for the woman and 14 for the man. Those ages were changed by the Age of Majority Act of 1929 when Parliament raised the age to 16 for both sexes, and at the same time rendered marriages of a couple of 12 and 14 to be void, not voidable. In the United States, the age at which a woman could marry without parental consent was 18 while a man had to be 21. However, a Utah court held that its marriage statute, which set different ages for men and women to marry, was unconstitutional.[36]

---

[34] 140 A.2d 65 (N.J. 1958).   [35] *See* N.J.S. 2A:34-20, N.J.S.A.
[36] *See* Lovato v. Evans, District Court of Utah (3rd Dist.) 1 Fam. L. Rep. 2848 (1975). Similarly, the U.S. Supreme Court held in *Stanton v. Stanton*, 421 U.S. 7 (1975) that Utah's statute that required parental support for women up to 18 and men up to 21 was unconstitutional.

In *Short v. Hotaling*,[37] the New York Supreme Court refused to annul the marriage of a 16-year-old girl and a 19-year-old boy who eloped and were married in Virginia. Following their marriage, the couple cohabited with each other—an important factor in cases dealing with the enforcement of an under-age marriage. With standing provided by a New York statute, the father, as the girl's guardian ad litem, brought the annulment suit. The court felt that the father's motivation was punitive in his pursuit of his son-in-law who displayed affection to his young wife, even willing to convert to her religion. The girl's father would not allow the couple to share a bed in his and his wife's house, but did suggest that the couple stay at a hotel the night after their wedding, even taking them to another hotel a day later. The court was convinced that the girl was a mature and responsible person who understood the meaning of marriage. The court went on to basically describe the essential foundation of marriage:

The marital status should be upheld, when the underaged persons involved show willingness and capacity for enduring marital life and for the building of a family unit. . . .

We know from our experience in the matrimonial courts that maturity of body alone is no sure foundation for a satisfactory marriage. What is needed is maturity of both body and mind, which quite often does occur in the case of a youthful couple while sometimes absent in people of age. Where it is present, as it is here, though it be a marriage without parental consent, the marriage deserves to be sustained.[38]

Prisoner's Marriage

To what extent does incarceration limit a person's right to marry? *In re Carrafa*[39] and *Turner v. Safley*[40] deal with this question. In *Carrafa*, Victor Carrafa, an inmate at Folsom State Prison, brought a habeas corpus petition to challenge the action of the Corrections Department that had temporarily prohibited him from marrying his fiancée. Prison authorities denied Mr. Carrafa's request to marry his fiancée because of her being denied visitation privileges. She had been accused of smuggling marijuana and a weapon into the prison as well as falsifying information on the questionnaire for visitors. The California Court of Appeal, citing *Loving*, held that '[t]he decision to marry is a fundamental right',[41] and that a prison may not deny an inmate his right unless there are security reasons. To the court there were other, less drastic measures, which the prison authorities could take in securing the prison. The court allowed the writ to be issued, thus directing the Department of Corrections to 'permit petitioner's marriage under such circumstances as will respect prison security'.[42]

Once again *Loving* was cited in *Turner v. Safley*[43] for the proposition that marriage is a fundamental right. Justice O'Connor, writing for the Court, held

---

[37] 225 N.Y.S.2d 53 (N.Y. Sup. Ct. 1962).   [38] *Id.* at 55.
[39] 77 Cal. App. 3d 788, 143 Cal. Rptr. 848 (1978).   [40] 482 U.S. 78 (1987).
[41] 143 Cal. Rptr. at 851.   [42] *Id.*   [43] 482 U.S. 78 (1987).

that not strict scrutiny, but 'a lesser standard of scrutiny is appropriate in determining the constitutionality of the prison rules' regarding marriage.[44]

In *Turner*, the Missouri prison officials had a regulation that prohibited inmates from marrying unless the prison superintendent 'approved the marriage after finding that there were compelling reasons for doing so'.[45] Turner, the superintendent of the prison, argued that allowing inmates to marry could affect concerns for security and rehabilitation. Justice O'Connor wrote that this justification for the denial of applications for marriage was inadequate. In fact, she thought that the rule denying marriages was too broad. Indeed, she went on to say that the rehabilitation [female inmates would be dependent on their husbands and would be subjected to abuse when they were released] objective was 'suspect'. Male inmates were routinely granted approval to marry whereas female inmates were subject to careful scrutiny before their requests to marry could be approved. The Court held that while 'prison officials may regulate the time and circumstances under which the marriage ceremony itself takes place',[46] they cannot completely ban marriages.

These prisoners' rights cases can be seen as an illustration of a strong public policy in favor of promoting marriage by not allowing administrative reasons for restricting it. In a way, the holdings in these cases represent a reversal of the old concept of 'civil death', a dated status reserved for prisoners who received a life sentence. These prisoners were not only denied the opportunity to marry, but their existing marriage could be considered terminated without taking any action—an extraordinary departure from divorce law, which requires an individual to sue for divorce.

Mental Competence

Mental incompetence may be used as a basis for an annulment if the incompetence existed before the marriage and the petition for annulment occurred soon after the discovery of that fact. To delay bringing a suit for an annulment may result in a decision like *Larson v. Larson*.[47] In that case, the plaintiff husband waited ten years, or perhaps slightly longer, from the date of his marriage before he sought an annulment. His basis was that his wife was mentally ill and had to be hospitalized from time to time. His wife had shown signs of her illness before his marriage to her. The case is important for its description of the necessary mental status for getting married in Illinois:

The [husband] has not satisfied the burden of proving, clearly and definitely, that the [wife] was an 'insane person' at the particular time of this marriage, . . . that she was at the time incapable of understanding the nature of the act, that she had insufficient mental capacity to enter into the status and understand the nature, effect, duties, and obligations of the marriage contract, that she was mentally incapable of giving an intelligent, understanding

---

[44] *Id.* at 81.   [45] *Id.* at 96.   [46] *Id.* at 99.
[47] 192 N.E.2d 594 (Ill. App. 1963).

consent, or that her mind could not and did not act rationally regarding the precise thing in contemplation, marriage, and this particular marriage in dispute.[48]

In *Larson*, because Mr. Larson lived with his wife for such a long period with knowledge of her mental problems, it might be said that he had 'ratified' her erratic behavior or was 'estopped' from raising it as a basis for annulment. The appropriate remedy for Mr. Larson might have been divorce if, in Illinois at that time, the facts could have fit into a ground for divorce.[49]

Incestuous Marriage

The ultimate origin of the nuclear family incest taboo is a mystery but the explanations for it in modern civilized society have been based on biological, sociological, and psychiatric considerations in addition to ethical and religious grounds. Each consideration has been subject to criticism and has been in vogue during various decades during the nineteenth and twentieth centuries. As more and more is learned about genetics, the laws regarding incestuous marriages may be revised.

The biological explanation, the one most often given and subject to change if genetic research results in findings that contradict conventional wisdom, is that the consequences of inbreeding (marrying close biologically related family relatives) decreases fitness and causes certain conditions and possibly incurable defects (like hemophilia, infertility, dwarfism, disfigurement, and mental retardation). As a result, incest has a serious impact on the survival of the individual and the human family. The sociological explanation is based on the theory that the family is the basic unit in society for socializing children. Sexual competition within the family interferes with the family's function. In addition, although inbreeding may be a means of preserving a family's assets, it prevents the addition of new ideas, new blood, and new ways of living. From a psychological point of view, incest is said to confuse family roles, underscore dependency and domination of the stronger family member (mother, father, or older sibling) over the weaker, and thus interfere with the normal sexual development of children. The Freudian explanation of the incest taboo is that it exists to condemn the normal unconscious sexual impulses children have for their adult parents.[50] All American jurisdictions have statutory prohibitions to marriages based on affinity and consanguinity.

---

[48] *Id.* at 598.

[49] In some states, Mrs. Larson's conduct might have been considered to be mental cruelty—that is if the wife's bizarre behavior caused the husband great suffering. Had Mr. Larson sued for divorce, among other legal responsibilities like alimony and property, he might have been responsible for all of Mrs. Larson's medical bills as well as her health insurance.

[50] For a full discussion on the origins of the incest taboo, see KARIN C. MEISELMAN, INCEST (1978).

A most interesting case concerning incest and its application to marriage is *Israel v. Allen*.[51] In that case the Supreme Court of Colorado was asked to decide whether a provision of its marriage law modeled after the Uniform Marriage and Divorce Law § 204, which prohibited adopted siblings the right to marry, was unconstitutional. The case concerned Martin Richard Israel and Tammy Lee Bannon Israel who were adopted siblings without a common biological parent. (Martin's father adopted Tammy, and Martin and Tammy had not been raised together nor had they lived together after Tammy's adoption). These facts complicated their legal status for purposes of obtaining a marriage license and marrying. The case arose after the clerk and recorder of deeds denied Richard and Tammy a marriage license. The lower court found Colorado's section of its marriage law that prohibited adopted couples the right to marry as an unconstitutional violation of the equal protection of the laws. The Supreme Court of Colorado affirmed the lower court's decision. It held that since the prohibition failed to satisfy minimum rationality requirements, the court did not need to reach the question whether the statute infringed on the couple's fundamental right to marry.

The court stated that while adopted children were to be treated like children born of the marriage, that status of equality did not extend to all purposes, including incest. The court treated adopted siblings like persons related by affinity and therefore not subject to the same restrictions as those related by consanguinity.

If one considers the conventional explanations for the incest prohibitions (biological, sociological, and psychological), and looks at the facts in *Israel v. Allen*, one would see that the court reached a correct result. Since the couple was not biologically related and not raised together as brother and sister, there is no great likelihood of defective offspring (caused by a biological relationship), no disruption of family harmony, and no fear of insularity. Nor, according to footnote 2 in the opinion, did the Roman Catholic Bishop of the Archdiocese of Denver find any moral or religious objections to the union.

A result different from *Israel v. Allen* occurred a year before in Pennsylvania whose marriage statute did not have a prohibition against the issuance of a marriage license to adopted siblings. In the case of *In re MEW and MLB*,[52] the judge took seriously the policy of Pennsylvania's adoption laws that made adopted children equal to biological children in that both kinds of children had the same legal obligations and disabilities. It mattered little to the judge that the adopted siblings were not raised together. He looked at the 'integrity of the family', the conventional justification for the incest taboos, and upheld the clerk's refusal to issue a marriage license to the adopted siblings. In a concurring opinion, the judge wrote that adopted siblings should not marry each other because 'the sanctity of the home should be maintained and there should not be

[51] 577 P.2d 762 (Colo. 1978).   [52] 4 Pa. D. & C.3d 51 (1977).

competition for sexual companionship between members of the same household or family'.[53] The dissenting judge wrote that he did not think that the marriage of the adopted siblings 'would undermine the fabric of family life'.[54] He felt that since the couple had not been raised to maturity in the same household, although they had lived in the same household for a short period, they could not be considered '*de facto* brother and sister'.[55]

What if after the decision in *MEW and MLB*, the disappointed couple went on a ski vacation to Colorado and got married in that state? The marriage would be valid in Colorado, but would it be valid in Pennsylvania? There are two views on the recognition of the validity of a marriage. Under the conventional choice of law rule of *lex loci contractus*, the validity of a marriage is determined by the law where it was contracted.[56] However, the Restatement (Second) of Conflict of Laws § 283 (1971) states that the 'validity of a marriage is to be determined by the local law of the state which, with respect to the particular issue, has the most significant relationship to the spouses and the marriage'. The Restatement's approach is consistent with the 'significant contacts' theory in conflict of laws, which is less formalistic than the conventional rule and allows for the weighing of factors.[57] Some states have enacted some form of the Uniform Marriage Evasion Act that provides that the domicile of the parties need not recognize a marriage of its domiciliaries if the couple went to another state to specifically avoid the laws of their home state.[58]

---

[53] *Id.* at 60.   [54] *Id.* at 62.   [55] *Id.*

[56] This is the conventional view. *See* 2 BEALE, CONFLICT OF LAWS 665–74 (1935); ALBERT EHRENZWEIG, CONFLICT OF LAWS 377 (1962); EUGENE F. SCOLES & PETER HAY, CONFLICT OF LAWS (2d) 436–43 (1992).

[57] Section 6 lists these factors:

> (a) the needs of the interstate and international systems, (b) the relevant policies of the forum, (c) the relevant policies of other interested states and the relative interests of those states in the determination of the particular issue, (d) the protection of justified expectations, (e) the basic policies underlying the particular field of law, (f) certainty, predictability and uniformity of result, and (g) ease in the determination and application of the law to be applied.

RESTATEMENT OF THE LAW 2ND, Conflict of Laws 2d, Vol. 1, § 6 (1969).

[58] Sixteen states have enacted the Act in some form. *See* HANDBOOK OF NATIONAL CONFERENCE OF COMMISSIONERS ON UNIFORM STATE LAWS 64 (1943); Charles W. Taintor, II, *Marriage in the Conflict of Laws*, 9 VAND. L. REV. 607, 629 (1956).
The Massachusetts Act reads as follows:

> If any person residing and intending to continue to reside in this commonwealth is disabled or prohibited from contracting marriage under the laws of this commonwealth and goes into another jurisdiction and there contracts a marriage prohibited and declared void by the laws of this commonwealth, such marriage shall be null and void for all purposes in this commonwealth with the same effect as though such prohibited marriage had been entered into in this commonwealth.

M.G.L.A. c. 207, § 10.

The conflicts issue arose in a decedents' estates context in *In re May's Estate*,[59] where the highest court in New York was asked to recognize a marriage between an uncle and his niece, both of the Jewish faith, that was celebrated in Rhode Island where such a marriage is specifically made legal. In the New York Domestic Relations Law, however, a marriage between an uncle and a niece or an aunt and a nephew is incestuous and void, and no exception is made for people of the Jewish faith. The New York provision is consistent with § 207 of the Uniform Marriage and Divorce Act that prohibits a marriage between an uncle and a niece regardless of their religion. The New York Court of Appeals, unwilling to extend its New York prohibition to an out-of-state marriage, upheld the validity of the marriage by stating that the New York statute did not expressly regulate 'within the domiciliary State marriages solemnized abroad', and 'the legality of a marriage between persons *sui juris* is to be determined by the law of the place where it is celebrated'.[60]

The dissent embraced the theory behind the Uniform Marriage Evasion Act and stated that the uncle and niece in the case were domiciliaries of New York where the marriage would be clearly void and went to Rhode Island for the specific purpose of avoiding the New York law. The dissenting judge went on to say that the marriage between an uncle and niece fell within the exception of the general rule of recognition because it was 'contrary to the prohibitions of natural law or the express prohibitions of a statute'.[61]

Eight years later in *Catalano v. Catalano*,[62] another decedents' estates case, the Connecticut Supreme Court would not recognize a marriage between a Connecticut man and his niece, an Italian citizen, that had taken place in Italy in 1951, seven years before the man's death. The issue before the Connecticut court was whether the decedent's niece could qualify as his widow and claim a widow's allowance for support under Connecticut law. In its opinion the court reaffirmed its position that a 'state has the authority to declare what marriages of its citizens shall be recognized as valid, regardless of the fact that the marriages may have been entered into in foreign jurisdictions where they were valid'.[63] The court went on to declare that Connecticut's policy toward incest, expressed in its criminal law, was and is so serious that one who engages in it is subject to being penalized by imprisonment up to ten years. Thus, the court

---

The application of this provision would result in Massachusetts not recognizing the marriage of a Massachusetts domiciliary who travels to another state so as to avoid the marriage laws of Massachusetts and returns to Massachusetts to live with his or her spouse. The same result would occur under an application of a conflict of laws rule that a marriage valid in the state of celebration is valid everywhere unless it conflicts with the public policy of the marital domicile. Another aspect of the Massachusetts Marriage Evasion Act provides that if a person is under a disability from marrying in his or her domicile, that person may not marry in Massachusetts. For a discussion of the Massachusetts experience, see KINDREGAN & INKER, *supra* note 32, at 461–62.

[59] 114 N.E.2d 4 (N.Y. 1953).   [60] *Id.* at 6.   [61] *Id.* at 8.
[62] 170 A.2d 726 (Conn. 1961).   [63] *Id.* at 728.

felt compelled to deny recognition of the marriage between an uncle and his niece even though the marriage took place in Italy where it was valid.[64]

In a dissenting opinion, the judge wrote that he thought the majority interpreted the Connecticut statute too broadly so as to prohibit the recognition of marriages that were valid in the jurisdiction where celebrated. He pointed out that Connecticut's marriage statute does not refer to evading its laws. And, if it had, the widow had been innocent of any intent to evade Connecticut laws. Indeed, she had remained in Italy and had given birth to a child following her marriage to the decedent. Further, he pointed out that the widow had not intended to emigrate to the United States. In addition, he felt that the result in the case would mean that the couple's relationship would be considered 'illicit' and their child would be illegitimate in Connecticut. The dissenting judge found such an outcome to be justified only if the Connecticut legislature had clearly expressed itself in one of its laws, which it had not.

Sex

Transsexualism

Surgically changing one's sex is not the shocking act that it was thirty years ago when sex classification was determined at birth by the examination of genitalia and recorded on a birth certificate. At that time, adults who changed their sex were considered by some to be freaks, and social acceptability was not easily obtained. Sexual classification was so fixed in the minds of society that it was thought to be immutable. The question for our purposes is what impact does the change from male to female, or female to male, achieved through surgery, have on the legal status of marriage?

In *M.T. v. J.T.*[65] a wife sued her husband for support. The unusual aspect of the case concerns the sexual identity of the wife, M.T., who was born a male and with the knowledge and financial support of her future husband, J.T., underwent a transsexual operation to become a female. After the operation M.T. and J.T. were married. J.T., the husband, defended the support action by denying the validity of the marriage. According to him, he had married a person born a male and such a marriage of two men is void. Ordinarily, the defense of estoppel would be applicable in a case where a person marries another knowing about a disability of the other person and who later wants to take advantage of the disability. But, the fact of transsexualism makes this case extraordinary.

The defendant presented the argument that won the day in the 1970 English case of *Corbett v. Corbett*,[66] that sexual identity is determined at birth and

---

[64] A marriage between an uncle and his niece is prohibited by § 87 of the Italian Civil Code. However, Italian legal authorities gave the couple legal dispensation in order to marry.   [65] 355 A.2d 204 (N.J. Super. 1976).

[66] 2 W.L.R. 1306, 2 All E.R. 33 (P.D.A. 1970). Notwithstanding the advances that have been made in medical science and technology since the *Corbett* case was decided,

changing a person's sexual classification is beyond human control. In taking into account the advances made in understanding the medical, psychological, and social aspects of transsexualism and the fact of the husband's cooperation in the sexual assignment surgery, the court decided that M.T. was a female, the marriage between the parties was valid, and the husband had a duty to support his wife. The court's concluding paragraph not only recognizes the transsexual status but affirms the heterosexual nature of marriage:

In this case the transsexual's gender and genitalia are no longer discordant; they have been harmonized through medical treatment. Plaintiff has become physically and psychologically unified and fully capable of sexual activity consistent with her reconciled sexual attributes of gender and anatomy. Consequently, plaintiff should be considered a member of the female sex for marital purposes. It follows that such an individual would have the capacity to enter into a valid marriage relationship with a person of the opposite sex and did so here. In so ruling we do no more than give legal effect to a fait accompli, based upon medical judgment and action which are irreversible. Such recognition will promote the individual's quest for inner peace and personal happiness, while in no way disserving any societal interest, principle of public order or precept of morality.[67]

Same Sex

During the 1970s and 1980s, four American state appellate courts were faced with the basic question of whether marriage should be restricted to hetero-sexual couples or whether same-sex couples could marry.[68] In the 1990s same-sex couples who had been refused marriage licenses and sought relief under state constitutional law in their state courts found some judicial support but not in their legislatures nor in the electorate. The closest proponents of same-sex marriage have come to being successful was in Hawaii and in Vermont under each of those state constitutions.

In *Baehr v. Lewin*,[69] Ms. Baehr applied for a marriage license to marry another woman. Mr. Lewin, the Director of the Department of Health, refused to issue her a license and Baehr filed a complaint against Mr. Lewin. Baehr sought (1) a declaration that Hawaii Revised Statutes (HRS) § 572–1 (1985) was unconstitutional because as 'construed and applied' by the Department of Health, it would not allow the marriage solely on the basis of the fact that the two persons seeking the license were of the same sex; and (2) 'preliminary and

---

twenty-six years later the Court of Appeal reaffirmed *Corbett* in the case of *J. v. S.T.*, The Times, Nov. 25, 1996.

[67] M.T. v. J.T., 355 A.2d at 211.

[68] These cases were: Jones v. Callahan, 501 S.W.2d 588 (Ky. Ct. App. 1973); Baker v. Nelson, 191 N.W.2d 185 (Minn. 1971), *appeal dismissed*, 409 U.S. 810 (1972); De Santo v. Barnsley, 476 A.2d 952 (Pa. Super. 1984); and Singer v. Hara, 522 P.2d 1187, *rev. denied*, 84 Wash. 2d 1008 (1974). During this same time, the U.S. Supreme Court decided *Bowers v. Hardwick*, 478 U.S. 186 (1986). For a discussion of *Bowers*, see accompanying text to note 137 *infra*.   [69] 852 P.2d 44 (Haw. 1993).

permanent injunctions prohibiting the future withholding of marriage licenses on that sole basis'.[70] The circuit court granted the defendant's motion for judgment on the pleadings on 'the basis that Lewin was "entitled to judgment in his favor as a matter of law" '.[71] The court dismissed Baehr's complaint with prejudice, and Baehr appealed to the Supreme Court of Hawaii.

Writing for the majority of the supreme court, Justice Moon vacated the circuit court's ruling, and remanded the case for further proceedings consistent with the reasoning of his opinion. The Supreme Court of Hawaii held that to deny a couple of the same sex the legal status of being married was an infringement on their rights to equal protection of the laws in Hawaii, rights guaranteed under the Hawaii State Constitution. And, because sex is a suspect category for purposes of equal protection analysis, any infringement on equal protection rights was subject to the strict scrutiny test. The court placed the burden on the defendant to justify a compelling state interest for the sex restriction and also to show that the marriage statute was 'narrowly drawn to avoid unnecessary abridgment of constitutional rights'.[72]

In his dissent, Judge Heen wrote that the Hawaii statute did not violate the state's constitution because the marriage law treated men and women equally. Since both sexes were treated alike, the law did not establish a suspect classification based on sex. Thus, a strict scrutiny test was unnecessary. There was only a need for the application of the rational basis test and that test was satisfied. On remand the case was litigated again in the circuit court and on December 3, 1996, the court handed down its decision in *Baehr v. Miike*.[73] That court held that the State of Hawaii did not meet its burden that a compelling state interest existed to deny a same-sex couple their right to marry, and that the Hawaii marriage law was narrowly drawn to avoid unnecessary abridgement of a citizen's equal protection of the law. Much of the circuit court's opinion is devoted to a discussion of appropriateness of gay men and lesbians as parents, the seriousness of the mutual commitment gay men and lesbian couples have to each other, and the stability of their monogamous relationship. In addition to the moral and cultural objections to same-sex marriage, these three issues seem to form the basis for arguments for and against the marriage of same-sex partners. These arguments are usually masked by constitutional doctrine. From reading the court's opinion, one gets the impression that the litigation must have involved a battle of psychology experts because of the conflicting testimony of psychologists concerning the impact of sexual orientation on child development and the permanency of same-sex unions.

The court concluded that:

14. The Defendant presented meager evidence with regard to the importance of the institution of traditional marriage, the benefits which that relationship provides to the community

---

[70] *Id.* at 48.   [71] *Id.* at 52.   [72] *Id.* at 68.
[73] 1996 WL 694235 (1996). The change in the name of the defendant was caused by the appointment of a new Director of the Department of Health.

and, most importantly, the adverse effects, of any, which same-sex marriage would have on the institution of traditional marriage and how those adverse effects would impact on the community and society. The evidentiary record in this case is inadequate to thoughtfully examine and decide these significant issues.[74]

. . .

17. In this case the evidence presented by Defendant does not establish or prove that same-sex marriage will result in prejudice or harm to an important public or governmental interest.

18. . . . Defendant has failed to present sufficient credible evidence which demonstrates that the public interest in the well-being of children and families, or the optimal development of children would be adversely affected by same-sex marriage. Nor has Defendant demonstrated how same-sex marriage would adversely affect the public fisc, the state interest in assuring recognition of Hawaii marriages in other states, the institution of traditional marriage, or any other important public or governmental interest.

The evidentiary record presented in this case does not justify the sex-based classification of HRS § 572-1.

Therefore, the court specifically finds and concludes, as a matter of law, that Defendant has failed to sustain his burden to overcome the presumption that HRS § 572-1 is unconstitutional by demonstrating or proving that the statute furthers a compelling state interest.[75]

Following the Circuit Court's decision, the Hawaii state legislature enacted the Reciprocal Beneficiaries Act.[76] The legislature also proposed an amendment to its constitution that would limit marriage to heterosexual couples. The state's electorate approved the amendment.[77] With that action, the case was essentially concluded.[78]

Following Hawaii's response to the same-sex marriage issue, three same-sex couples applied for marriage licenses in Vermont. They were denied the licenses, and thereupon sued the State of Vermont, the Towns of Milton and Shelburne, Vermont, and the City of South Burlington. They sought a declaratory judgment that the refusal of marriage licenses to them violated the marriage statutes and the Vermont Constitution. The couples lost in the trial court and appealed their case to the state's supreme court.

The opening paragraphs of the supreme court's opinion in *Baker v. Vermont*[79] captures the issues presented and the court's conclusion:

May the State of Vermont exclude same-sex couples from the benefits and protections that its laws provide to opposite-sex married couples? That is the fundamental question

---

[74] *Id.* at 20.   [75] *Id.* at 21.

[76] For a discussion of the Reciprocal Beneficiaries Act, see Chapter 1.

[77] Haw. Const. art. 1, § 23.

[78] The second appeal to the state supreme court was dismissed as moot. *See* Baehr v. Miike, 994 P.21d 566 (Haw. 1999). For a full discussion of the case and its place in constitutional law, see Jerome A. Barron, *The Constitutionalization of American Family Law, in* CROSS CURRENTS—FAMILY LAW AND POLICY IN THE UNITED STATES AND ENGLAND 257–78 (Sanford N. Katz, John Eekelaar & Mavis Maclean eds., 2000) [hereinafter CROSS CURRENTS].   [79] 744 A.2d 864 (Vt. 1999).

we address in this appeal, a question that the Court well knows arouses deeply-felt religious, moral and political beliefs. . . . The issue before the Court, moreover, does not turn on the religious or moral debate over intimate same-sex relationships, but rather on the statutory and constitutional basis for the exclusion of same-sex couples from the secular benefits and protections offered married couples.

We conclude that under the Common Benefits Clause of the Vermont Constitution, which, in pertinent part reads:

> That government is, or ought to be, instituted for the common benefit, protection, and security of the people, nation, or community, and not for the particular emolument or advantage of any single person, family, or set of persons, who are a part only of that community . . .

We hold that the state is constitutionally required to extend to same-sex couples the common benefits and protections that flow from marriage under Vermont law. Whether this ultimately takes the form of inclusion within the marriage laws themselves or a parallel 'domestic partnership' system or some equivalent statutory alternative, rests with the Legislature. Whatever system is chosen, however, must conform with the constitutional imperative to afford all Vermonters the common benefit, protection, and security of the law.[80]

It is important to note that the Vermont Supreme Court viewed the case as a question of same-sex couples' sharing the same benefits, protection, and security as married couples under the state's constitution, not the Federal Constitution. Essentially the court passed the opportunity to provide these couples with these benefits to its legislature. The legislature could choose to change its marriage laws to enable same-sex couples to secure licenses to marry, thus achieving the actual status of marriage, or to provide the couples with benefits and protections equal to marriage but without the title. The legislature chose the latter with the passage of the Vermont Civil Unions Act.[81]

In 2002 the Commonwealth of Massachusetts became the next battleground for same-sex proponents to secure the legal status of marriage and the recognition that marriage enjoys. In *Goodridge v. Department of Public Health*,[82] seven same-sex couples were denied marriage licenses in their respective cities, and thus sought relief in the Massachusetts Superior Court. Their argument was that they were denied their rights under the Massachusetts Constitution. The plaintiffs' motion for summary judgment was denied, and the defendant's motion for summary judgment was allowed. The plaintiffs sought direct appeal to the Supreme Judicial Court of Massachusetts where the case will be decided in 2003.

In the Superior Court's decision, Justice Connolly reviewed the history of marriage in Massachusetts, and his opinion sets down the traditional arguments for limiting marriage to heterosexual couples. In writing about the word 'marriage', he quoted the nineteenth-century case of *Inhabitants of Milford v.*

---

[80] *Id.* at 867.

[81] Vermont Civil Unions Act, Pb. Act. 91 H. 847, 2000 Vt. Acts & Resolves. For a discussion of the Act, see Chapter 1.   [82] 2002 WL 1299135 (Mass. Super.).

Inhabitants of Worcester,[83] where the Supreme Judicial Court defined marriage as a 'civil contract founded in the social nature of man, and intended to regulate, chasten, and refine intercourse between the sexes; and to multiply, preserve, and improve the species.'[84] He then supported this definition by citing contemporary same-sex marriage cases, which restricted marriage to heterosexual couples.

In addition, Justice Connolly used statutory construction rules to interpret Massachusetts's marriage statute so as to restrict the status to one man and one woman. Supported by legal history and judicial precedent, he interpreted the state's Declaration of Rights (which embraces the values of liberty, freedom, equality, free speech) in its constitution in such a way as not to include the right to marry. Further, the justice discussed and seemed to place a great deal of importance on the extent to which heterosexual marriage is deeply rooted in the social, legal, and political history as well as the traditions of Massachusetts. He concluded with a statement that 'marriage's central purpose' was to procreate, and that marriage should be limited to couples who, 'theoretically, are capable of procreation'.[85] Like Vermont Supreme Court, the Superior Court in Massachusetts stated that the state legislature was the appropriate forum to regulate the formation requirements for marriage.

The statement that the 'central purpose' of marriage is procreation found in the Massachusetts and Vermont cases and the discussion about child development issues and same-sex parents in the Hawaii case are subject to criticism. If one were to take seriously the procreation argument, one would have to ask the question of whether a marriage license could be denied to a couple, one or both of whom were sterile or impotent. In truth, there is no official inquiry into the reproductive capabilities of couples who wish to marry. Nor is there any prohibition on a man and a woman, each beyond child-bearing age, obtaining a marriage license. Marriage licensing statutes provide a minimum age, but not a maximum one. The procreation justification is aspirational, not actual.

The child development argument, which states that children are best raised in a family of a mother and father, is in a sense also aspirational because of the fact that such a goal is not always possible. Divorce, death, and war, are at least three reasons for not achieving the goal. Yet children survive all three events.

The state constitutional law issues raised in Hawaii, Vermont, and Massachusetts are different because of special provisions in each state's constitution. But the principle argument that a person has a fundamental right to

---

[83] 7 Mass. (1 Tyng) 48 (1810).   [84] *Id.* at 51.

[85] Goodridge v. Dep't of Pub. Health, 2002 WL 1299135 at 14. The court cited the following cases to support its conclusion: Baker v. State of Vermont, 744 A.2d 880 (1999); Commonwealth of Mass. v. Stowell, 449 N.E.2d 357 (Mass. 1983); Inhabitants of Milford v. Inhabitants of Worcester, 7 Mass. (1 Tyng) 48 (1810); Adams v. Howerton, 486 F. Supp. 1119 (D. Cal. 1980); Singer v. Hara, 522 P.2d 1187 (Wash. Ct. App. 1974); Dean v. D.C., 653 A.2d 307 (D.C. 1995).

marry whomever he or she chooses may be weakened by countervailing arguments that have shown the number of areas in which the state has limited that right with persuasive justification. The statement about history and tradition of a people as justification for maintaining marriage as a complimentary heterosexual relationship should not be underestimated. It supports the position that allowing same-sex marriage is not just a matter of semantics. Rather it would be changing a model of marriage that may have in the past supported the domination of the husband and the dependency of the wife, but has developed into its contemporary form as an egalitarian relationship (if the couple wishes it to be) that fulfills many human needs and instincts. This modern model of marriage preserves the mystery inherent in the heterosexual relationship.

Although it can be argued that both history and tradition in certain parts of the United States produced miscegenation statutes, the counter-argument is that barring interracial marriage as part of a racially motivated scheme that was certainly neither universally nor nationally recognized. Nor had it been part of the Judeo-Christian tradition that has been incorporated into American marriage laws. Miscegenation was, as mentioned, limited to a certain part of the country. Same-sex marriage has never been a part of the English law upon which American marriage law is based. Nor has it been a part of Roman law.[86]

An important point made in both the Vermont and the Massachusetts cases concerned the institution empowered by law and history to either limit or broaden the requirements for marriage. It is, in the words of Justice Connolly, 'the people's elected representatives' who should make the ultimate determination. He wrote, 'While this court understands the reasons for the plaintiffs' request to reverse the Commonwealth's centuries-old legal tradition of restricting marriage to opposite-sex couples, their request should be directed to the Legislature, not the courts.'[87] That statement is certainly consistent with what Justice Field's wrote in *Maynard v. Hill*.[88] Whether the holding in *Goodrich* will be upheld or reversed remains to be seen when the Supreme Judicial Court of Massachusetts renders what is sure to be a historic decision and may be a bellwether sign of the outcome of future same-sex marriage cases before other state supreme courts.

Number (Bigamy)

If one were to ask the question as to whether an American citizen, man or woman, living in the United States can with knowledge have more than one

---

[86] *See* SUSAN TREGGIARI, ROMAN MARRIAGE 5 (1991), where the author writes, 'Matrimonium is an institution involving a mother, mater. The idea implicit in the word is that a man takes a woman in marriage, in matrimonium ducere, so that he may have children by her. He joins her to him by marriage, or by his marriage, or by marriage with himself.'   [87] Goodridge v. Dep't of Pub. Health, *supra* note 85, at 11.
[88] *See* Maynard, *supra* note 1.

spouse at a time, the answer is not simply 'yes' or 'no'. One must first ask whether the multiple marriages took place in a country where it is legal, and second what is the purpose and in what context is recognition sought? The case cited for the proposition that a bigamous marriage is unenforceable in the United States is *Reynolds v. U.S.*[89] In that nineteenth-century case, the U.S. Supreme Court held that religious freedom did not give Mormons the right to have more than one wife at a time. The Court was unwilling to legally sanction polygamy, which was allowed in the Church of Jesus Christ of Latter-Day Saints. To do so, according to the Court, would be to make religious beliefs superior to the law of the land. Chief Justice Waite wrote:

Polygamy has always been odious among the northern and western nations of Europe, and until the establishment of the Mormon Church, was almost exclusively a feature of the life of Asiatic and of African people. At common law, the second marriage was always void . . . and from the earliest history of England polygamy has been treated as an offence against society. . . .

So here, as a law of the organization of society under the exclusive dominion of the United States, it is provided that plural marriages shall not be allowed. Can a man excuse his practices to the contrary because of his religious belief? To permit this would be to make the professed doctrines of religious belief superior to the law of the land, and in effect to permit every citizen to become a law unto himself. Government could exist only in name under such circumstances.[90]

Seventy years after *Reynolds*, a District Court of Appeal in California was faced with the issue of which of two wives, both married at the same time to the same man in India, and who had not lived with the man in California, could claim a widow's share of his estate. In *In re Estate of Dalip Singh Bir Estate*,[91] Dalip Singh Bir, an Indian national, had emigrated to California and died intestate. Two women, living in India, both claiming to have been legally married to the decedent in India, petitioned to be declared his heir. While the trial court applied the law that the first wife was the legal widow because of the lack of evidence proving a divorce, the Court of Appeal reversed the decision and held that both women should share equally in the estate.

The interesting point to *In re Estate of Dalip Singh Bir* is this statement:

The decision of the trial court was influenced by the rule of 'public policy': but that rule, it would seem, would apply only if decedent had attempted to cohabit with his two wives in California. Where only the question of descent of property is involved, 'public policy' is not affected. . . . 'Public policy' would not be affected by dividing the money equally between the two wives, particularly since there is no contest between them and they are the only interested parties.[92]

The California court was sympathetic to the two women and suggested that since they had married in India, and would not be both living with their

---

[89] 98 U.S. 145 (1878).   [90] *Id.* at 164–67.
[91] 188 P.2d 499 (Cal. App. 1948).   [92] *Id.* at 502.

husband in California, a sight that might be offensive to the community, the court was willing to interpret public policy very narrowly.

Basically, the rule against bigamy is local substantive law, because under certain procedural rules and conflict of law rules, bigamy can be recognized. In addition to a fact pattern like that found in *In re Estate of Dalip Singh Bir*, other examples include the application of presumptions, like the presumption of the most recent marriage being valid, and the putative spouse doctrine where one of the spouses may in fact have a spouse living at the time he or she enters into a new marriage. Yet, in protecting the innocent spouse, usually in a decedents' estate matter, a court, by using presumptions find that the second marriage, being the most recent, is valid as to the bona fide spouse.[93]

Another, less obvious situation is raised by *Frambach v. Dunihue*,[94] where a Florida court in a property dispute awarded Mr. Dunihue an interest in the house in which he, his children, and Mr. and Mrs. Frambach had lived for about nineteen years. Mr. Dunihue had sought an equitable lien on the property, claiming that Mr. and Mrs. Frambach had promised him a home for the rest of his life in exchange for his working for them. The Court of Appeal reversed the lower court's decision and instead of awarding Mr. Frambach an undivided one-half interest in the house, remanded the case to the lower court to determine either the value of the plaintiff's contribution to the improvement of the house or the value of his services and award him an appropriate amount of money. The court's aim was to prevent the Frambachs from being unjustly enriched through Mr. Dunihue's efforts. For our purposes, the following statement is relevant: 'The trial court determined that the two families had operated as a single family. While emphasizing that he was not making such an inference, the judge opined that the association of the parties was almost as close as though there had been a single wife and two husbands.'[95] Given that idea, one wonders whether there could be a masked case of bigamy by virtue of a married couple's entry into a formal contractual relationship with a third person (perhaps employing the third person as a housekeeper, handyman, etc.) with all three people living together?

MAINTAINING THE MARRIAGE RELATIONSHIP: FROM INEQUALITY TO EQUALITY IN MARRIAGE

Once established, marriage becomes a special complementary relationship in which the state has tried to protect and maintain certain values like economic security, obligation, trust, fidelity, loyalty, affection, equality, and personal

[93] See discussion of presumptions and putative wife *infra*.
[94] 419 So. 2d 1115 (Fla. Dist. Ct. App. 1982).   [95] *Id.* at 1117.

autonomy.[96] Economic security is the reason for laws regulating financial support during marriage, upon divorce, and laws regulating the distribution of wealth on death.[97] The values of equality and autonomy can be seen in the U.S. Supreme Court abortion cases.[98] The values of loyalty and trust are reflected in evidentiary rules, by which the state's attempts to promote the free and confidential communication between husband and wife. For example, spouses are privileged not to testify against one another in criminal cases, and private conversations between spouses are rendered inadmissible in civil and criminal trials by a spousal disqualification.[99]

---

[96] Professor Scott FitzGibbon has written about the importance of obligation in marriage. He writes,

> Marriage would not be fully marriage without obligation. Marriage comes into its own as man and wife embrace obligation to one another. Marriage seeks obligation, fosters it, and even rejoices in it. Marriage involves obligation just as fundamentally as it involves respect, mutual knowledge, and love.

See Scott FitzGibbon, *Marriage and the Good of Obligation*, 47 AM. J. JURIS. 41, 42 (2002).

[97] *See* 26 UNIF. PROBATE CODE § 2-202(a) (amended 1993), 8 Part I U.L.A. 102-03 (1998). Professor Madoff has written:

> Limitations on freedom of testation are imposed on married individuals directly through marital property laws and more subtly through federal tax statutes. Marital property laws impose limitations on freedom of testation in both community [Arizona, California, Idaho, Louisiana, Nevada, New Mexico, Texas and Washington. In adopting the Uniform Marital Property Act, Wisconsin has made its laws similar to community property states]. In community property states each spouse has a fifty per cent ownership interest in all property acquired during the marriage. Therefore, upon death each spouse can only control the disposition of her separate property and half of the community property. In separate property states, spouses are limited in their ability to control the disposition of their property at death through formal elective share statutes. If a married testator in a separate property state disinherits her spouse, the spouse can make an election against the estate for a portion of the decedent's estate. In states that have adopted the most recent version of the Uniform Probate Code, this election can affect as much as fifty percent of the decedent's property.
>
> Federal tax laws provide additional significant limitations on any individual's ability to control the disposition of property after death by providing that married participants in a qualified retirement plan must transfer those plan assets to a spouse unless the spouse consents to an alternative disposition. It is not uncommon for retirement benefits to represent the single largest asset in a decedent's estate, so the effect of this provision is substantial.

See Ray Madoff, *Lurking in the Shadow: The Unseen Hand of Doctrine in Dispute Resolution*, 76 S. CAL. L. REV. 161, 184–85 (2002).

[98] *See* text accompanying notes 130–32 *infra*.

[99] For a discussion of these privileges, see PAUL LIACOS, MARK S. BRODIN & MICHAEL AVERY, HANDBOOK OF MASSACHUSETTS EVIDENCE § 13.2 (7th ed. 1999).

Through the years the marital relationship has changed from a dependent and unequal one, which the state supported through the unity theory of marriage, to one of more independence and equality with special regard for the individual rights of each spouse. As stated earlier, the unity theory is basically a legal fiction that, upon marriage, a man and a woman become one—the husband.

Property Ownership and Control

Compared with men, the legal status of a woman under the common law was extremely limited, and these limitations were incorporated into American law. A married woman was under major disabilities. For example, she could not own property in her own name; she could not enter into commercial relationships with others; and she could not sue her husband except in matrimonial matters. A further limitation was the fact that under the common law, upon marriage, a woman's property became her husband's. Domination and control basically described a husband's relationship to his wife. That was changed to some extent by the enactment of Married Women's Property Acts in the mid-nineteenth century, led by Arkansas in 1835 and Mississippi in 1839. Those Acts were originally designed to allow a wife to own the plantation and slaves, thus insulating what was the husband's original property from creditors.[100] Although the early Married Women's Property Acts had certain limitations,[101] the revised Acts did allow a married woman to acquire property in her own name, enter into contracts with others, retain her own earnings, as well as, sue and be sued in her own name.[102] It would appear that the laws on the books diminished married women's dependence on their husbands by giving her a legal personality. The Acts brought a certain amount of equality to them, but in reality women still suffered from economic discrimination in the marketplace for about a century and a half following the Arkansas Act.[103] For about four years during World War II,

[100] *See* Richard Chused, *Married Women's Property Law: 1800–1850*, 71 GEO. L.J. 1359, 1399–1403 (1983).

[101] Professor Singer has written that the Married Women's Property Acts

Failed to achieve the aims of nineteenth century women's rights advocates who 'sought to emancipate wives' labor in the household as well as in the market, and to do so, advocated "joint property" laws that would recognize wives' claims to marital assets to which husbands otherwise had title.' The husband's income earned outside the home was still owned by the husband alone and wives who did not work outside the home therefore had no earnings of their own.

See JOSEPH W. SINGER, INTRODUCTION TO PROPERTY 378–79 (2001).

[102] For a full and excellent discussion of the Married Women's Property Act and its impact on women's rights, see HOMER H. CLARK, JR., THE LAW OF DOMESTIC RELATIONS IN THE UNITED STATES 286–305 (2d ed. 1987).

[103] Professors Clark and Estin have written:

The purpose of these [Married Women's Property] Acts was to place married women on an equal footing with their husbands with respect to contracts,

between 1941 and 1945, the economic conditions of women changed. But, that period turned out to be an anomaly. When veterans returned home, they resumed their positions in the workforce, displacing women.[104]

Perhaps the change that has had the greatest impact on marriage was the abandonment of the unity theory of marriage. In the last half of the twentieth century, married women emerged as individuals with their own legal identity and their independent rights. This independence was manifested in ways that had more to do with custom than law, and in major civil and criminal matters. An illustration of the former is the matter regarding a married woman's name.

There has been a conflict in authority as to whether a wife takes her husband's name as a matter of custom or as a matter of law. The former position seems to be the dominant one. In *Stuart v. Board of Supervisors*,[105] an action was brought by Mary Emily Stuart challenging the action of the Board of Supervisors of Elections for Howard County in Maryland, which had cancelled her registration to vote because she had registered in her own name, not her

---

earnings, the ownership of property and the right to sue or be sued, but as they were construed by the courts they frequently failed to accomplish the intended reforms. It was not until the 1960s that a vigorous and effective attack upon sex discrimination began to eliminate all of married women's legal disabilities. This was accomplished by federal legislation, state legislation, the Supreme Court's broader application of the Equal Protection Clause of the Fourteenth Amendment and the adoption of Equal Rights Amendments in about seventeen states. These amendments to state constitutions generally provide that equal rights under the law shall not be denied or abridged on the ground of sex. A federal Equal Rights Amendment was proposed as the Twenty-Seventh Amendment to the United States Constitution in 1972, with a requirement that ratification had to be concluded within seven years. At the end of that period only thirty-five of the needed thirty-eight states had ratified the Amendment. Congress then extended the time to June 30, 1982, but the extension time expired without ratification. Resolutions proposing the Amendment have again been introduced in both Houses of Congress, but have been passed in neither house.

HOMER H. CLARK, JR. & ANN LAQUER ESTIN, DOMESTIC RELATIONS—CASES AND PROBLEMS 8 (6th ed. 2000).

[104] Elsewhere I have written:

In mid-century family law was stagnant. Little law reform occurred in the 1940s. For one thing, few legislators were thinking about family law during World War II and immediately afterwards. In 1945 the country was concerned with rebuilding its economy and providing opportunities for veterans to enter colleges and return to their jobs. Reentering the work force meant displacing women who had been an important and vital part of industry during the wary years. During that period children of servicemen were raised by their working mothers, a fact soon forgotten. After the war, women who lost their jobs resumed their traditional role in the family.

See Sanford N. Katz, *PROLOGUE*, 33 FAM. L.Q. 435, 436 (1999).
[105] 295 A.2d 223 (Md. Ct. App. 1972).

husband's. Her actions violated Maryland law, which stated that 'a woman's legal surname becomes that of her husband upon marriage'. Mary Emily Stuart had not completed a change of name form, which the Board ruled was necessary. An interesting aspect to the case is that the couple had entered into an oral prenuptial agreement before marrying in Virginia. The couple had agreed that the wife would use her birth name. Yet, the court did not seem to be concerned with a choice of law problem, but apparently assumed that Maryland law governed voting registration.

The court reviewed the conflict between custom and law and recognized what it called the 'common law right of any person, absent a statute to the contrary, to "adopt any name by which he may become known, and by which he may transact business and execute contracts and sue or be sued" '.[106] In his dissent, Judge Smith cited an 1891 text, Bishop on *Marriage, Divorce and Separation*, which stated: 'The rule of law and custom is familiar, that marriage confers on the woman the husband's surname.'[107] The judge believed that it was a matter of both law and custom for a wife to assume her husband's name, and for the court to hold otherwise was 'judicial legislation which is forbidden by the Maryland Declaration of Rights'.[108]

Though the question of whether a woman assumes her husband's name upon marriage by operation of law, or by the volition of the individual woman may seem to be unimportant when reviewing the whole realm of laws regulating marriage, the symbolism is not unimportant. The choice of name is a matter of identity. Imposing the husband's surname on a wife reflects the law's perpetuation of the dependency and inferior position of the wife. This may have been the common law view of marriage, but since the women's movement, which began during the 1970s, there has been a major shift. Women now have a choice upon marriage and upon divorce.[109] Contemporary culture accepts, and may even expect, that women maintain their birth name upon marriage as well as a certain amount of independence including the maintenance of separate bank accounts, separate credit card accounts, etc. The lack of a common name may cause difficulty with presumptions of marriage and substantive rules for the legality of a common law marriage. In both instances, one of the indices of marriage was a common name, a common residence, and the pooling of finances. Those may no longer be a useful guide. More important may be evidence of a common residence and a sustained mutual commitment.

---

[106] *Id.* at 231.　　　[107] *Id.* at 230.　　　[108] *Id.* at 231.

[109] For a full discussion of the common law history of the law relating to names of married and divorced women, see *Secretary of the Commonwealth v. City Clerk of Lowell*, 366 N.E.2d 717, 723–24 (Mass. 1977), where Justice Braucher concluded that

> a woman, like a man, may change her name at will, without resorting to legal proceedings, provided that this is done for an honest purpose. . . . It has been held that such freedom of choice is not compelled by the United States Constitution. . . . But the results indicated accord with the overwhelming weight of recent authority in other states. . . .

Just as a woman may choose whether to assume her husband's name or not, so may parents choose their child's surname even when the name may be different from either of its birth parent's names.[110] This is true even though the custom in the United States has been to give a child the surname of his or her father. Children of unmarried parents have by custom been given the name of their birth mother. However, some states allow an illegitimate child to take the father's surname when the child has been legitimatized, in other defined circumstances, or where the naming would be in the child's best interest.[111]

REGULATING THE MARRIAGE THROUGH PRIVATE CONTRACTS: POSTNUPTIAL AGREEMENTS

As discussed earlier, privately negotiated prenuptial agreements, which serve to regulate marriage prior to entering into the relationship, are valid as long as the negotiating process and the terms meet the standard of fairness.[112] But what about agreements that attempt to regulate a marriage after the parties have entered into the relationship? Ordinarily postnuptial agreements would be enforced if they were a prelude to divorce or if they related to reconciliation contemporaneously with, or after an actual separation. The consideration for the contract would be the exchange of promises—in exchange for a spouse's promise to return to the marriage, the other spouse would make an independent promise. Now, however, during marriage, married spouses may contract with each other about matters relating to divorce, death, or the designation of property as separate or marital so long as the contract is based on consideration.[113] They may even modify their prenuptial agreements. The most important element of these postnuptial contracts, like prenuptial ones, is the necessity of a fair process because of the possibility of coercion.

Interspousal Immunity

Under the marital unity theory, it would not be possible for a spouse to sue another spouse because the result would be like suing oneself. It has not been

---

[110] For example, in *Sydney v. Pingree*, 564 F. Supp. 412 (S.D. Fla. 1982), the U.S. District Court in Florida held that a Florida statute that required parents to name their legitimate child with the child's father's surname to be an unconstitutional violation of the right of a parent to choose the name of their child. In that case, the mother, Chris Ledbetter and the father, Dean Skylar, chose to combine their last names and name their child 'Skybetter'.

[111] For a state by state listing of legal standards for name changing of children, see Deborah M. Baumgarten, (*Chart 9*) *Child's Name Change Standards*, 35 FAM L.Q. 625–6 (2002).   [112] *See* discussion of prenuptial agreements *infra*.

[113] Cases that deal with postnuptial agreements are: Peirce v. Peirce, 994 P.2d 193 (Utah 2000); Pacelli v. Pacelli, 725 A.2d 565 (N.J. 1999); and Bronfman v. Bronfman, 229 A.D.2d 314, 645 N.Y.S.2d 20 (1996). In each of these cases, the courts stressed the importance of a process, free from coercion.

unusual for states to take a step-by-step approach to abrogating interspousal tort immunity, an old-fashioned doctrine that justified under the additional theory, actually a fiction, that such lawsuits would undermine marital harmony. The reason for considering the immunity doctrine as a fiction is that it assumed that one spouse actually sues another. In reality, most tort lawsuits involve insurance companies and their lawyers. The second assumption is that all couples pool their resources and because of that, for example, a husband tortfeasor might benefit from his tortious act against his wife who would deposit the money damages awarded in her tort case in a joint bank account. The pooling of resources is the basis for the assumption, not necessarily supported by any empirical data, that in tort cases involving insurance companies, spouses might be in collusion to defraud the companies.

Three California cases illustrate the movement from dependency to independence in a period of sixty-three years. In *Peters v. Peters*,[114] Mr. Peters sued his wife for battery, claiming that Mrs. Peters had shot him in the leg, causing him to be bedridden for a month and unable to work for several more months. The California court held that a husband could not sue his wife in tort because of the unity theory of marriage. The court went on to state that in a case like the one at bar the only remedy, other than under a criminal statute, would be divorce or maintenance. For many years, divorce was often the only remedy for assault and battery within a marriage. The general feeling was that if a husband beat up his wife, the marital relationship was probably not worth continuing and termination was the proper outcome. Advocates for divorce as a remedy for what we would call 'domestic violence' probably gave little thought to the cost of pursuing a divorce and, perhaps more importantly, to the social, psychological, and economic disruption that divorce brings to a family. Nonetheless, that was the law for over fifty years.

In 1962 the Supreme Court of California decided two cases on the application of the defense of interspousal immunity on intentional and negligent torts. In *Self v. Self*,[115] Mrs. Self suffered a broken arm as a result of her husband's assaulting and battering her. She sued her husband in tort, and he moved for a summary judgment on the ground that a wife cannot sue her husband for tort in California. The motion was granted in the trial court and the wife appealed. The Supreme Court of California held that interspousal immunity was outdated, and considering the fact that women have a 'separate legal personality', which gives them a separate legal estate in their own property, free from the control of their husbands, Mrs. Self could sue her husband.[116] In reversing the lower court's decision, the Supreme Court of California made new law: interspousal immunity was no longer available in cases of intentional torts between spouses.

[114] 103 P. 219 (Cal. 1909). [115] 376 P.2d 65 (Cal. 1962). [116] *Id.* at 66.

In the same year, the Supreme Court of California extended its position on abolishing interspousal immunity to negligent torts in *Klein v. Klein*.[117] In that case, a wife sued her husband during marriage for his negligence in not warning her that the deck of their pleasure boat was slippery, causing her to fall. Apparently the defendant must have contended that abolishing the defense would encourage collusion, fraud, and perjury. The court was not convinced by that argument and held that, unless there was a statute or compelling public policy to the contrary, a person who is harmed by either willful or negligent conduct of another should be compensated for such a wrong. That the parties were husband and wife should not defeat the action.

Personal Safety

Domestic violence—acts of physical and psychological abuse occurring within the marriage relationship—is seen today as a major public health problem.[118] Indeed that was reflected in the U.S. Congress's passage of the Violence Against Women Act in 1994.[119] That Act provided victims of gender-motivated violence a civil remedy in the federal courts. Although the U.S. Supreme Court found the Act unconstitutional because such congressional action was not authorized by the Commerce Clause,[120] thus denying victims civil remedies, it did not strike down other aspects of the Act, such as the provision making it a federal crime to cross state lines to commit an act of domestic violence,[121] or federal funding for programs proposed by the Act.

Psychiatrists state that often the abuser attempts to assert power and control over his victims by the use of physical force whether this force takes the form of rape or assault and battery. The battered child and the battered wife syndromes that are discussed in Chapter 4 are now part of the legal and psychiatric lexicon. The family, often romanticized in literature, art, and films, can be an

---

[117] 376 P.2d 70 (Cal. 1962).

[118] For a full discussion of violence against women, *see* Elizabeth M. Schneider, *The Law and Violence against Women in the Family at Century's End: The US Experience,* in Cross Currents, *supra* note 78, at 471–94. For a discussion of domestic violence generally, see *Note, Developments—Domestic Violence,* 106 Harv. L. Rev. 1498 (1993).

[119] 42 U.S.C. § 13981 (1994).

[120] *See United States v. Morrison,* 529 U.S. 598 (2000), where Chief Justice Rehnquist, writing for the majority, stated,

> Gender-motivated crimes of violence are not, in any sense of the phrase, economic activity. . . . We . . . reject the argument that Congress may regulate noneconomic, violent criminal conduct based solely on that conduct's aggregate effect on interstate commerce. The Constitution requires a distinction between what is truly national and what is truly local.

Id. at 617–18.

[121] 18 U.S.C. § 2261(a)(1).

enclosure for the worst kinds of brutality. Such brutality has often been shielded from public view and state intervention because of American notions of family privacy. As stated earlier, in cases where a husband beats his wife, the remedy was not a private tort action but divorce. If one reads old divorce cases, one is often struck by the matter of fact approach taken by judges when they relate the abusive conduct in the marital relationship that defines cruelty.[122]

It is common knowledge that when a spouse is murdered, the first major suspect will usually be the other spouse; when a child is found drowned or beaten to death, a parent, step-parent, or a parent's companion is usually the prime suspect.

A major issue in domestic violence is the extent to which civil or criminal law is an effective means to deal with violence within the family. Another is whether the gender-based orientation of certain domestic violence laws—protection of women—is justified.

In *Warren v. State*,[123] the Supreme Court of Georgia held that marriage does not give a husband license to engage in sexual intercourse and other sexual practices with his wife without her consent. Since the Georgia rape statute was silent as to a marital exemption, the court interpreted the silence as not signifying a common law spousal exclusion. Thus, the husband in *Warren v. State* had committed rape and aggravated sodomy with his wife. The court summarized three theories for the marital rape exemption: Lord Hale's (Hale was Chief Justice of the Court of King's Bench from 1671 until 1675) contractual theory, which basically maintained that a wife impliedly and irrevocably consented to the actions of her husband; a wife was the property of her husband who could make whatever use of his property that he desired; the unity theory of marriage.

---

[122] *See, e.g., Warner v. Warner*, 283 P.2d 931 (Idaho 1955), where an issue was whether a husband was estopped from denying the validity of his marriage so that his wife could sue him for divorce on ground of extreme cruelty. In the course of relating the facts, the court wrote:

> [he] was good to her about a month after their return, but thereafter pursued his previous course of cruelty, slapping her and striking her with his fist; that on several occasions she asked him to enter into a ceremonial marriage and that 'if I ever mentioned it he got mad, and usually slapped me around.' As to the occasion which caused the final separation, she testified:
> Well, he—the last time he hit me in the head, and I couldn't hardly eat, or open my mouth, and he laughed and thought it was real funny, but it wasn't, and I decided that I am getting too old to take those beatings any longer, I can't take them.
> It knocked me down the last time he hit me. He hit me right here on the side of the head (Indicating). I had pains for about two months. I was even afraid he had injured me some way.

Id. at 932.
Today Mr. Warner's hitting and knocking his wife down would be treated as domestic violence.
[123] 336 S.E.2d 221 (1985).

The court went on to list modern reasons for the exemption, which included the prevention of (1) fabricated charges, (2) the use of rape as revenge, and (3) the possibility of reconciliation. All the theories, old and new, were thought to be invalid in the twentieth century.

The marital rape exemption still exists in a number of states and although there seems to be a legislative trend toward abolishing or limiting the exemption, the Model Penal Code takes the position that a spousal exemption for rape applies to 'persons living as man and wife, regardless of the legal status of their relationship' until legal separation.[124]

How can women be protected from men who threaten them? One civil remedy is the civil restraining order.[125] Another is through a stalking law. The Massachusetts Stalking Law[126] was enacted in 1992 as a result of a number of publicized cases in the state that resulted in women being murdered by obsessive lovers with whom the victims had broken off relationships. The problem with stalking laws, in general, is that they can provide only temporary relief. Moreover, under the Massachusetts statute the maximum prison term is five years. It is doubtful whether a first offender would receive the maximum punishment. What happens when he is released from prison? The usual situation is that the stalker returns to his prey and continues to threaten her. That being the usual scenario, the victims of stalkers usually are forced to move to secret locations. The price American society pays for allowing men to harass women—a man's freedom of movement—may be the murder of the women or women having to go into hiding, thus forcing them to give up their normal lives, friendships, family, and jobs.

Privacy, Equality, and Autonomy: Sexual Intimacy in Marriage

Under the common law, wives were treated as servants to their husbands. Not only did wives have a duty to serve their husbands in terms of keeping house and raising children, but they also lost control over their bodies. Major changes began in the 1970s and continued for twenty years. These changes were the result of U.S. Supreme Court cases that transformed the relationship of husband and wife by recognizing the individual rights and autonomy of each spouse,

[124] Model Penal Code §§ 213.1, 213.6(2)(1980).
[125] For example, the Massachusetts Abuse Prevention Act, M.G.L.A. c. 209A, § 3 sets out various forms or relief:

> A person suffering from abuse from an adult or minor family or household member may file a complaint in the court requesting protection from such abuse, including, but not limited to, the following orders:-
> (a) ordering the defendant to refrain from abusing the plaintiff whether the defendant is an adult or minor;
> (b) ordering the defendant to vacate forthwith the household ...

[126] M.G.L. c. 265, § 43 (1992).

especially the procreative rights of a woman, and the privacy of the marital
relationship. The values of equality, privacy, and autonomy may seem to be
neutral. However, their application may have positive and negative consequences in terms of men and women's rights. Personal autonomy, for example,
supports a woman's personal decision to become pregnant if she so chooses. It
would also support a man's right to be notified of an abortion and involve him
in the woman's decision to have an abortion. Privacy in marriage might give a
husband the opportunity to take advantage of his wife by imposing his will on
her within the confines of their home.[127] On balance, however, the U.S. Supreme
Court's decisions in family law have supported the concept of individual rights
as contrasted with community interests. In so doing, the Court has followed
history and tradition.[128]

In *Griswold v. Connecticut*,[129] the U.S. Supreme Court recognized a fundamental right to marital privacy. Griswold had violated a statute prohibiting the
distribution of contraceptives except for the prevention of disease when he gave
some information to a married couple at a New Haven, Connecticut clinic.
Justice Douglas, writing for the Court, found the right to marital privacy
emanating from a 'penumbra' of specific rights to association, security from
government in the home, from self-incrimination, and the Ninth Amendment's
catch-all recognition that rights not enumerated are retained by the people. In a
concurring opinion, Justice Goldberg focused on the statute's failure to survive
strict scrutiny review due to its inability to fulfill a compelling interest. He
dismissed the rationality of the state's purpose of discouraging extramarital
affairs as doubtful, and the statute as overly broad by intruding into marital
privacy, but he also noted that the Court's decision does not interfere with a
state's regulation of promiscuity and misconduct.

Griswold supports privacy in marriage but not necessarily any type of sexual
relations within the marriage. The Court's opinion seems to represent a preference for equality of women in their relations to men. The result of the Court's
opinion was to make contraceptives more accessible by lessening the burden of
obtaining them.

In *Roe v. Wade*,[130] the U.S. Supreme Court struck down a Texas statute criminalizing abortion. It held that the right to privacy includes a woman's decision
whether to have an abortion. Justice Blackmun found the right to exist in the

---

[127] *See* Katherine T. Bartlett, *Feminism and Family Law*, 33 FAM. L.Q. 475 (1999).
[128] Elsewhere I have written that the progress women have made in the United States
has been associated with the movement for individual rights.

'Individual rights' refers to the relationship of the individual to the state wherein the
individual's interests take precedence over the state's. In family law, the progress made
in protecting individual rights, especially those of women and children, through the
interpretation of the due process and equal protection clauses of the U.S. Constitution,
has required membership in the family to be redefined. *See* Sanford N. Katz, in
Individual Rights and Family Relationships CROSS CURRENTS, *supra* note 78, at 634–35.
[129] 381 U.S. 479 (1965).   [130] 410 U.S. 113 (1973).

Fourteenth Amendment's concept of personal liberty and restrictions upon state action. He reasoned that the right to choose to terminate a pregnancy is crucial in light of the possible mental and physical harms that may come with early pregnancy or the eventual burden of an unwanted child. But he also recognized the state's interest in the health of the woman and in protecting the 'potentiality of human life'. As a result of this conflict, Justice Blackmun evaluated the abortion statutes in terms of their effect on the three trimesters of pregnancy and the consideration of the maternal health and the judgment of the attending physician. In the first trimester, the woman's decision is left to the judgment of the physician; in the second, the state is allowed to regulate consistent with maternal health; and, in the third trimester, the state may regulate or proscribe abortion except where it is considered medically necessary to protect the mother's health.

In *Webster v. Reproductive Health Services*,[131] the U.S. Supreme Court upheld the constitutionality of a Missouri state abortion law. The Missouri Act included prohibition of the use of public facilities or employees to perform abortions, the prohibition of public funding of abortion counseling, and the requirement that physicians conduct viability tests prior to performing abortions. In the plurality opinion Chief Justice Rehnquist rejected Justice Blackmun's trimester analysis. He emphasized the lack of trimesters and viability protection in the words of the Constitution, and recognized that the decision would encourage state legislatures to regulate abortion procedures more heavily than thought possible following *Roe*. The Court, however, limited its decision to recognizing the particular Missouri law as constitutional and did not specifically overturn *Roe*. Concurring in the judgment of the Court, Justice O'Connor used an 'undue burden' analysis and asked whether each new regulation and the cost it placed on a pregnant women placed an undue burden on a woman's decision. Justice O'Connor also noted that judicial respect for 'stare decisis' compelled upholding *Roe*.

Justice O'Connor's analysis came to the foreground in *Planned Parenthood v. Casey*,[132] in which she wrote the opinion for a considerably divided court. In that case, the U.S. Supreme Court upheld part of a Pennsylvania Act restricting abortion but struck down a provision requiring any married woman to swear that she had notified her husband of her impending abortion. The Court upheld requirements that a pregnant woman give her informed consent prior to an abortion based on information that she received at least twenty-four hours prior to the procedure, and that a minor seeking an abortion received parental consent, unless a judicial bypass was obtained.

With the undue burden analysis, Justice O'Connor reasoned that a state is allowed to encourage childbirth over abortion, even if the means do not further a health interest. The spousal notice provision, however, created too great of an obstacle or, in her words, an 'undue burden'. In so finding, Justice O'Connor

---

[131] 492 U.S. 490 (1989).   [132] 505 U.S. 833 (1992).

wrote of the history of woman battering and again relied heavily on judicial restraint principles to avoid overturning *Roe*. *Roe*, she noted, stood for the principle that viability, not the trimesters, is the mark when the weight of competing interests shift in favor of state regulation of abortion to protect potential life. Justice Blackmun hailed the opinion's upholding of *Roe*, but reiterated that state restrictions on abortion violate a woman's right of privacy, a term noticeably absent from Justice O'Connor's undue burden analysis.

Sexual Intimacy Outside of Marriage

Unlike *Griswold*, which concerned the use of contraceptives in marriage, *Eisenstadt v. Baird*,[133] is concerned with the privacy of unmarried persons. In that case, the U.S. Supreme Court held that a Massachusetts statute prohibiting distribution of contraceptives to unmarried persons but allowing distribution to married persons violated the Equal Protection Clause of the U.S. Constitution. Baird was convicted under the statute when he gave vaginal foam to a woman at a lecture to Boston University students. The Court affirmed a dismissal of the charges against Baird, first noting that no grounds exist for treating married and unmarried persons differently in regards to receipt of contraceptives. As a result, the statute violated the Equal Protection Clause. The state's claim that the statute was intended to deter premarital sex was rejected, particularly since it did not deter extramarital affairs, another supposed statutory purpose. The Court found *Griswold* controlling, and noted that while it recognized the right of privacy in the marital relationship, the right of privacy essentially is the right of an individual, married or not, to be free from government intrusion into matters fundamentally affecting a person.

Further freedom to engage in sexual activity was granted by the Supreme Court of Pennsylvania in *Fadgen v. Lenkner*.[134] That court abolished the action of criminal conversation, an action in which a spouse sues a third party for having had sex with their spouse. Criminal conversation had been made available to wives only fifteen years prior to the decision, but had been available to husbands for hundreds of years. The court reasoned that the defenses to the action—denial or the accusing spouse's consent—failed to take account for the cheating spouse, specifically noting a wife, who initiated and pursued the extramarital affair and the unsuspecting man who did not know the wife was married. The court also found troubling the inexactness of the damages, including possible punitive damages, for loss of social position and honor. The concurring opinion, however, was more persuaded by the then current decisions in *Roe v. Wade* and *Cleveland Board of Education v. LaFleur*,[135] the latter holding that a mandatory maternity leave based on the school board's desire to have continuity of instruction as well as the protection of the health of the pregnant teacher and

---

[133] 405 U.S. 438 (1972).   [134] 365 A.2d 147 (Pa. 1976).
[135] 414 U.S. 632 (1974).

the unborn child was unconstitutional under the Due Process Clause under the U.S. Constitution. In his concurring opinion in *Fadgen*, Justice Manderino wrote:

> If a married man or woman chooses to engage in sexual activity with one other than his or her spouse, I believe such a choice is protected by the right to privacy guaranteed by the Constitution and there is no 'compelling state interest' involved which would justify the state's limiting the exercise of such rights.[136]

In *Bowers v. Hardwick*[137] the U.S. Supreme Court drew the line for the right of privacy's encompassing with sexual freedom with homosexual acts. Hardwick was charged with violating a Georgia statute criminalizing sodomy, a statute applying to any person, not just same-sex relations. The Court rejected any possibility of a fundamental right of consenting men to engage in sodomy. The U.S. Supreme Court, upholding the conviction, left open the question of whether a fundamental right to commit sodomy existed for married persons. The Court distinguished *Griswold* and the subsequent cases as involving family, marriage, or procreation. The Court noted that proscriptions against sodomy have ancient roots and that to find a fundamental right to that kind of activity may be pushing the limit of the Court's ability to find substantive rights in the Due Process Clause.[138]

Seventeen years after *Bowers* was decided, the U.S. Supreme Court overruled it in *Lawrence v. Texas*.[139] In *Lawrence*, the Houston police entered a private residence in response to a report of weapons disturbance and found two adult

---

[136] 365 A.2d at 153.   [137] 478 U.S. 186 (1986).

[138] Since that case was decided, however, the Georgia Supreme Court held that the Georgia sodomy statute violated an individual's right to privacy under the state constitution. *See* Powell v. State, 510 S.E.2d 18 (Ga. 1998). In 1996 the U.S. Supreme Court held that an amendment to the Colorado constitution that prevented the enforcement of laws or ordinances prohibiting discrimination against gays, lesbians, and bisexuals was unconstitutional as a violation of the Equal Protection Clause of the federal constitution. *See* Romer v. Evans, 517 U.S. 620 (1996).

[139] —S.Ct.—, 2003 WL 21467086. This case was decided on June 26, 2003. Justice Scalia, Chief Justice Rehnquist, and Justice Thomas dissented. In the conclusion to his stinging dissent, Justice Scalia wrote:

> Today's opinion dismantles the structure of constitutional law that has permitted a distinction to be made between heterosexual and homosexual unions, insofar as formal recognition in marriage is concerned. If moral disapprobation of homosexual conduct is 'no legitimate state interest' for purposes of proscribing that conduct . . . and if, as the Court coos (casting aside all pretense of neutrality), '[w]hen sexuality finds overt expression in intimate conduct with another person, the conduct can be but one element in a personal bond that is more enduring,' . . . what justification could there possibly be for denying the benefits of marriage to homosexual couples exercising '[t]he liberty protected by the Constitution,' . . .? Surely not the encouragement of procreation, since the sterile and the elderly are allowed to marry. This case 'does not involve' the issue of homosexual marriage only if one entertains the belief that principle and logic

males engaging in sexual intercourse. The men were arrested and convicted of a crime under a Texas statute that criminalized same-sex sodomy (the Texas statute differed from the Georgia statute, which applied to both sexes). Relying on the Due Process Clause of the Fourteenth Amendment to the U.S. Constitution, not the Equal Protection Clause, which would have been the expected basis of the opinion, considering the decision in *Bowers*, and which Justice O'Connor relied on in her concurrence, the Court struck down the Texas statute. Justice Kennedy, writing for a six to three majority, in a surprisingly broad opinion with far-reaching consequences, wrote that the issue of private sexual conduct in *Lawrence* went beyond consideration of a particular sexual act. It concerned the state's intruding into the most intimate of personal conduct, sexual relations, in a private place, thus violating a person's liberty to choose to enter into relationships in the privacy of their own home. Justice Kennedy went on to dispute the contention in *Bowers* that there was a long-standing history of regulating homosexual conduct in the United States. He noted that the history of laws prohibiting sodomy and cases of prosecution of the crime involved the actions of adults with minor girls and boys, not actions between consenting adults. The Court mentioned the trend in state statutes, legal literature, model acts, and in an unusual reference to decisions in the European Court of Human Rights, all of which have rejected the reasoning and judgment in *Bowers*. In a powerful conclusion to his opinion Justice Kennedy emphasized the distinguishing facts in the case, and stated that there is a 'realm of personal liberty which the government may not enter'. He wrote:

The present case does not involve minors. It does not involve persons who might be injured or coerced or who are situated in a relationship where consent might not easily be refused. It does not involve public conduct or prostitution. It does not involve whether the government must give formal recognition to any relationship that homosexual persons seek to enter. The case does involve two adults who, with full and mutual consent from each other, engaged in sexual practices common to a homosexual life style. The petitioners are entitled to respect for their private lives. The State cannot demean their existence or control their destiny by making their private sexual conduct a crime. Their right to liberty under the Due Process Clause gives them the full right to engage in their conduct without intervention of the government. . . .

Had those who drew and ratified the Due Process Clauses of the Fifth Amendment or the Fourteenth Amendment known the components of liberty in its manifold possibilities, they might have been more specific. They did not presume to have this insight. They knew times can bind us to certain truths and later generations can see that laws once thought necessary and proper in fact serve only to oppress. As the Constitution endures, persons in every generation can invoke its principles in their own search for greater freedom.

Whether a fundamental right of a same-sex couple to engage in intimate sexual relations in one's home can be the predicate to a fundamental right to

have nothing to do with the decisions of this Court. Many will hope that, as the Court comfortingly assures us, this is so.

marry a person of the same sex remains to be seen. Regardless of the answer, the U.S. Supreme Court's recognition of contemporary sexual mores in *Lawrence v. Texas* represents a major advancement for gay rights.

INDIVIDUAL RIGHTS AND EQUALITY IN MARRIAGE

The theme that seems to describe contemporary laws regulating the marriage relationship is the emphasis on individual rights, the right of each partner to a marriage to define her or his role within certain legal boundaries. In the past when marriage was considered a union of a man and a woman in which the couple became 'one', the reality was that the husband dominated the relationship at the expense of his wife. The modern concept of marriage as a special kind of partnership has given rise to the idea that marriage as partnership means marriage as a contract between two individuals who maintain their individuality, psychologically, socially, and legally. At first blush, the focus on individual rights may seem to diminish marriage, perhaps even pitting a husband against a wife, or of supporting Professor Milton Regan's description of marriage as 'alone together'.[140] However, the concept of individual rights in marriage need not support selfishness or alienation. It can promote mutual respect and equality. As the concept of individual rights in marriage becomes imbedded in the fabric of our society and takes the place of the old-fashioned idea of domination and dependency on the husband, which described marriage for over a century, marriage will have earned its position, as I think it has, as the foundation of the family and worth preserving.

---

[140] *See* MILTON C. REGAN, JR., ALONE TOGETHER: LAW AND THE MEANINGS OF MARRIAGE (1999).

3

Divorce

Introduction

American divorce laws and procedure have undergone enormous changes during the past half century and seem to be stable in the beginning of the present century. The reasons for the changes are complex. Essentially, they have a great deal to do with changes in the nature of marriage and the social and legal acceptance of formal and informal alternatives to marriage, both of which have been discussed in an earlier chapter. Equally important have been the changes in cultural norms, particularly with regard to societal attitude toward divorce, population movement from one area of the country to another, shifts in the political climate as a result of the impact of various of the civil rights movements—children's rights, women's rights, and father's rights—and changes that have occurred in the legal profession, access to legal representation, court structure, and the availability of alternative methods of dispute resolution especially with the use of negotiation and the wider acceptance of mediation.[1]

Divorce can be seen as both the legal termination of the husband and wife relationship as well as the legal, social, and psychological reorganization of that relationship and the parent–child relationship established through the marriage. The reason for the word 'reorganization' is that the divorced couple may have a continuing relationship, although altered, because of the post-divorce property and child custody arrangement. Alimony and the assignment of property may continue the adult relationships, but on a level different from marriage. The judicial award of a child's custody to one parent or another changes the

---

[1] Various aspects of these changes are discussed in the following works: Jerome A. Barron, *The Constitutionalization of American Family Law: The Case of the Right to Marry, in* Cross Currents—Family Law and Policy in the United States and England 257–78 (Sanford N. Katz, John Eekelaar & Mavis Maclean eds., 2000) [hereinafter Cross Currents]; Ira Mark Ellman, *Divorce in the United States, in* Cross Currents, at 341–62; Grace Ganz Blumberg, *The Financial Incidents of Family Dissolution, in* Cross Currents, at 387–404; Barbara Bennett Woodhouse, *The Status of Children: A Story of Emerging Rights, in* Cross Currents, at 423–40; Walter J. Wadlington, *Marriage: An Institution in Transition and Redefinition, in* Cross Currents, at 235–56; Walter O. Weyrauch, Sanford N. Katz & Frances Olsen, Cases and Materials on Family Law—Legal Concepts and Changing Human Relationships 1–2, 157–61, 309–10, 483–84 (1994); Sanford N. Katz, *Introduction, in* Negotiating to Settlement in Divorce xiii–xxvii (Sanford N. Katz ed., 1987).

relationship from what it was during marriage. During marriage, the mother and father were the child's natural and joint legal custodians. Within certain legal boundaries, their relationship to their child was basically self-defined. The petition for divorce not only restricts the personal autonomy of the couple, but also limits their relationship with their children at least until they reach their majority. With divorce comes the loss of individual freedom and the addition of judicial regulation.

It should be noted, however, that conflicts in the great majority of divorce cases are resolved in lawyers' offices where negotiation between lawyers takes place in an informal setting without adherence to rules of evidence. The cases reach the courts only for judicial affirmation of the resulting agreement.

At first glance a negotiated settlement may seem to be beneficial to the parties who have managed to avoid the time and costs of a lengthy court battle. If both the husband and wife are represented by equally qualified counsel who negotiate against the background of the law as found in statutes and in the cases, then the result may very well be fair. But is that likely? I believe that divorce is one area of legal practice where the oral legal tradition may play as important, perhaps even more important, a role in negotiating a divorce settlement than official law found in statutes and cases. By that I mean that the oral tradition is very much a part of law practice and lawyers tend to advise clients on the basis of their experience, perhaps more than on what they read in statutes or cases. For example, a lawyer might advise his female client to accept a small sum in lieu of alimony because of his belief that particular judges do not award any alimony to marriages of less than two years. That fact may not be found anywhere except in the lawyer's mind. Or, a lawyer might advise his male client not to seek custody but to accept a reasonable visitation schedule because of his belief that a particular judge does not award a female infant to a father. Again, that fact may be found nowhere but in the lawyer's mind and may indeed be contrary to the law's statement of excluding any presumptions in custody laws. Interestingly enough, it is the oral legal tradition that laymen often believe to be 'the law' and rely on for making their own decisions about their case. There are, therefore, two systems at work in divorce sometimes supporting each other, sometimes running parallel and sometimes modifying or contradicting each other. One is the oral tradition or the unwritten law. The other is the official law, which judges refer to in making their decision. It is the latter system that is the subject of this chapter.[2]

---

[2] I am grateful to Walter O. Weyrauch for sharing his insights with me on the theoretical implications of the oral legal tradition as they relate to official law in family law. For an illuminating analysis and discussion of the interrelationship between oral tradition and official law generally, see Lynn M. LoPucki, *Legal Culture, Legal Strategy, and the Law in Lawyers' Heads*, 90 Nw. U. L. Rev. 1498 (1996) and Lynn M. LoPucki & Walter O. Weyrauch, *A Theory of Legal Strategy*, 49 Duke L.J. 1405 (2000).

DIVORCE PROCEDURE

Fault

Until the introduction of no-fault divorce, American divorce procedure had been, and in instances where the action is for a fault divorce still is, based on the adversarial model. This model assumes protagonists: each party, free of fault, suing the other in court. American law has never adopted a transactional approach to divorce, which would allow a husband and wife to enter into a private divorce agreement without any official involvement (like a judge or a court clerk) at all.[3] With the adversarial model came a body of law based on English equity principles.[4] For example, under a fault system, among other limitations, divorces could not be consensual and a divorce could be defended and defeated because of the conduct of the plaintiff (the moving or petitioning party). Defenses to a divorce included connivance (consenting to or being involved with the ground for divorce, particularly adultery), collusion (agreement by the couple to commit the act, which will support the ground for divorce), and condonation (forgiveness for the wrong). In addition, if both plaintiff and defendant were guilty of fault, theoretically, unless changed by statute, neither could get a divorce under the doctrine of recrimination, later modified to comparative rectitude.[5] These defenses supported the old English adages: one must do equity to receive equity and one must come into court with clean hands. Divorce actions have been described as resembling those for torts. In order to recover in tort one must show that one was not at fault or has not contributed to the wrong.

When a fault-based system of divorce was the exclusive method of obtaining a divorce, evidence for formally proving grounds, for example, cruelty, desertion, or adultery was critical. If the ground was not proven, no divorce could

---

[3] This is not to say that some people assume they are divorced because they desert their spouses or go through certain motions or sign legal documents in a lawyer's office thinking they are legally divorced. Legally they are not divorced. In a 1961 law review article the late Professor Henry H. Foster coined the phrase 'common law divorce', which he defined as 'the private termination of marriage, independent of judicial action, which may be relied upon by the parties as carrying with it a privilege to remarry'. There is no such doctrine as 'common law divorce' in American law. *See* Henry H. Foster, *Common Law Divorce*, 46 MINN. L. REV. 43, 58–62 (1961).

[4] For a history of the law of divorce procedure, see HOMER H. CLARK, JR., THE LAW OF DOMESTIC RELATIONS IN THE UNITED STATES 405–19 (1987). For a discussion of equity in American colonial history, see Stanley N. Katz, *The Politics of Law in Colonial America: Controversies over Chancery Courts and Equity Law in the Eighteenth Century, in* PERSPECTIVES IN AMERICAN HISTORY 258–72 (Doland Fleming & Bernard Bailyn eds., 1971).

[5] The defense of recrimination has been abolished in the United States. *See* Sanford N. Katz & Marcus G. Raskin, *The Dying Doctrine of Recrimination in the United States of America*, 35 CAN. BAR REV. 1046 (1957).

be granted. Because of the strict requirements for cruelty and adultery, the grounds were often difficult to prove unless there was secret collaboration with the defendant. In the case of adultery, which was the only ground for divorce in New York until 1967,[6] it was not uncommon for a spouse to fake an adultery scene. The situation was so bad in New York that as early as 1945, the Committee on Law Reform of the Association of the Bar of the City of New York recommended divorce reform to the state legislature. A portion of the report read: 'We . . . urge a liberalization of the divorce laws under proper legal sanctions. We do so in the hope that we may thus eliminate what has come to be recognized as a scandal, growing out of widespread fraud, perjury, collusion, and connivance which now pervade the dissolution of marriages in this State.'[7]

In states where there were a number of divorce grounds and a judge wanted to grant a divorce but was not presented with persuasive evidence, the judge might interpret the ground for divorce broadly. For example, a judge could interpret the ground of cruelty, which customarily required some evidence of physical force, to mean emotional or mental distress without any physical manifestations such as a slap or a punch. The result was that divorce cases were often considered illustrations of two processes occurring at the same time. On the level that could be observed in court there was the formal process of a divorce case: lawyers and litigants going through the motions of a civil law suit. On another level there was private understanding between lawyers and litigants that there would be a certain amount of lying and perjury. Because of this, divorce practice was considered to be low level, and judges assigned to hear divorce cases were often thought to be part of the legal charade, thus not very competent or persons with little respect for the legal system.[8]

Fault-based divorce, the model that existed in the United States for years and still exists (in some instances side by side with no-fault) in thirty-three states,[9]

---

[6] The Divorce Reform Act of 1966 changed the law to broaden the grounds. The Act became effective on September 1, 1967. *See* NEW YORK LAW 1966 Ch. 244, § 15.

[7] This passage is cited in Richard H. Wels, *New York: The Poor Man's Reno*, 35 CORNELL L. REV. 303–04 (1950). In his article Mr. Wels discussed 'the mockery and the fraud attendant upon divorce proceedings' in New York.

[8] Mr. Wels wrote:

> Our present laws [referring to the laws of New York] from a lawyer's viewpoint, are bad because of the corrupting effect which their administration has had upon our courts. The keystone of our Western democracy is the integrity and honesty of our courts, and the knowledge that any citizen who has been aggrieved will obtain just and honest dealing there. Our divorce practice has become an evil in that it has corrupted and degraded those courts.

Id. at 326.

[9] These states are: Alabama, Alaska, Arkansas, Connecticut, Georgia, Idaho, Illinois, Indiana, Kansas, Louisiana, Maine, Maryland, Massachusetts, Mississippi, Missouri, Nevada, New Hampshire, New Jersey, New Mexico, New York, North Dakota, Ohio, Oklahoma, Pennsylvania, Rhode Island, South Carolina, South Dakota, Tennessee, Texas, Utah, Vermont, Virginia, West Virginia.

affected not only grounds for obtaining a divorce but also influenced the assignment of children and property.[10] It was hard to separate the evidence for proving a ground like cruel and abusive conduct or adultery from the litigation over who was assigned custody of what child and how much a spouse would have to pay in alimony unless the procedure was bifurcated. Appellate case law is filled with cases denying a spouse custodial rights in the first instance or after a modification hearing on the basis of moral turpitude.[11]

In the 1960s and early 1970s, the legal profession and state legislatures came to realize the deplorable state of divorce laws and practice.[12] Respect for divorce law and procedure, if there ever really was any, had declined. Reform was needed not only in terms of changing substantive laws, like grounds for divorce, but also with regard to the process of divorce. The thought was that the law should not mask deception but should, as far as possible, reflect reality. It was at that time that the Governor's Commission in California found that the fault-based divorce laws in effect in California were no longer viable and should be replaced with laws that allowed a divorce without a showing of fault. Thus, in 1969 California became the first state to implement a divorce law without any fault-based grounds for divorce. Although, due to strong resistance from some segments of society, only a few states have entirely done away with fault as a basis for divorce, by 2001 all fifty states have enacted some type of no-fault provisions as part of their divorce laws.[13]

Residency

At the same time that no-fault divorce laws were being enacted, a major procedural reform was taking place: changes in residency laws. Prior to 1970 it was

[10] Twenty-eight states still consider marital fault when determining alimony awards. They are: Alabama, Arizona, Connecticut, Florida, Georgia, Idaho, Kentucky, Louisiana, Maryland, Massachusetts, Michigan, Mississippi, Missouri, Nevada, New Hampshire, New Jersey, New York, North Dakota, Pennsylvania, Rhode Island, South Carolina, South Dakota, Tennessee, Texas, Utah, Virginia, West Virginia, and Wyoming. The source for this information is: Linda D. Elrod & Robert G. Spector, *Family Law in the Fifty States 2000–2001*, 35 FAM. L.Q. 577, 617 (2002).

[11] A case that illustrates this point is *Jarrett v. Jarrett*, 400 N.E.2d 421 (Ill. 1979), where the Illinois Supreme Court held that a divorced mother who lived with a man to whom she was not married was denied custody of her child because of her immoral conduct. To the Illinois Supreme Court, such conduct 'debases public morality'. Mrs. Jarrett appealed the decision to the U.S. Supreme Court, which denied certiorari. However, Justices Brennan and Marshall dissented. *See Jarrett v. Jarrett*, 449 U.S. 927 (1980), *infra* note 101.

[12] The reform movement, especially in California, is discussed in Herma Hill Kay, *Beyond No-Fault: New Directions, in* STEPHEN D. SUGARMAN & HERMA HILL KAY, DIVORCE REFORM AT THE CROSSROADS 6–36 (1990).

[13] The states that have enacted no-fault as the exclusive method for obtaining a divorce are: Arizona, California, Colorado, Delaware, Florida, Hawaii, Iowa, Kentucky, Michigan, Minnesota, Montana, Nebraska, Oregon, Washington, Wisconsin, and Wyoming. The source for this information is: Elrod & Spector, *supra* note 10, at 620.

not uncommon for a state to have a one- or two-year residence requirement before a person could file for divorce. The idea behind such residence requirements is that a state should have an interest in the status of marriage before it allows its courts to be used for dissolving a marriage. In addition, residence requirements provide a certain amount of time to consider divorce. Further, for practical reasons, long residence requirements, like two years, act as a deterrent to divorce and reflect a policy of marriage being a serious undertaking, not easily dissolved.[14] Nevada had the dubious distinction of being the 'divorce mill' state and the 'road to Reno' became another way of saying 'the road to divorce'.[15]

Reducing the length of time a person must live in a state before he or she may petition for a divorce is a reflection of that state's view of marriage and divorce. It stands to reason that the longer the residence requirement the more likely it is that the state takes marriage as a serious institution worth preserving. In addition, a long residency requirement discourages persons who have not lived in the state for a certain length of time from seeking a divorce there. The theory, rightly or wrongly, is that a state has an 'interest' only in marriages of its domiciliaries. The general view has been that a divorce action should not be like a transitory tort action—allowing the damaged party (plaintiff) to sue the wrongdoer (tortfeasor) wherever he or she can be found in a state that has no contact with the marriage at all. No state takes that position, although the statutory trend seems to be clearly in the direction of shortening the time necessary to live in a state before one can sue for a divorce.[16] As more and more states either relax their grounds for divorce, adopt grounds similar to those in sister states, or enact a liberal no-fault system, the need to leave a state or travel to a foreign country to obtain a divorce—what the law terms (with negative connotations) migratory divorce—becomes less and less important.

As fewer couples seek divorces in jurisdictions that are not their marital domicile, the less there is litigation over the recognition of a sister state's divorce

[14] The same can be said for grounds of divorce. For example, in writing about New York divorce law when adultery was the only ground for divorce, Mr. Wels wrote:

> In establishing adultery at the time [in 1787] as the sole ground for divorce, the Legislature then intended to make divorce as difficult as possible for the purpose of preserving the family unit. For many years this result was attained, and the statute exercised a severe restraint upon divorce actions.

See Wels, *supra* note 7, at 306.

[15] NELSON M. BLAKE, THE ROAD TO RENO (1962). In the 1940s Arkansas, Idaho, and Florida had a reputation of 'key[ing] their laws to the revenue of the divorce trade, [seeking] such traffic to compensate for the lack of real gold mines within their boundaries'. *See* Wels, *supra* note 7, at 304.

[16] A chart (Number 4) that lists the durational residency requirements of most states (6 weeks to 1 year) can be found in Linda Elrod & Robert G. Spector, *A Review of the Year in Family Law: Redefining Families, Reforming Custody Jurisdiction, and Refining Support Issues*, 34 FAM. L.Q. 656 (2001).

decree. Two famous cases, *Williams v. North Carolina I*[17] and *Williams v. North Carolina II*,[18] dealt with the question of the extent to which a divorce decree issued in one state (where only one spouse was before the court and the other spouse was given notice of the divorce hearing), not the marital domicile, must be given full faith and credit in another state. In *Williams I*, a bigamy case, the U.S. Supreme Court held that a divorce decree that was obtained in a state (Nevada) where one of the spouses was domiciled for purposes of divorce is entitled to full faith and credit in the couple's marital domicile (North Carolina). The case was remanded to the North Carolina courts to determine the issue of domicile. In *Williams v. North Carolina II*, the U.S. Supreme Court held that North Carolina should respect Nevada's finding that it had jurisdiction over the Williams's divorce. However, this did not mean that North Carolina could not examine the matter itself and reach its own judgment on whether Nevada's jurisdictional requirements were met. That is what North Carolina did, and it found that Nevada was without jurisdiction. Throughout the case, the justices emphasized the importance of domicile. The result of the *Williams* cases is that a divorce can be granted in one state (Nevada) and be legal there. However, that same divorce need not be recognized in the marital domicile of the divorcing parties (North Carolina).[19] It should be emphasized, however, that if both parties to a marriage appear personally in another state and participate in obtaining a divorce there, neither can attack the divorce.

In the *Williams* cases, only one party to the marriage, Mr. Williams, was present in Nevada. That kind of *ex parte* proceeding can give the court jurisdiction to terminate only the marriage. Without personal jurisdiction over both spouses, a court cannot either impose or limit obligations (like alimony)[20] or restrict rights (like issuing a custodial order restricting the rights of the absent parent).[21]

No-Fault Divorce

It is an oversimplification to say that once a no-fault system of divorce is in place, the idea of fault is abandoned. Many states and the Uniform Marriage and Divorce Act do specifically state that the division of marital property should be assigned 'without regard to marital misconduct'.[22] But, words like 'unfitness' in child custody matters or 'conduct of the parties' (as it affects the marital assets), 'dissipation of assets', 'misuse or mismanagement of marital

---

[17] 317 U.S. 287 (1942).   [18] 325 U.S. 226 (1945).

[19] The Williams cases, including a chronology of the cases and the impact of the cases on the persons involved, are discussed in WEYRAUCH ET AL., *supra* note 1, at 1010–14.

[20] *See* Vanderbilt v. Vanderbilt, 354 U.S. 416 (1957).

[21] *See* May v. Anderson, 345 U.S. 528 (1953).

[22] *See* Uniform Marriage and Divorce Act § 307 (Alternative A & Alternative B), i.e. *see* Appendix.

assets' may be a mask for the concept of 'fault'. However, the idea is the same.
In addition, some states specifically mention that a court may consider fault in
determining alimony and child custody.[23] Also, an abused spouse who was
awarded a no-fault divorce, if allowed under state law, might have preserved
her right to seek a tort action for assault and battery after her divorce unless she
specifically waives that right in a divorce settlement.[24]

It is important to note that there are two kinds of no-fault divorce statutes:
those that allow one of the spouses to contest the claim that the marriage is
'irretrievably broken' or that the spouses are 'incompatible', and those that do
not allow any contest. In the first kind, if one spouse claims that her marriage
is 'irretrievably broken' and her husband claims it is not, the wife must prove
her allegation by what amounts to factors that might have been satisfactory
to show a fault ground.[25] Where there is no contest, one spouse's allegation of
'incompatibility' might be sufficient for a judge to grant a divorce. The pure
no-fault model—that which does not provide for a contest—basically allows
one spouse to leave the marriage at will. It also minimizes the role of the
judge.[26] But it must be emphasized that no-fault in this context only operates to
terminate the marital relationship. It does not affect the assignment of property
or the custody of children, both of which are separate issues.

There has been a great deal of discussion in the academic literature as to the
effect of no-fault divorce on the divorce process and on society as a whole. It is
generally believed that no-fault divorce has decreased the acrimony and hostility
between the spouses and civilized the process.[27] There is no more need for

[23] For a full discussion and state by state analysis of the impact of fault on property
and alimony in most of the states, see PRINCIPLES OF THE LAW OF FAMILY DISSOLUTION:
ANALYSIS AND RECOMMENDATIONS 67–85 (Amer. Law Inst. 2002).

[24] Because a separate action for tort that occurred during the marriage, like assault,
battery, intentional infliction of emotional distress or fraud, still exists in many states,
lawyers often include a provision in the property settlement agreement that prohibits any
and all separate actions arising out of the marriage from being brought following the
divorce.

[25] An illustration of this point is the Florida case of *McClelland v. McClelland*, 318 So.
2d 160 (Fla. Dist. Ct. App. 1975), where the District Court of Appeals permitted the wife
to plead adultery as the cause of an irretrievably broken marriage.

[26] This was emphasized in the Florida case of *Ryan v. Ryan*, 277 So. 3d 266
(Fla. 1973), where the Supreme Court of Florida wrote that a judge is more than a ministerial officer in divorce cases. To the Supreme Court of Florida a judge must make a
'proper inquiry' in order to determine whether a marriage is irretrievably broken (the no-
fault basis for divorce in Florida).

[27] Deborah L. Rhode and Martha Minow wrote that although decreasing acrimony
and hostility between the parties was a worthy goal, the early reforms in no-fault divorce
did not pay sufficient 'attention to vulnerable groups'. They stated:

> Early no-fault reforms gave no special attention to the concerns of particularly
> vulnerable groups such as displaced homemakers with limited savings, insur-
> ance, and employment options; families with inadequate income to support two
> households (a problem disproportionately experienced by racial minorities); or

charades. Two questions have been raised with regard to the social implications of no-fault divorce. The first concerns the rate of divorce: Has the advent of no-fault divorce increased the divorce rate? A second question is whether a pure no-fault divorce economically favors one spouse over another.

Professor Morrison has written:

During the decade from 1950 to 1960, the rate of divorce was considerably lower than would have been expected based on the historical trend. But this period of high marital stability did not last. In the late 1960s the rate of divorce made a sharp ascent which continued through the late 1970s. Like the 1950s downturn that preceded it, this surge was more radical than what would have been predicted from the trend line over time. Given that during this span of fifteen years divorce rates more than doubled from 17 per 1,000 single women ages 15 to 54 in 1963 to 1965 to 40 in 1978 to 1980, it is not surprising that this pattern was dubbed the 'Divorce Revolution'. Observers attribute the rise in divorce rates during this period to several things, including the sexual revolution, the availability of modern contraception to control fertility via artificial means, and the legalization of abortion, each of which may have increased marital infidelity. *Moreover, both the introduction of no-fault divorce laws and the increased labor market involvement of women (and hence their improved economic independence) may have made it easier for couples to sever their marital ties. The rate of divorce began to level off in the 1970s and actually declined during the 1980s. More recently, the divorce rate has remained high, but steady.*[28] (emphasis added)

As to whether no-fault divorce favors one spouse or another, again it can be said that it is not absolutely clear because most of the research on divorce trends was published in the 1980s. One researcher has maintained that at least in California, divorced women are economically worse off than their divorced husbands, perhaps because judges, using their discretion, have awarded inadequate support orders.[29] Another study concludes that the effects of no-fault on

couples with no children, no significant property, and no need for a formal adjudicative procedure. Nor was child support central to the reform agenda; it appeared only as a side issue, buried within custody and other financial topics.

Reformers also neglected the impact of post divorce property divisions—such as the forced sale of the family home—on dependent children. And what was most critical, no-fault initiatives omitted criteria for assessing the outcomes of divorce, outcomes affecting not only the parties and their children but subsequent marriages, stepfamilies and public welfare responsibilities.

Deborah L. Rhode & Martha M. Minow, *Reforming the Questions, Questioning the Reforms, in* DIVORCE REFORM AT THE CROSSROADS, *supra* note 12, at 196.

[28] Donna Ruane Morrison, *A Century of the American Family, in* CROSS CURRENTS, *supra* note 1, at 64–65.

[29] LENORE J. WEITZMAN, THE DIVORCE REVOLUTION: THE UNEXPECTED SOCIAL AND ECONOMIC CONSEQUENCES FOR WOMEN AND CHILDREN IN AMERICA 366 (1985). Weitzman's research received early praise, but then was highly criticized. For example, Herbert Jacob wrote:

Weitzman does not distinguish between the effects of no-fault and the new property division rules because an equal division rule was adopted along with

the economic condition of divorced women 'were either modestly benign or neutral'.[30]

While no-fault divorce may not have a major adverse effect on women, this does not mean that the same can be said about divorce itself.[31] There seems to be no dispute in the literature about divorce's negative impact on women.[32] The reasons for this latter phenomenon have much to do with the fact that the social and financial position of the wife who usually has custody of the children tends to be frozen at the time of divorce, while the husband's position is more fluid. In other words, a working husband may have his alimony and child support payments calculated on the basis of his salary for his existing job at the time of divorce. There may or may not be consideration of his future finances such as his working overtime, receiving a promotion, or taking a second job.[33] If any of these eventualities do occur and a divorced wife needs additional support for herself and her child, she must seek a modification of her alimony decree and child support order on the basis of 'changed circumstances', defined as events that have occurred following the divorce decree that have materially altered the status quo.

If a divorced wife chooses to work outside the home after divorce, she may find that her years out of the commercial workforce have put her in an economically disadvantageous position compared with men and women who did not leave the labor force to raise children.[34] Divorced husbands do not

no-fault in California, where she obtained most of her data. . . . Another problem is that . . . the Weitzman . . . analyses focus almost entirely on asset division, alimony, and child support. . . . There are good reasons, however, to surround a discussion of these resources with caveats, because they may reflect changes in the property division and child support statutes as well as the impact of no-fault.

Herbert H. Jacob, *Another Look at No-Fault Divorce and the Post Divorce Finances of Women*, 23 Law & Soc'y Rev. 95, 96–97 (1989).

[30] *Id.* at 111.

[31] In his full discussion of the legal and sociological aspects of fault and no-fault divorce, and a thoughtful presentation of the arguments for not reviving fault in divorce, Professor Ira Mark Ellman writes that the 'claim that no–fault divorce hurt women financially is probably wrong. On balance there seems little empirical evidence in its support . . . ' Professor Ellman believes that the change in divorce laws has not had a major impact on divorce rates. *See* Ellman, *supra* note 1, at 341–50.

[32] *See* Morrison, *supra* note 28. *See also* Suzanne M. Bianchi & Daphne Spain, American Women in Transition (1986).

[33] Some judges do, however, consider not only the husband's earnings, but his earning capacity in setting alimony and child support orders. If the husband has made a pattern of 'over-time' or a having a second job, and the family had lived on the additional money, a judge would consider that additional income in calculating the husband's financial obligation. Some men consider that approach as unfair, claiming it basically interferes with the husband's ability to change his way of life or his job. The judicial response has been that the family relied on the additional income. In a way, the result suggests the application of the estoppel principle.

[34] There is a distinction between working in the home and working outside of the home in the 'commercial workforce'. Whether a person (usually the wife and mother)

necessarily have the same experience. In fact men who stayed in the workforce throughout their marriage may have more opportunities to increase their income by taking advanced training in their particular career and being promoted. In addition, more divorced men tend to remarry than divorced women.[35] These men may benefit financially from their new wives. These wives may be making the major financial contribution to their husband's second marriage because of the husband's financial obligation to his first family, which many judges feel is the husband's primary obligation.[36] This is especially true if the new wives are professional women in the commercial world.[37]

Distribution of Economic Resources

With the inclusion of no-fault divorce in American law, the emphasis in a divorce case has shifted from determining and proving fault grounds for divorce to determining what are marital assets and how should they be assigned. For the most part the economic aspects of divorce constitute the main concern in divorce negotiation in lawyers' offices and the major time in litigation. Divorce that involves a couple with substantial financial resources has become complex. In order to prepare such a case, lawyers must hire not only accountants but experts in special types of valuations, such as those who specialize in valuing the position (including benefits and advancement possibilities), which a spouse holds and the industry in which a spouse's business is located.[38] The reason for

works in the home or out of the home, it is still 'work'. The difference is that working at home is devalued in our society while working outside the home or in the commercial world is not. *See* Rhode & Minow, *supra* note 27, at 193–94.

[35] *See* ANDREW J. CHERLIN, MARRIAGE DIVORCE REMARRIAGE 29 (1981).

[36] *See* discussion of child support, *infra*.

[37] A 1995 Harris survey showed that more than half the employed single and married women in the United States supply at least half of their household's income. *See* Tamar Lewin, *Women Are Becoming Equal Providers*, N.Y. TIMES, May 11, 1995, at A27. The article went on to state that the findings of the Bureau of Labor Statistics revealed that in 1993 married women who were working full time 'contributed a median of 41 percent of the family's income'. A 2003 report of the U.S. Census conducted in March 2002 revealed that of the 282.1 million residents in the United States 51 percent were women of whom 12 percent of women 65 and older live in poverty compared with 7 percent of men. It continued that women were more likely to be widowed than men. It also stated that men reach the highest salary brackets compared with women. For example, according to the report about 20 percent of men earned $50,000 to $75,000 a year compared with 12 percent of women. *See Census Study Finds That Men Earn the Most, Women Are Becoming Equal Providers*, N.Y. TIMES, March 25, 2003, at A13.

[38] Divorce cases are much more complicated now than they were thirty years ago. The growth of state statutes and uniform acts that set standards for equitable distribution and child custody and the enormous amount of reported cases have required lawyers to do more legal research, collect a great deal of information about their clients and present complex material to a court. Lawyers who are not current in the latest reported cases and statutory modifications in their jurisdiction as well as judicial and statutory trends in the

this change in divorce practice and litigation is, as has been discussed earlier, that marriage is now considered a special economic partnership in which each spouse may have contributed to and have an interest in the other spouse's business or career.[39]

Property Distribution

Two kinds of marital property systems have existed side by side in the United States: the common law system and the community property system.[40] The common law property system is based on evidence of title. In other words under the common law property system the motto: 'He who holds title takes the property' has a ring of truth to it. Under the community property system, found in nine states in the western and southwestern part of the country, the distribution of marital property (accumulated during marriage) upon divorce is theoretically based on the principle that each spouse owns an undivided one-half interest in each community property item. While four of the community property states seem to conform to the fifty–fifty split (assuming there has not been a prenuptial agreement that assigns property according to a different formula), the other five incorporate equitable distribution principles (that is, a judge considers the equities of a case), which may result in a different formula than an equal split.[41]

In the last twenty years there has been a major decline in the number of states that either by statute or case law adhere to the old common law property system. Now, the prevailing method of assigning marital property upon divorce is called 'equitable distribution'. Basically equitable distribution has changed the

country can expect malpractice actions filed against them if their failures result in loss of money for their clients. In *Smith v. Lewis*, 530 P.2d 589 (Cal. 1975), for example, the Supreme Court of California held that a lawyer was negligent in failing to assert his client's community interest in her husband's retirement benefits. The failure to consider the retirement benefits had a direct bearing on the outcome of the assignment of property to the wife, since the husband's retirement benefits were the only significant asset available to the community. The question of whether a lawyer was negligent or not is usually determined by a jury who may be sympathetic to the wives who are more likely than men to be the victims of their lawyer's ignorance. The reason for this is that women who have a limited amount of money to spend on the divorce may not be able to finance complicated discovery matters in uncovering a husband's hidden assets. Or they may be forced to hire inexperienced lawyers who may miss out on claims that would have been raised by more experienced lawyers.

[39] See text accompanying note 50 *infra*.

[40] For a discussion of both systems, see MARY ANN GLENDON, THE TRANSFORMATION OF FAMILY LAW 116–47 (1989).

[41] The five community property states referred to are: Arizona, Idaho, Nevada, Texas, and Washington. The four are California, Louisiana, New Mexico, and Puerto Rico. For a discussion of the principles of community property, see W. S. MCCLANAHAN, COMMUNITY PROPERTY LAW IN THE UNITED STATES 531–36 (1982).

nature of the judicial inquiry when making an assignment of property. Instead of asking the question: Who holds title? The questions asked are: What is considered marital property and what is considered separate property regardless of title? When and how was the property in dispute acquired: while the parties were single or before marriage but while the couple was living together, during the marriage, or after the separation? Who has contributed to the enhancement of its value or who has depreciated the property? When should it be valued (e.g. at the time of separation, initial court petition for divorce, or the time of the divorce trial) and what is its value? Who should value it, the parties themselves or experts? If the property was acquired by gift or inheritance, should it be considered separate? If either of the parties enhanced the value of the gifted or inherited property during the marriage by keeping the property in good repair or rehabilitating the property, were those activities sufficient to change its nature from separate (if that was the case) to marital? The key word to equitable distribution is 'contribution': and the ultimate question is: Who should be assigned the property?

A whole body of law has developed to give courts guidance in determining whether assets are separate or marital. Courts have come up with three concepts: tracing, commingling, and transmutation. Tracing of assets consists of determining the source of the asset, that is whether the asset was acquired through inheritance, gift, or by the use of marital funds. Commingling takes place when separate funds are brought into the marriage but are mixed with other assets so as to be untraceable. Transmutation of an asset is the term used to describe the change in character of the property from separate to marital or from marital to separate, usually accomplished by use, gift, or contract.[42]

But the fundamental assumption of equitable distribution is the fact that the marriage is an economic partnership in which there is a shared enterprise. In some respects the modern American marriage is an investment in a relationship, which at times pays off by being successful. That success has been measured by its bringing mutual happiness to the couple, being productive in the sense that joint aspirations have been realized, and that it has been of a long duration.

---

[42] In *Quinn v. Quinn*, 512 A.2d 848 (R.I. 1986), the Supreme Court of Rhode Island applied these terms to a case in which a portion of the total price of the marital domicile had been purchased with money from the husband's inheritance. This resulted in the property being transmuted from separate to marital property by the intent of the parties and by the placement of the title to property in joint tenancy. The court used notions of equity and fairness to offset the husband's argument that the placing of the names of the couple on the title to the property was for convenience and nothing more. Further, the court stated that the couple's investments made during the marriage involved commingling of inherited and non-inherited funds. These funds were exchanged for other property, which became marital property. The court went on to state that the husband's inherited furniture that had been brought into the marital home and used during the thirty-year marriage was marital property, while the furniture that had not been taken out of storage retained their inherited and separate nature. Inherited jewelry that the husband had given to his wife, who possessed the jewelry at the time of divorce, was considered the wife's by virtue of the husband's gift to her.

At other times the marriage turns out to be unsuccessful for many reasons and results in a divorce.

Over a decade ago, marital property was thought of as mainly tangible items like a house, an automobile, or a painting and salary, cash in the bank, and investments. Today, the definition of marital property goes beyond these items to include less obvious ones like, for example, pensions (vested and non-vested),[43] deferred income, unused vacation or sick leave payments, stock options, interests in a spouse's business, including its good will and a spouse's reputation, celebrity status, or career,[44] income from a patent, a law suit, and

---

[43] In *In re Marriage of Grubb*, 745 P.2d 661 (Colo. 1987), the Supreme Court of Colorado held that the husband's contribution and his unmatured right to the employer's contribution (to the extent that the employee/employer contributions were made during the marriage) are marital assets that can be distributed upon divorce. The court rejected the argument advanced by the husband that the vested but unmatured pension rights were a mere 'expectancy' until such time as a right actually matures.

Valuing pension plans for purposes of the assignment of marital property is highly technical. Two methods have been proposed: (1) assigning a percentage of the present actuarial value of the pension; or (2) making the apportionment to the non-retiring spouse elective if, as and when the person receives the pension benefits. The advantages of the first method are (1) that by determining a figure for the present actuarial value of the pension and paying the amount allows the parties to enjoy a 'clean break' in their financial relationship; (2) the employee spouse is left with an unencumbered pension plan; (3) a court is relieved of the responsibility of supervising any payments; and (4) at the time the pension is to be paid, the recipient is the contributing spouse, not a non-employee.

Some states prohibit the assignment of any portion of a pension. For example, in Massachusetts, under M.G.L. ch. 32, § 19, assignment of retirement funds in general is prohibited. However, the provision does expressly allow for such an assignment to satisfy a support order under the M.G.L. ch. 204, § 34, the Massachusetts property distribution statute.

With regard to disability benefits, as contrasted with retirement benefits, there is a split of authority. A number of courts have held that disability benefits should be considered marital assets and thus able to be divided in some equitable fashion between the parties. Other courts look to the nature of the disability benefit and consider some portion of the disability payments as marital property. Some courts have characterized disability benefits as separate property to be considered only in awarding alimony and child support. An illustration of this third position is *Thompson v. Thompson*, 642 A.2d 1160 (R.I. 1994), where the Rhode Island Supreme Court held that a disability pension (based on an injury that the husband suffered in 1975, approximately nine years before the divorce) that had been paid to the husband during the marriage was not a marital asset subject to equitable distribution, but could be 'considered as a source of income to the disabled spouse from which alimony and child support can be paid'.

For a full discussion with formulae for the assignment of pensions and employee stock options in divorce, see J. THOMAS OLDHAM, DIVORCE, SEPARATION AND THE DISTRIBUTION OF PROPERTY §§ 7.10–11 (2002). *Also see* Elizabeth Barker Brandt, *Valuation, Allocations, and Distribution of Retirement Plans at Divorce: Where Are We?*, 35 FAM. L.Q. 469 (2001).

[44] A recent illustration of this principle is the case of *Elkus v. Elkus*, 572 N.Y.S.2d 901 (A.D. 1 Dept. 1991), in which the New York Supreme Court (Appellate Division) held

royalties from the present or future sale of books.[45] Disability benefits and personal injury awards or causes of action for personal injury may or may not be marital property. Ordinarily, if the disability benefit or personal injury award related to payment for disfigurement or compensation for pain and suffering, and is not related to lost wages, the benefit or award is usually considered separate property. A cause of action may be marital or separate depending on the substance of the action and whether recovery is too speculative.[46] Recovery from a cause of action for sexual harassment, for example might be personal property if the damages relate to pain, suffering, and humiliation. The important point is that for the most part in equitable distribution states, marital property consists of assets earned (sometimes gifts and inheritance acquired during marriage and remain in their original form are separate, depending on the facts or a statutory exclusion) during the marriage and while the couple live together, whether the assets are fully realized during the marriage or after divorce.[47] It should also be noted that debts can be marital if they were incurred for joint benefit during the marriage.[48]

Professional degrees and licenses present special problems. One state, New York, by statute, considers a professional license marital property if it was obtained during the marriage.[49] Generally, however, a professional degree or a professional license is not considered marital property subject to division because it does not conform to the traditional definition of property. A professional degree or license is personal to the holder, and cannot be bought, sold, mortgaged, or transferred. Judges consider the degree or license as having enhanced the earning capacity of the person holding the degree or license, and

that Mr. Elkus, the husband of Metropolitan Opera star Frederica von Stade, had a property interest in Ms. von Stade's operatic career.

[45] For a discussion of intellectual property as marital property, see Ann Bartow, *Intellectual Property and Domestic Relations: Issues to Consider When There Is an Artist, Author, Inventor, or Celebrity in the Family*, 35 FAM. L.Q. 383 (2001).

[46] *See* BRETT R. TURNER, EQUITABLE DISTRIBUTION OF PROPERTY 388–94 (2d ed. 1994).

[47] Timing is important. The critical period is during the marriage and while the couple reside together. For example, if after separation and before a divorce one spouse invests his or her own separate money in some venture that proves to be successful, the fruits of that investment would ordinarily be separate property. On the other hand, if an asset was completed during the marriage, like a piece of art, sculpture, or a novel, but sold after the divorce, the proceeds from the work would ordinarily be marital, since it was produced during the marriage.

[48] *See* TURNER, *supra* note 46 at 455–67.

[49] *See O'Brien v. O'Brien*, 489 N.E.2d 712 (1985), where the Court of Appeals of New York held that a husband's medical license was marital property within the meaning of its equitable distribution law. The court interpreted its statute, Domestic Relations Law § 236(b)(1)(c), which defined marital property to include 'all property acquired by either or both spouses during the marriage and before the execution of a separation agreement or commencement of a matrimonial action, regardless of the form in which title is held' to include a professional license.

thus a factor in the determination of alimony generally,[50] or 'reimbursement alimony'. In addition to alimony, a supporting spouse could also seek restitution for repayment of her expenses (such as tuition), or if there was some sort of implied or expressed contract that could be proven, she could have an independent breach of contract cause of action. The major problem with seeking recovery in any action, including quasi-contractual relief, rather than a property division or alimony award is overcoming the presumption that spouses contribute to each other's lives, including the payment of educational debts, with a donative intent and not with the expectation of being reimbursed.

The uncovering and consideration of marital assets have a great deal to do with the changes that have occurred in society. For most Americans today (although this may be changing because of the present economic conditions and downsizing of companies) one's job—the workplace—generates one's property, not one's family (by way of inheritance).[51] Thus, instead of accumulating

---

[50] *See Downs v. Downs*, 574 A.2d 156 (Vt. 1990), where the Supreme Court of Vermont in what it labeled the 'diploma dilemma' held that where a wife had sacrificed her own career opportunities to advance her husband's, she should be compensated through a just maintenance award. In *Mahoney v. Mahoney*, 453 A.2d 527 (N.J. 1982), the Supreme Court of New Jersey held that a way of compensating a wife for supporting her husband while he obtained his MBA. was through 'reimbursement alimony'. The court went on to limit its holding and basically define 'reimbursement alimony'. Such alimony would be available to one spouse who supports his or her spouse through professional school having had mutual and shared expectation that their marriage will materially benefit through the advanced education. Both *Downs* and *Mahoney* include full discussions of the professional degree and license as marital or separate property.

[51] Professor Mary Ann Glendon was one of the first scholars to bring this phenomenon to the attention of others. *See* MARY ANN GLENDON, THE NEW FAMILY AND THE NEW PROPERTY (1981). In 1981 she wrote that employment ties (the employer's inability to fire an employee without cause) were more secure because of family ties (because of no-fault divorce where a spouse may leave another spouse without cause). Professor Glendon's observations were truer in the 1970s and early 1980s than they would be today. Over the past two decades the employment bond itself has loosened considerably. The employment relationship today appears little more stable than the marital relationship itself. The fastest growing area in the employment sphere is multiple job holding and contingent employment arrangements. On this phenomenon, see Thomas C. Kohler, *Individualism and Communitarianism at Work*, 1993 BYU L. REV. 727. Professor Kohler wrote:

> It may be that instability increasingly characterizes many of the significant relationships among Americans: employment relationships in the U.S. now last an average of 4.5 years, while the average marriage lasts but seven. Trends are not wholly clear, but the average length of both may be on the way down.

Id. at 736.

Professor's Kohler's statement that the average marriage lasts seven years is supported by divorce epidemiologists who write: 'Currently, most people who divorce do so early in their marriage so that half of the divorces occur by the seventh year of marriage.' *See* Patricia H. Shiono & Linda Sandham Quinn, *Epidemiology of Divorce*, 4 THE FUTURE OF CHILDREN 15, 18 (No. 1 Spring 1994).

wealth in investments in land and in stocks and bonds, and inheriting money from relatives, most Americans derive their present and future assets (especially their pensions and other retirement benefits) and status from their employment. In addition, economic contributions to the marital enterprise are not limited to those directly created by employment outside the home (such as a salary) but by contributions made within the home itself. Thus, in the context of a divorce, a value may be placed on a wife's (or husband's) household services, which include caring for the marital house and raising children. The percentage of the marital property awarded to a spouse who performs household services during the marriage and does not work outside of the home varies according to the facts of the case.[52] One state considers homemaker services only to the extent that they contributed to 'the acquisition, preservation and maintenance, or increase in value of marital property'.[53] Considering the value of a wife's homemaker services for purposes of determining her contribution to the marital enterprise is a major change in the law. It must be remembered that under the common law, a wife's duty was to perform such services. A husband's promise to compensate his wife for those services or to consider their value for determining her share of marital property in a way would violate notions of pre-existing duty, a firmly established doctrine that would deny recovery in contract law.

The nature and provision of equitable distribution statutes vary from state, to state although the Uniform Marriage and Divorce Act provides a framework for most of the statutes.[54] Basically state statutes contain a list of factors

---

[52] Lawrence J. Golden, Equitable Distribution Of Property 262–65 (1983). *See also* Brett R. Turner, Supplement To Equitable Distribution Of Property 248–49 (1990).

[53] *See* W. Va. Code § 48-2-32 (1996), cited and discussed in Mark Ellman, Paul M. Kurtz & Elizabeth S. Scott, Family Law Cases, Text, Problems 276 (3d ed. 1998). The authors have written:

> If that requirement were really applied as written, the homemaker would not often do well. While it may be easy to show that the homemaker wife contributed greatly to her husband's comfort or happiness. It is less easy to show that her services yielded a significant contribution to . . . 'the acquisition, preservation and maintenance, or increase in value of marital property.' Married men do earn more, on average, than do bachelors, but that is not necessarily because having a wife increases a man's earning potential. One can just as plausibly hypothesize that men with better earnings prospects have more success in attracting a wife, or that certain traits help a man both in courting women and in earning money . . .
>
> It thus matters greatly whether a 'homemaker' statute is read to create an irrebuttable presumption that the homemaker's economic contribution is equal, or merely to create an opportunity for the homemaker to try to show how her services contributed to the parties' assets.

[54] The Uniform Marriage and Divorce Act is reproduced in the Appendix.

that a court must consider in order to properly determine the assignment of property.[55] By enacting such legislation, one goal was to provide guidance to judges. A second was to provide some uniformity in decisions. Although at first blush stating factors that must be considered for making an assignment of marital property might seem to be a method to limit judicial discretion, the history of the application of state statutory provisions has not proved this to be the case. In other words, even though judges are governed by statutory provisions, there is still wide discretion in interpreting statutory factors and applying them to a particular set of facts. One commentator has gone so far as to label equitable distribution as 'discretionary distribution of property'.[56]

The factors that are considered in the assignment of property are not weighted equally. Nor does an equitable distribution provision provide a formula. The statutes merely state that certain factors are to be considered, thus allowing the judge to set his or her own priority of importance. Some attempts have been made to create either a presumption of equal division or a fifty–fifty starting point for division. A handful of state statutes contain a presumption that marital property will be divided equally.[57] As a check on judicial discretion, some states require judges to make specific findings explaining their award. These findings not only present lawyers with reasons for the division, but also provide a basis for appeal.

We have had nearly a quarter of a century experience with some form of equitable distribution. Has the existence of statutory factors reduced judicial discretion? What trends can be discerned? Equitable distribution legislation has limited judicial discretion to some extent, but has certainly not eliminated it.[58] A review of the statutes and case law suggests that absent statutory guidance, courts are generally more likely to divide property equally in the case of long-term marriages (fifteen years and longer) and, conversely, less likely to presume equal division for short-term marriages (one to three years).[59]

---

[55] These factors include: duration of the marriage, the age, health, station, occupation, amount and sources of income, vocational skills, employability, estate, liabilities, and needs of each of the parties, custodial provisions, whether the apportionment is in lieu of or an addition to maintenance, and the opportunity of each for future acquisition of capital assets and income. Statutes also state that consideration should be given to the contribution or dissipation of each party to the acquisition, preservation, depreciation, or appreciation in value of the respective estates, and as the contribution of a spouse as a homemaker or to the family unit. Uniform Marriage and Divorce Act, § 307, Alternative A. *See* Appendix.　　　　　[56] *See* GLENDON, *supra* note 51, at 228.

[57] *See* TURNER, *supra* note 46, at 554–64.

[58] *See* ELLMAN, KURTZ & SCOTT, *supra* note 53, at 278–86.

[59] Indeed, the length of a marriage is one of the factors that judges must consider in making an equitable assignment of marital property. *But see* TURNER, *supra* note 46, at 586–88. For recent cases comparing the duration of marriage with the percentage of the marital estate awarded to each spouse, see TURNER, 2001 SUPPLEMENT, *supra* note 52, at 702–04.

The assignment of property upon divorce is only part of the economic consequences of divorce. Alimony and child support are additional financial considerations. Both have undergone major changes in the last thirty years.

Alimony

As stated earlier, before the passage of the Married Woman's Property Acts in the mid-nineteenth century in the United States, a woman's property became her husband's upon marriage. A husband, then, had the duty to support his wife during marriage. Upon divorce that duty continued under the legal term, 'alimony'. It was customary to say that alimony was based on a balance between the husband's ability to pay and the wife's needs.[60] Today, however, alimony may be awarded to a husband as well as a wife.[61] The amount of an alimony award was based on the station of life that the wife enjoyed during her marriage and to some extent the value of the property she lost control over and which the husband acquired upon marriage.[62] Alimony can be awarded periodically, which can be modified if there are changed circumstances, as a lump sum or as a lump sum paid out periodically, which normally cannot be modified (unless the modification is mutually agreed upon), since the lump sum is a debt. If the alimony was determined by agreement, the method of payment is ordinarily determined by the parties themselves, depending on the financial circumstances of the debtor and the tax consequences.

Unlike today's equitable distribution laws, which include factors for judges to consider in assigning property,[63] and before the enactment of laws based on the Uniform Marriage and Divorce Act,[64] there were no standardized statutory guidelines. The result was that judges used their own discretion in making awards. Discretion could mask biases for which the only procedure to question the discretion was through appellate review that might be both time-consuming

---

[60] The reporters of the ALI's Principles of the Law of Family Dissolution suggest an alternative approach to determining an alimony award based on need is to think of such an award as 'compensatory payment' or 'compensatory award', which is based on compensation of losses occasioned by the marriage and its breakup. *See* PRINCIPLES OF THE LAW OF FAMILY DISSOLUTION, *supra* note 23, at 785–804.

[61] The U.S. Supreme Court held in *Orr v. Orr*, 440 U.S. 268 (1979), that the Alabama alimony statute that imposed an alimony obligation on husbands, but not wives, was an unconstitutional denial of a husband's equal protection under the U.S. Constitution.

[62] *See* CLARK, *supra* note 4, at 619.

[63] Massachusetts sets out factors, based on the Uniform Marriage and Divorce Act, to be considered in its statute. *See* M.G.L. ch. 208, § 34.

[64] Although only eight states—Arizona, Colorado, Illinois, Kentucky, Minnesota, Missouri, Montana, and Washington—have enacted all or parts of the Uniform Marriage and Divorce Act, that Act has been the model for other statutory schemes. By 2003 Wisconsin was the only jurisdiction to enact the Uniform Marital Property Act, see W.S.A. §§ 766.001 to 766.97.

and costly.[65] At that time, no thought was given to the now accepted idea that a wife may have contributed something of value to the economic well-being of the family (as she did in the past, although this is often lost sight of, by bringing her own property into the marriage) by her household services or by giving up certain opportunities in the commercial workforce and that the husband's payment of alimony was really repaying what was really owed to the wife. In other words, today alimony is considered to be a wife's entitlement, not a privilege that may or may not be judicially recognized.

In reading appellate cases decided over thirty years ago and earlier, it is not unusual to find cases where a wife who divorced her husband after ten years of marriage (during which time she did not work outside the home) received alimony for the rest of her life. Why was lifetime alimony awarded in the past, but uncommon today? One thought is that if a wife never worked outside the home, she would not have qualified for any benefits like a private pension or social security. Thus, if she were divorced without any financial support from her husband and unable to find a job, she would become a 'public charge'.[66] Perhaps, in those old cases (before thirty years ago) alimony could have been thought of as a substitute for a pension or social security except that instead of a pension or government social security check, a wife would receive one from her former husband. Another view is that alimony serves as severance pay paid out in a lump sum or in installments. If one viewed alimony either as a government benefit or severance check, one would have to think of the marriage relationship as similar to that of an employer and employee with the husband acting as the employer.

Alimony is the economic link that continues a relationship between divorced spouses especially in the case of periodically paid alimony. That is to say, if a husband has a duty to pay alimony, he is forced to have some kind of relationship with his former wife. In other words, he has to communicate with her, even if it is by mailing her a check. If the divorced husband remarried, that fact alone

[65] Appellate review of alimony, judicial assignment of property, and child custody decisions is usually based on the abuse of discretion. Unless a state court system has an expedited review process whereby a spouse can get a hearing and a decision on a disputed judicial ruling within days and then resume the trial, appealing a trial court's decision is likely to be impractical. It is because of the inability to obtain appellate relief quickly, the cost of an appeal and the statistical unlikelihood of a reversal that trial judges have enormous power and their rulings during trial and their ultimate judgment are usually final.

[66] The words, 'public charge', often used in appellate cases during the first quarter of the twentieth century are totally out of date. In the last half of the past century, one could use the phrase 'a candidate for public assistance'. In 2003 in the United States, however, the availability of public welfare funds to support unemployed and unemployable destitute women without children is completely unavailable unless the woman is mentally or physically disabled, which, if substantiated with the proper documentation, would qualify her for special government-sponsored funds.

does not ordinarily discharge his alimony obligation. He has to consider his first wife (and first family if he had children) in all his economic planning. Permanent alimony means that a divorced wife can passively receive her former husband's alimony without any effort to reduce her financial dependency on him. As attitudes toward the role of men and women in marriage as well as the definition of marriage itself changed so has the concept of alimony.

Today long-term permanent alimony is an unusual outcome of a divorce except in the case of a very long marriage (of twenty years or more) where the wife is of an age, e.g. 50 years old, when she has been out of the commercial workforce for so long that she is now unemployable or is not in good health. In its place is short-term alimony (for a few years in order to help a wife through the difficult period of post-divorce adjustment) or rehabilitative alimony.

Rehabilitative alimony is a phenomenon derived from the application of judicial discretion in alimony cases.[67] The thought is that divorced wives should actively attempt to reduce the husband's alimony obligation by developing skills to become employable.[68] In a way, conceptualizing rehabilitative alimony in this way suggests the idea of mitigation of damages in contract law—that is that a contracting party should try to reduce the amount owed her under a contract. In the case of divorce, it would mean that the divorced wife would have to eventually seek employment and if the wife needed additional education to obtain a position, the husband would support his divorced wife in order to secure the education.[69] In a way, rehabilitative alimony is designed to take into account

---

[67] *See* WALTER O. WEYRAUCH & SANFORD N. KATZ, AMERICAN FAMILY LAW IN TRANSITION 319–20 (1982).

[68] The 1963 Supreme Court of Washington case of *Dakin v. Dakin*, 384 P.2d 639 (Wash. 1963), illustrates this point:

> The record shows that the plaintiff [wife] has no children to support or care for; that she was 53 years of age at the commencement of this action; that she was extremely nervous and upset at the time of the trial; but, otherwise she is an able-bodied woman; that, because of her past condition, she has been unable to maintain steady employment; that she attended teacher's college for two years and taught school for four years thereafter; that she has had considerable experience as a social worker, although no formal training.
>
> It is the policy of this state to place a duty upon the wife to gain employment, if possible.
>
> . . .
>
> . . . We think that [the plaintiff] should be encouraged to rehabilitate herself and that, within a reasonable period, she may become self supporting. Although she may have been nervous and upset prior to her decree of divorce, there is no evidence which indicates this condition is of a permanent nature. Except for this condition, she appears to be an able-bodied woman capable of future employment. We conclude that alimony should be awarded which is adequate for the purpose of providing for her during her transitional period.

[69] An early case that illustrates this point is *Morgan v. Morgan*, 81 Misc. 2d 616, 366 N.Y.S.2d 977 (1975). This New York case involved a wife who had financially helped to

the spouse's (usually the wife's) lost opportunities for either education or employment advancement.

Whether alimony as maintenance terminates when a wife remarries is not necessarily automatic, unless there is a state statute that requires the termination or the parties themselves agreed to remarriage as the event that ends alimony. Further, if alimony was established as a special method for long-term payment of a debt or for compensation for the wife's contribution to her husband's career or for other reasons, the wife's remarriage may be irrelevant. Parties do have some flexibility in their settlement agreement regarding the conditions that will affect the amount and duration of alimony. However, these conditions are subject to judicial review, which would occur if the husband sought a modification of the alimony provision because of his interpretation of the agreement.

Agreements about alimony can be the vehicle in which a husband can control his wife's conduct after a divorce. The issue of control was raised in *Gottsegen v. Gottsegen*,[70] where a settlement agreement included two provisions that were the basis of the litigation before the Supreme Judicial Court of Massachusetts. The provisions read as follows: (1)'[i]n the event of the wife's remarriage (as hereinafter defined) at any time prior to the fifth . . . anniversary of the date of execution hereof, the husband's support obligation . . . shall thereupon terminate and be substituted by an obligation to pay the wife, or for her benefit, for her support and maintenance $30,000, at the rate of $833.33 per month for three years'; (2) The 'remarriage of the wife shall, for purposes of this Agreement, be deemed to include her cohabitation with the same unrelated man with whom the wife has a romantic relationship for more than two . . . consecutive months.'[71]

put her husband through law school. After divorce, the wife wanted to enter medical school. Her husband refused to support the endeavor. The trial court judge wrote:

> In my opinion, . . . under these circumstances, the wife is also entitled to equal treatment and a 'break' and should not be automatically relegated to a life of being a well-paid, skilled technician laboring with a life-long frustration as to what her future might have been as a doctor, but for her marriage and motherhood.
> I am impressed by the fact that the plaintiff [wife] does not assume the posture that she wants to be an alimony drone or seek permanent alimony. Rather she had indicated that she only wants support for herself until she finishes medical school in 5 1/2 years (1 1/2 years more in college and 4 years in medical school) and will try to work when possible. In this regard, she merely seeks for herself the same opportunity which she helped give to the defendant [husband].
> Accordingly, I am directing that the defendant shall pay a total sum of $200 weekly for alimony and child support . . .

The trial court judge's decision was appealed. On appeal the alimony award of $100 was reduced to $75 a week. The case is reprinted and discussed in WEYRAUCH ET AL., *supra* note 1, at 95–98, 113–15.

[70] 492 N.E.2d 1133 (Mass. 1986). [71] *Id.* at 1135.

When the divorce was first heard in the Massachusetts Probate Court in 1981, the probate court judge granted the divorce *nici* (not final) and included the cohabitation clause in the divorce judgment. In 1983 and after the divorce judgment became final, the plaintiff wife filed a complaint for civil contempt,[72] against the defendant husband for failing to fulfill his financial obligation. The defendant husband denied that he was in contempt of the divorce judgment and in fact counterclaimed to request to declare that his former wife's cohabiting with another man for a two-month period constituted 'remarriage' within the meaning of the agreement.

In an opinion that traced the history of alimony in the Commonwealth of Massachusetts, Justice Ruth Abrams restated the conventional view that alimony is based on reaching an equitable balance between the needs of the dependent spouse and the ability of the supporting spouse to pay. She held that the divorce judgment that incorporated the agreement empowered the judge to modify the financial provision of the agreement if the recipient spouse's economic circumstances had materially changed. The mere fact that Mrs. Gottsegen 'cohabited' with another man did not warrant a judge's discontinuance of the alimony award. Had Mrs. Gottsegen proven that the man with whom she was cohabiting had supported her, a different result might have been obtained.

The case is interesting because of the discussion of the cohabitation clause that was ordered to be struck from the divorce judgment. The important point in the case is that the agreement was merged into the decree, thus allowing the judge to examine the provision and determine its fairness under the judge's discretionary powers.

If the agreement had not been merged with the decree but had maintained all of its contractual characteristics (this can be accomplished by a provision that states that the agreement will not be merged and has been approved by the judge at the time of divorce), the anti-cohabitation clause still might have been struck, but for reasons relating to the enforcement of contracts.[73] One attack

---

[72] Civil contempt is the customary remedy the court uses for a party who violates a court order. It differs from criminal contempt in that in civil contempt when the defendant conforms to the decree he can be released from prison.

It is often said that in civil contempt the defendant holds the keys to his cell in his pocket, which means that he, himself, can determine when he wishes to be released, namely by conforming to a judicial order.

[73] An agreement that is merged with the judgment becomes part of the judgment. The remedy for failing to fulfill a provision is civil contempt. If the agreement is not merged, but maintains its independent status, the remedy would be breach of contract. A breach of contract may not be desirable in many cases, particularly with regard to custody agreements. What would be more desirable would be a suit for specific performance.

That equitable remedy of specific performance is often inappropriate in family law matters because judges, adhering to equitable principles, are very reluctant, perhaps unwilling, to order anyone to perform a personal act. For example, it would be unlikely that a judge would specifically order a father to follow a provision in a custody agreement that

might have been to argue for the unconscionability of the provision because it restricted a wife's freedom of association. Another, less general, would be that unless the agreement contained additional consideration for the burdensome anti-cohabitation provision (like a higher alimony amount than would have been expected), the provision would fail for consideration reasons. Indeed, such a provision not attached to any mention of the cohabitant's providing the wife with support might be considered overreaching on the part of the husband, since it provides him with a benefit that is unrelated to the purpose of the agreement. In other words, the anti-cohabitation clause provides the husband with more than he bargained for.

Child Support

Child support has been revolutionized.[74] It is no longer a simple matter of a negotiated settlement in a lawyer's office or a judge's own determination of what constitutes an adequate amount of money to support a child. In the past, court-ordered child support tended to greatly undervalue the true costs of raising children. Today, child support is governed by standardized guidelines to which judges must conform or express reasons for their deviation.[75]

required him to conform to a visitation schedule or to show affection for his children. Another unlikely order would be to enforce an antenuptial agreement that had a provision that would require a divorced parent to raise a child in a particular faith (possibly unenforceable because of vagueness) or order a divorced spouse to obtain a religious divorce. Judges are inclined not to cross the line between religion and state. However, some courts might cross that line and enforce an agreement requiring a parent to cooperate in the religious education (clearly defined) of his or her child. For a collection of cases holding both ways, see HOMER H. CLARK, JR. & ANN LAQUER ESTIN, DOMESTIC RELATIONS—CASES AND PROBLEMS, 1052–53 (2000). Some courts have found ways to enforce promises between adults in an antenuptial agreement or in the religious marriage contract itself. For example, in *Avitzur v. Avitzur*, 446 N.E.2d 136 (N.Y. 1983), *cert. denied* 464 U.S. 817 (1983). The New York Court of Appeals (with a dissent) did uphold a provision in a Ketubah (Jewish marriage contract) in which the husband promised to cooperate in obtaining a 'get' (Jewish divorce). In holding that the provision did not violate the First Amendment, the highest court in New York stated that it was not ordering the husband to obtain a get, but enforcing a promise. The court analogized the provision to a promise to arbitrate, which courts ordinarily enforce. The case had an impact on the New York Legislature, which passed the 'Avitzur' statute, requiring a divorcing couple to show that they have taken the appropriate steps to remove any barriers to remarriage. That would include cooperating with a request to obtain a religious divorce. *See* N.Y. McKinney's DOM. REL. LAW § 253 (Supp. 1984–85). *See also Goldman v. Goldman*, 554 N.E.2d 1016 (Ill. App. 1990), where an Illinois Appeals Court ordered specific performance of the Ketubah that bound the husband to obtain a Jewish divorce.

[74] For a full legal discussion of child support with cases, statutory references, and formulae, see PRINCIPLES OF THE LAW OF FAMILY DISSOLUTION, *supra* note 23, at 410–643.

[75] For a full discussion of the guidelines and a state by state analysis of their application, *See* LAURA W. MORGAN, CHILD SUPPORT GUIDELINES—INTERPRETATION AND APPLICATION (1996).

Prior to 1984 when the U.S. Congress passed the Child Support Enforcement Amendments, child support orders very often bore no relationship to the cost of supporting a child, were not complied with after a few years, and were not zealously enforced. For example, child support obligors, mostly fathers, failed to fulfill their support obligation at the rate of $4 billion annually. In addition, half of the divorced custodial parents did not have a support order to enforce.[76] With no other means of support, divorced women turned to departments of public welfare to assist them in raising their fatherless children. This placed an unusually severe financial burden on public welfare agencies and ultimately the taxpaying public. In order to reduce divorced women's (as mothers) dependency on public funds, the federal government's Child Support Enforcement program provided creative ways of forcing fathers to comply with court orders and ultimately supporting their families. For example, specific enforcement remedies include wage withholding, imposition of bonds, securities or other guarantees, liens on real and personal property, and interception of federal and state income tax refunds.

Even with the new legal machinery in place and support laws on the books by way of child support guidelines, recent data indicates that a large number of children were still not receiving support from the parent with the obligation.[77] The explanations for the custodial parent's failure to pursue a support order or the obligor's failure to meet his obligation are said to include reasons like a mother's seeking support from the father is futile, or a mother's desire not to communicate with a former husband, or a father's feeling that the order is unfair.[78] In cases of non-support, if the mother sought assistance from the welfare department and the department provided assistance to the mother, the department would seek reimbursement from the delinquent father if the father could be found and he had funds. Of course, if the current economic conditions persist and parents with support obligations are unable to find employment, non-support of children will continue to be a major social problem as well as a drain on public welfare funds.

[76] *See* Robert M. Horowitz, *The Child Support Enforcement Amendments of 1984*, 36 JUV. AND FAM. COURT J. 1 (1985).

[77] ELLMAN, KURTZ & SCOTT report:

> Despite the law's assignment of support responsibilities to both parents, empirical data indicates a significant proportion of children do not receive support from an absent parent. According to the most recent Census Bureau data based on a 1992 survey, only 54% of the 11.5 million parents living with children under 21 whose other parent was not living in the household reported having either a decree or an agreement for child support. . . . While approximately 69% of divorced parents reported an award or agreement, fewer than half (44%) of separated parents and barely one-quarter (27%) of never-married parents reported an order or agreement.

See ELLMAN, KURTZ & SCOTT, *supra* note 53, at 573.

[78] *Id.* at 573–75.

In the present economic climate, judges have a difficult time arriving at an economic balance between the divorced spouses when there just are not enough finances to support the reorganized family. Attempts are made to preserve some assets like the family home. And in most cases where possible and economically practical the spouse who will be raising the children usually is assigned title to the home.[79] Further, child support obligations may not necessarily be abruptly stopped in some states when a child reaches 18 if he or she is in college.[80]

There are two recurring problems in child support. With serial marriages so prevalent coupled with fathers who abandon their financial responsibility for their children, the question of the liability of stepfathers becomes important. The fact pattern that would give rise to the question of liability would concern a man who marries a woman with an infant. Upon his wife's remarriage, the father fails to fulfill his child support obligation, and the wife's new husband, the child's stepfather lives with the child and assumes the obligation. After five years of marriage, the couple divorces and the stepfather refuses to support his stepchild for whom he has been the de facto father. If the state has no statute making a step-parent liable for support if he stood in a *loco parentis* relationship with the child or if there is no statute and a judge took a particularly narrow view of parental financial responsibility, he or she might very well determine that the step-parent has no financial obligation to the child. Another judge might apply the doctrine of *in loco parentis* or the doctrine of estoppel to such a fact pattern. She might decide that since the father voluntarily assumed the role of a parent for five years, took financial responsibility for the child, and the mother relied on that conduct, the step-parent should have some obligation for child support.[81]

The second problem, associated with serial marriages, is the responsibility of a father for the support of his children from his first and second marriages. The alternative approaches are to consider the child of the father's first marriage as

---

[79] Golden writes,

> Frequently, the marital home (if classified as marital property) will be awarded to the custodial parent. This is so even though the other spouse may have strong family or sentimental ties to the residence. Many states specifically list the desirability of awarding the marital home to the custodial parent as a factor for the court to consider in making the final equitable distribution.

See GOLDEN, *supra* note 52, at 201.

[80] Linda Elrod & Robert G. Spector list the following states as supporting child support obligation to continue education: Alabama, Arizona, California, Connecticut, Delaware, Florida, Indiana, Iowa, Kentucky, Massachusetts, Michigan, Mississippi, Nevada, New Hampshire, New Jersey, New York, North Carolina, North Dakota, Ohio, Oregon, Pennsylvania, Rhode Island, South Carolina, Tennessee, Vermont, Virginia, West Virginia, Wisconsin. *See* Elrod & Spector, *supra* note 16, at 657. *See also* ALI § 3.12, which provides that child support rules should include support for postsecondary education and vocational training. *See* PRINCIPLES OF THE LAW OF FAMILY DISSOLUTION, *supra* note 23, at 513.   [81]*See id.*

his primary obligation. This seems to be the generally accepted position and the position taken by the American Law Institute.[82] The second alternative is to equalize the financial obligation for all the father's children. This would mean that when the father married his second wife who bore him a child, the obligation to his child from his first wife would have to be adjusted, most likely downward. This may not be possible from a procedural point of view, since the first family may not be before the court. There is also the position that when a man remarries, and his second wife knows of his child support obligation, she enters the relationship with her eyes open and should not be surprised at the amount of her husband's disposable income. The fact pattern that would give preference to children of a father's first marriage over those of his second marriage, which has also ended in divorce, is to deduct the support obligation to the children of his first marriage in figuring his income for determining the amount of child support for his second family. But there is always that underlying thought that a father's children, no matter born of the first, second, or third marriage, are all his responsibility and should be treated equally. The father divorced the children's mother, he did not divorce them.

CHILD CUSTODY

Judicial Discretion and Codification

As stated earlier, negotiation is the most common way of resolving divorce conflicts. Most divorces are uncontested and judges review and approve divorce agreements more than they conduct trials. There is no way of knowing how and why custodial arrangements are settled. The reasons may relate to the financial condition of the spouses and the need to reach an agreement quickly and out of court; they may relate to the talents and power of persuasion of lawyers or perhaps to the individual personalities of the spouses and how they perceive their post-divorce lives.

Before the trend toward codifying standards and setting statutory guidelines for judges to follow in child custody cases within state divorce laws, the award of a child to one parent or another was based on a judge's interpretation of the standard, 'the best interests of the child', which may have been included as a statement in a state divorce statute or found in case law. That standard had no uniform definition, and its application was both contextual and case-specific. For example, the application of the standard would be different, even in terms of the burden of proof, in cases involving termination of parental rights, adoption, interpretation of contracts concerning child custody, or divorce. Application of the standard would also be different depending on who the claimants were and their relationship to the child. While the standard may have

[82] *See id.* at § 3.14(3).

been indeterminate and speculative, it served as a convenient and useful justification for a decision that may have been reached on another level. For example, even though a state may have abrogated the maternal preference rule or the tender years presumption,[83] the application of either gave a procedural and substantive advantage to the mother and discriminated against the father. A judicial decision to award an infant to the mother could be made not because of the rule or the presumption, but because it was in 'the best interests of the child'.

During the 1970s there was a movement by state legislatures to enact detailed child custody statutes, which had the effect of limiting judicial discretion when interpreting and applying the best interests of the child standard.[84] These laws which are now in effect mandate judges to use certain statutory standards. The Uniform Marriage and Divorce Act, a model proposal for many state statutes, enumerated factors, focusing mainly on the child, his wishes, and his relations and relationships with others, for a judge to consider in a child custody dispute.[85] In contrast to this straightforward approach, some state statutes now

[83] The tender years presumption and the maternal preference rule coexisted with the best interests of the child standard and were incorporated in state statutes and case law. The presumption could be rebutted by proof of the mother's unfitness. Unfitness might be difficult to prove as well as being an undesirable legal strategy between a mother and a father who would most likely have a post-divorce relationship through their children. Because the presumption and preference by their very definition denied both parents an equal opportunity to claim custody, most states have either abolished the presumption by statute or the presumption and preference have been judicially abandoned. Some state supreme courts found that the tender years presumption violated the state's Equal Rights Amendment and others that it violated the Equal Protection Clause of the Fourteenth Amendment to the U.S. Constitution. *See* ANN M. HARALAMBIE, 1 HANDLING CHILD CUSTODY, ABUSE AND ADOPTION CASES 233–38 (1993); HOMER H. CLARK, JR., THE LAW OF DOMESTIC RELATIONS IN THE UNITED STATES 786–849 (2d 1988).

[84] For a discussion of how judicial discretion is controlled through presumptions and statutory guidelines, see WEYRAUCH ET AL., *supra* note 1, at 838–43.

[85] Section 402 of the Uniform Marriage and Divorce Act reads:

Section 402. [Best Interest of Child]. The court shall determine custody in accordance with the best interest of the child. The court shall consider all relevant factors including:
(1) the wishes of the child's parent or parents as to his custody;
(2) the wishes of the child as to his custodian;
(3) the interaction and interrelationship of the child with his parent or parents, his siblings, and any other person who may significantly affect the child's best interest;
(4) the child's adjustment to his home, school, and community; and
(5) the mental and physical health of all individuals involved.
The court shall not consider conduct of a proposed custodian that does not affect his relationship to the child.

Since the 1970s, when only sixteen states statutorily mandated judges to consider a child's preference in custody disputes, thirty-two states have included some reference to the child's preference, depending on the child's age. Of prime importance is the child's age. Statutes range from mere consideration to increased weight as the child matures to

include elaborate schemes requiring lawyers to prepare detailed parenting plans.[86] To lawyers, the effect of such statutes has been to require thought, planning, and organization of evidence in the preparation of a child custody case. These statutes have the result of trying to put order in the trial, and in many instances, forcing judges to spend time reviewing documents and studying plans; upon reaching a decision, the judges must also make findings of fact with reasons for their decisions. The requirement of writing a trial opinion, which relates evidence to the statutory factors and which states reasons for a decision has a positive result. Expressions of bias may be minimized or at least open to scrutiny. Additionally and ideally, the likelihood of a trial judge's decision being reversed on appeal for abuse of discretion or for being unsupported by the facts is considerably diminished.[87]

The Primary Caretaker Preference

The 1980s saw the emergence of the concept of the primary caretaker preference in child custody disputes, a concept which captured the interest of family law scholars, judges, and law reformers.[88] The primary caretaker is defined as the person who before the divorce managed and monitored the day-to-day

granting controlling weight to the child's preference. *See* Kathleen Nemechek, *Child Preference in Custody Decisions: Where We Have Been, Where We Are Now, Where We Should Go*, 84 IOWA L. REV. 437, 445 (1998); Randi L. Dulaney, *Children Should Be Seen and Heard in Florida Custody Determinations*, 25 NOVA L. REV. 815, 821, 823 (2001).

[86] *See, e.g.*, WASH. REV. CODE ANN. § 26.09.181 (West Supp. 1991).

[87] In *Pikula v. Pikula*, 374 N.W.2d 705, 712 (Minn. 1985), Justice Wahl wrote:

> The inherent imprecision heretofore present in our custody law has, in turn, diminished meaningful appellate review. We have repeatedly stressed the need for effective appellate review of family court decisions in our cases, and have required specificity in writing findings based on the statutory factors. . . . We are no less concerned that the legal conclusion reached on the basis of those findings be subject to effective review. We recognize the inherent difficulty of principled decision-making in this area of the law. Legal rules governing custody awards have generally incorporated evaluations of parental fitness replete with ad hoc judgments on the beliefs, lifestyles, and perceived credibility of the proposed custodian. . . . It is in these circumstances that the need for effective appellate review is most necessary to ensure fairness to the parties and to maintain the legitimacy of judicial decision-making.

[88] *See, e.g.*, Katharine L. Mercer, *A Content Analysis of Judicial Decision-Making— How Judges Use the Primary Caretaker Standard to Make a Custody Determination*, 5 WM. & MARY J. WOMEN & L. 1 (1998); David Chambers, *Rethinking the Substantive Rules for Custody Disputes in Divorce*, 83 MICH. L. REV. 477 (1984); Jon Elster, *Solomonic Judgments: Against the Best Interests of the Child*, 54 U. CHI. L. REV. 1 (1987); Martha Fineman, *Dominant Discourse, Professional Language and Legal Change in Child Custody Decisionmaking*, 101 HARV. L. REV. 727 (1988).

activities of the child and met the child's basic needs: feeding, clothing, bathing, and arranging for the protection of his or her health. It is assumed that the primary caretaker would continue in that role after the divorce. This standard for a custodial disposition seemed to single out continuity of care, a standard proposed by Joseph Goldstein, Anna Freud, and Albert J. Solnit in their book, *Beyond the Best Interests of the Child*, to trump all other consideration.[89]

In a law review article that has been instrumental in advocating the primary caretaker rule and providing insight in divorce negotiation, Chief Justice Neely of West Virginia, wrote that such a rule spells 'mother'.[90] After reviewing the research in the field and using his own experience as a lawyer and judge, he concluded that mothers are 'more likely than fathers to feel close to their children'. But his major arguments supporting the primary caretaker presumption were rooted in his mistrust of negotiation in divorce, of the divorce process itself, and of the use of experts. He believed that if the presumption was established the likelihood of using child custody litigation as a bargaining chip in negotiation would be diminished. In addition, he stated that having the presumption minimizes elaborate and time-consuming custody trials where a costly battle of experts dominates the litigation, and women are disadvantaged because they lack the finances to underwrite lengthy and complex litigation. He also believed that determining who is the primary caretaker is a simpler task than delving into the elaborate factors used to determine who was and will be a good parent. For him, the answer is basically: mother.

The primary caretaker presumption has been attacked by asking some critical questions. Why should the primary caretaker presumption be considered the exclusively reliable means of choosing a custodian? In other words, is past conduct—the maintaining and monitoring of day-to-day activities of the child—the only true test for choosing who should be the child's custodian? Is there a rational connection between the presumption and the nurturing activities of the custodian? Does the presumption emphasize quantity of care at the expense of quality of care? Does 'primary caretaker' define the strongest bond between parent and child? Will the presumption really deter litigation and promote fairer negotiations between parents? If the presumption is established and known, will it promote co-parenting, a desirable social goal? Since today more and more parents are both working outside the home so that they must utilize various forms of day care, does this not pose difficulties in identifying the primary caretaker? Moreover, with the current economic situation causing changes in parental roles because of loss of employment, the primary caretaker

---

[89] *See* JOSEPH GOLDSTEIN, ANNA FREUD & ALBERT J. SOLNIT, BEYOND THE BEST INTERESTS OF THE CHILD 31–34 (1973); JOSEPH GOLDSTEIN, ANNA FREUD, ALBERT J. SOLNIT & SONJA GOLDSTEIN, IN THE BEST INTERESTS OF THE CHILD 66–67 (1986).

[90] *See* Richard Neely, *The Primary Caretaker Parent Rule: Child Custody and the Dynamics of Greed*, 3 YALE L. & POL'Y REV. 168, 180 (1984).

may not necessarily be the mother.[91] In order to answer any of these questions, the judge must make an inquiry into the particular facts of the case and examine the quality of the parent–child relationship.

The primary caretaker presumption once again focuses custody disputes on custodians rather than on the child. It also fuels political fires by declaring even before a case is heard that one parent has the advantage. If that parent is the mother, one might ask whether the primary caretaker presumption is 'a thinly disguised form of the tender years presumption'.[92] If this is the case, will there be a return to the ugly disputes concerned with the unfitness of the primary caretaker? Will there be a resurgence of the old arguments for gender neutrality?

The Best Interests of the Child

Where a state statute does not include any presumptions but states that 'the best interests of the child' standard should guide decisions along with the consideration of other factors like the child's preference,[93] how should that standard be applied? Stated another way, what questions should a judge ask in a divorce case and what evidence should she obtain to help her reach a decision? Elsewhere I have written about the initial inquiry in a custody dispute in divorce. I emphasize 'initial' because once a custody award has been made and

---

[91] The issues raised in these questions are discussed in Bruce Ziff, *The Primary Caretaker Presumption: Canadian Perspectives on an American Development*, 4 INT'L J.L. & FAM. 186 (1990). For full exploration of the arguments for and against the primary caretaker preference and citations to cases and statutes to the preference, see Gary Crippen, *Stumbling Beyond Best Interest of the Child: Reexamining Child Custody Standard-Setting in the Wake of Minnesota's Four Year Experiment with the Primary Caretaker Preference*, 75 MINN. L. REV. 427 (1990); HARALAMBIE, *supra* note 83, 238–39.

[92] *See* HOMER H. CLARK, JR. & CAROL GLOWINSKY, DOMESTIC RELATIONS: CASES AND PROBLEMS 1075 (4th ed. 1990). Justice Wahl answers this question in the negative. Writing in *Pikula v. Pikula, supra* note 87, at 712 n. 2, she stated:

> The primary parent preference, while in accord with the tender years doctrine insofar as the two rules recognize the importance of the bond formed between a primary parent and a child, differs from the tender years doctrine in significant respects. Most importantly, the primary parent rule is gender neutral. Either parent may be the primary parent; the rule does not incorporate notions of biological gender determinism or sex stereotyping. In addition, the rule we fashion today we believe will encourage co-parenting in a marriage unlike the tender years doctrine which, for fathers, meant that whatever function they assumed in the rearing of their children would be deemed irrelevant in a custody contest.

> In 1990, the Minnesota Legislature abolished the primary caretaker presumption. *See* MINN STAT § 518.17(1)(a)(1990).

[93] For example, § 46b–56 of the Connecticut Statute provides, in relevant part:

> (b) in making or modifying any order with respect to custody or visitation, the court shall be guided by the best interests of the child, giving consideration to the wishes of the child if he is of sufficient age and capable of forming an intelligent preference, provided in making the initial order the court may take into consideration the causes for dissolution of the marriage or legal separation.

a child is living with one parent, a different inquiry would be necessary. In other words, in a motion for a modification, consideration of attachments and how a new arrangement will affect those attachments may be critical. I approach the ideal placement in terms of values being promoted through the application of 'the best interests of the child' standard.[94] Underlying these values is the principle that parents should promote a positive relationship with both. Stated another way, neither parent should try to alienate the child from the other, since child development research supports the position that children thrive best when they have a positive relationship with both parents.

The values that I see as pouring content into 'the best interest of the child' standard can be formulated into asking two basic questions: (1) what placement and with whom can a child, with major consideration to the child's age and level of maturity, be provided with an environment (family unit, broadly defined, and community) in which he is wanted and where he is safe, secure, and accepted; (2) what adult or adults can provide the child with continuity of a relationship or relationships[95] where affection, stimulation, and nurturing is

---

[94] *See* Sanford N. Katz, *Foster Parents versus Agencies: A Case Study in the Judicial Application of 'The Best Interests of the Child' Doctrine*, 65 MICH. L. REV. 145, 154–69 (1966).

[95] I use the word 'relationship' and 'relationships' not 'continuity of care', because I do not wish to totally embrace the primary caretaker presumption. A child can have a positive relationship with a non-resident adult as well as with more than one adult. This includes the non-custodial parent.

It is also very important to consider a child's relationship with relatives, especially siblings, grandparents, aunts, uncles, and cousins, and friends as well as with the community in which he and his family of origin identifies. Relationships can change over time and the positive aspect of modification of a custody decree is that if a child's needs change a custody decree can be modified to reflect that change. This is particularly true during the adolescent period when these children make strong attachments to friends and also may need a closer relationship to the parent of the same sex because of the belief that that parent can better understand the whole range of physical, emotional, and intellectual changes that are occurring in the adolescent. For a full discussion of the adolescent's interactions with parents, and how adolescents view their parents based on the results of the authors' empirical studies, see JAMES YOUNISS & JACQUELINE SMOLLAR, ADOLESCENT RELATIONS WITH MOTHERS, FATHERS, AND FRIENDS (1985).

When the custody of an infant (under 3 years old) is in dispute, an inquiry into the attachment relationships the infant has with his or her parents is crucial in making a decision. In reporting on the research in child development that has an impact on child custody decisions, Joan B. Kelly and Michael E. Lamb state that infants benefit from regular interaction with both of their parents to promote their attachments. They also write that the parent's interaction should occur in all phases of the infant's day to day activities. They emphasize the need for both parents to be involved in the infant's life. Divorce, of course, causes insecurity in the infant–parent attachments. Lessening the insecurity is a difficult task and calls for supportive and cooperative parents post-divorce. Lessening the insecurity should be one of the goals a judge tries to advance in making a child custody decision. *See* Joan B. Kelly & Michael E. Lamb, *Using Child Development Research to Make Appropriate Custody and Access Decisions for Young Children*, 38 FAM. & CONCILIATION CTS. REV. 297–311 (2000).

present along with the necessary financial support,[96] either actual or potential, so that the child will thrive intellectually and become a moral, ethical, respect-ful, and responsible adult? If a priority must be set, the paramount values are safety, and physical and emotional health. Other values, like intellectual achievement, morality, and ethics flow from a child's emotional and physical well-being promoted in a supportive environment.[97] The individual factors that illustrate each of these values depend on the case and the context of the dispute. The mechanisms by which these factors are gathered, and who should provide the facts, also depend on each case. For example, mental health specialists, teachers, friends, the parents themselves as well as the child whose custody is in dispute, depending on the child's age and comprehension, are ordinarily the people to whom a judge turns to provide her with the information to make a decision.

The Lawyer for the Child and the Guardian ad Litem

Unlike juvenile delinquency and child protection proceedings where represen-tation is mandated under the federal law,[98] no such mandate exists in divorce. However, independent counsel for children can play a useful role in both the negotiation of custody agreements as well as in the litigation of a contested case and in hearings for modification,[99] especially in petitions for relocation.[100] The reason for independent representation is that the interests of children and

---

[96] By financial support I am not proposing that a judge weigh the relative economic strengths of the claimants and award custody to the parent who is more affluent. In divorce, child support is separate from the assignment of custody. What is important is that the parent (or another adult) who is awarded custody take financial support seriously and if necessary pursue a parent delinquent in his child support obligation.

[97] In attempting to define 'the best interests of the child', I have been influenced by the work of JOSEPH GOLDSTEIN, ALBERT SOLNIT & ANNA FREUD, BEYOND THE BEST INTERESTS OF THE CHILD (1973). They introduced three concepts, which have become part of the child custody legal vocabulary: continuity of care, the psychological parent, and the least detrimental alternative. For a discussion of these concepts in an appellate case, see *Seymour v. Seymour*, 433 A.2d 1005 (Conn. 1980).

[98] In *In re Gault*, 387 U.S. 1 (1967), the U.S. Supreme Court held that children have a right to counsel in delinquency cases. Under the federal Child Abuse Prevention and Treatment Act as amended in 1996, representation for children is required in child protection cases. *See* 42 U.S.C.A. § 5106a(b)(2)(A)(ix) (West Supp. 1999). The Act is discussed in Chapter 4.

[99] Some states require that a period of time elapse before a motion to modify a custody decree. The Uniform Marriage and Divorce Act sets a two-year period unless the child's health or safety is being threatened. *See* Uniform Marriage and Divorce Act § 409(a) in the Appendix.

[100] Wallerstein and Tanke strongly advocate that children should be heard in removal cases. *See* Judith S. Wallerstein & Tony J. Tanke, *To Move or Not to Move: Psychological and Legal Considerations in the Relocation of Children Following Divorce*, 30 FAM. L.Q. 305, 322–23 (1996).

the interests of the parents in divorce may not be the same. In negotiation, the independent lawyer can represent only the child's interests, especially with regard to such important matters as to what kind of custodial arrangement is desirable and what amount of support is adequate, especially with regard to fulfilling a child's educational goal beyond high school. Often the idea of independent representation for a child comes later in the divorce process when a judge, recognizing the intensity of the custodial dispute, recommends that the children be independently represented. The belief is that the child needs his or her own wishes to be heard and the child's own lawyer can provide that voice.

The appointment of a guardian ad litem (GAL) serves a different function. The guardian ad litem is appointed by a judge to make an independent investigation of the facts of a case. The GAL might be a lawyer who has training in child development and psychological issues, or a mental health professional, like a social worker or a clinical psychologist. Sometimes, in addition to the investigation, a judge will ask the GAL to recommend an appropriate custodial disposition that will advance the child's best interests. In performing her investigation, the GAL ordinarily spends as much time as is necessary with the child whose custody is in issue in order to learn about the child's primary attachments. The GAL also would interview people (recommended by each parent) who interact with the child and the parents, such as teachers, pediatricians, clergy, neighbors, and friends. If the GAL is not a mental health professional, she might seek the assistance of a psychologist to perform psychological tests or a child psychiatrist who may be able to learn more about the child than the GAL can. The difference between an attorney for the child and a GAL is, as stated earlier, that the attorney represents the child whereas the GAL represents the GAL's opinion as to the child's best interests.

A Child-Focused Inquiry

It should also be said that the focus of child custody cases should be on the child interests. Such a focus would include an inquiry into the extent to which continuity of care with one or both parents who themselves are emotionally stable promotes those interests, as well as continuity with the community (including family, friends, and school) in which the child was being raised before the divorce, continuity of religion or racial identification, if those are issues, not on the rights of those seeking custody. Emphasis on rights to a child tends to analogize children as property, which is an outdated concept. That being said, if an issue is raised about the lifestyle of the claimant, the inquiry should be on the question of whether the lifestyle has a negative or positive impact on the values being promoted.[101] A fundamental goal for a judge who must make a custodial

---

[101] In discussing Illinois's conclusive presumption that a divorced mother who fornicates with a man to whom she is not married is unfit to continue to have custody of her child, Justices Brennan (who was joined by Justice Marshall) wrote in his dissent in the

decision is the security of the decree. By that I mean that a judge should be convinced that she has listened to the evidence, perhaps if appropriate considering the child's age and level of maturity, interviewed the child in her chambers, and received some idea of the child's preference or at least the child's feelings about the divorce and the issues that affect him or her. The interview,

U.S. Supreme Court's denying a writ of certiorari in *Jarrett v. Jarrett*, 449 U.S. 927 (1980):

> Nothing in the record or in logic supports a conclusion that divorced parents who fornicate, for that reason alone, are unfit or adversely affect the well-being and development of their children in any degree over and above whatever adverse effect separation and divorce may already have had on the children.
> . . .
> Moreover, not only is there no basis for conclusively presuming that [the mother's] cohabitation would adversely affect her children sufficiently to justify modification, but also any such conclusion is unequivocally rejected by the record which affirmatively shows that the 'children were healthy, well adjusted, and well cared for.' . . . There was no evidence of actual harm; nor was there evidence, statistical or otherwise, to suggest that the children's current exposure to their mother's cohabitation might result in harm to them that might become manifest only in the future. Surely, in any event, it is no more likely that divorced mothers who fornicate are unfit than are unwed fathers. Thus, this case squarely presents the question whether the Due Process Clause entitles [the mother] to a meaningful hearing at which the trial judge determines, without use of conclusive presumption, whether violation of the fornication statute adversely affects the well-being of the children.

The American Law Institute's Principles of the Law of Dissolution prohibits decision-making based on race, ethnicity, sex, or religious practices of the child or parent, sexual orientation of a parent, extramarital sexual conduct of a parent (unless it can be shown to harm the child), or the parents' relative earning capacities or financial circumstances. *See* Principles of the Law of Family Dissolution, *supra* note 23, at § 2.12.

Professor Lynn Wardle argues for a rebuttable presumption in child custody and visitation cases that parental infidelity *causes* harm to a child. *See* Lynn D. Wardle, *Parental Infidelity and the 'No-Harm' Rule in Custody Litigation*, 52 Cath. U. L. Rev. 81 (2002).

With regard to using race as a determinative factor in child custody decisions, the U.S. Supreme Court has held in *Palmore v. Sidoti*, 466 U.S. 429 (1984), that it violates the Equal Protection Clause of the Fourteenth Amendment to the U.S. Constitution. However, the facts in *Palmore* are important to consider, and the application of the case may be limited. The facts did not present a conflict between an interracial couple where the issue was whether the child should be awarded to one parent or another, but concerned a modification of a child custody decree brought by a white father against the white mother because of changed circumstances: the mother's living with a black man, then marrying him and thus raising the white child in an interracial setting. The lower Florida court chose to base its decision on the fact that the white child would be socially stigmatized by living in the interracial family. There was some reference in the lower court's opinion to the mother's morality in first living with a man without being married to him. To the U.S. Supreme Court, the government has a 'substantial' interest in protecting a child's welfare. However, the possible effects of racial prejudice did not justify the transfer of the child from a fit mother to her father, and therefore the Florida court's consideration of biases that a child may face was not a permissible judicial inquiry.

which is usually at the judge's discretion, may be in the presence of counsel for the parents or with their permission in private with a stenographer recording the event. Whether the written record of the interview becomes a part of the official court record may depend on individual state statutes. On the basis of all the evidence, the judge should reach a fair and balanced decision that will find acceptance with the claimants. The successful decree is one that is lasting and not subject to the disappointed claimant's filing motions for a rehearing, modification, or request for a contempt citation.

Alternative Custodial Dispositions

Matters dealing with the custody of children are mostly settled by the spouses' lawyers either in their offices or at the beginning of or midway through the litigation. The final agreement defines each parent's relationship to his or her child and spells out the specific responsibilities of each. Lawyers may use any terminology to describe the arrangement, or merely categorize the whole issue as 'custodial arrangement'.

The conventional custodial arrangement was for one parent to be named the legal custodian and guardian with whom the child lived and who usually had a whole range of rights, which basically allowed her to make all the decisions about the child's day-to-day life. The non-custodial parent usually had defined rights including a visitation schedule. At the divorce hearing, if the judge found the custody agreement that had been worked out by lawyers suitable and in the child's best interests, the judge would approve it.

Joint or Shared Custody

Joint custody (or as some jurisdictions label it 'shared custody') became an alternative disposition to custody to one parent and visitation to another and was advanced in part in the late 1970s by fathers who thought that they had been excluded from serious consideration as a primary custodian in child custody cases.[102] The arrangement can either be agreed upon by the couple and reflected in a custody agreement or judicially imposed upon a couple as a decision in a contested case. At first some judges felt they were not authorized to award joint custody, even if agreed upon, because of its not being included in any state statute or because of the lack of judicial precedent. This has changed, and now almost all states authorize or refer to joint or shared custody as a possible dispositional alternative. A few states express a statutory preference for the disposition by making it a presumption.[103]

---

[102] For a discussion of joint custody, see Joan Kelly, *The Determination of Child Custody*, in THE FUTURE OF CHILDREN, *supra* note 51, at 121.

[103] For a detailed discussion and list of state statutes as well as an analysis of cases on joint custody, see HARALAMBIE, *supra* note 83, at 260–61.

Today joint custody generally means that both mother and father are jointly responsible for making decisions about their child. They are equally responsible for the upbringing of the child who has an ongoing relationship with both of them. In a certain sense, a joint custody agreement or disposition is an attempt to re-create the intact family. It is obvious that joint custody requires unusually cooperative and financially sound parents and a child who is agreeable to the arrangement to make it succeed. The child's participation in the decision to work out a joint custody arrangement is extremely important and is often overlooked.

Various kinds of joint custodial arrangements have developed. Joint legal custody might mean that both parents have the legal authority to make decisions about the child, but the child lives with one parent but visits the other on certain days of the week. This arrangement might have been identical to the old method of custody to one parent and visitation to the other, except that in a joint custody arrangement as stated earlier, both parents are legally responsible for making decisions about their child's life. Another arrangement is joint physical and legal custody, which means that the child lives with each parent for certain period of time. This physical arrangement would require, of course, two homes.

The findings of empirical research on joint custody have resulted in a new look at the disposition, especially as to whether in fact joint custody is truly joint and whether it lessens conflict.[104] Some feminist writers have felt that an award of joint custody may reflect a minimization of the role a mother has played in rearing her children. These writers have called for major changes, some recommending the revival of the maternal preference rule and others for statutory enactment of the primary caretaker standard.[105] Joint custody may not have fulfilled the strong expectations that it was desired to meet—including equal child-rearing responsibilities. Good intentions by lawyers, judges, and litigants are not enough for a successful disposition. The realities of everyday living can prove to be extremely difficult in a divorced family where each of a child's activities may need joint parental approval, whereas in an intact family one parent can and ordinarily does act on behalf of both parents. In addition, any number of unforeseen factors and events can enter into the equation for success. Perhaps one of the most important unforeseen facts is that human relations are not frozen. Time and events prompt change. Spouses remarry; they relocate with the new spouses, children mature, resulting in their having different needs and a different relationship with adults.

---

[104] *See* Robert Mnookin et al., *Private Order Revisited—What Custodial Arrangements are Parents Negotiating, in* SUGARMAN & KAY, *supra* note 12, at 37–74.

[105] For a discussion of the feminist approach, see Katharine T. Bartlett, *Feminism and Family Law*, 33 FAM. L.Q. 475, 483 (1999); June R. Carbone, *A Feminist Perspective on Divorce, in* THE FUTURE OF CHILDREN, *supra* note 51, at 183.

Continuity of a Relationship with Both Parents: Relocation

The conventional rule in child custody is that unless there has been a custodial agreement allowing the custodial parent to leave the jurisdiction with her child and that agreement has been approved by the court, a spouse who wishes to move with her child must first notify the non-custodial spouse that she is seeking court approval for the move and give him an opportunity to be heard in a court proceeding. The reason for the judicial approval is that in domestic relations matters, courts jealously guard their jurisdiction, and do not want to lose it. Ordinarily, the parent who has sole custody and seeks to relocate, over the objection of her former husband, has the burden of proving that circumstances have changed since the initial award. She would file a motion for a hearing to permit her to move. The focus of the hearing would be to determine what affect the changed circumstances would have on the initial award. Conversely, if a non-custodial father hears that his former wife is planning on moving out of the jurisdiction, and he would like to prevent the move, he may file a motion for a modification of the custody decree to change custody from his former wife to him, again on the basis of changed circumstances.[106] If the initial award was joint custody of the child, the hearing may require a court to engage in a full hearing on custody similar to the original hearing. Indeed, the issue in relocation cases is generally whether the judicial inquiry is limited to the changed circumstances issue, whether, as in joint custody, it is wider and looks at the whole matter of the child's interests, or whether there should be any presumptions or preferences for continuation of the person with custody.

Relocation cases pose difficult legal and painful emotional problems for both children and parents. Since there has not been any solid national empirical data or longitudinal studies on the effects of relocation on a child's adjustment so as to predict the outcome of a child's moving from one location to another, psychologists have had to rely on their clinical practice, using basic principles of child development to generalize on the issue. As in custody generally, the child's age, developmental needs, and quality of the attachments to both parents, and to siblings, relatives, and friends are important considerations. Relocation

---

[106] Joan B. Kelly and Michael E. Lamb have written that the focus in relocation cases should be on the child, not the parents. They propose that decision-makers inquire into the costs and benefits of the move, heavily weighing the strength of the child's relationship with each parent. They point out that courts should consider the following: 'the age and developmental needs of the children, the quality of parent–child relationships, the psychological adjustments of the parents, the likely effects of moving on the children's social relationships, as well as the cultural and educational opportunities in both locations.' They underscore the effect of a move on very young children and the need for those children to continue to have meaningful contact with both parents, delaying the move if that is necessary. *See* Joan B. Kelly & Michael E. Lamb, *Developmental Issues in Relocation Cases Involving Young Children: When, Whether, and How?*, 17 J. FAM PSYCHOLOGY 193, 202 (2003).

cases, however, present the additional comparative inquiry into the social and educational opportunities available to the young child in both locations. Further, if the custodial spouse has remarried and wishes to relocate to be with her new husband, an examination of the child's relationship with that new spouse and his children if they are to be involved in the child's life, would be appropriate. The extremely difficult problems are presented when a spouse, in good faith, wishes to relocate for reasons relating to career advancements or to be close to her family who will act as a support system for her during the post-divorce period. One can see how one can be sympathetic to the move because it would benefit the custodial spouse in any number of ways including the spouse's emotional well-being and a potentially financially secure parent, both having a positive influence on a child's welfare. These benefits have to be weighed against the impact the move would have on the quantity and quality of the contact the non-custodial spouse would have with his child as well as the ease with which the noncustodial spouse could continue his relationship with his child at a distance.

For adolescents, relocation may present issues different from those considered in the initial custody award.[107] Relocation cases may pose equal protection issues if one parent's sex is preferred over another. Some parents have argued that a court's denial of a parent's motion to relocate interferes with that parent's constitutional right to travel. If the choice is between that constitutional right and the best interests of the child in a divorce setting where children are so vulnerable, the best interests test seems to trump a parent's constitutional right to travel.[108]

To bring about some uniformity in the relocation cases and avoid a case by case approach, some states have enacted legislation to guide judges in making these decisions.[109] These statutory guides range from standards that limit the

---

[107] In writing about relocation decisions, Judith Wallerstein and Tony J. Tanke stated that adolescents should be treated differently from younger children. For reasonably mature adolescents who are well-adjusted, they wrote that:

> stability may not lie with either parent, but may have its source in a circle of friends or particular sports or academic activities within a school or community. These adolescents should be given the choice, if a choice is to be made, as to whether they wish to move with the moving parent. It should also be made clear to them that their decision can be changed, if parents can arrange this. . . . It would seem appropriate to their age and development that mature adolescents be encouraged to exercise their free choice about whether they wish to live, provided parenting and supervision are available in both homes, and the arrangements are otherwise feasible.

See Wallerstein & Tanke, *supra* note 100, at 322–23.

[108] For balancing a parent's right to travel with the child's best interests see: Everett v. Everett, 660 So. 2d 599 (Ala. Civ. App. 1995); Holder v. Polanski, 544 A.2d 852 (N.J. 1988); Watt v. Watt, 971 P.2d 608 (Wyo. 1999).

[109] Many of these statutes and cases interpreting them are discussed in Carol S. Bruch & Janet M. Bowermaster, *The Relocation of Children and Custodial Parents: Public Policy, Past and Present*, 30 FAM. L.Q. 245 (1996).

custodial parent and give great weight to the rights of the non-custodian to those that permit the custodial parent greater freedom to relocate. Some include a presumption that custody should continue with the primary caretaker. The trend in state statutes is toward greater flexibility and allowing the relocation. Case law has also reflected the range, with New York as an example.

A case that illustrates the old restrictive view of New York is *Elkus v. Elkus*.[110] In that case Mrs. Elkus, whose professional name is Frederika von Stada, the famous international opera singer, who had been awarded joint custody in her divorce from Mr. Elkus, remarried and wished to move to California to be with her new husband who could not relocate. The lower court allowed her request to relocate, and her husband appealed to a New York appellate court (not the highest court in New York). The appellate court reversed the holding, stating that the facts in the case neither conformed to the 'exceptional circumstances' standard nor would the move be in the best interests of the children. The court was not sympathetic to the opera singer's reducing her concert schedule that would have taken her away from her children, hiring a housekeeper, nor was the court impressed with her support for Mr. Elkus's visiting the children in California. To the court, the move would create a substantial hardship on the father and his relationship with his children who did not want to move. It would also remove the children from the environment to which they had adapted so well. There was, in the words of the New York court, no 'compelling reason or exceptional circumstances to justify relocation to California'.

Four years after *Elkus*, the Court of Appeals of New York, the highest court in New York, decided *Tropea v. Tropea*[111] in which it took a broader approach, and set down standards for that state's lower courts to follow in relocation cases. Interestingly enough, that court cited *Elkus* for the narrow proposition that a 'spouse's remarriage or wish for a "fresh start" can never suffice to justify a distant move'.[112]

The court in *Tropea* criticized the lower courts in setting up an analysis in relocation cases that seemed to emphasize the impact the move would have on the non-custodial parent so that he would not have regular access to his child. If the move would not deprive the non-custodial parent of his visitation rights, the court need not make further inquiries into the custodial parent's motive for moving. If the move would disrupt the non-custodial parent's access to his child, then the custodial parent must show the exceptional circumstances that would justify the relocation.

The New York Court of Appeals found the analysis too mechanical and difficult to apply. It took a broader approach and placed emphasis on the child. To that court, the factors judges should make an inquiry into are: (1) each parent's reasons for moving or opposing the move; (2) the child's relationship with both parents; (3) the impact the move would have on the child's relationship with the

---

[110] 588 N.Y.S.2d 138 (App. Div. 1992).
[111] *See* Tropea v. Tropea, 667 N.E.2d 145 (1996).   [112] *Id*. at 151.

non-custodial parent; (4) the extent to which both the custodial parent's and the child's lives will be economically, emotionally, and educationally advanced by the move; and (5) the feasibility of preserving the relationship between the child and the non-custodial parents through reasonable visitations. Ultimately, using the preponderance of the evidence standard, the court should determine whether the move would further the child's best interests.[113] Basically, the approach taken by the New York Court of Appeals allows the removal if it is in the best interests of the child and sufficient recognition is given to the impact the move will have on the non-custodial spouse's maintaining contact with his child.[114]

In the same year that *Tropea* was decided, the Supreme Court of Colorado decided *In re the Marriage of Francis*.[115] In that case the custodial mother wished to relocate from Colorado to New York where she could pursue a two-year program that would train her to become a physician's assistant. No other school had accepted her, making the move a necessity to pursue a career anticipated by the couple. In fact a clause in the separation agreement provided that the husband support his wife in her career goal. By moving, she would be depriving the child's father of his joint custodial rights. Relying on its state statute that emphasized the importance of the stability of a child's relationship with the primary caretaker, the court adopted a presumption in favor of the custodial parent. In so doing, Colorado joined states that tip the scale in favor of the custodial parent unless the non-custodial parent can show that the move would be detrimental to the child or that the custodial parent's motives are questionable.[116] In a certain sense the approach taken by Colorado and other states reflects the value of continuity of care so long as that continuity has been positive and breaking it would be seriously detrimental to the child's well-being.

---

[113] *Id.* at 152.

[114] The ALI Principles takes a realistic position on the complicated issue of relocation. The Principles define relocation of a parent as constituting 'a substantial change in circumstances . . . only when the relocation significantly impairs either parent's ability to exercise responsibilities the parent has been exercising or attempting to exercise under the parenting plan.' In order to guide judges in making a decision about relocation, the Principles recommend that the judge take into account the extent to which the relocating party is the primary caretaker or the parent who has been exercising the clear majority of custodial responsibility, the nature of the move, whether the move is valid and in good faith, the impact the move will have on the child, and the extent to which the move will interfere with the non-custodian's rights. The thrust of the Principles seem to allow relocation, especially in light of what the Principles state as one of the primary purposes of modern divorce is 'to allow each party to go his or her own way'. *See* PRINCIPLES OF THE LAW OF FAMILY DISSOLUTION, *supra* note 23, at § 2.17(a).

[115] 919 P.2d 776 (1996).

[116] These states include: California, Montana, Minnesota, South Dakota, Tennessee, Washington, Wisconsin, and Wyoming. See PRINCIPLES OF THE LAW OF FAMILY DISSOLUTION, *supra* note 23, at 371–84.

Unilateral Removal of the Child from the Jurisdiction

The issue of removal that has been discussed concerned parents who seek a judicial modification of their custody decree so that they can move to another state with their child. Once a child moves from one state to another, the question is which state has jurisdiction over the case. Ordinarily, if a child moved from the home state to another, the home state would continue to have jurisdiction over the case and the second state would also have jurisdiction. Before the adoption of the Uniform Child Custody Jurisdiction Act, any number of states could assert jurisdiction if, for example, the child and one parent were present in the state, regardless of the circumstances surrounding the move to the second state. Since the second state did not have to recognize the original custody order, which was not necessarily final and could be modified, theoretically the judge in the second state could revisit the question of custody, notify the absent parent, and make a new determination. This state of affairs led to great uncertainty and confusion about the integrity of the custody decree. And that uncertainty had the effect of providing the child and his custodial parent with insecurity. In addition, the availability of alternative jurisdictions to hear custody cases was almost an open invitation to parental kidnapping.

In light of this state of affairs, the Commissioners on Uniform State Laws promulgated the Uniform Child Custody Jurisdiction Act (UCCJA) in 1968, which by 1984, all states adopted, and which was designed to address the problem of multiple jurisdiction over child custody cases. In 1997 the Commissioners promulgated the Uniform Child Custody Jurisdiction and Enforcement Act (UCCJEA) (1) to harmonize the provisions of state child custody laws with the federal Parental Kidnapping Prevention Act (PKPA); (2) to clarify the provisions of the UCCJA that have met with conflicting interpretations in state courts; and (3) to expand the enforcement of custody decrees issued by state courts and foreign countries.[117]

The UCCJA was created to ensure that only one state assumes jurisdiction over a single custody case at a time. However, the Act allows certain exceptions to a second state assuming jurisdiction. For example, a second state can assume jurisdiction if it is significantly connected with the child and one parent, there is substantial evidence in that state, and assuming jurisdiction would be in the

---

[117] For a discussion of the early history of the UCCJA, the application of the full faith and credit clause to custody decrees, and civil and criminal remedies available to the custodial spouse when her child has been abducted, see SANFORD N. KATZ, CHILD SNATCHING—THE LEGAL RESPONSE TO THE ABDUCTION OF CHILDREN (American Bar Association, 1981). For a full discussion of the basis for custody jurisdiction, the UCCJA, UCCJEA, and the Federal Parental Kidnapping Prevention Act (PKPA), with citations to cases that have interpreted the acts, see RUSSELL J. WEINTRAUB, COMMENTARY ON THE CONFLICT OF LAWS 327–40 (4th ed. 2001). For an analysis of the major provisions of the UCCJA, see ELLMAN, KURTZ & SCOTT, *supra* note 53, at 758–97. The UCCJA, UCCJEA, and the PKPA can be found in the Appendix.

best interest of the child. Another reason for assuming jurisdiction is in a situation where a child has been abandoned. Additionally, there is an exception if no other state has jurisdiction to hear the case or a state court has refused to hear the case.

The Commissioners stated its nine general purposes in Notes to § 1:

(1) to avoid jurisdictional competition and conflict between states in custody matters;
(2) to promote cooperation between courts of various states;
(3) to assure that litigation concerning the custody of the child takes place in the state with which the child and his family have the closest connection;
(4) to discourage continuing litigation over child custody;
(5) to deter abductions of children by their parents;
(6) to avoid litigation of a case in their states;
(7) to facilitate the enforcement of custody decrees;
(8) to promote the exchange of information and mutual assistance between states;
(9) to make the laws of the states which adopt the Act uniform.

In 1980 the Federal Congress passed the Federal Parental Kidnapping Prevention Act, which provides that one state must give full faith and credit to custody decisions of the rendering state. In addition, the federal courts, usually not the forum for family law cases, can take jurisdiction over these interstate custody disputes.

In 1985 the U.S. Senate approved the Hague Convention on the Civil Aspects of International Child Abduction. The aim of that Convention was to facilitate the return of abducted children from the United States to a foreign country.[118]

Continuity of a Relationship with Others

How important is it for a child of divorce to continue to have a relationship with an adult with whom the child has had a strong attachment? This is the question posed by step-parents and grandparents. There is no issue if the divorcing parents agree to continue the relationship, but if the custodial spouse interferes with the relationship the child has with his or her step-parent or grandparent, what rights do these people have?

It had been the custom to technically treat a step-parent, even if he or she were a de facto parent, and grandparents as strangers in so far as having any custodial rights in divorce cases.[119] Neither had standing to raise the issue of

[118] For a full discussion and analysis of the Hague Convention, see Linda Silberman, *The Hague Children's Conventions: The Internationalization of Child Law, in* CROSS CURRENTS, *supra* note 1, at 589–617.

[119] As we have seen, step-parents may or may not have child support obligations. *See* accompanying text to note 81.

their visitation rights in litigation. Unless a judge relied on his residual equity powers to do justice and promote the best interests of the child, or interpreted a visitation statute broadly to include a non-parent, a step-parent would be without rights.[120]

Grandparents differ from step-parents or de facto parents in that they are biologically (if there is a blood tie) or legally (if the child was adopted) related to the child. Yet for years they, too, were considered legal strangers. It took a massive effort on the part of grandparents to convince state legislatures that they should have standing to assert their rights to visitation with their grandchildren.

The major legal problem grandparents faced was the fundamental principle in American law, based on a series of U.S. Supreme Court cases that protect the liberty interests parents have in the care, custody, and control of their children.[121] In American law, parents are the lawful custodians of their children, and unless the state can show that the parents are unfit, family privacy should be protected. Thus, the tension is between grandparents desiring standing to assert their rights to have a relationship with their grandchildren versus the rights of parents to determine for themselves the persons with whom their children can associate.

This conflict, although not in the divorce context, finally reached the U.S. Supreme Court in *Troxel v. Granville*.[122] The case arose in the State of Washington, which had a statute that allowed 'any person to petition a superior court for visitation rights at any time and authorizes that court to grant such visitation rights whenever visitation may serve the best interests of the child'.[123] In *Troxel*, the dispute was between paternal grandparents who wished to increase their visitation schedule with their dead son's illegitimate children and the mother of those grandchildren who refused their request. The mother did not want to terminate the visits, but limit the visitation to one short visit a month and special holidays. In a lower court ruling the grandparents were successful in obtaining the schedule they desired, but they lost in their first appeal because the court stated that the grandparents did not have standing. That court did not address the constitutionality of the Washington visitation statute.

---

[120] *But see, e.g.*, COLO. REV. STAT. ANN. § 14-10-123(1)(c) (2000); CONN. GEN. STAT. ANN. § 46b–59 (West 1995), which states that 'any person may be awarded visitation'. OR. REV. STAT. § 109.119 (1999), which states that any person who has 'maintained an ongoing personal relationship with substantial continuity for at least one year, through interaction, companionship, interplay and mutuality' may petition for visitation.

[121] These historic cases are: Meyer v. Nebraska, 262 U.S. 390 (1923); Pierce v. Society of Sisters, 268 U.S. 510 (1925); Prince v. Massachusetts, 321 U.S. 158 (1944); Stanley v. Illinois, 405 U.S. 645 (1972); Wisconsin v. Yoder, 406 U.S. 205 (1972); Parham v. J.R., 442 U.S. 584 (1979); Santosky v. Kramer, 455 U.S. 745 (1982); Washington v. Clucksberg, 521 U.S. 702 (1997).

[122] 530 U.S. 57 (2000).   [123] WASH. REV. CODE ANN. § 26.10.160(3) (West 1997).

The grandparents appealed that decision to the Supreme Court of Washington, which held that the visitation statute was unconstitutional because it unduly interfered with parental decision-making. That decision was appealed to the U.S. Supreme Court, which affirmed the state supreme court's decision. Justice O'Connor, writing for a plurality of the Court, with other justices filing concurring and dissenting opinions,[124] held that the visitation provision as applied to the mother of the children was 'breathtakingly broad'. The statute, as applied, did not afford the mother's decision any weight including a presumption of validity, thus giving the judge too much power in making his decision. Justice O'Connor wrote that the effect of the statute was basically to disregard the rights of a fit parent when a third party seeks to gain visitation rights to her child. For those reasons, Justice O'Connor wrote that enforcing the statute violated the due process rights of the mother, since allowing the grandparents visitation rights interfered with her fundamental liberty in raising her children. Justice O'Connor made it a point to state that the Court was putting the broad language of the Washington visitation statute to the constitutional test. It was not deciding 'whether the Due Process Clause requires all nonparental visitation statutes to include a showing of harm or potential harm to the child as a condition precedent to granting visitation'.[125]

Justice Scalia's dissent presented a major departure from the opinions of the other justices. He expressed a fundamental disagreement with them and questioned the present value of the historic parental rights cases in stating that the Washington visitation law was no burden to a fundamental constitutional right.

To Justice Scalia, the right to raise a child is not a constitutional right enforceable by the courts, but is 'among the "unalienable Rights" with which the Declaration of Independence proclaims "all men . . . are endowed by their Creator." And in my view that right is also among the "othe[r] [rights] retained by the people" which the Ninth Amendment says the Constitution's enumeration of rights "shall not be construed to deny or disparage." '[126]

Because of the seven separate opinions in *Troxel*, it is difficult to determine its future application.[127] It appears that one reading of the case is that family

---

[124] Briefly and in summary, Justice Souter, while concurring in the judgment, would have affirmed the Supreme Court of Washington's decision, holding the statute to be facially unconstitutional. Justice Thomas, also concurring in the judgment, agreed that the statute had been applied unconstitutionally, but felt that the Court should have stated the appropriate standard of review for the rights in question, which to him was strict scrutiny. Justice Stevens dissented from the decision, asserting that the statute had a legitimate sweep and that nothing in the Court's precedent indicated that a third party should have to show harm before a court can award visitation. Justices Kennedy and Scalia dissented. Justice Kennedy argued that a showing of harm should not be required before a court can award visitation rights to a third party, and asserted that the best interests of the child standard is the most appropriate tool in domestic relations law when dealing with visitation proceedings. The major point of Justice Scalia's dissent is discussed in the text above.

[125] 530 U.S. at 74.   [126] *Id.* at 91.

[127] Professor David Meyer has analyzed the case and produced a chart that compares all the opinions and provides the general statements, based on the number of judges who

privacy is protected, at least with regard to a court ordering visitation by any third parties. Another interpretation is that a plurality of the justices favors a constitutional presumption in favor of parental judgments about the child's best interests. However, that presumption is reputable by case-specific factors.

What effect the case will have on the fifty grandparent visitation statutes remains to be seen? What is important in any analysis of the impact of *Troxel* will be the context in which grandparents seek visitation rights. For example, is the context an intact family, namely an attempt by grandparents to seek visitation rights while their children are living together with their parents; is the context divorce in which grandparents seek to visit their children over the objection of one or both of the divorcing couple; or are the grandparents seeking visitation rights after the death of one of the child's parents who was the grandparent's child; is the request to visit the illegitimate child of their own son? Also important is the precise wording of the grandparent visitation statute. No matter what context, the basic question concerns the rights of parents to raise their children without interference from third parties, even grandparents. With that question often come two others: whether there must be a showing of parental unfitness before any interference and whether the best interests of the child are served by allowing the third party visitation.

Following *Troxel*, the Supreme Court of Iowa was faced with a case that questioned the constitutionality of the Iowa grandparent statute under its state constitution. In the case of *Santi v. Santi*,[128] parents in an intact family denied grandparents visitation rights under a statute that allowed grandparents to petition a court to visit their grandchildren if the grandparents have established a substantial relationship with their grandchild and the visitation would be in the best interests of the grandchildren.[129] The statute was broad and was not

---

agree on each issue. *See* David D. Meyer, Lochner *Redeemed: Family Privacy after* Troxel *and* Carhart, 48 UCLA L. Rev. 1125, 1143 (2001). Professor Meyer points out that only Justice Souter and Justice Thomas considered the Washington statute facially unconstitutional, and Justices O'Connor, Rehnquist, Ginsburg, Breyer, Souter, and Thomas, either expressly or impliedly, found the statute unconstitutional as applied to the parent, the mother, in the case.

See also, JEROME A. BARRON, C. THOMAS DIENES, WAYNE MCCORMACK & MARTIN H. REDISH, CONSTITUTIONAL LAW: PRINCIPLES AND POLICY—CASES AND MATERIALS 515–16 (6th ed. 2002).

[128] 633 N.W.2d 312 (Iowa 2001).

[129] The Iowa statute reads as follows:

The grandparent or great-grandparent of a child may petition the district court for grandchild or great-grandchild visitation rights when any of the following circumstances occur:

. . .

7. A parent of the child unreasonably refuses to allow visitation by the grandparent or great-grandparent or unreasonably restricts visitation. This subsection applies to but is not limited in application to a situation in which the parents of the child are divorced and the parent who is the child of the grandparent or who is the grandchild of the great-grandparent has legal custody of the child.

limited to situations where the parents were divorced. The Iowa court first pointed out that the law in the state protected the liberty interest in fit, married parents to oppose visitation by third parties, and that it would review its grandparent visitation statute under the strict scrutiny standard under the Iowa state constitution. The strict scrutiny standard requires that the parental liberty interests implicated by the statute be narrowly tailored to serve a compelling state interest. Under the strict scrutiny standard, the court held that fostering close relations between grandparents and grandchildren was not a compelling state interest to justify intruding into the privacy of an intact family. To the court, its statute failed to require a threshold finding of parental unfitness before proceeding to the best interest analysis. For these reasons the court found the Iowa statute unconstitutional. One interesting discussion in the case was its comments about an *amicus curiae* brief submitted by a retired persons organization (presumably comprised of many grandparents) who argued for the importance of strengthening extended family bonds. To this reasonable argument, the court responded by saying something equally reasonable: that imposing a court-ordered grandparent visitation hardly results in strengthening extended family bonds. Indeed, one might add that intra-family and intergenerational litigation might exacerbate differences.

Many of the cases that have been decided by state supreme courts since *Troxel* have not been concerned with divorce, but with the visitation rights of grandparents in cases where they seek to visit their grandchildren who may be living with one parent. In a number of the cases, the child is illegitimate and is either living with the child's biological mother or father who refuses to allow the child's grandparent to visit with the child.

As a general rule, state supreme courts have held that the status of grandparent does not give that person standing by itself. Rather, the grandparent or third party must prove that he or she has had a parent-like relationship with the child, that the child will be harmed by the lack of the grandparent's visitation, and that the visitation is in the child's best interests. State statutes that include those factors seem to be held constitutional under state constitutions. The most important point that dominates the cases is the court's respect for parental autonomy and the protection of children from harm.[130]

> A petition for grandchild or great-grandchild visitation rights shall be granted only upon a finding that the visitation is in the best interests of the child and that the grandparent or great-grandparent had established a substantial relationship with the child prior to the filing of the petition.

See IOWA CODE § 598.35 (7).

[130] In *Blixt v. Blixt*, 774 N.E.2d 1052 (Mass. 2002), the Supreme Judicial Court of Massachusetts found its grandparent visitation statute, M.G.L. ch. 119, § 39D to be constitutional. That statute reads as follows:

> If the parents of an unmarried minor child are divorced, married but living apart, under a temporary order or judgment of separate support, or if either or both

DIVORCE AND DECISION-MAKING

Summary Dissolution

Throughout this chapter I have referred to lawyers and judges as the major decision-makers in the divorce process. This is so because, as stated previously, lawyers advise their clients on their prediction of outcomes, and those predictions play an important role in their client's decisions on whether to settle or proceed to trial. Divorce uses a judicially managed adversarial model in a court setting for determining an outcome. The adversarial process has been subject

> parents are deceased, or if said unmarried minor child was born out of wedlock whose maternity has been adjudicated by a court of competent jurisdiction or whose father has signed an acknowledgment of paternity, and the parents do not reside together, the grandparents of such minor child may be granted reasonable visitation rights to the minor child during his minority by the probate and family court department of the trial court upon a written finding that such visitation rights would be in the best interest of the said minor child; provided, however, that such adjudication of paternity or acknowledgment of paternity shall not be required in order to proceed under this section where maternal grandparents are seeking such visitation rights. No such visitation rights shall be granted if said minor child has been adopted by a person other than a stepparent or such child and any visitation rights granted pursuant to this section prior to such adoption of the said minor child shall be terminated upon such adoption without any further action of the court.

In *Blixt* the maternal grandfather sued his daughter and the father of his daughter's illegitimate child for visitation rights to his grandchild. The child's parents who were living with their child objected to the visitation. The mother filed a motion to dismiss her father's action on the grounds that the visitation statute was unconstitutional on its face because it violated the Fourteenth Amendment and its Massachusetts counterpart, and also violated the equal protection provisions of the state and federal constitutions. The Family and Probate Court granted the mother's motion to dismiss, finding the statute unconstitutional. The case went up to the Supreme Judicial Court of Massachusetts.

The Supreme Judicial Court, however, held that its statute was constitutional. To a majority of the court, the mother was not denied due process or equal protection. The court first differentiated the Massachusetts statute and its limitation to the broadness of the Washington statute in *Troxel*. The court mentioned the context in which this case arises (illegitimate child living with the child's biological mother and father). The court also stated 'that the Massachusetts statute satisfied strict scrutiny because the court's interpretation narrowly tailors it to further the compelling State interest in protecting the welfare of a child who has experienced a disruption in the family unit from harm'. The court's construction of the statute requires that a parental decision concerning grandparent visitation be given presumptive validity, and that such presumption assumes the fitness of the parent. To rebut the presumption that a parental decision concerning grandparent visitation is valid, grandparents must prove by a preponderance of the crucible evidence that the failure to grant visitation will cause the child significant harm, thus affecting the child's health, safety, or welfare. The court stated that if grandparents do not have a pre-existing relationship with their grandchild, they must prove that the visitation is nevertheless necessary to protect the child from significant harm.

to major criticisms in divorce because it has been thought of as creating antagonists.

A question that is asked is whether the judicially managed adversarial model is appropriate for divorce? On the one hand, as we have seen, the economic considerations raised when the divorcing couple has complicated financial interests may resemble the dissolution of a business partnership. Such issues may require the formalism of court procedure with strict adherence to rules of evidence. On the other hand, child custody cases raise major psychological issues where court procedures and rules of evidence may actually hinder the search for a resolution that is in the best interests of the child.

Because the legal costs of divorce, like other civil matters, have increased dramatically due to such factors as attorney's fees and the costs of hiring experts, there has been a consumer demand to both simplify the divorce procedure and to make divorce available without using a lawyer. In response to that demand, some states[131] have enacted legislation providing for summary dissolution of marriage, a form of divorce that does not require the parties to make a court appearance or to use a lawyer (although they may still do so), but merely to file a form with the appropriate government body. The legislation addresses uncomplicated divorce. Thus, as a general statement, it may be said that summary dissolution provisions apply to cases in which the parties have been married for a short length of time, have limited assets, have no children, and mutually desire a divorce. It should be emphasized that summary dissolution is a formal method of terminating a marriage because public documents must still be completed and officially filed and approved. (Indeed, no American jurisdiction permits a private, informal, unregulated contract of divorce.) But unlike the conventional formal adversarial model managed by a judge who makes the decision, it is the parties themselves who are the principal actors and decision-makers, not lawyers or judges.

Summary Process and Divorce by Registration

A development related to summary dissolution is the simplified divorce procedure. A simplified divorce procedure (called summary process or divorce by mutual consent in some jurisdictions), unlike summary dissolution, requires a court appearance. However, the divorce is granted on the basis of mutual consent of the parties, rendering the court appearance a mere formality. Such a process also lessens or eliminates the need to procure a lawyer. Some form of simplified divorce procedure has been adopted by seventeen states.[132]

---

[131] *See, e.g.,* California (CAL. FAM. CODE § 2400), Colorado (C.R.S. 14-10-120.3), Indiana (Burns IND. CODE ANN. § 31-15-2-13), Iowa (IOWA CODE § 598.8), Minnesota (MINN. STAT. § 518.195), Nevada (NEV STAT. 125.181), and Oregon (OR. REV. STAT. § 107.485).

[132] *See, e.g.,* ALASKA STAT. § 25.24.220(B); ARIZ. REV. STAT. § 25–316; DEL. CODE ANN. tit. 13, § 1517; FLA. STAT. ANN. § 61.052; GA. CODE ANN. § 19-5-10(a); HAW. REV.

Surprisingly, there has been little commentary or analysis concerning summary dissolution or simplified divorce. Therefore, it is difficult to assess how many couples have used these procedures with or without legal counsel. However, the advantages of summary dissolution and simplified divorce are clear. They decrease the costs of obtaining a divorce by streamlining the divorce process and by rendering it less time-consuming both for the divorcing couple and court personnel. These procedures may be an attractive model for many states to adopt if the costs of divorce continue to rise out of the reach of an increasing number of people.

In complex divorce cases—those in which the custody of children is in dispute and where complicated property issues are to be resolved—divorce by registration or summary dissolution procedures may be inappropriate. A major question is how can complex cases be resolved in the most efficient and civilized manner?

Mediation

There is no question that people tend to respect decisions in which they have had some input, or at least the opportunity to be heard and to have presented their views. This is true when concerned with complying with laws on a broad scale or decisions on a personal level. Applying this principle to divorce means that spouses who jointly participate in the decisions about their children and about their finances are more likely to comply with those decisions than are those who have a decision imposed upon them without their having had an opportunity to participate in the process of formulating the decision.

In contrast to decisions imposed by lawyers and judges, mediation promotes party self-determination and decision-making by consent. Although mediation has been a major method of resolving disputes in the labor and employment fields as well as in family counseling settings, its use in divorce on such a large scale is only about thirty years old. Its focus in divorce is on resolving a variety of family issues, which become crucial for a divorce but may continue to exist in some form or another after a divorce decree is issued. Therefore, unlike mediation in many other settings, mediation in divorce must take into account that the parties may continue to have a relationship after the divorce judgment.

The mediation process facilitates the effectuation of a formal agreement in a relatively informal atmosphere, using a neutral third party as mediator. The mediator, in helping the parties to come to an agreement, may help clarify issues, suggest possible accommodations and alternatives, assist the divorcing

STAT. § 580–42(a); IDAHO CODE § 32–716; 750 ILL. COMP. STAT. 5/453; KY. REV. STAT. ANN. § 403.170; MASS. GEN. LAWS ANN. ch. 208, § 1A; MISS. CODE ANN. § 93-5-2; MONT. CODE ANN. § 40-4-130 to 133; NEB. REV. STAT. ANN. § 42–361; OHIO REV. CODE ANN. § 3105.63; TENN. CODE ANN. § 36-4-103; WASH. REV. CODE ANN. § 26.09.030(1); and WIS. STAT. § 767.12 (2).

couple to develop their own parental, financial, and property agreements, and help promote decision-making within the family. Mediation differs from courtroom litigation in that it is not adversarial in nature. Instead of each party retaining a lawyer who advocates for them, the parties speak for themselves and there is usually only one neutral mediator.

There are several other advantages to the mediation process with an experienced mediator. It may be less expensive and more expeditious than protracted courtroom litigation. Mediation may be a more humane process than an adversarial proceeding and, in some instances, may be better able to discover and address the emotional issues that may be having a negative effect on resolving practical legal problems. Lawyers (especially those who specialize in litigation) in an adversarial proceeding are often accused of actually reinforcing conflict between the parties and creating obstacles to settlement. In some instances this may be true. Because mediation is non-adversarial, many technical legal issues, like procedure and rules of evidence, are set aside, and this may cause some problems.

The leading writers in the field suggest that mediation between people of unequal bargaining power tends to lead to agreements reflecting that inequality.[133] Therefore, mediation is particularly appropriate for parties who have already achieved some independence and have relatively equal bargaining power, but may be less appropriate for parties of unequal bargaining power.

The concept of divorce mediation has not yet gained universal acceptance by the general public because many divorcing couples seek lawyers first, and the lawyer's initial response may be to rely on traditional litigation strategies. Generally, the highest level of participation is found in compulsory mediation programs such as those found in California, which, in 1980, made such mediation mandatory for contested custody and visitation issues. Since then a number of states have authorized courts to assign mediation in contested cases.[134]

---

[133] For a discussion of mediation in divorce and decedents estates conflicts, see Ray D. Madoff, *Lurking in the Shadow: The Unseen Hand of Doctrine in Dispute Resolution*, 76 S. CAL. L. REV. 161 (2002). *See also* H. Jay Folberg, *Divorce Mediation—The Emerging American Model, in* THE RESOLUTION OF FAMILY CONFLICT 193–232 (John M. Eekelaar & Sanford N. Katz eds., 1984).

[134] In some states, mediation is a prerequisite to a hearing in cases of contested custody and visitation issues. *See, e.g.*, CAL. CIV. CODE § 4607 (West 1983 & Supp. 1990); DEL. FAM. CT. C.R. (16)(a)(1); ME. REV. STAT. ANN. tit. 19, § 752 (West 1981 & Supp. 1990); N.C. GEN. STAT. § 50-13.1 (1989) (mediation required if custody or visitation issue involved); OR. REV. STAT. ANN. §§ 107.755–795 (Butterworths 1990). Other states permit the court to order mediation. *See, e.g.*, ALASKA STAT. § 25.24.060 (Michie 1983); FLA STAT. ANN. § 44.101 (Harrison Supp. 1989); ILL. REV. STAT. ch. 40, 607.1(c)(4) (Smith-Hurd 1980 & Supp. 1990); IOWA CODE ANN. §§ 598.41, 679.1–.14 (West 1987 & Supp. 1990); KAN. STAT. ANN. §§ 23–601 to -607 (1989); LA. REV. STAT. ANN. §§ 9:351– :356 (West Supp. 1990); MICH. COMP. LAWS § 552.505 (West 1988 & Supp. 1990); MINN. STAT. ANN. § 518.619 (West 1990); MONT. CODE ANN. §§40-4-215, 301 (2002); N.H. REV. STAT. ANN. § 328-C (Butterworths Supp. 1989); N.M. STAT. ANN.

Voluntary mediation programs do not attract a substantial number of participants. This has been attributed to the legal community's somewhat neutral attitude toward mediation, and the public's lack of information about mediation as
an alternative to the adversarial process. However, researchers find that those
who undergo the mediation process achieve a more successful outcome both in
the short term and the long term than their adversarial counterparts.[135] Because
parties are often more satisfied with the agreements, which they, themselves,
have forged through mediation, they are more likely to follow the terms of
those agreements than court-imposed settlements. That being said, mediation
may not be appropriate for divorcing couples who during their marriage were
unable to reach agreements about domestic matters especially dealing with
finances and child-rearing. It may also not be appropriate for a couple, one or
both of whom have unresolved emotional problems, or who are ambivalent
about the divorce, or who are litigious.[136]

When mediation was first suggested as an alternative conflict resolution
mechanism, it was criticized by some lawyers who saw it as an intrusion by
non-professionals. It was said that just at a time when divorce was becoming
highly complicated because of the newness of equitable distribution, lay people
were becoming involved with decision-making in the divorce process. How can
a non-lawyer know the complexities of marital property law when lawyers
themselves may be unaware of the answers?[137] Such criticism has waned only
within the last decade as mediation has matured into a conventional method of
resolving disputes and a mediation industry has developed in the metropolitan
areas of the country. Lawyers themselves can be mediators (although they may
not act as lawyers in the case, if they are) and non-lawyers can be trained in the
complexity of the law so as to assist spouses properly.[138]

Some states have built into their divorce system procedural stop lights in
order to attempt to resolve disputes along the way toward an actual trial. For
example, in Massachusetts some probate courts have established pre-trial
conferences that have the effect of trying to reach consensus on divorce matters.
These pre-trial conferences, led by the judge who will hear the case with lawyers
and their clients present, are not meant to mediate the dispute, but are designed
to give the judge a fair assessment of where the parties are in their negotiation.
The judge can then attempt to have the lawyers reach an agreement on all or
certain issues, thus minimizing the length of a trial.

§ 40-12-5 (1988); R.I. GEN. LAWS § 15-5-29 (1988); TEX. CIV. PRAC. & REM. CODE ANN.
§§ 152.001–.004 (Vernon 1985); WASH. REV. CODE ANN. § 26.09.015 (West Supp.
1990); WIS. STAT. § 767.11(3) (West Supp. 1990).

[135] *See* H. JAY FOLBERG AND ANN MILNE, DIVORCE MEDIATION—THEORY AND PRACTICE
431–49 (1988).

[136] For a discussion of these issues and other alternative methods of resolving conflicts
in divorce, see Janet R. Johnston, *High-Conflict Divorce, in* THE FUTURE OF CHILDREN,
supra note 51, at 165, 176–78.   [137] *See, e.g.*, Smith v. Lewis, *supra* note 38.

[138] *See* JAY FOLBERG & ALISON TAYLOR, MEDIATION (1984).

THE FUTURE OF DIVORCE

Although fault and no-fault divorce exists in the United States, there is some thought being given to whether the states should abandon no-fault divorce and return to a fault-based divorce system. On one hand, there is a feeling that divorces should be prevented or at least made difficult because of the belief that divorce results in a number of social ills including juvenile delinquency.[139] Just over thirty years ago, the late Professor Max Rheinstein responded to conclusions of this sort by writing that it was not divorce that caused social ills, but marriage breakdown. He wrote, 'If we are concerned about the good of society, we must focus our attention on the prevention or minimization of the incidence of factual marriage breakdown rather than upon stemming the tide of divorce.'[140] Professor Rheinstein's advice would support programs and services like marital counseling, which are probably more available now and used more often than when he wrote about divorce in the late 1960s and early 1970s. Some legislatures are constantly reviewing substantive laws and procedures in order to improve them by making the laws more realistic and the process more efficient.

No-fault divorce is now a part of American law. There seems to be no returning to the past when divorce was difficult to obtain because of our reliance on English law that reflected a culture and customs of a different time and place. With no formally established national church in the United States where we have a more heterogeneous population than in Great Britain, we are not held hostage to a single religious dogma, although some states in the United States have been dominated by particular religious groups who have influenced divorce legislation. If the immediate past history of divorce is any indication of the future, future reforms may take the direction of further relaxing substantive and procedural divorce laws. I do believe, however, that the requirement of the presence of at least one spouse at the divorce hearing will not be abandoned. In other words, it is hard to imagine that divorce by proxy or divorce by mail either in the United States or in a foreign country, like renewing a license or a passport, will become attractive alternatives because of our fundamental belief in marriage and family as serious American institutions requiring personal attention and the investment of time and concern. Divorce by registration or summary procedure—the wave of the future—requires the presence of both parties and the involvement of some official who reviews documents and issues a divorce.

---

[139] This is manifested from time to time when legislatures either refuse or are reluctant to reduce the periods between the time a divorce decree is issued and when it is final. For example, in Massachusetts 90 days must elapse between the time a decree is granted and when it becomes final. (See M.G.L. ch. 208, § 21). Attempts at reducing the period have been unsuccessful. The reason for the time period is supposedly to give the spouses time to reconcile. It is generally believed (although there are no definitive studies to prove the point) that such a goal is unrealistic.

[140] *See* MAX RHEINSTEIN, MARRIAGE STABILITY, DIVORCE AND THE LAW 5–6 (1972).

Divorce by the conventional adversary method is expensive. Although it is difficult to quantify because of the lack of national data, reports from judges suggest that at the present time courts are seeing an inordinate amount of litigants pursuing their cases themselves, that is, acting as their own attorneys—*pro se*.[141] This presents difficulties for the court system (because *pro se* cases do not move through the system in an orderly fashion as compared to cases handled by lawyers) and for the judges who, according to judicial ethics, must be neutral and are not allowed to act as counsel to litigants, yet are confronted with the reality that the litigants need assistance. Institutional responses for *pro se* cases are varied. One is to refer the litigants to lawyers who are willing to represent them at a reduced rate. A court in one state features a video that runs continuously and provides litigants with basic information about divorce procedure. Some courts have volunteer lawyers (in the court building) not to represent litigants but to be available to them as consultants or aids. A project in Massachusetts involves utilizing retired partners of law firms to assist litigants with limited means to obtain a divorce.

Just as important as it is to litigants with uncomplicated divorces to provide them with inexpensive and timely divorces, it is vital to those going through a complex divorce to provide a setting that reduces, to the extent possible, the anxiety of getting a divorce. The hope is that family courts can fulfill that function, although the establishment of family courts in each state has been diminished because of the current economic slump. Family courts as conceived by thoughtful reformers would provide a milieu that is conducive to the informal processes, like mediation, that are important in divorce if the goal is to humanize the process.[142] The tension that exists in divorce is that, on one hand, the economic and child custody aspects of divorce are extremely complex requiring the use of traditional procedural mechanisms for discovering facts. On the other hand, there is a desire to simplify, expedite, and reduce the financial and emotional costs of the divorce process by utilizing as many alternative conflict resolution methods as are appropriate. Additionally, family courts can serve as a community-based institution that coordinates all legal matters dealing with the family in a holistic manner. That is, it can provide necessary social and psychiatric services that may be incident to the divorce on the site of the court. It can be the institution to which divorced spouses as well as children of divorce can turn for future services such as post-divorce counseling.

It is difficult to come to any other conclusion but that divorce is an emotional experience that can leave lasting scars on husbands, wives, and children. The

---

[141] The author has derived this information from his participation in judicial education both in the Commonwealth of Massachusetts and with the Council of Juvenile and Family Court Judges, a national organization that holds educational programs for judges from many states.

[142] *See* SANFORD N. KATZ & JEFFREY A. KUHN, RECOMMENDATIONS FOR A MODEL FAMILY COURT (National Council of Juvenile and Family Court Judges, 1991).

goal of any divorce law whether in the assignment of property or the award of custody is to promote fairness and justice, which the parties themselves feel have been achieved. The goal of divorce process, including negotiations in a lawyer's office, mediation in an informal setting, and formal procedure in a court, should be to lessen that scarring process in a humane system.

4

Child Protection

INTRODUCTION

Child abuse and neglect are not unknown in American social history and can be traced as far back as the founding of the country.[1] Children have suffered at the hands of parents, teachers, social agencies, and even the state, although the suffering has often been justified as in the child's best interests. A law in the Massachusetts Bay Colony during the seventeenth century and taken directly from the Book of Deuteronomy provided that if a son did not 'obey the voice of his father', he could be stoned.[2] Children were as vulnerable in certain respects as enslaved people.

During the eighteenth and nineteenth century children were exploited in the workforce. It took the child labor laws of the nineteenth century to free children from the control of their employers who took advantage of the children subjecting them to all sorts of dangers. The nineteenth century was a period in which American state legislatures enacted child neglect laws that gave the government the legal authority to intervene into the parent–child relationship. Some of those laws are still on the books today.[3]

Children were subject to all sorts of indignities. Late in the nineteenth century and early in the twentieth, many children found on the streets in Boston, New York, and Philadelphia, whether homeless or not, were subject to being rounded up and sent to the midwest and west where they were sold to farmers to assist them in their work. These children who were later to be called 'the children of the orphan trains' were basically kidnapped by social service agencies in the name of advancing children's welfare. The agencies said

---

[1] *See* JEANNE M. GIOVANNONI & ROSINA M. BECERRA, DEFINING CHILD ABUSE 31–75 (1979); Shippen L. Page, *The Law, the Lawyer, and Medical Aspects of Child Abuse, in* CHILD ABUSE 105–11 (Eli Newberger ed., 1982). Much of the major social science and legal research on child abuse and neglect began in the 1960s and continued during the 1970s and early 1980s. The results of that research are still considered sound, and many of the books and articles published during those decades are considered classics in the field.

[2] *See* Sanford N. Katz & William A. Schroeder, *Disobeying a Father's Voice: A Comment on Commonwealth v. Brasher*, 57 MASS. L.Q. 43 (1973). For a discussion of father's rights in Colonial America, see MARY ANN MASON, FROM FATHER'S PROPERTY TO CHILDREN'S RIGHTS, 1–47 (1994).

[3] *See* SANFORD N. KATZ, MELBA MCGRATH & RUTH-ARLENE W. HOWE, CHILD NEGLECT LAWS IN AMERICA (American Bar Association Press, 1976).

that the children would be freed from the foul air of the cities and experience the openness of the midwest and west where the air was clean and the opportunities limitless. Such statements were, of course, nonsense. Children of the orphan trains were lied to and sold to farmers for farm hands or kitchen maids.[4]

Throughout the history of the laws governing the complex relationship of parent, child, and state, there has been a struggle between parental authority and family privacy, on the one hand, and the state's responsibility of guarding the best interests of the child, on the other. The rhetoric has been that parents have the basic right to raise their children as they see fit, subject to their not overstepping the bounds of reasonableness in all aspects of child-rearing. Parental rights are not unlimited. Historically the state, the ultimate parent who looks after all the children in society under the *parens patriae* concept, has a right to subject parents to public scrutiny and legal examination. In the United States, in the main, child protection in the form of child welfare services in the latter part of the twentieth century and the beginning of the twenty-first is basically the responsibility of the states, although earlier in the past century those services were performed by local authorities, like counties or cities. State social service agencies under the executive branch deliver certain social services themselves but more commonly for reasons of economy contract for foster care and adoption services with private social service agencies, which they monitor.[5]

The executive and legislative branches of the federal government also play a role in child protection. The executive branch through the U.S. Department of Health and Human Services develop model laws for states to adopt if they wish and technical services in order for states to conform to federal legislation including social security. The legislative branch through the U.S. Congress enacts laws that basically fund child welfare programs but provide certain requirements for states to fulfill in order to meet federal mandates. State and federal courts hear cases involving child protection depending on the issues involved. Normally, a state court is the venue for a child protection case brought under a state statute, i.e. child neglect and abuse law, a domestic violence law, or criminal law, but if a federal statute is involved, then the federal courts have jurisdiction to hear the case.[6]

In this chapter, I shall explore the struggle that exists between parental rights to rear their children and the state's responsibility to look after the best interests

---

[4] For a full discussion of the orphan train children, see MARILYN IRVIN HOLT, THE ORPHAN TRAINS—PLACING OUT IN AMERICA (1992) and LINDA GORDON, THE GREAT ARIZONA ORPHAN ABDUCTION (1999).

[5] State contracting with private social service agencies is part of a national trend, begun in the latter part of the twentieth century, to privatize services traditionally delivered or performed by the state.

[6] *See* discussion of *DeShaney v. Winnebago County Dept. of Social Services*, 489 U.S. 189 (1989) in this chapter.

of all children. I shall begin by examining the historical basis for the state's intervention into the parent–child relationship, and then I shall briefly summarize the federal government's impact on the child protection systems in the states. That influence cannot be underestimated.

THE CONCEPT OF PUNISHMENT

In American law, parents have used 'parental immunity' as a defense in criminal and civil actions brought by the state's (or county's, depending on the jurisdiction) attorney or a department of social services in actions against them for child abuse. The parents' argument usually is stated in terms of their right to discipline their children according to their own religious beliefs or culture. Over the past century, parents have become less and less successful in justifying their abusive behavior on religious grounds.

The maxim, 'Spare the rod and spoil the child', thought to be based on the Old Testament, but actually from Samuel Butler's poem 'Hudibras', has been part of American child-rearing for centuries[7] and has even been incorporated into American law. The idea is that parents and those in authority over children have the right to punish a child in order to inculcate values of obedience and respect. In the nineteenth-century North Carolina case of *State v. Jones*,[8] Mr. Jones was tried for an assault and battery on 16-year-old Mary C. Jones. During the trial, the young woman testified that Mr. Jones had a severe temper and when angry whipped her without any reason. She said that on one occasion he gave her

about twenty-five blows with a switch, or small limb, about the size of one's thumb or forefinger with such force as to raise welts upon her back, and then going into the house, he soon returned and gave her five blows more with the same switch, choked her, and threw her violently to the ground, causing dislocation of her thumb joint.[9]

Mr. Jones's defense, substantiated by his wife, Mary's stepmother, was that Mary was habitually disobedient, had several times stolen money, and was chastised at the time spoken of for stealing some cents from her father, that he never whipped her except for correction, and this he was often compelled to do for that purpose, and that he had never administered punishment under the impulse of high temper or from malice.[10]

The judge's instruction to the jury expressed the North Carolina law at the time:

a parent had the right to inflict punishment on his child for the purpose of correction, but the punishment must not be 'excessive and cruel,' nor must it be 'to gratify malicious motives;' that if the whipping was such as described by the daughter, there would arise a

---

[7] Professor Philip Greven discusses the religious roots of punishment in his excellent study, *see* PHILIP GREVEN, SPARE THE CHILD 48 (1990).

[8] State v. Jones, 95 N.C. 588 (1886).   [9] *Id.*   [10] *Id.*

question as to the severity and extent of the punishment; that if the jury was convinced that it was cruel and excessive, the defendant would be guilty; that it was not necessary that it should result in a permanent injury to her, and if it was *excessive and cruel* it would be sufficient to make the defendant guilty.[11]

Mr. Jones was found guilty.

In setting aside the trial court's verdict, Chief Justice Smith of the North Carolina Supreme Court stated the nineteenth-century view of family privacy that would allow for parents to have enormous discretion in raising their children, and at the same time minimize governmental supervision. He wrote:

It will be observed that the test of the defendant's criminal liability is the infliction of a punishment *'cruel and excessive'* and this it is left to the jury without the aid of any rule of law for their guidance to determining.

It is quite obvious that this would subject every exercise of parental authority in the correction and discipline of children—in other words, domestic government—to the supervision and control of jurors, who might, in a given case, deem the punishment disproportionate to the offence, and unreasonable and excessive. It seems to us, that such a rule would tend, if not to subvert family government, greatly to impair its efficiency, and remove restraints upon the conduct of children. If, whenever parental authority is used in chastising them, it could be a subject of judicial inquiry whether the punishment was cruel and excessive—that is, beyond the demerits of the disobedience or misconduct, and the father himself exposed to a criminal prosecution at the instance of the child, in defending himself from which he would be compelled to lift the curtain from the scenes of home life, and exhibit a long series of acts of insubordination, disobedience and ill-doing—it would open the door to a flood of irreparable evils far transcending that to be remedied by a public prosecution. Is it consistent with the best interests of society, that an appeal should thus lie to the Court from an act of parental discipline, severe though it may be, and unmerited by the particular offence itself, perhaps but one of a series of evincing stubbornness and incorrigibility in the child, and the father punished because the jurors think it cruel and immoderate?[12]

Although the opinion is short, it includes the assumption that physical punishment may reflect parental affection. The linkage of physical pain with affection may have been an acceptable proposition in the nineteenth century, but it is clearly thought to be misguided today. For example, Chief Justice Smith stated that physical punishment as a manifestation of parental affection 'must be tolerated as an incident to the relation, which human laws cannot wholly remove or redress'. He adopted the position taken by another judge in another case who wrote that the relationships of master and apprentice, teacher and pupil, parent and child, and husband and wife should not be interfered with by trivial complaints 'not because these relations are not subject to law, but because the evils of publicity would be greater than the evil involved in the trifles complained of; and because they ought to be left to family government'.[13]

---

[11] *Id.*   [12] *Id.*
[13] State v. Rhodes, 61 N.C. (Phil. Law) 349, 453 (1868).

Following that policy, the North Carolina Supreme Court held that although 'the punishment seems to have been needlessly severe', it refused to consider it a criminal act, believing that 'it belongs to the domestic rather than legal power, to a domain into which the penal law is reluctant to enter, unless induced by an imperious necessity'.[14] It is this kind of attitude that has given currency to the statement that the family can be an enclosure for all kinds of violence between husband and wife and parent and child, and one in which the state (the police) is reluctant to enter.

In many of the cases dealing with punishment, defendants often invoke the Bible for support of the proposition that corporal punishment is justified by the Old and New Testament, and thus proper parental conduct. As late as 1988, in a South Carolina case, the parents' lawyer quoted Proverbs: 'Withhold not correction from the child; for if thou beatest him with the rod, he shall not die' to justify the father's beating of his 13-year-old daughter while her mother stood by because the daughter had lied about her whereabouts instead of telling her parents that she had been to a friend's party.[15] Her punishment included the father's whipping her with his belt and beating her until she was black and blue. He also slapped her in the face causing his daughter to have ringing in her ears for a day.

The case arose because the parents had been reported to a social service agency for child abuse. The agency investigated the case and thought the allegations serious enough to bring an action under the South Carolina child protection law. The lower court found that there had been child abuse and ordered both parents to participate in an agency counseling program.[16]

To support the defendants' argument that the Old Testament justified punishment, a clergyman acted as a witness and testified that the Bible was the 'ultimate binding authority'.[17] The defendants claimed that the free exercise of religion was constitutionally guaranteed to them. The South Carolina court addressed the argument with the following:

the First Amendment embraces two concepts: the freedom to believe and the freedom to act. The first is absolute, but the second is not. The law cannot regulate what people believe, but the law can regulate how people act, even if how they act is based on what they believe. . . . Indeed if the law were otherwise, the father in this case could beat his daughter into submission.[18]

In the concluding paragraph the court stated:

We believe the mother and father love their daughter and, despite what had happened, we believe she loves them. We also believe the mother and father can, if they will, learn to express their love in better ways, and the child can, if she will, learn to obey her parents—a requirement, coincidentally, of both the Bible and the law.[19]

---

[14] Jones, *supra* note 8.
[15] South Carolina Dept. of Social Services v. Father and Mother, 366 S.E.2d 40 (S.C. 1988). [16]*Id.*
[17] *Id.* [18] *Id.* [19] *Id.*

The court did not accept the parents' justification. However, equating affection with physical pain is a curious child-rearing principle. It suggests that children will learn positive behavior through experiencing pain. There appears to be no contemporary research results that confirm this conclusion.[20] To what extent has the Bible justified corporal punishment? Professor Greven argues that while the Old Testament is replete with references to physical violence and punishment against children, the New Testament generally speaks of love, emphasizing paternal restraint and advocating the affectionate nurturing of children rather than punishing them. Nowhere does he find corporal punishment ascribed either to the teaching of Jesus or to Paul.[21]

Culture was used as a defense in the New York case of *Dumpson v. Daniel M.*[22] In that case the New York Commissioner of Social Services brought an action to remove three children from their mother and father's home because of the father's use of excessive force in punishing one of them. The father had allegedly struck his 7-year-old son 'with his hands, a belt and his feet'. The result was that the boy suffered a cut lip and bruises.

An interesting fact in the case (for cultural understanding) was that the father was a taxi driver and was taking courses at Brooklyn College in order to become an engineer. His wife was a high school teacher of chemistry and biology in the New York school system. Thus, the parents were educated and upwardly mobile.

The father claimed that his actions were a response to his son's poor school behavior, which he said brought shame on the family. The father said that according to his Nigerian culture, 'if a child misbehaves in school and causes shame to the family, the parent has the duty to punish immediately and in any manner he sees fit'. He further testified that in Nigeria if a 'villager is summoned to court for any reason, he cannot return home until he has purified himself by way of a special cleansing ritual. No matter what the reason, it is a cause for embarrassment and shame if one has to appear in court.'

The New York Family Court decided that the father's form of corporal punishment was 'excessive' and as such would be considered 'neglect' under New York law. The judge ordered that the father and mother should undergo counseling; that the father should not physically punish his children; and three of the four children who had been temporarily removed from the custody of their parents should be returned to their parents' home. Further the court ordered that the child who had been beaten should remain under the care of the department for the present.

The case raises interesting questions about the role of custom and culture in defining child-rearing and the extent to which American law will tolerate or even sanction customs that deviate from the dominant American methods of

---

[20] *See* GREVEN, *supra* note 7, at 155 n. 6 and 174.   [21] *See id.* at 46–54.
[22] N.Y. LAW J., at 17, c7 (16 October 1974).

child-rearing if such methods can be defined.[23] Eunice Uzodike states that 'the Nigerian Criminal Code authorizes parents and school teachers to inflict a "blow or other force" for the purpose of correcting children under the age of sixteen'.[24] The author then states that Nigerian law does not authorize physical punishment that would 'exceed reasonable physical chastisement'.

According to Uzodike, children are considered the personal property of their parents in Nigerian culture and consequently incidents of physical force on children are ordinarily not of great concern to the police who would be the proper authority to intervene. As of 1990, Uzodike states that there have been no recorded cases of physical abuse in Nigeria.

If Uzodike is correct about Nigerian culture, the father in *Dumpson v. Daniel M.* was truthful about the treatment of children in Nigeria. Uzodike makes the point, however, that physical punishment is more prominent among the poor, uneducated, and illiterate in Nigeria. The father in the *Dumpson v. Daniel M.* case did not have any of those characteristics.

THE DEFINITION OF CHILD ABUSE

Is there a dominant American practice of child-rearing that could be used to define appropriate punishment and differentiate it from child abuse? The answer is probably 'no'. The research that comes closest to determining whether there is a consensus on what kind of parental misconduct should be reported to social service agencies for investigation to determine if there has been child abuse is that conducted by Giovannoni and Becerra in the late 1970s.[25] They reported that child maltreatment is 'not an absolute entity but, rather, is socially defined and cannot be divorced from the social contexts in which it occurs.'[26] In trying to discover whether there was a consensus on the definition of child maltreatment, the researchers developed vignettes and presented them to lay persons and professionals to determine how they would categorize the conduct of the parents in each vignette. Giovannoni and Becerra reported that:

Although the respondents concurred on the boundaries of different kinds of mistreatment, there was not always agreement about the valuations placed on each. Community members saw most kinds of mistreatment as more serious than did professionals, and among professionals, lawyers especially dissented from the other groups, generally regarding mistreatment as less serious than the others did. However, there was amazing similarity in the judgments of the relative seriousness of different *kinds* of mistreatment.

---

[23] For a discussion of cultural differences regarding child-rearing and the ways in which such differences should be assessed by the state, see Michael Freeman, *Cultural Pluralism and the Rights of the Child, in* THE CHANGING FAMILY (John Eekelaar & Thandabantu Nhlapo eds., 1998).

[24] Eunice Uzodike, *Child Abuse and Neglect in Nigeria—Socio-Legal Aspects*, 4 INT'L J.L. & FAM. 83, 86 (1990).   [25] GIOVANNONI & BECERRA, *supra* note 1.

[26] *Id.* at 239.

There were some notable exceptions to this general pattern. Among the professionals, police and social workers saw most kinds of mistreatment as more serious than did lawyers or pediatricians. This difference in opinion was most clearly related to the roles they play in the protective network as gatekeepers who make the initial decision as to whether a situation will be defined as one of mistreatment at all. This role provided them with particular kinds of responsibilities and experiences. Among the community respondents, differences in opinions related to ethnicity and social class. Contrary to common speculation, Black and Hispanic respondents, and those of lower socio-economic statuses exhibited greater concern about all kinds of mistreatment. Further, socioeconomic status of the respondents, while shown to be related to their perceptions of mistreatment, was not a factor that operated independently of their ethnicity. Rather, the ways in which social class and cultural values affected opinions about mistreatment were demonstrated to be very complex and not uniform across all ethnic groups.[27]

The Giovannoni and Becerra study is over twenty years old. Yet it confirms generally held beliefs about the lack of uniformity in defining child abuse. The debate over definitions and the question of state intervention in the parent–child relationship took place in the early 1970s and was prompted by the federal government's concern about violence in the home that occurred in the 1960s.[28]

Indeed, violence in the home was a phenomenon that was not widely studied or taken very seriously before about 1970, although reported divorce cases are filled with wife abuse that was not even discussed in terms of domestic violence, but whether the abuse justified a ground for divorce. Husbands could beat up their wives or subject them to sexual assaults with legal immunity for all practical purposes because of the old notion that wives were essentially the property of their husbands as well as the adage that a man is king in his household. Wives were supposed to serve their husbands and not question his authority.[29] Children were in a worse position than their mothers because children could be dominated by both parents and could be subjected to all sorts of abusive conduct in the name of parental rights. Domestic violence, whether between adults or adults and children, is really an expression of power and aggression over the dependent and vulnerable.

While the issue of child abuse generated legislative reform and response relatively quickly once it became a widely acknowledged problem, violence against women did not. The problems revolving around violence against

---

[27] GIOVANNONI & BECERRA, *supra* note 1. at 241.

[28] For a discussion of the problem of state intervention that was a major issue in the 1970s, see SANFORD N. KATZ, WHEN PARENTS FAIL (1971) and Michael S. Wald, *State Intervention on Behalf of Neglected Children*, 27 STAN. L. REV. 985 (1975).

[29] These issues are discussed in WALTER O. WEYRAUCH, SANFORD N. KATZ & FRANCES OLSEN, CASES AND MATERIALS ON FAMILY LAW—LEGAL CONCEPTS AND CHANGING HUMAN RELATIONSHIPS 212, 348 (1994). For an illustration of wife battering that is not even discussed as such, see *Warner v. Warner*, 76 Idaho 399, 283 P.2d 931 (1955) reproduced and commented on in that book.

women were finally recognized and addressed by Congress through the Violence against Women Act of 1994. Among its major purposes were the encouragement of mandatory arrest of domestic abusers and increased awareness of the pervasiveness and severity of violence against women.[30]

THE ROLE OF THE FEDERAL GOVERNMENT

The federal government's role in child welfare is basically twofold: (1) to provide technical assistance to states by developing model legislation for states to use in their law reform; and (2) to provide financial assistance for federal or federal and state child welfare programs, but with the mandate that the states fulfill certain requirements. It is because of the second role that the federal government can influence state legislation. To put it bluntly, if the states do not enact certain laws or promulgate certain administrative regulations, they are not eligible to receive funds for a number of vital state child welfare programs.

The role of government in child protection is enormous and the power of a judge who decides child protection cases is profound. Often, the concept of *parens patriae* is invoked not necessarily to justify the governmental role, but to explain it.[31] With all that power, does the government have any responsibilities? To help answer that question, one should look to history.

In his study of wardship jurisdiction,[32] John Seymour explains the origins of the law of wardship and its relationship to the concept of *parens patriae*. He discusses the conflict in English cases between those judges who believed that the Chancery Court judge stood in the shoes of the parents and those who held to the idea that the jurisdiction of the Chancery Court was wider than parents and was not derivative from parents but from the Crown. Seymour quotes from Lord Donaldson's observation in *Re R*: The jurisdiction of the Chancery Court 'is not derivative from the parents' rights and responsibilities, but derives from, or is, the delegated performance of the duties of the Crown to protect its subjects and particularly children.'[33] In other words, with the invocation of *parens patriae* comes the duty to protect children. But what kind of duty did Lord Donaldson mean?

---

[30] *See* Elizabeth M. Schneider, *The Law and Violence against Women in the Family at Century's End: The U.S. Experience, in* CROSS CURRENTS—FAMILY LAW AND POLICY IN THE UNITED STATES AND ENGLAND (Sanford N. Katz, John Eekelaar & Mavis McClean eds., 2000) [hereinafter CROSS CURRENTS]; ELIZABETH M. SCHNEIDER, BATTERED WOMEN AND FEMINIST LAWMAKING (2000). *See also* discussion of personal safety on p. 67 Violence Against Women.

[31] For a discussion of *parens patriae* and its origins, see HOMER H. CLARK, JR., THE LAW OF DOMESTIC RELATIONS IN THE UNITED STATES 335 (2d ed. 1988); SANFORD N. KATZ, WHEN PARENTS FAIL 17 n. 17 (1970).

[32] John Seymour, *Parens Patriae and Wardship Powers: Their Nature and Origins*, 14 OXFORD J. LEGAL STUDIES 159 (1994). [33] *Id.*

From the 1960s until the 1980s, child welfare specialists and American legislators interested in the plight of children struggled with the question of what can government do to prevent the break-up of families and if such a phenomenon occurs, how to reorganize them in such a way as to facilitate a child's entry into another family where the child can be safe and thrive. Leadership from the federal government took the form of the U.S. Department of Health, Education, & Welfare providing a Model Mandatory Child Abuse and Neglect Reporting Law,[34] Model State Subsidized Adoption Act,[35] and the Model Act to Free Children for Permanent Placement.[36] Congress enacted the Child Abuse Prevention and Treatment Act of 1974[37] and the Adoption Assistance Act of 1980.[38]

MODEL MANDATORY CHILD ABUSE REPORTING STATUTE

It is interesting to observe that child abuse and neglect became important in the public consciousness about twenty years before violence against women. In 1962 the research of Dr. C. Henry Kempe and his associates in Colorado was published and their article that coined the phrase 'battered child syndrome' was widely read and recognized by both the medical, psychiatric, and social work communities.[39] At about the same time, Children's Bureau of the then U.S. Department of Health, Education, & Welfare (now called the Department of Health and Human Services) held a conference to discuss what the legal response should be to the phenomenon that Dr. Kempe and his associates described. In 1963 the Model Mandatory Child Abuse Reporting Law developed from the conference.

To develop a mandatory child abuse reporting law was not without problems. It affected not only family privacy, but it also was at first seen as an

[34] Children's Bureau, U.S. Department of Health, Education & Welfare, The Abused Child-Principles and Suggested Language for the Reporting of the Physically Abused Child (1963).

[35] Reproduced in Sanford N. Katz & Ursula M. Gallagher, *Subsidized Adoption in America*, 10 FAM. L.Q. 1, 11 (1976). The brief summary of the Act is based on that article. The authors of the article, a law professor and a social worker, were the drafters of the model act, which has been the foundation upon which subsidized adoption in the United Sates is based.

[36] The Act is reproduced in Sanford N. Katz, *Freeing Children for Permanent Placement through a Model Act*, 12 FAM. L.Q. 203 (1978). The brief summary of the Act is based on that article.

[37] Pub. L. No. 96-272, 94 Stat. 500 (codified as 42 U.S.C. §§ 620–28 & 670–79).

[38] Pub. L. No. 96-272, 94 Stat. 500 (codified as amended in scattered sections of 42 U.S.C.). This chapter will discuss aspects of §§ 620–28 & 670–79.

[39] C. Henry Kempe et al., *The Battered Child Syndrome*, 18 JAMA 17 (1962). This is a classic article responsible for describing the syndrome of unexplained injury to a child and causing the label 'battered child syndrome' to become part of the medical and legal vocabulary.

intrusion into the confidential relationship between doctor and patient. Thus, the first laws were limited in scope and in the number of professional persons who were required to report abuse. As the concept of reporting was accepted, the number of mandated reporters grew.[40] For example, initially only physicians and surgeons were mandated to report in California. Now it can be said that mandated reporters often include all health care professionals, school personnel, clergy, day care operators, and even film developers.[41] Some statutes include a catch-all category such as other persons who regularly come into contact with children in the scope of their employment[42] and at least one state includes anyone with reasonable cause to believe a child has been abused.[43]

One of the major issues that met with resistance in persuading states to enact mandatory reporting laws was the extent to which those mandated to report were protected from cases where initial observation or diagnosis of the child's injury later proved to be something other than abuse. The resolution of that issue was to give immunity to mandated reporters whose report to the appropriate agency was made in good faith. For those mandated reporters who failed to report criminal sanctions (usually the crime is a misdemeanor with a fine and/or jail sentence) were put in place. The basic elements of mandatory reporting statutes include:

(1) definition of reportable conditions;
(2) persons required to report;
(3) degree of certainty reporters must reach;
(4) sanctions for failure to report;
(5) immunity for good faith reports;
(6) abrogation of certain communication privileges; and
(7) delineation of reporting procedures.[44]

Although there is no absolute uniformity in all American reporting laws, their passage has, to some extent, accomplished one of its primary goals, which is to make child abuse a public concern. The studies about child abuse reporting laws were mostly completed in the 1980s. One study indicates that nearly ten times the number of cases reported in 1965 were reported in 1985, totally 1.5 million.[45] According to a U.S. Census Bureau abstract, reports of child abuse increased from 669,000 in 1976 to 2,086,000 in 1986[46] and to 3,000,000

---

[40] *See* Douglas J. Besharov, *Gaining Control over Child Abuse Reports*, 48 PUBLIC WELFARE 34 (1990).

[41] *See, e.g.*, CAL. PENAL CODE §§ 11165, 11166 (1990).   [42] *Id.*

[43] ALASKA STAT. § 47-17-020.

[44] Educational Commission of the States, Report No. 106. *Trends in Child Protection Laws—1977*, at 18–21 app. (1978).

[45] *See* generally Douglas J. Besharov, *Doing Something about Child Abuse: The Need to Narrow the Grounds for State Intervention*, 8 HARV. J.L. & PUB. POL'Y 540, 542–50 (1985).

[46] BUREAU OF THE CENSUS, U.S. DEPT OF COMMERCE, STATISTICAL ABSTRACTS OF THE UNITED STATES 186 (1992).

in 1996.[47] The prediction that 2.5 million reports would be expected each year during the 1990s was an underestimation.[48] Even with these statistics, studies show that a majority of child abuse and neglect cases remain unreported. And, there is the ever present problem of unsubstantiated reports, which had comprised of about one half million each year.[49]

That child abuse is a public concern was highlighted in 2002 by the discovery of the number of Roman Catholic priests who had sexually abused children under their guidance in educational activities, church functions, sports activities, or in counseling sessions at church or in the child's home.[50] These priests, mostly from Kentucky and Massachusetts, had not only been protected by the local church hierarchy by keeping secret the claims of abuse, but were assigned to different parishes within the state or transferred to parishes in other states without reference to the priests' conduct.[51] In some instances the priests were placed on medical leave and sent to special mental health facilities or rehabilitation centers.[52]

The Massachusetts state legislature shared the outrage of the general public and saw the pressing need to protect children from further abuse. For the first time since 1997, the legislature amended its reporting statute to include clergy.[53] Mindful of the sanctity the religious practice of the Roman Catholic Church and the importance of religious autonomy, they were careful to preserve the confidentiality between Roman Catholic priests and penitents in the confessional, and excluded from the mandate information gained through confession in the confessional booth or in another area but clearly intended to be a personal confession.[54] Thus, the change in Massachusetts law requiring priests

---

[47] See Patricia A. Schene, *Past, Present and Future Roles of Child Protective Services*, 8 THE FUTURE OF CHILDREN 23, 29, citing the U.S. House of Representatives Committee on Ways and Means, *1996 Green Book: Background Material and Data on Programs within the Jurisdiction of the Committee on Ways and Means* 733 (U.S. Gov't Printing Office 1996).

[48] U.S. ADVISORY BOARD ON CHILD ABUSE & NEGLECT, OFFICE OF HUMAN DEVELOPMENT SERVICES, CRITICAL FIRST STEPS IN A NATIONAL EMERGENCY 2, 15 (1990).

[49] See Douglas Besharov, *The Legal Aspects of Reporting Known and Suspected Child Abuse and Neglect*, 23 VILL. L. REV. 458, 556–57 (1978). U.S. DEP'T OF HEALTH & HUMAN SERVICES, STUDY FINDINGS: NATIONAL STUDY OF INCIDENCE AND SEVERITY OF CHILD ABUSE AND NEGLECT 34 (DHHS 1981); Amy Buchele-Ash et al., *Forensic and Law Enforcement Issues in the Abuse and Neglect of Children with Disabilities*, 19 MENTAL & PHYSICAL DISABILITY L. REP. 115 (1995).

[50] Approximately 218 priests were reportedly removed in 2002, with another 34 known offenders remaining in active service. *See* Alan Cooperman & Lena H. Sun, *Survey Finds 218 Priests Have Been Removed This Year*, BOSTON GLOBE, June 9, 2002, at A1.

[51] *Id.*

[52] *See, e.g.*, Sacha Pfeiffer, *Memos Reveal Trail of Charges*, BOSTON GLOBE, June 5, 2002, at A16.   [53] MASS. GEN. LAWS ANN. ch. 119, § 51a (West 2002).

[54] For a discussion of the Massachusetts law as well as the issue of the clergy–penitent privilege, see R. Michael Cassidy, *Sharing Sacred Secrets: Is it (past) Time or a Dangerous Exception to the Clergy–Penitent Privilege?*, 44 WM. & MARY L. REV. 1627 (2003).

to reveal information not obtained in the confessional restricts the confidentiality between Roman Catholic priests and their parishioners that has traditionally applied to all communications. In so doing, the state may be seen as infringing upon the practices and traditions of the Church. However, in cases of child abuse, the state's compelling interest in protecting children outweighs certain constitutional guarantees.[55]

OTHER MODEL ACTS

During the 1960s and 1970s, when government intervened in the parent–child relationship such intrusion was often the result of a report of child abuse. Once the child was removed from her parent's control, she was often placed in foster care. In many instances, public social service agencies saw their job as having been completed since the child was now safe. Little thought was given to the ultimate disposition of the case. The reason was that there were so many cases that agencies were just not able to process all of them or even to keep track of where the child had been placed and the duration of the placement.

Out of the research that revealed the growing number of children in foster care and the lack of services provided for them came the Model Subsidized Adoption Act and the Model Act to Free Children for Permanent Placement.[56] To the question, why were so many children in foster care, one response that was often given was that the longer a child stayed in foster care, the more difficult it was to place him or her for adoption and those persons who might be willing to adopt the foster child were not financially able to adopt. Another response was that the children who might be able to be adopted were not legally free.

The Model Subsidized Adoption Act was designed to provide a financial benefit for children who were candidates for adoption but for whom adoptive parents could not be easily found. Usually such children, labeled children with special needs, were in foster care and were medically handicapped, had been abused or neglected and were physically and emotionally scarred, were part of a sibling group, were older children, perhaps from ages 6 to 12, or from an

---

[55] *See, e.g., City of Baltimore v. Bouknight*, 493 U.S. 549 (1990), where the U.S. Supreme Court upheld the state's overwhelming interest in protecting children over a mother's right to remain silent about the whereabouts of her child. In that case, the Court recognized that the state's interest in protecting children trumped the mother's Fifth Amendment right against self-incrimination.

[56] The number of children in foster care rose sharply after promulgation of the Model Child Abuse and Neglect Reporting Act, reaching 296,000 in 1966. By 1977 more than 500,000 children were living in foster care. The 1966 figures were found in DAVID FANSHEL & E. SHINN, CHILDREN IN FOSTER CARE 29 (1977). The 1977 figures were found in Ruth-Arlene W. Howe, *Development of a Model Act to Free Children for Permanent Placement: A Case Study in Law and Social Planning*, 13 FAM. L.Q. 257, 330 (1979).

ethnic group and difficult to place. The theory was that once these children were approved for a subsidy, they would become attractive candidates for adoptive parents. During the years that adoption subsidies have been made, there has been only marginal progress if any.

The Model Act to Free Children for Permanent Placement was meant to provide state legislatures with a model to replace their outdated termination of parental rights provisions. It had three goals: (1) to provide judicial procedures for freeing children for adoption or other placement by terminating parental rights; (2) to promote permanent placements of children freed from their parents; and (3) to insure that each party's constitutional rights and interests were protected.

Although state legislatures did not adopt the Model Act to Free Children for Permanent Placement as they did the Model Subsidized Adoption Act, the permanent placement model act along with social science research dealing with the idea of the need for permanency planning for children in foster care provoked the states and Congress to face the crisis in foster care. The Congress responded by enacting the Child Abuse Prevention and Treatment Act of 1974.

CHILD ABUSE PREVENTION AND TREATMENT ACT OF 1974

Under the leadership of the then Minnesota Senator Walter Mondale who would later become the U.S. Vice President, Congress held hearings on the plight of abused children. After the hearings he later wrote that he found the evidence of child abuse at his hearings to be 'horrifying'.[57] Through his efforts, Congress passed the Child Abuse Prevention and Treatment Act of 1974. The Child Abuse Prevention and Treatment Act of 1974 had two central elements (1) the establishment of a National Center on Child Abuse and Neglect; and (2) the establishment of minimum standards for state child protective systems. The National Center on Child Abuse and Neglect serves as a clearing house for information for developing and disseminating information about child protection research. In addition it provides funding for research, demonstration, training, and technical assistance for funded projects.[58]

---

[57] Walter Mondale, *Introductory Comments*, 54 CHI.-KENT L. REV. 535, 536 (1978).

[58] The Act also required individual states seeking to qualify for a grant offered through the Act to provide for the dissemination of information to the public regarding child abuse and neglect and available services, essentially creating individual state Centers on Child Abuse and Neglect, Pub. L. 93-247, at § 4(b)(2)(I). The Child Abuse Prevention and Treatment Act was amended in 1996. In order to receive federal funds for child abuse and neglect prevention and treatment programs, a state must submit to the federal government a plan that outlines the provisions and procedures for representation for the child (whether an attorney, a guardian ad litem, or a special child

In order for a state to acquire funding for its child protection programs, it had to comply with certain federal requirements. For example, the Act required that states 'provide for the reporting of known and suspected instances of child abuse and neglect', broadening in some states the types of abuse reported to include all forms of child maltreatment. The Act also required states to streamline their child protection system to conform to the federal government's model of what a proper system should include.

THE ADOPTION ASSISTANCE
AND CHILD WELFARE ACT OF 1980

Six years after the Child Abuse Prevention and Treatment Act of 1974 became a federal law, the U.S. Congress passed another child protection law with far-reaching consequences: The Adoption Assistance and Child Welfare Act of 1980. This Act was directed to once again get control of the continuing crisis in foster care. With all the federal intervention in the child protection field, with all its financial incentives to states to manage the problem of child abuse and neglect, still there were far too many children in foster care. The challenge that had to be met was to resolve the conflict that can arise between parental rights to rear their children and society's responsibility to care for children. How can these rights and responsibilities be balanced?

Once again the Act was a funding vehicle for states to obtain money for the structuring and implementing a foster care system according to the Act's requirements. The Act was concerned with family situations before a child enters the foster care system, the child's situation while in the foster care system, and the child's situation at the end of foster care. The Act attempted to improve these situations by providing for the following: (1) the provision of sufficient replacement services to families to prevent the need for children to enter the foster care system; (2) the protection and provision of services for children in the foster care system; and (3) the return of children to their homes or their placement in a permanent setting like adoption.

The most important aspect of the Act was its introduction of the concept of 'reasonable efforts'.[59] The Act required that social service agencies must make reasonable efforts to prevent a child from being removed from her parents, and

---

advocate) in child protection proceedings. *See* 42 U.S.C.A. § 5106a(b)(A)(ix) (West. Supp. 1999). For a discussion of the statutory basis for affording children some kind of representation in child protection proceedings and selected writings on the role of representation of children including passages from the Model Rules of Professional Conduct and the American Bar Association Standards of Practice for Lawyers Who Represent Children in Abuse and Neglect Cases, see ROBERT D. GOLDSTEIN, CHILD ABUSE AND NEGLECT—CASES AND MATERIALS 937–53 (1999).

[59] 42 U.S.C.A. § 671(a)(15).

if removed, the agency must make reasonable efforts to provide services to the parents and the child within a certain time-frame in order to facilitate the child's return to her family.

The reasonable efforts concept was designed to place an affirmative duty on the part of the agencies to try to rehabilitate those parents whose children had been removed from their care. The hope was that by providing parents with services (e.g. referral to drug and alcohol addiction programs) that the agency would pay for, and giving the parents a specific time (e.g. eighteen months) to become able to provide proper care for their child, family reunions could occur. In order to protect parents, the Act required that states have in place a procedure by which cases could be reviewed, either administratively or judicially, each six months. In this way, it was thought that families would not be lost in the bureaucracy of an agency. If, within the time-frame (e.g. eighteen months), a parent did not rehabilitate herself, then termination of parental rights would be appropriate.

ADOPTION AND SAFE FAMILIES ACT OF 1997

As a result of the shortcomings of the application of the 1980 Act, Congress updated it in 1997. Recognizing the reality that family reunification is not possible in many situations, Congress returned to the concept of the permanent placement of children that had been articulated and dealt with in the 1970s. To that end, the 1997 Adoption and Safe Families Act provides more specific definitions of 'reasonable efforts', including delineation of 'aggravating circumstances', which are so egregious that reasonable efforts to reunify need not be made. In such a case, the Act requires that the state hold a 'Permanency Hearing' within thirty days of the determination that such aggravating circumstances exist, where agency representatives are required to present a plan for the child's long-term placement. In addition, the Act includes requirements that a state move to terminate parental rights when a child has been in foster care for a given length of time (e.g. fifteen out of the last twenty-two months). This provision is designed to remedy the broad and various applications of the reasonable efforts standard of the 1980 Act by creating a specific timetable for parental rehabilitation. Further, the 1997 Act creates increased incentives for adoption and looks to adoption as a primary means of addressing the inadequacies of the foster care system. The great difficulty with quantifying periods for parental rehabilitation is that in the case of drug-addicted parents (a common ground for termination of parental rights), recovery may be difficult to assess. In addition, drug-addicted persons often experience a relapse and that event would, no doubt, extend the duration of rehabilitation. The emphasis on adoption as the solution for reducing the foster care population in the United States has met with both support and criticism. Basically the question is whether focusing on adoption as the answer to permanent placement takes into account serious mental health and social problems, like poverty, unemployment, and inadequate housing, that are associated with child neglect.[60]

CHILD PROTECTION PROCESS

The process by which a child protection case moves through the judicial system is designed to balance the interests of the child and the constitutional rights of parents. This balance is reflected in the procedure during each stage of the process from the decision to report child abuse, to the evidentiary issues during trial, and at the dispositional phase. For example, during the investigation phase of alleged abuse cases, some states require not only a decision by the child protection worker that the child is in danger, but also a court order before a child can be removed from parental custody.[61] Some states also have guidelines regulating the circumstances under which a child protection worker can interview an allegedly abused child, effectively preventing children from being interviewed at school without notice to the parents.[62] If the Department of Social Services finds evidence of abuse but the parents refuse to cooperate with it, then the court becomes involved through an adjudicatory hearing. The adjudicatory hearing requires the state to show, by a preponderance of the evidence or clear and convincing

---

[60] *See, e.g.*, ELIZABETH BARTHOLET, NOBODY'S CHILDREN: ABUSE AND NEGLECT, FOSTER DRIFT AND THE ADOPTION ALTERNATIVE (1999), where the author presents the case for adoption as the best means of providing permanent homes for children in the foster care system. Professor Bartholet suggests that through adoption, children in the foster care system can be given a new start in a permanent, loving home. Professor Martin Guggenheim, critical of that solution, argues that adoption is not the answer. In fact, he believes that adoption serves to aggravate some of the problems in the system. For example, Professor Guggenheim points out that an inordinate number of those children placed in foster care and ultimately relinquished for adoption come from economically disadvantaged homes. He suggests that, many times, state social workers mistakenly assess poverty as neglect. The result of this designation is the removal of a child from his family when the family is providing all they can within their means. He argues that this trend of removing children from their homes in an attempt to place them in a more advantaged setting results in disparate treatment of parents and children from poor communities, and many times results in unnecessary removal. *See* Martin Guggenheim, *Somebody's Children: Sustaining the Family's Place in Child Welfare Policy*, 113 HARV. L. REV. 1716 (2000). Professor Guggenheim has written about the consideration of child protection in the United States as a problem of parental failure, using the medical model to categorize issues. He suggests that classifying child protection in that way prevents an opportunity to examine the root causes of child maltreatment. *See* Martin Guggenheim, *Child Welfare Policy and Practice in the United States, in* CROSS CURRENTS, *supra* note 30, at 563–64.   [61] *See, e.g.*, IOWA CODE § 234 (2002).

[62] *See* DAVID HECKLER, THE BATTLE AND THE BACKLASH: THE CHILD SEXUAL ABUSE WAR (1988).

evidence, that its petition alleging child abuse or neglect should be sustained. These evidentiary standards serve to protect the rights of parents and other caretakers.[63] If the Department's petition is sustained, the case moves to the dispositional phase at which the court decides who should have custody of an abused child. In making that determination, the court considers the particular problems and needs facing the family at hand, and assesses the best interest of the child. Federal guidelines mandate that a state make reasonable efforts to prevent the removal of children from their families except in the most aggravated circumstances of abuse. The goal is to insure parental rights are respected, on the one hand, and the best interest of the child is served, on the other.[64]

If a child is not returned to his birth parents and termination of parental rights occurs, the dispositional alternatives are limited to either long-term foster care or adoption. Depending upon the age of the child, long-term foster care usually means that a child will be living with a foster family related (kinship placement) or unrelated to the child, group home, or orphanage until the child reaches the age of majority when he or she is no longer supported by government funds. Adoption is designed to provide the child with a permanent attachment. If the neglected child has been living with foster parents and the placement has been successful, those parents are ordinarily given priority in adopting the child if they so desire, and the child's best interests would be furthered. Subsidized adoption programs were designed to support that outcome.[65]

As one studies the role that government now plays in the area of child protection, one comes away with the observation that punishing one's own children, once a private family matter, if interpreted as abuse by neighbors, school personnel, or governmental officials can become a public matter. That is to say, when a parent strikes a child for being disobedient and the injury that the child sustains is seen by a third person (e.g. a school teacher or a school nurse) who thinks the injury requires medical attention, the result might be the reporting of the incident to a social service agency. In cases defined as serious by agency officials, the result may be for the parents and the child to become involved with child protection process. Such a process might conclude a court hearing and a disposition that may involve the child's removal from her home and her placement with foster parents.

I have attempted to review federal legislation in child protection because the federal government has really been the impetus for states to reform its child protection laws and procedures. Now I wish to turn to a famous case, which tested the state's responsibility to children.

[63] *See, e.g.,* In re Juvenile Appeal, 189 Conn. 276 (1983); In re Adoption of K.L.P., 735 N.E.2d 1071 (2000).
[64] *See* discussion of Adoption and Safe Families Act in this chapter.
[65] *See* discussion of Subsidized Adoption Act in this chapter.

DeShaney v. Winnebago County Department of Social Services

When Joshua DeShaney was 1-year-old, his parents divorced in the State of Wyoming, and his father, Randy, was awarded custody of him. Shortly thereafter Randy DeShaney and his son moved to Winnebago County, Wisconsin. Randy remarried and soon after was divorced again. About two years after Randy had moved to Wisconsin, the Winnebago County Department of Social Services learned that Joshua might be experiencing abuse. Randy denied any abusive conduct and the department did not pursue the matter.

About one year later, Joshua was admitted to a local hospital because of his having multiple bruises and abrasions. The examining physician suspected that Joshua had been abused and notified the department. After investigating the matter, the department sought legal action by placing the child in the temporary custody of the hospital. During this time the department entered into a voluntary agreement with Randy to enroll Joshua in a preschool program, seek counseling, and to have his girlfriend move out of his house. Randy agreed and the court dismissed the child protection case and returned Joshua to his father's custody.

One month later Randy was again seen in the emergency room of a hospital, and again the medical personnel reported Randy's injuries to the department. With this evidence, the caseworker decided that no action needed to be taken. However, for the next six months the caseworker visited Joshua in his home. Randy had not enrolled Joshua in the school program and he had not asked his girlfriend to leave the house. In addition, the caseworker noticed bruises on Joshua. The caseworker recorded all of this in Joshua's file and took no action. In the same year, Joshua was once again treated in the emergency room of the local hospital. The caseworker took no action. Nor did she take any action when she was not allowed to visit Joshua in his home because she was told that he was too ill.

Four months later, Joshua was admitted to the hospital because Randy had beaten him so badly that he suffered hemorrhages in his brain. Joshua survived brain surgery but suffered so much brain damage that he had to be confined to an institution for profoundly retarded children. Joshua's father was tried and convicted of child abuse.

The criminal action that the state brought against Randy DeShaney and that resulted in his conviction amounts to a certain kind of justice. Joshua's father was punished for the monstrous abusive acts he committed on his child. But the more important question concerns the liability of the state department of social services. Under the common law a parent has a positive duty to care for his child. If the state stands in the shoes of the parent, does the state have a positive duty to protect children?

In *DeShaney v. Winnebago County Department of Social Services*,[66] Chief Justice Rehnquist, writing for the majority of the U.S. Supreme Court held that

---

[66] 489 U.S. 189 (1989). *DeShaney* has been commented upon widely. Mostly the academic response has been critical. For a full discussion of *DeShaney*, see Aviam Soifer,

it did not. The case arose when Joshua and his mother brought an action under the federal civil rights act against the Winnebago County Department of Social Services in which they claimed that the department through its employees had deprived Joshua of his liberty without due process of law, in violation of his rights under the Fourteenth Amendment, by failing to actively prevent Joshua from harm from his father. Joshua and his mother claimed that the department knew or should have known that while in his father's care, Joshua was at an enormous risk of being abused.

Specifically, the Court, held that the State of Wisconsin could not be liable under the Federal Civil Rights Act[67] because the conduct of the state social worker and any other state employees involved in making decisions about Joshua was not considered 'state' action (the Fourteenth Amendment to the U.S. Constitution covers state, not private, actions). Because Joshua was injured by his father (in whose custody he had been placed), a private actor, and not by any state worker, Joshua's rights under the Constitution or federal law had not been violated, Chief Justice Rehnquist wrote:

nothing in the language of the Due Process Clause itself requires the State to protect the life, liberty, and property of its citizens against invasion by private actors. The Clause is phrased as a limitation on the State's powers to act, not as a guarantee of certain minimal levels of safety and security."[68]

Chief Justice Rehnquist would not interpret that clause to impose an affirmative obligation on the state to protect Joshua.

Justices Brennan, Marshall, and Blackmun dissented in the case. Justice Brennan stated that the state agency's actions were not merely passive but active state intervention. He thought that with such active intervention came a duty to protect Joshua.

The case is important in that it is an example of the Court's unwillingness to constitutionalize a tort. One can see the economic consequences of the case if Joshua and his mother had won. If state social service agencies were to be held financially liable for the negligence of its caseworkers and supervisors, the federal courts would be inundated with cases, and the federal courts would be placed in a position of trying to second guess decisions reached by social workers. And, it is probably safe to say that the budgets for state social service agencies would have to take into account the contingencies of lawsuits. States would probably have to become self-insurers as they normally do when they have to pay victims of the brutality of the police, prison guards, and state mental health caretakers—all state actors. Chief Justice Rehnquist stated that if states do want to make themselves liable for the negligence of its state employees that is up to the states, not the U.S. Supreme Court.

Moral Ambition, Formalism, and the 'Free World' of DeShaney, 57 GEO. WASH. L. REV. 1513 (1989).

[67] 42 U.S.C.A. § 1983.   [68] 489 U.S. at 196.

Following *DeShaney*

The Court's holding in *DeShaney* gave rise to several questions about the nature of the relationship between the state and those providing care for children. In particular, when is a state or its agents liable for violations of civil rights stemming from abuse that occurs after the state has placed a child in foster care? The answer is not clear. In *Taylor v. Ledbetter*,[69] the 11th Circuit Court of Appeals held that a child in state custody has liberty interests guaranteed by the Fourteenth Amendment, which include reasonably safe living conditions, and that if foster parents with whom the state has placed a child injure the child, a deprivation of liberty caused by the state's action or inaction may be shown. However, the same court in *Rayburn v. Hogue*,[70] held that foster parents were not state actors, and that consequently parents whose children had been abused in foster care could not recover damages. In 1990 the 7th Circuit Court of Appeals held in *K.H. v. Morgan*[71] that state workers who removed a child from her natural parents and placed her in a foster home where she was subsequently abused would only be liable if the state agency had, without due consideration or justification, placed the child in hands they knew to be dangerous or unfit.

A similar question exists regarding the liability of the state or its agents where the state removed a child from the home of one parent and placed the child with the other parent, and that parent harmed or killed the child. In 1990, the 4th Circuit Court of Appeals found in *Weller v. City of Baltimore*[72] that *DeShaney* prevented recovery where a father voluntarily surrendered his son to DSS who then placed the child with the mother, who subsequently abused the child. However, in 1995, a U.S. District Court in Pennsylvania distinguished *DeShaney* from a situation where the state has created the danger. In *Ford v. Johnson*,[73] the court held that where the state had taken custody of a child and then returned the child to her abusive father who beat the child to death, no special relationship existed between the state and the child so as to allow relief under *DeShaney*. However, the court found liability for violations of the child's due process rights on the theory that the abuse was the result of a state-created danger. Similarly, in 1998, a U.S. District Court for New Mexico held in *Currier v. Doran*[74] that where the state removed a child from his mother's custody and placed the child with the father who then killed him by scalding him with boiling water, the fact that the child was not in state custody at the time of his death did not preclude liability because the state had a duty not to consign the child to another dangerous situation.

With the enormous power of government to intervene in the parent–child relationship, one can ask if the state has any accompanying responsibilities.

---

[69] 791 F.2d 881 (11th Cir. 1986), *aff'd in part, rev'd in part on reh'g*, 818 F.2d 791 (11th Cir. 1987) (en banc), *cert. denied*, 489 U.S. 1065 (1989).
[70] 241 F.3d 1341 (2001).   [71] 914 F.2d 846 (1990).   [72] 901 F.2d 387 (1990).
[73] 899 F. Supp. 227 (1995).   [74] 23 F. Supp.2d 1277 (1998).

Federal mandates have made state agencies more cognizant of the need to try to keep families together and if separated, the need to reunify them. The courts have underscored the need for social service agencies to provide services. But when the ultimate test came to decide the liability of a state social service agency that failed every test of good social work practice, the U.S. Supreme Court got the state agency off the hook. The U.S. Supreme Court decided *DeShaney* by interpreting the U.S. Constitution narrowly and by distinguishing away cases that were relevant by their specific facts. The hairline distinction between a child's being in the custody of his father and not the state, even though the state social worker intervened in the relationship by visiting the home, meant the difference between abdication of responsibility and responsibility itself.[75] One is left with the feeling that the historic concept of *parens patriae* in contemporary child protection law may be pure rhetoric.

[75] Chief Justice Rehnquist wrote in a footnote in *DeShaney*: 'Had the State by the affirmative exercise of its power removed Joshua from free society and placed him in a foster home operated by its agents, we might have a situation sufficiently analogous to incarceration or institutionalization to give rise to an affirmative duty to protect.' 489 U.S. at 201.

5

Adoption

INTRODUCTION

In 1972 the U.S Supreme Court set in motion the first fundamental change in American adoption laws in many decades. Ironically, this transformation occurred in a passing reference in a footnote in a dependency case.[1] In that footnote, the Court mentioned that an unwed father should be afforded notice and an opportunity to be heard in his illegitimate children's custody or adoption proceeding. By including adoption in the sentence, it overturned long-standing adoption law, which did not require the consent of a father if his illegitimate child was to be adopted, nor entitle him to notice of the proceeding.

That the U.S. Supreme Court should have referred to adoption procedure so casually in a case not concerned with adoption was unusual. The Court may not have realized that the immediate effect of a footnote in its opinion could delay adoptions in Illinois and prompt every state legislature to revise its adoption statute, to provide some kind of notice—personal service or service by publication—to putative fathers who had met certain requirements like registering with a state agency. In addition, it forced every adoption agency to set new policies and procedures regarding their participation in the adoption process where they previously had been invisible or only shadow figures.[2]

The Supreme Court's decision in *Stanley v. Illinois* illustrates how modern adoption law has been influenced by the Court's expansion of the protection of

---

[1] In *Stanley v. Illinois*, 405 U.S. 645 (1972), the U.S. Supreme Court held that excluding a father from a dependency proceeding that would make state wards of his illegitimate children who lived with him deprived him of the equal protection of the laws guaranteed under the Due Process Clause of the U.S. Constitution. Footnote 9 read:

> We note in passing that the incremental cost of offering unwed fathers an opportunity for individualized hearings on fitness appears to be minimal. If unwed fathers, in the main, do not care about the disposition of their children, they will not appear to demand hearings. If they do care, under the scheme here held invalid, Illinois would admittedly at some later time have to afford them a properly focused hearing in a custody or *adoption* proceeding.
>
> Extending opportunity for hearing to unwed fathers who desire and claim competence to care for their children creates no constitutional or procedural obstacle to foreclosing those unwed fathers who are not so inclined.

Id. at 657 (emphasis added).

[2] Professor Jerome A. Barron was the first constitutional law scholar to recognize the difficulties raised by the ambiguities in footnote 9 in *Stanley*. The questions he asked about implementing the Court's comments, for example, whether notice had to be given to all

individual rights during the civil rights movement of the 1960s and 1970s.[3] Since then, instead of a social issue having an impact on adoption, adoption, itself, has been used to promote social goals like racial assimilation or integration or even for recognizing the changes in the composition of some American families.[4]

unwed fathers or only those, like Mr. Stanley, who had 'sired and raised' his children, are still not completely and clearly answered by state case law and statutes. *See* Jerome A. Barron, *Notice to the Unwed Father and Termination of Parental Rights: Implementing* Stanley v. Illinois, 9 FAM. L.Q. 527 (1975); *see also* Joan Heifetz Hollinger, *Consent to Adoption, in* 1 ADOPTION LAW AND PRACTICE § 2.1–2.12 (Joan Heifetz Hollinger & Dennis W. Leski eds., 1998).

In order to bring some uniformity to the issue of notification of a putative father in an adoption case, the Commissioners on Uniform State Laws promulgated the Uniform Parentage Act. That Act requires service by publication or posting only where the court finds that such service would be likely to lead to the identification of the father. See Uniform Parentage Act § 24 in the Appendix.

In 1988 the Commissioners promulgated the Uniform Putative and Unknown Fathers Act. The Commissioners recommended that the UPUFA should be enacted to replace the UPA or in addition to UPA. The questions the Act was designed to cover are: notice, visitation, custody and termination of parental rights in connection with adoption and other proceedings. The Act contains notice provisions §§ 3(a) and (g) and 4(a) are meant to give guidance in implementing *Stanley*. *See* Uniform Putative and Unknown Fathers Act in the Appendix.

Some states have enacted laws that establish putative father registries. Under those laws, notice must be given to men who register as fathers of particular children. The Uniform Putative and Unknown Fathers Act does not include a provision for such registries. In its Comment to § 3 dealing with notice, the Commissioners stated:

> The Act does not include a putative fathers registry requirement for, essentially three reasons: (1) while 'ignorance of the law is no excuse,' most fathers or potential fathers—even very responsible ones—are not likely to know about the registry as a means of protecting their rights . . . (2) individual state registries do not protect responsible fathers in interstate situations; and (3) since registries rely on unsupported claims, their accuracy is in doubt and their potential for an invasion of privacy and for interference with matters of adoption, custody, and visitation is substantial. . . .

Comments to § 3, at 16.

---

[3] After *Stanley*, the U.S. Supreme Court decided a number of cases that concerned illegitimate children and the rights of unwed fathers. *See, e.g.*, Lehr v. Robertson, 463 U.S. 248 (1983), holding that a statute which requires that putative fathers, and other possible classes of fathers who have acknowledged a relationship to their illegitimate child, be provided advance notice of the adoption proceeding of their illegitimate child, but fails to notify fathers who made no such efforts, is consistent with both the Due Process and Equal Protection Clauses; Quilloin v. Walcott, 434 U.S. 246 (1978), holding that a state statute recognizing the biological mother as the only parent, unless the father legitimates the child and granting her exclusive authority to consent to adoption of an illegitimate child, to be consistent with the Due Process and Equal Protection Clauses; Caban v. Mohammed, 441 U.S. 380 (1979), holding that a statute that enables only an unwed mother, and not the unwed father who had a relationship with his child, to prevent the adoption of her illegitimate child by withholding consent, violates the Equal Protection Clause; Lalli v. Lalli, 430 U.S. 762 (1977), holding that a probate court statute that allows illegitimate children to inherit by intestate succession only from their mothers, and not their fathers, violates the Equal Protection Clause.

[4] *See* note 37 *infra* and accompanying text.

This was not always the case. In mid-century, through placement standards that were designed to match a child's physical characteristics and ethnic background with those of his or her adopted parents, adoption was meant to create a traditional nuclear family that looked natural. Once adoption was finalized the child's past history was often literally eradicated by changes in the birth certificate. By keeping secret the child's previous life and terminating the child's relationship with his or her birth parents for almost all purposes, adoption created a legal fiction. Until about 1960, to mention that a person had been adopted was taboo.

During the twentieth century, adoption has been a specialized child welfare service performed by social workers in private and public child welfare agencies. Whether a birth mother relinquishes her infant for adoption voluntarily or whether adoption is the final outcome of a child dependency proceeding, the articulated goal sometimes achieved and sometimes mere rhetoric, is to advance the best interests of the child. In the former case, court involvement occurs as the last judicial act (ordinarily in a judge's chambers) of formally approving the adoption and issuing an adoption decree. In the latter, it is a disposition, often at a separate proceeding, for example, a waiver of consent hearing, following the involuntary termination of parental rights because of parental abuse or neglect.

These two tracks—voluntary relinquishment and involuntary termination of parental rights—resulting in adoption have given rise to dual systems in the past forty years. For the most part, one system—voluntary relinquishment—is consensual and private, involving non-governmental, non-profit or profit-making agencies, or individuals;[5] the other system—involuntary termination of parental rights—is non-consensual and public, involving state agencies with major funds provided for foster care and adoption programs by the federal government. Even though the ultimate outcome of adoption for children from either system may be the same in terms of a court establishing the adoptive status, there is a major difference in goals. The goal of the voluntary system may well be to provide a childless couple with an infant so as to continue the adoptive family name. The aim of dependency proceedings resulting in the termination of parental rights is to protect children, and the disposition of adoption is a vehicle for providing a child with a permanent attachment to a family.

A social class distinction tends to exist between the participants in the two systems. Infants voluntarily relinquished by their birth mothers and placed with adoptive parents tend to move into the middle class of which their new parents are a part. Children who are the subject of termination proceedings tend to be the offspring of poor parents from deprived backgrounds whom the state claims have neglected[6] or abandoned them, or from parents who have been judicially declared

---

[5] Some state social service agencies also include adoption among their services. Some enter into contracts with private child welfare agencies to provide adoption services. Private agencies, some of which have a religious affiliation, receive funds from individual donors, private foundations, community charities, and through fees for services.

[6] The definition of 'neglect' varies greatly and usually means that the parent has failed to protect her child. *See* Sanford N. Katz, Ruth-Arlene W. Howe & Melba McGrath,

unfit because of abuse, alcoholism, drug addiction, or serious and chronic mental illness. For the most part, couples who adopt these children are their foster parents. In some instances, however, the children are placed with relatives (kinship adoption) or under certain circumstances with middle-class couples or individuals.

Although there have been two major efforts to enact a uniform adoption law, they have been unsuccessful.[7] Perhaps the reason for this may be that adoption laws reflect local practice and policies. It also may be an area of family law where it is difficult to reach a consensus because of conflicting interests of the participants in the adoption process.[8] Thus, to understand adoption in the

Child Neglect Laws in America, 9 FAM. L.Q. 1 (1975). There can be social neglect, defined as society's (or a community's) failure to respond to the needs of poor families. Social neglect is not found in state statutes. To what extent there is social responsibility for caring for the poor is, of course, a question that has been around for many decades. In contemporary times it is usually raised during years close to elections both on the state and national level.

The announcement of a policy about homeless people in New York City illustrates how the status of being poor can be used to define 'neglect'. On December 4, 1999, the New York Times reported that the Commissioner of Welfare for the City of New York warned all homeless families that they were subject to having their children removed from their care for neglect if they failed to work or meet shelter and welfare requirements. The Commissioner apparently qualified his threat by saying that there would, of course, be a judicial hearing, presumably after an emergency removal and temporary foster care placement for the children had occurred. *See* Nina Bernstein, *City May Remove Children from Families in Shelters*, N.Y. TIMES, December 4, 1999, at A13.

On December 9, 1999, the New York Times reported that the previous day, a state court had temporarily halted the plan to place the children of homeless parents who refused to work or failed to meet welfare requirements in foster care. *See* Nina Bernstein, *Work-for-Shelter Requirement is Delayed by New York Judges*, N.Y. TIMES, December 9, 1999, at A1.

[7] In 1953 the Commissioners on Uniform State Laws promulgated the first Uniform Adoption Act. Alaska (1974), Arkansas (1977), Montana (1957), North Dakota (1971), and Ohio (1976) enacted parts of the 1969 Revised Uniform Adoption Act. In 1994 the Commissioners on Uniform State Laws approved a new Uniform Adoption Act. Two years later, Vermont enacted it, and as of 2002 remains the only state that has done so. The Revised Uniform Adoption Act (1969) can be found in 9 U.L.A. (Part I) 15–78 (1988). The 1994 Uniform Adoption Act can be found in 9 U.L.A. Part I (West Supp. 1999).

[8] One illustration of the difficulty of drafting a model state adoption act is evidenced by the actions of the Family Law Section of the American Bar Association, the largest organization of family law lawyers in America. From 1981 to 1985, the Section attempted to reach a consensus among its members so that it could draft an act that would be acceptable to lawyers. One of the major issues of contention was the extent to which adoption agencies would control the placement of children. The model act that was eventually drafted was not enacted in any state. For two views on the Act, *see* William M. Schur, *The ABA Model State Adoption Act: Observations from an Agency Perspective*, 19 FAM. L.Q. 131 (1985) and David Keene Leavitt, *The Model Adoption Act: Return to a Balanced View of Adoption*, 19 FAM. L.Q. 141 (1985).

United States, it is important to realize that there are fifty-one adoption laws, one in each American state and the District of Columbia.

This chapter will be divided into two major parts: adoption resulting from the voluntary placement of infants by the birth mother, which I shall label 'Voluntary System', and adoption as the judicial disposition following the termination of parental rights, which I shall call 'Involuntary System'. The unifying theme in this chapter will be an examination of the recurring tension between individual autonomy and state regulation in the placement of children for adoption, and how it is reflected in the major developments in adoption in the past half century.

VOLUNTARY SYSTEM

The Role of Personal Autonomy

In 1851 Massachusetts enacted the first American adoption statute, which required a public judicial process for conferring the status of adoption on a child.[9] Before then, adoption in the United States was created by a contract or deed or in some states by a private statute.[10] By regulating adoption, the Massachusetts Act eliminated a parent's unrestricted power to contract away her parental rights or transfer them to others through a deed. It required the consents of the immediate parties to the adoption. In addition, a court had to consider the welfare of the child and the qualifications of the adopters before it approved an adoption and issued an adoption decree.[11] The result was that

---

[9] *See* Massachusetts Adoption of Children's Act of 1851, 1851 Mass. Acts, ch. 324 (May 24, 1851).

[10] Since there was no common law of adoption, a state statute was required to establish the status. The closest analogy to a common law of adoption is 'equitable adoption'. Equitable adoption is a term used in probate proceedings to describe a relationship between an adult and a child who was not formally adopted by the adult but who lived in a de facto parent–child relationship with him or her for an extended period of time. Because the child was neither the biological nor legally adopted child of the adult, the child would not qualify as an heir. In some states, however, where a decedent dies intestate, a probate judge will allow the child to inherit from the de facto parent, but rarely through the parent. This can occur if the judge finds that there is sufficient evidence, usually 'clear and convincing', to show that the decedent promised to adopt the child or was in the process of adopting the child but never completed all the formalities. For a comprehensive analysis of the history of adoption laws in the United States, see Joan Heifetz Hollinger, *Introduction to Adoption Law and Practice, in* 1 ADOPTION LAW AND PRACTICE, *supra* note 2, at § 1.01–1.06; *see also* 2 ANN M. HARALAMBIE, HANDLING CHILD CUSTODY, ABUSE AND ADOPTION CASES § 14 (1993).

[11] Five years after the Massachusetts Adoption Act was enacted, the Massachusetts Supreme Judicial Court reflected this approach when it wrote that '[adoption] is not a question of mere property, . . . the interests of the minor is the principal thing to be considered'. Curtis v. Curtis, 71 Mass. (5 Gray) 535, 537 (1856).

Massachusetts limited the personal autonomy of birth parents and prevented them from exploiting their children for economic gain.

For nearly one hundred and fifty years, a major question in adoption has been: when a birth mother voluntarily relinquishes her infant, how much decision-making power can she reserve, and at what stage in a state-regulated system of adoption may she exercise it? May she decide herself, or delegate to another, who can adopt her child? Once her consent is given, even though voluntarily, can she revoke it? May she maintain a connection with her child by requiring that she be given post-adoption visitation rights? Years after an adoption decree has been issued, may she have access to adoption records and locate her child? Answers to these questions not only measure the amount of personal autonomy with which the state endows birth parents, but also reflect society's concept of adoption.

Independent and Agency Adoptions

Allowing a birth parent to place a child directly with adoptive parents or to delegate that power to another, such as a lawyer, physician, or clergyman has been called 'independent' or 'private' adoption. Requiring her to relinquish her rights to a public or private child welfare agency for placement has been labeled 'agency adoption'.[12] Most American jurisdictions permit private adoption. Only four restrict placement to agencies in non-relative adoptions.[13] Preference for private adoption over agency adoption reveals a general bias toward market mechanisms in American society. It also can be seen as anti-regulation or anti-governmental intervention, even though in all American jurisdictions,

[12] For a discussion of research that inquired into the risks of independent adoptions, see WILLIAM MEEZAN, SANFORD N. KATZ & EVA MANOFF RUSSO, ADOPTIONS WITHOUT AGENCIES—A STUDY OF INDEPENDENT ADOPTIONS (1978). For an attorney's perspective, see Jed Somit, *Independent Adoptions in California: Dual Representation Allowed, in* 1 ADOPTION LAW AND PRACTICE, *supra* note 2, at § 5.01–.04.

[13] As of 2002, these four are: Colorado: COLO. REV. STAT. §§ 19-5-204(2), 19-5-206 (West 1999); Connecticut: CONN. GEN. STAT. ANN. §§ 45–63(3), -69(d) (West 1993); Delaware: DEL. CODE ANN. tit. 13, § 904 (Michie 1993); and Massachusetts: MASS. ANN. LAWS ch. 210, § 2A (1994). The Massachusetts provision reads:

> No decree of adoption shall be entered for the adoption of a child below the age of fourteen until one of the following conditions has been met:
> (A) The child sought to be adopted has been placed with the petitioners for adoption by the department of social services or by an agency authorized by said department for such purpose, . . .

Massachusetts allows the direct placement of a child with a blood relative, step-parent, or with the petitioner if that person was nominated as a guardian or adoptive parent in the will of the child's deceased birth parent.

In addition, Kentucky requires the permission of the state Department of Human Resources for non-relative adoption (Ky. Rev. Stat. Ann. § 199.473); Minnesota requires an agency for non-relative adoption, but the court may waive this requirement if it is in the best interest of the child (Minn. Stat. Ann. § 259.22); Wisconsin permits non-relative placement only in a state licensed foster home (Wis. Stat. Ann. § 48.62).

adoption must ultimately be state sanctioned by judicial approval. Private adoption can also be viewed purely as a preference for preserving individual autonomy and the state's reluctance to restrict parental choice.

In reality, the forces that have been successful in promoting private adoption are individuals and groups, especially the adoption bar, whose focus is on locating a child for parents rather than finding parents for a child, resulting in a primary concern for birth mothers and adoptive parents.[14] They argue that a birth mother should be free to place her child with whomever she wants, and for whatever reason she chooses.[15] Indeed, such an approach might be similar to the unregulated sale of human organs.[16] In the past thirty years, an adoption industry has developed. The private placement of children has taken on the characteristics of a business, basically trading in children,[17] even though the sale

---

[14] Jed Somit has written:

Various reasons are postulated for the comparative popularity of independent adoption:

- less bureaucratic involvement in the placement process;
- the birth mother's ability to select the adopting parent or parents;
- the expertise developed by attorneys in 'networking,' 'outreach' or otherwise marketing their adoption practice and their clients;
- the perceived relative generosity of support payments made in an independent adoption; and
- the greater freedom to structure the adoption to meet the needs and demands of each particular birth mother.

. . .

Independent adoption . . . allows the most flexibility in making arrangements (within legal limits) for financial support of the birth mother, for the prospective adoptive parents and the birth mother to form a relationship before the birth of the child, and for the parents to discuss their relationship after the birth. The birth mother's sense of having some control of her child's, and her own destiny may help in her forming a commitment to the adoption, and later in dealing with the loss that is inevitable when placing a child.

Jed Somit, *Independent Adoptions in California: Dual Representation Allowed, in* 1 ADOPTION LAW AND PRACTICE, *supra* note 2, at § 5.01[1]5–7, 8; [2] 5–9.

[15] It is unclear whether it is a birth mother who is really placing an infant for adoption or the person to whom she has delegated that power, e.g., a lawyer, physician, or clergyman.

[16] *See* David E. Jefferies, *The Body as Commodity: The Use of Markets to Cure the Organ Deficit*, 5 IND. J. GLOBAL LEGAL STUD. 621 (1998); William Boulier, *Sperm, Spleens, and Other Valuables: The Need to Recognize Property Rights in Human Body Parts*, 23 HOFSTRA L. REV. 693 (1995).

[17] 'Making money from adoptive placements, while at odds with the idealized image of adoption as an altruistic service, is not inherently evil. Reputable adoption agencies, attorneys, and psychologists do this daily, with beneficial effects on adoption placements.' Somit, *supra* note 14, at § 5.02[4]5–17; *see also* Tamar Frankel & Frances Miller, *The Inapplicability of Market Theory to Adoptions*, 67 B.U. L. REV. 99 (1987); Richard A. Posner, *The Regulation of the Market in Adoptions*, 67 B. U. L. REV. 59 (1987); RICHARD A. POSNER, ECONOMIC ANALYSIS OF LAW 139–44 (3d ed. 1986); Elizabeth M. Landes & Richard A. Posner, *The Economics of the Baby Shortage*, 7 J. LEGAL STUDIES 323 (1978); *but see* J. Robert S. Prichard, *A Market for Babies*, 34 U. TORONTO L.J. 341 (1984).

of children is prohibited, and state statutes limit fees relating to adoption to administrative costs and are often monitored by the courts. Yet questions have been raised about whether such limitations are effective given the broad definition of administrative costs.

Restricting the placement of children to licensed private or public adoption agencies is thought to lessen the risks of flawed placements. Nationally accredited agencies, staffed with experienced and knowledgeable social workers are able and equipped to screen applicants, and after the completion of a home study, select the most appropriate adoptive couple for the child. It would be unusual for a lawyer, physician, or clergyman to have the same kind of education, skill, and experience as adoption agency social workers who historically have held graduate degrees in social work. Since an agency must be licensed by the state in which it is located, it must conform to state regulations and periodic monitoring. If the monitoring is effective, it would be the vehicle to assure placement decisions advance a child's welfare rather than the special interests of other participants, like the birth mother or the adoptive couple.

The advantages of the involvement of reputable agencies in the adoption process also relate to their administrative structure with a built-in system of accountability and to their delivery of services, both missing in private placements. Agencies keep records. They also have internal procedures whereby placement decisions can be reviewed. Agencies provide social and psychological services to a birth mother (and father if he is identified and involved in the mother's life) in counseling her about her decision to relinquish her child and to prospective adoptive parents in their decisions about undertaking adoption as a way of having a family. They are available for post-adoption services to all the participants, including the child. This aspect of adoption services is particularly important if and when the birth parents and adopted child seek information about each other.

However, agencies have been criticized for not being creative in developing strategies to reach minority couples as prospective adoptive parents, for being too rigid in their placement requirements, following only certain theories about child development, or for being less than candid about the social and psychological history of a birth mother or a child. In addition, it has been said that if agencies alone are permitted to place children, a monopoly will be created with the result that they will be overburdened and unable to provide adequate services.[18] Whether an adoption is ultimately more successful if arranged through an agency or privately has not been proven. Success is difficult to define and to measure.

There is also the matter of the legal responsibility for adoption placement. Wrongful adoption is a cause of action first recognized in Ohio in 1986,[19]

---

[18] *See* MEEZAN ET AL., *supra* note 12, at 232–33.

[19] *See* Burr v. Board of County Comm'rs, 491 N.E.2d 1101 (Ohio 1986). Breach of contract has also been argued in cases in which adoptive parents have alleged that by not disclosing information about the child, the agency had failed to fulfill its side of the adoption placement agreement. Breach of contract actions brought against agencies

which extended the common law torts of negligence, fraud, and misrepresentation to adoption. It arises from an agency's failure to fulfill its duty to disclose facts about a child's past history, including genetic information, which would have affected the child's placement. While the tort would also be applicable to a private placement, the likelihood of actually recovering compensatory damages to cover present and future medical bills from a birth mother or a third party compared with a licensed and insured private or public agency would seem remote.

Surrogacy

The complex interplay between private autonomy and regulation was placed in a new perspective in the 1980s with the phenomenon of surrogate motherhood. When *In re Baby M*,[20] the first nationally publicized surrogacy case, was decided in New Jersey in 1988, there was no single legal model to which a court could turn to resolve the conflict resulting from this new method of family formation. Because of the relationship of the three adult parties to each other and to the child in that case and because of the nature of the transaction the parties chose, surrogacy concerned the common law of contracts and statutes relating to adoption, paternity, and termination of parental rights. As surrogacy became less of a novelty during the 1990s, the question of whether, like adoption, it should be regulated by the state was raised. States have taken a variety of approaches regarding both the process of entering into a surrogacy arrangement and the enforcement of the surrogacy contract.[21]

It is difficult to determine how extensive a formal (with a written contract) or informal (without any contract) surrogacy arrangement is used as a substitute for adoption since national statistics are unavailable. Surrogacy laws are in flux. Some state legislatures have declared surrogacy contracts valid if the surrogate is not compensated; some declare them void, even making it a crime to enter into an agreement or brokering one. A few states require the intended mother to be infertile. At least two states require judicial approval of a surrogacy agreement in advance of performance.[22] An aim of many of the state statutes is the prevention, by way of an imposition of civil or criminal penalties, of selling

---

have been less successful than tort actions. For a full discussion of the tort of wrongful adoption and other possible remedies for misrepresentation in adoption placement, see D. Marianne Blair, *Liability of Adoption Agencies and Attorneys for Misconduct in the Disclosure of Health-Related Information, in* 2 ADOPTION LAW AND PRACTICE § 16.01–08 (Joan Heifetz Hollinger & Dennis W. Leski eds., 1998).

[20] 537 A.2d 1227 (N.J. 1988).

[21] For a full discussion of the statutory provisions regulating surrogacy, see IRA MARK ELLMAN, PAUL M. KURTZ & ELIZABETH S. SCOTT, FAMILY LAW—CASES, TEXT, PROBLEMS 1498–1500 (3rd ed. 1998).

[22] *See* N.H. REV. STATE. ANN. §§ 168-B:1 to B:32 (1994 & Supp. 1996) and VA. CODE ANN. § 20–156 et seq. (Michie 1995).

babies born to a surrogate through a surrogacy arrangement. The Uniform Status of Children of Assisted Conception Act, promulgated by the National Conference of Commissioners on Uniform State Laws in 1988, has provided states with guidance in the legislative regulation of surrogacy, even with a provision, proposed as Alternative B, making surrogacy agreements void.[23]

A host of problems have developed from surrogacy agreements, which include determining who the legal parents are and issues regarding the timing of consent.[24] For example, in *R.R. v. M.H.*,[25] the Supreme Judicial Court of Massachusetts, applying the time-frame concerning consent (consent can be given on the fourth calendar day after the date of birth of the child to be adopted) from the Massachusetts adoption statute[26] held that the provision in the surrogacy agreement regarding the mother's promise to surrender her baby before the infant was four days old, was unenforceable.

Because a surrogacy agreement concerns the custody of an infant, the Massachusetts court went on to say that enforcement of such an agreement must be determined by the application of best interests of the child test. The

---

[23] The Uniform Status of Children of Assisted Conception Act, Alternative B, Section 5 reads as follows:

> Section 5. Surrogate Agreements. An agreement in which a woman agrees to become a surrogate or to relinquish her rights and duties as parent of a child thereafter conceived through assisted conception is void. However, she is the mother of a resulting child, and her husband, if a party to the agreement, is the father of the child. If her husband is not a party to the agreement or the surrogate is unmarried, paternity of the child is governed by [the Uniform Parentage Act].

[24] The Uniform Status of Children of Assisted Conception Act takes the following position on these issues:

> Section 2. Maternity. [Except as provided in Sections 5 through 9,] a woman who gives birth to a child is the child's mother.
>
> Section 3. Assisted conception by married woman. [Except as provided in Sections 5 through 9,] the husband of a woman who bears a child through assisted conception is the father of the child, notwithstanding a declaration of invalidity or annulment of the marriage obtained after the assisted conception, unless within two years after learning of the child's birth he commences an action in which the mother and child are parties and in which it is determined that he did not consent to the assisted conception.
>
> Section 4. Parental status of donors and deceased individuals. [Except as otherwise provided in Sections 5 through 9:]
> (a) A donor is not a parent of a child conceived through assisted conception.
> (b) An individual who dies before implantation of an embryo, or before a child is conceived other than through sexual intercourse, using the individual's egg or sperm, is not a parent of the resulting child.

[25] 426 Mass. 501 (1998).

[26] MASS. ANN. LAWS ch. 210, § 2 (1994) reads: '[W]ritten consent shall be executed no sooner than the fourth calendar day after the date of birth of the child to be adopted.'

court concluded by suggesting that judicial approval of a surrogacy contract before conception would be a wise policy.[27]

Feminist scholars have raised special concerns about surrogacy arrangements and surrogacy contracts. A major question that is discussed in the literature is whether surrogacy is a part of a woman's individual reproductive rights, which

[27] The court referred to laws in New Hampshire and Virginia requiring judicial approval in advance of the child's birth. *See supra* note 22. That requirement is built into the Uniform Status of Children of Assisted Conception Act Alternative A. Sections 5,6, and 9. Those sections read as follows:

Section 5. Surrogacy agreement.

(a) A surrogate, her husband, if she is married, and intended parents may enter into a written agreement whereby the surrogate relinquishes all her rights and duties as a parent of a child to be conceived through assisted conception, and the intended parents may become the parents of the child pursuant to Section 8.

(b) If the agreement is not approved by the court under Section 6 before conception, the agreement is void and the surrogate is the mother of a resulting child and the surrogate's husband, if a party to the agreement, is the father of the child. If the surrogate's husband is not a party to the agreement or the surrogate is unmarried, paternity of the child is governed by [the Uniform Parentage Act].

Section 6. Petition and hearing for approval of surrogacy agreement.

(a) The intended parents and the surrogate may file a petition in the [appropriate court] to approve a surrogacy agreement if one of them is a resident of this State. The surrogate's husband, if she is married, must join in the petition. A copy of the agreement must be attached to the petition. The court shall name a [guardian ad litem] to represent the interests of a child to be conceived by the surrogate through assisted conception and [shall] [may] appoint counsel to represent the surrogate.

(b) The court shall hold a hearing on the petition and shall enter an order approving the surrogacy agreement, authorizing assisted conception for a period of 12 months after the date of the order, declaring the intended parents to be the parents of a child to be conceived through assisted conception pursuant to the agreement and discharging the guardian ad litem and attorney for the surrogate, upon finding that:

(1) the court has jurisdiction and all parties have submitted to its jurisdiction under subsection (e) and have agreed that the law of this State governs all matters arising under this [Act] and the agreement;

(2) the intended mother is unable to bear a child or is unable to do so without unreasonable risk to an unborn child or to the physical or mental health of the intended mother or child, and the finding is supported by medical evidence;

(3) the [relevant child-welfare agency] has made a home study of the intended parents and the surrogate and a copy of the report of the home study has been filed with the court;

(4) the intended parents, the surrogate, and the surrogate's husband, if she is married, meet the standards of fitness applicable to adoptive parents in this State;

would allow them to control their own bodies, or whether there is a broader social policy concern that should trump personal autonomy. To some feminists, women should be able to make decisions about their own bodies and outlawing surrogacy would be an infringement on that right. To others, hiring poor women, the usual surrogacy candidates, to act as surrogates for affluent

(5) all parties have voluntarily entered into the agreement and understand its terms, nature, and meaning, and the effect of the proceeding;

(6) the surrogate has had at least one pregnancy and delivery and bearing another child will not pose an unreasonable risk to the unborn child or to the physical or mental health of the surrogate or the child, and this finding is supported by medical evidence;

(7) all parties have received counseling concerning the effect of the surrogacy by [a qualified health-care professional or social worker] and a report containing conclusions about the capacity of the parties to enter into and fulfill the agreement has been filed with the court;

(8) a report of the results of any medical or psychological examination or genetic screening agreed to by the parties or required by law has been filed with the court and made available to the parties;

(9) adequate provision has been made for all reasonable health-care costs associated with the surrogacy until the child's birth including responsibility for those costs if the agreement is terminated pursuant to Section 7; and

(10) the agreement will not be substantially detrimental to the interest of any of the affected individuals.

(c) Unless otherwise provided in the surrogacy agreement, all court costs, attorney's fees, and other costs and expenses associated with the proceeding must be assessed against the intended parents.

(d) Notwithstanding any other law concerning judicial proceedings or vital statistics, the court shall conduct all hearings and proceedings under this section in camera. The court shall keep all records of the proceedings confidential and subject to inspection under the same standards applicable to adoptions. At the request of any party, the court shall take steps necessary to ensure that the identities of the parties are not disclosed.

(e) The court conducting the proceedings has exclusive and continuing jurisdiction of all matters arising out of the surrogacy until a child born after entry of an order under this section is 180 days old.
. . .

Section 9. Surrogacy: Miscellaneous Provisions.

(a) A surrogacy agreement that is the basis of an order under Section 6 may provide for the payment of consideration.

(b) A surrogacy agreement may not limit the right of the surrogate to make decisions regarding her health care or that of the embryo or fetus.

(c) After the entry of an order under Section 6, marriage of the surrogate does not affect the validity of the order, and her husband's consent to the surrogacy agreement is not required, nor is he the father of a resulting child.

(d) A child born to a surrogate within 300 days after assisted conception pursuant to an order under Section 6 is presumed to result from the assisted conception. The presumption is conclusive as to all persons who have notice of the birth and who do not commence within 180 days after notice, an action to assert the contrary in which the child and the parties to the agreement are named as

couples is demeaning to women who are used merely as child-bearing vessels. This treatment of women raises major social policy considerations. The role of governmental regulation in this area would be the balancing of individual rights of women with the broader policy issues of protecting the exploitation of vulnerable women, as well as the best interests of the child born of the arrangement. In regulating surrogacy, there is the additional consideration of the procreative liberty of the couple seeking parenthood and the surrogate herself.[28]

In re Baby M was the first surrogacy mother contract case to be decided by an American state supreme court. The issue before the court was the legality and enforceability of a surrogacy contract between a married woman, Mrs. Whitehead, and a man, Mr. Stern, not her husband (a party to the contract) but married to another woman (not a party to the contract). The terms of the contract included an exchange of promises in which Mr. Stern promised to pay Mrs. Whitehead $10,000 in exchange for her promising to be artificially inseminated with Mr. Stern's semen, conceiving a child, carrying the child to term and after the birth of the child, surrendering her to Mr. Stern and his wife. In addition Mrs. Whitehead promised to fulfill the legal requirements for the termination of her rights so that Mrs. Stern could adopt the child. After the child was born, her birth records indicated that Mrs. Whitehead was her mother and, contrary to fact, Mr. Whitehead was her father. Following the terms of the contract, Mrs. Whitehead gave the newborn infant (referred to by the court as Baby M but named Melissa) to Mr. and Mrs. Stern.

Four days after she had relinquished Melissa to her new parents, the birth mother asked to have her newborn returned for a week. The Sterns agreed not fully realizing that Mrs. Whitehead had changed her mind. With her baby, Mrs. Whitehead fled to Florida and refused to return Melissa to her new parents, thus violating the terms of the surrogacy contract.

Four months later through various legal maneuvers, the Sterns secured possession of Melissa. In New Jersey, Mr. Stern sued for the enforcement of his contract with Mrs. Whitehead and for the custody of Melissa. He also sought the termination of Mrs. Whitehead's parental rights and an order allowing Mrs. Stern to adopt the child. The lower court held that the surrogacy contract was valid. It ordered the termination of Mrs. Whitehead's parental rights in

> parties. The action must be commenced in the court that issued the order under Section 6.
> (e) A health-care provider is not liable for recognizing the surrogate as the mother before receipt of a copy of the order entered under Section 6 or for recognizing the intended parents as parents after receipt of an order entered under Section 6.

[28] These issues along with others dealing with the reproductive rights of women are explored in Katharine T. Bartlett, *Feminism and Family Law*, 33 FAMILY L.Q. 475, 492–94 (1999). For a commentary on surrogacy literature including articles and books on the economics of the arrangement as well as the constitutional issues, see ELLMAN ET AL, *supra* note 21, at 1499–1500.

Melissa, granted custody to Mr. Stern, and after a brief hearing allowed the adoption of Melissa by Mrs. Stern. Mrs. Whitehead appealed.

After invalidating the surrogacy contract (which had provided for the termination of Mrs. Whitehead's parental rights by the surrogacy contract), the New Jersey Supreme Court remanded the case to the Superior Court to determine which of the two legal parents—Mrs. Whitehead or Mr. Stern—should be granted custody. To the New Jersey Supreme Court, the surrogacy contract violated two state statutory provisions: one that barred the payment of money for an adoption, and the other which prevented the enforcement of a pre-birth adoption agreement. The Superior Court held that the best interests of Melissa would be served by her custody being awarded to Mr. Stern with visitation rights to Mrs. Whitehead. The outcome was a legal anomaly. It had some of the characteristics of a failed adoption as well as of a custodial arrangement after divorce with the husband being awarded physical and legal custody and the wife receiving visitation rights. It was also like a resolution of a conflict between an unmarried couple where the father of the illegitimate child born of that relationship was awarded custody of his daughter.

The case is exceptional in a number of ways. Ordinarily a child born to a married couple is presumed to be the legitimate child of the husband.[29] If that child is relinquished for adoption, the parents must formally consent. Many jurisdictions allow for the revocation of consent within a certain time-frame.[30] In New Jersey, a birth mother can change her mind within a short period of time after she relinquishes her child to a couple and she has been notified of the adoption proceeding.[31] There is also the inheritance aspect to the case's outcome. Generally, when birth parents' rights are terminated to allow for adoption, the termination is for all purposes including inheritance and succession rights. This

---

[29] American law adopted the English common law presumption that a child born in wedlock is the legitimate child of the couple. *See* Michael H. v. Gerald D., 491 U.S. 110, 124–25 (1989); MICHAEL GROSSBERG, GOVERNING THE HEARTH 201–02 (1985); T. E. James, *The Illegitimate and Deprived Child: Legitimation and Adoption, in* A CENTURY OF FAMILY LAW 42–43 (R. H. Graveson & F. R. Crane eds., 1957).

[30] For example, Alaska allows birth parents to revoke their consent within ten days after consent has been executed if a court finds it to be in the child's best interest. Revocation is not allowed after the adoption decree has been issued. *See* ALASKA STAT. § 25.23.070(b) (Lexis 1998). Arkansas allows a consent to be revoked within ten calendar days of the consent having been signed or within ten calendar days of the child's birth. *See* ARK. CODE ANN. § 9-9-209 (1998). Maine requires a three-day waiting period after a consent or surrender has been executed before it is valid. *See* ME. REV. STAT. ANN. tit. 18-A, § 9–202 (West 1998). Missouri requires written consent to adoption to be reviewed by a judge. The consent cannot be obtained before the infant is 48 hours old. *See* MO. ANN. STAT. § 453.030 (West 1997).

[31] In New Jersey, once a birth mother validly surrenders her child to an agency, she cannot revoke her consent. In a private placement, she can object to the adoption within twenty days of her receiving notice of the adoption proceeding. *See* N.J. STAT. ANN. § 9:3–41, 9.3–46 (West 1993); *see also* Matter of Adoption of Child by D.M.H., 641 A.2d 235 (N.J. 1994); Sees v. Baber, 377 A.2d 628 (N.J. 1977).

was not always the case[32] but occurred over time as adoption became more and more socially acceptable and the adopted child became fully integrated into his or her new family. There are still some residual effects of the period when adopted children were treated quite differently from children not adopted. For example, at least six state statutes still allow adopted children to inherit from their biological parents.[33] In *In re Baby M* as long as no termination of parental rights had occurred, Melissa would be the statutory heir of Mrs. Whitehead and Mr. Stern, but not of Mrs. Stern nor Mr. Whitehead.

If Melissa had been born to Mr. and Mrs. Whitehead as their legitimate child, and then properly relinquished for adoption to the Sterns, in the 1960s or before, it would have been unusual, but not impossible, for the birth parents to have contact with their child after her adoption. However, from the 1970s into the 1990s, adoption of newborns or infants with visitation rights in the birth parents—called 'Open Adoption'—has become less and less uncommon but by no means standard practice.

Open Adoption: Visitation Rights for Birth Parents

In non-relative adoptions, the conventional agency practice in mid-century was not to allow a birth mother to have contact with the adoptive family, now referred to as one aspect of 'Open Adoption'. Adoption agencies followed a theory of child development that the successful integration of an adopted child into the new adoptive family would be complicated if the child's relationship with her birth parents were to continue. It was thought that the child would be

---

[32] After reviewing adoption decisions and legislation in the United States, a 1936 Note in the IOWA LAW REVIEW concluded with these statements:
1. The adopted child may inherit from his natural parents and relatives, and from his adoptive parents, but not from his adoptive relatives.
2. Rights of inheritance from the adopted child are given to adoptive parents and relatives, but not to the natural family; in some states the property is divided according to its source.

Two unfortunate results are apparent. The adopted child is in a better situation than other children are, for he can inherit from four parents. The framers of the general adoption statutes surely never intended this . . .
The second injustice is that the adoptive relatives may inherit from him, but he may not inherit from them.

Note, *Legislation and Decisions on Inheritance Rights of Adopted Children*, 22 IOWA L. REV. 145, 153 (1936). In sixty-three years, the inheritance rights of adopted children have changed dramatically, reflecting the attitudinal change about fully integrating the adopted child into his or her adoptive family.

[33] *See, e.g.*, KAN. STAT. ANN. § 59–2118(b) (1994); LA. CIV. CODE ANN. art. 214 (West 1993); R.I. GEN. LAWS § 15-7-17 (Michie 1993); TEX. PROB. CODE ANN. art. 40 (West Supp. 1999); VT. STAT. ANN. tit. 15, § 448 (1993); WYO. STAT. ANN. § 2-4-0107 (Lexis 1999). Wyoming has an unusual provision that allows biological relatives to inherit from the adopted person. *See* WYO. STAT. ANN. § 2-4-107 (Lexis 1999).

confused as to her loyalties and the objects of her affection. To allow a birth mother to conditionally relinquish her child would support her ambivalence toward giving her child up, if she had any, and prevent her acceptance of the finality of adoption. Also, the adoptive parents would have a feeling of being observed and even scrutinized, thus finding it difficult to form a complete and lasting attachment to their adopted child. In a certain sense, open adoption is like some forms of joint custody in divorce without the birth mother and the adoptive couple having had a previous relationship to support the new arrangement.

A birth mother who chose to place her child privately would not be subject to an agency's rules about contact. In the 1990s if she entered into an open adoption agreement as the consideration for relinquishing her child to an adoptive couple, the agreement could be enforced if a state statute specifically allowed visitation rights. Absent a statutory provision a judge, using his discretionary power, could enforce the agreement if it advanced the child's best interests.

Whether a state legislature should modify its adoption statute to allow open adoption or whether a judge should interpret an adoption statute in such a way as to allow it poses a fundamental question: should the model of adoption that has resulted in the complete termination of the birth parents rights in their child and has been part of American law for many years continue, or should the model be changed? Traditionalists would say that adoption requires termination of parental rights for all purposes. If a birth parent does not want her rights fully terminated, she can agree to relinquish her child to a legal guardian. Guardianship is a flexible status allowing for a variety of ways of dividing responsibilities between her and the court-appointed guardian. Long-term foster care with visitation may be another alternative if a state or private agency would accept the child and if an appropriate foster family was available. The major drawback of these alternatives is financial. Unless the birth mother has the means to support these alternatives, she might be forced to relinquish her child for adoption.

Open adoption introduces a new model of adoption and an alternative to the traditional family model of one set of parents and their children. It removes the mystery of the birth parents' identity, thus eliminating the need for secrecy in the adoption process and closed adoption records. In some respects allowing open adoption supports personal autonomy by preserving a birth mother's decision-making powers. She can control the terms of the adoption.

Open Adoption: Access to Adoption Records

During the 1970s and again in the late 1990s, the issue of whether identifying information from adoption records should be disclosed to adult adopted children and birth parents received national attention in the media.[34] Making

---

[34] For a full discussion of open records, *see* E. WAYNE CARP, FAMILY MATTERS (1998). For the personal stories of adopted adults who searched for their birth parents and the experiences they had, *see* TIM GREEN, A MAN AND HIS MOTHER—AN ADOPTED SON'S SEARCH (1997); FLORENCE FISHER, THE SEARCH FOR ANNA FISHER (1973).

adoption records accessible to parties to the adoption is complicated because there might be two sets of records: one in the possession of the placement agency or person who arranged the adoption and the other in the court where the adoption decree was issued. Identifying information including a family and medical history about birth parents and the adopted child would be recorded in a licensed and reputable agency. However, such information might not be available in a private placement unless the lawyer or physician obtained it and safely secured it. Court adoption records are impounded and access to them is not a matter of right, but dependent on a judicial determination that the individual seeks the information for a good cause.

Whether adoption records should be open to adult adopted children as a matter of right was raised in 1979 when a group of adult adoptees sued the Director of Vital Records in the City of New York, certain New York judges, and adoption agencies in the federal court in New York.[35] They claimed that the New York statutes that required the sealing of adoption records were a violation of the Due Process and Equal Protection Clauses of the Fourteenth Amendment to the U.S. Constitution. In addition, the adoptees argued that the Thirteenth Amendment also applied in that the sealing of adoption records imposed on them an incident of slavery by abolishing the parental relationship. The Federal Court of Appeals affirmed the lower court's decision and held that the New York sealed records statutes did not violate substantive due process in that the state recognized the privacy interests of both birth parents and adopted children. Further, the court held that equal protection was not violated either because New York had an important state interest in advancing the social policy of protecting the confidentiality afforded birth parents when they place

Mike Leigh's prize-winning 1996 British film, Secrets and Lies, examined the issue of a young woman, the illegitimate child of a lower-class white mother and black father, who had been adopted by a middle-class black family. Following the death of her adopted mother, she began to search for her birth mother, first obtaining information from the agency that placed her and then arranging to meet her mother. She had not known that her mother was white, nor had the mother known the race of her daughter because of events at the child's birth. The film demonstrates in an artistic way the extent to which blood ties are so important to both the adopted child and the birth mother, regardless of the race of either. It also portrayed quite vividly the initial underlying hostility toward race even within a family, and how this lessens and perhaps evaporates once the adopted child becomes better known and integrated into the family.

The act that prompted the young woman's search, the death of her adoptive mother, illustrated an important point made in John Triseliotis's book, In Search of Origins (1973) that an adopted person's seeking the identity of her birth parents usually follows some personal loss. That loss, he writes, triggers the person's earliest loss, that of a birth mother. Triseliotis's study has important implications for the law, particularly for the issue of open records and for social work in dealing with adult adopted children and the meaning of their search.

[35] *See* ALMA Society Inc. v. Mellon, 601 F.2d 1238 (2d Cir.), *cert denied*, 100 S. Ct. 531 (1979).

children for adoption. The court rejected the adult adoptees' slavery argument when it held that the sealed records statutes did not divest birth parents of their children. It was the adoption laws which accomplished that, and those laws were not challenged. In the last sentence of the opinion the court basically said that to open adoption records adult adoptees had either to conform to the requirements of the New York statute by obtaining official approval first or seek legislative changes.

Between 1979 and 1999 legislative changes occurred in New York and beyond. At least seven jurisdictions allow identifying information to be released by the court either because of the consent of the adopted child and her birth parents or for good cause. About the same number of jurisdictions allow access to an adopted child's birth certificate when he or she is an adult, and twenty-four states have statutory provisions that set up mutual consent registries.[36]

In 1997 the 1996 Tennessee statute that allowed adult adoptees to have access to their adoption records was challenged in the federal courts by adoptive parents and birth mothers. They sought to enjoin state officials from enforcing the statute that would have the effect of disclosing confidential information to the adopted child. They argued that the new law violated their right of privacy, which they interpreted to encompass family privacy, reproductive privacy, and privacy against disclosure of confidential information under the federal constitution. The Federal District Court denied the injunction, as did the Court of Appeals. To the Court of Appeals, the open adoption records controversy involved competing interests: the interest of a child adopted during her infancy to know the identity of her birth parents and the birth parent's interest in secrecy. The court held that the child's interest outweighed those of the birth parents'.

The court added that if the plaintiffs thought that the Tennessee Constitution provided them with greater protection, they should sue in the state court.[37] The plaintiffs filed an action in the Tennessee Court of Appeals and were successful in arguing that the statute impaired their vested legal expectations in the adoption statute (before the 1996 amendment), as well as their privacy rights under the state constitution.[38]

The state of Tennessee appealed that decision to the Supreme Court of Tennessee, which upheld the validity of the 1996 amended statute. To the court, the 1996 adoption statute did not violate the parents' privacy rights nor did it impair any vested legal expectations under the former adoption statute.[39]

---

[36] *See Appendix 13-A, State Procedures for Obtaining Identifying Information from Confidential Adoption Records, in* 2 ADOPTION LAW AND PRACTICE, *supra* note 19.

[37] *See* Doe v. Sundquist, 106 F.3d. 702 (6th Cir. 1997).

[38] *See* Doe v. Sundquist, 1997 W.L. 354786 (Tenn. Cir. Ct. May 2, 1997) (No. 97C-941).

[39] *See* Doe v. Sundquist, 2 S.W.3d 919 (Tenn. 1999).

Placement

In a jurisdiction that allows private placement, a birth mother who places her child for adoption can choose anyone she likes as adoptive parents. However, if a birth mother relinquishes her infant to an agency, that agency will follow its own regulations regarding placement factors. In certain respects placement factors reflect larger cultural assumptions about parenthood and the family both of which change in time. They also have been and are used to promote certain values such as religion and ethnic and racial integrity. Whether a placement is arranged privately or through an agency, the placement is subject to judicial approval according to statutory standards.

Since the 1950s and into the 1970s agency placements in voluntary relinquishment cases used the nuclear family model as the standard placement for an infant. Agencies tended to prefer married couples of childbearing ages, who were well educated, financially secure, and who could provide a child with all the necessities of life in order for him or her to mature into a productive adult. In addition, agencies tried to match the child with the adoptive parents so that the new family would look like it had been created through biology not the law. If a religiously affiliated private agency placed the child, that agency would require the adoptive couple to be a member of its religion or, in certain instances, to promise to raise the child in the religion associated with the agency.

By the 1990s, adoption practice had changed because of a number of factors. They included the decrease in the number of newborns available for adoption because of the availability of abortion and increased social tolerance for unwed mothers and their children.[40] Agency placement criteria also changed, particularly for private religiously affiliated agencies. The reason was that they could no longer choose adoptive placements on a religious basis if they accepted funds from community charities, like the United Way, which conditioned its financial support on non-discrimination policies. In addition, agencies generally recognized the social acceptance of new forms of families such as single parent and same-sex parents. However, the principle that an adopted child should be loved, wanted, and feel secure in his or her new family and community has remained constant.

During the 1950s, religion was the factor that was controversial and the subject of litigation. At issue in two widely publicized cases, one in New York[41] and the other in Massachusetts,[42] was the interpretation of adoption statutes that directed the court 'when practicable' to award custody only to persons of the same religious faith as that of the child. The highest court in New York held that 'when practicable' gave the court discretion and included a concern for the best interests of the child, that is whether the current placement with a couple

---

[40] For this reason, many American couples have sought to adopt foreign children. The whole issue of international adoption is beyond the scope of this chapter.

[41] *See* In re Maxwell, 151 N.E.2d 484 (N.Y. 1958).

[42] *See* In re Goldman, 121 N.E.2d 843 (Mass. 1954), *cert. denied*, 348 U.S. 942 (1955).

of a different religion from the child was more beneficial than any available alternatives. The Supreme Judicial Court of Massachusetts court held that 'when practicable' should be interpreted as a mandate to search for an adoptive couple of the same religion as the child. Thus, to the Massachusetts court placing a child of one religion with a family of a different religion would be approved only if no families of the child's religion could be located.

Forty years later, race replaced religion not so much as a subject of litigation, but as a major concern of African Americans. Basically the question is: under what circumstances should children of one race who are *voluntarily* relinquished for adoption by their birth mothers be placed with adoptive parents of another race?[43] Some advocates of transracial placements base their position on the interpretation of the best interests of the child, which they define as advancing the child's psychological need for affection, stimulation, nurturing, safety, and stability. To them such a goal can be achieved regardless of the race of the adoptive parents. Others justify their preference for transracial adoption because of their strong belief in antidiscrimination and their view that racially mixed families provide the first step toward national harmony.[44]

Opponents of transracial adoption (except in unusual circumstances) have suggested that advocates take too narrow a view of the psychological needs of children and fail to understand the extent to which race defines the person in twentieth-century America. They also claim that proponents may be naive about racial tensions and thus are unrealistic about the abilities of adoptive parents to fully appreciate the difficulties the adopted child raised in a family of a different race will face during the child's youth and adulthood. Further, it has been said that placing African American children with white adoptive parents robs these children of their heritage, which includes a deep respect for the

---

[43] By transracial adoption, I am referring to the placement for adoption of a child clearly identified as having been born of parents of the same race with an individual or a couple of a different race. I am not referring to mixed race children or mixed race parents. I am also emphasizing 'voluntary' relinquishments in this discussion. The issue of transracial adoption under the involuntary system is discussed later in this chapter.

[44] Professor Randall Kennedy has written:

> Race matching ought not to be permitted. Eradicating it would have several beneficial consequences. Abolishing race matching would redound to the immediate benefit of children in need of foster care or adoptive homes by removing an impediment that currently slows or prevents child placements when parents of the 'correct' race are not on hand. Getting rid of race matching would also have a broader, long-term beneficent consequence by signaling in a vivid way that, in the eyes of the law, monochromatic families are no better than, and certainly entitled to no preference over, racially mixed families . . . People who are persuaded by my approach should insist that administrators and judges *enforce* antidiscrimination norms in the context of family law.

Randall Kennedy, *How Are We Doing with* Loving? *Race, Law, and Intermarriage*, 77 B. U. L. Rev. 815, 821 (1997).

family and its special educational role for African Americans.[45] There is also the wider issue of the place of the African American family in American life. Transracial adoption may add to the disintegration of that family precisely at a time when its stability is being threatened by social and economic forces.

Some scholars, questioning the conscious or unconscious motives behind placing African American infants with white adoptive parents, have asked: Is transracial adoption another form of racial annihilation? Is transracial adoption a replay of the historical place of African Americans in American life, namely of African Americans serving white Americans? These are important questions raising legitimate concerns about how a history of racial oppression affects adoption policies.[46]

Consider the position of the leading American child welfare organization whose standards were used to accredit adoption agencies in the 1950s on using religion and race as factors in adoption placement:

A child should ordinarily be placed in a home where the religion of adoptive parents is the same as that of the child, unless the parents have specified that the child should or may be placed with a family of another religion. Every effort (including interagency and interstate referrals) should be made to place the child within his own faith, or that designated by his parents. If however such matching means that placement might never

---

[45] Thirty-two years ago, Andrew Billingsley, who was Assistant Chancellor for Academic Affairs and Associate Professor of Social Welfare at the University of California at Berkeley, wrote in a book that received a great deal of attention at the time:

For the Negro family, socialization is doubly challenging, for the family must teach its young members not only how to be human, but also how to be black in a white society. The requirements are not the same.

Negro families must teach their children very early in life, sometimes as early as two years of age, the meaning of being black.

ANDREW BILLINGSLEY, BLACK FAMILIES IN WHITE AMERICA 28 (1968).

[46] Professor Linda Gordon has written:

[M]ixed race adoptions, even more than mixed-race couples, occur only in one direction: there is debate about whether whites should adopt children of color, but adoptions of white children by parents of color are so rare they are not even debated. This dimension of racial policy in child welfare suggests something of the degree to which race is about hierarchy, not difference.

LINDA GORDON, THE GREAT ARIZONA ORPHAN ABDUCTION 309 (1999).

For a full discussion (with extensive references) of the social, historical, and legal context in which transracial adoption has developed and for responses to the empirical research on the subject, see Ruth-Arlene W. Howe, *Transracial Adoption (TRA): Old Prejudices and Discrimination Float under a New Halo*, 6 B.U. PUB. INT. L.J. 409 (1997); Ruth-Arlene W. Howe, *Redefining the Transracial Adoption Controversy*, 2 DUKE J. OF GENDER LAW & POL'Y 131 (1995); see also David S. Rosettenstein, *Transracial Adoption and the Statutory Preference Schemes: Before the 'Best Interests' and after the 'Melting Pot'*, 68 ST. JOHN'S L. REV. 137 (1994). For discussion of empirical research supporting the positive aspects of transracial adoption, see generally RITA J. SIMON ET AL., THE CASE FOR TRANSRACIAL ADOPTION (1994); RITA J. SIMON & HOWARD ALSTEIN, ADOPTION, RACE, AND IDENTITY 1–55 (1992).

be feasible, or involves a substantial delay in placement or placement in a less suitable home, a child's need for a permanent family of his own requires that consideration should then be given to placing the child in a home of a different religion.[47]

. . .

It should not be assumed that difficulties will necessarily arise if adoptive parents and children are of different racial origin. At the present time, however, children placed in adoptive families with similar racial characteristics, such as color, can become more easily integrated into the average family group and community.[48]

The peculiar wording of the race provision in terms of the negative assumption reveals a perspective common for the time. Why is it not assumed that difficulties will necessarily arise if adoptive parents and children are of different religions? Substituting the word 'race' for 'religion' in the provision on religion is more reflective of the last decade of this century when race matters.

A child should ordinarily be placed in a home where the *race* of adoptive parents is the same as that of the child, unless the parents have specified that the child should or may be placed with a family of another race. Every effort (including interagency and interstate referrals) should be made to place the child within his own *race*, or that designated by his parents. If however such matching means that placement might never be feasible, or involves a substantial delay in placement or placement in a less suitable home, a child's need for a permanent family of his own requires that consideration should then be given to placing the child in a home of a different *race*.

Although placement factors have remained fairly consistent in the past forty years, the priority given to individual factors has changed depending on the circumstances of the relinquishment and the availability of adoptive parents. The nuclear family of a man, woman, and child that was thought of as conventional or as an ideal is now one model among others: single parent, unmarried heterosexual parents, unmarried parents of the same sex. The preference given to placement factors used to place infants voluntarily relinquished to adoption agencies differs from those used to place neglected or abused children whose parents' rights have been terminated. The major reason is that unlike the involuntary system where agencies report a shortage of prospective adoptive applicants, the number of married heterosexual couples waiting to adopt healthy white newborns far exceeds the supply of those infants, and therefore agencies give priority to those couples.

Step-parent and Second Parent Adoptions

With serial marriages now more common than in the past, step-parent adoption has become more prevalent. The fact pattern of such adoptions might involve a woman who has divorced her first husband or whose husband has died. Her second husband's seeking to adopt her child usually removes the adoption from

[47] Child Welfare League of America, Standards for Adoption Services 25 (1958).
[48] *Id.* at 24.

the requirements of an agency involvement in those states that mandate agency placements. Judicial approval is still required although a home study report by a court official or an agency designated to perform the investigation and a waiting period, normally required in adoption, are ordinarily waived. Adoption terminates the child's statutory inheritance rights from and through his birth father.

The conflict that might arise as a result of a step-parent adoption would concern the visitation rights of blood relatives of the divorced or deceased husband over the objection of the child's mother. Since the second husband's adoption of his wife's child would have severed the child's legal relationships with his divorced or deceased father's blood relatives, he would have no legal ties with his paternal grandparents. All American states have grandparent visitation statutes, which were enacted to provide grandparents standing and the opportunity to maintain a connection with their grandchildren particularly after the children's parents had divorced. These statutes have been challenged on constitutional grounds as violating parents' right to raise their children without interference from the state, absent abuse or neglect. During the 1990s, four state supreme courts held that grandparent visitation statutes were unconstitutional under their state constitutions.[49] Since the grandparent visitation statutes do not directly relate to adoption, grandparents, technically no longer legally related to their grandchildren, would have to appeal to the judge's discretion or in some states his or her broad equitable powers to grant them visitation rights. The judge would have to balance the privacy and liberty interests of the parents to raise their children without interference from others with the interests of the grandparents and the child to maintain a connection with each other.

A phenomenon of the past decade is second parent adoption. Two New England cases decided in 1993[50] raised the same issue: whether the state law required the termination of a birth mother's parental rights as a prerequisite to her child being adopted by her partner of the same sex. In both cases, the state supreme courts held that termination was not required, and that the adoption by the birth mother's partner should be allowed. These cases are important for the courts' statements about a same-sex couple as parents. The practical result of a court's approving such an adoption by a birth mother and her female partner is the legal recognition given to them as parents. Since the Hawaii and Vermont

[49] *See* Beagle v. Beagle, 678 So. 2d 1271 (Fla. 1996); Brooks v. Parkerson, 454 S.E.2d 769 (Ga. 1995), *cert. denied*, 516 U.S. 942 (1995); Von Eiff v. Azicri, 720 So. 2d 510 (Fla. 1998); Hawk v. Hawk, 855 S.W.2d 573 (Tenn. 1993). For a discussion of Troxel v. Granville, 530 U.S. 57 (2000), and its application to third party visitation cases, see Chapter 3. For cases holding that grandparent visitation statutes are constitutional, *see* King v. King, 828 S.W.2d 630 (Ky. 1992), *cert denied*, 506 U.S. 941 (1992); Herndon v. Tuhey, 857 S.W.2d 203 (Mo. 1993); *see also* Brooks v. Parkerson, 454 S.E.2d 769, 775 (dissenting opinion by Justice Bentham).
[50] *See* In re Adoption of Tammy, 619 N.E.2d 315 (Mass. 1993); Adoption of B.L.V.B. & E.L.V.B., 628 A.2d 1271 (Vt. 1993).

Supreme courts in two major American cases on same-sex marriage[51] discussed whether a same-sex couple could raise a child effectively, implying that parenthood, or at least the potential for it, was a test for marriage, these cases are valuable. They could provide the legal precedent for the proposition that female partners can be parents who will promote the best interests of the birth mother's infant. The Vermont and Massachusetts adoption cases may signal the beginning of social and legal acceptance of unconventional families beyond adoption.[52]

INVOLUNTARY SYSTEM

The Role of the Federal Government and the Absence of Personal Autonomy

Unlike the infants relinquished for adoption by their birth mothers to agencies or directly to an adoptive couple, children who are freed for adoption after a termination of parental rights proceeding in state courts are or have been in foster care. Because state foster care programs are part of a federally funded child welfare system, the federal government through the U.S. Department of Health and Human Services, a part of the executive branch of government and the U.S. Congress, the legislative branch, plays a very important role. The Department of Health and Human Services (formerly called the Department of Health, Education, & Welfare) develops model legislation for states to enact. It provides technical assistance to states, supports research, sets standards, and promulgates regulations for various child welfare programs in the states; the U.S. Congress enacts legislation authorizing funding for these programs.

The 1960s and 1970s were decades in which child neglect and abuse began to be recognized as matter for public concern.[53] Major federal initiatives were

---

[51] *See* Baehr v. Lewin, 852 P.2d 44 (Haw. 1993) and Baker v. State of Vermont, 744 A.2d 864 (Vt. 1999). These cases are discussed in Chapter 2.

[52] The Supreme Judicial Court of Massachusetts cited *Adoption of Tammy, supra* note 43, when it held that a woman who had established herself as a de facto parent of her female partner's child had visitation rights to that child after the termination of her relationship with the child's mother and over the mother's objection. *See* E.N.O. v. L.M.M., 711 N.E.2d 886 (Mass. 1999). Justice Ruth Abrams wrote:

> The recognition of de facto parents is in accord with notions of the modern family.
> An increasing number of same gender couples, like the plaintiff and the defendant are deciding to have children. It is to be expected that children of nontraditional families, like other children, form parent relationships with both parents, whether those parents are legal or de facto . . .

Id. at 891.

[53] One of the important studies at that time was LEONTINE R. YOUNG'S WEDNESDAY'S CHILDREN: A STUDY OF CHILD NEGLECT AND ABUSE (1964); *see also* DAVID GIL, VIOLENCE AGAINST CHILDREN (1970); JEANNE M. GIOVANNONI AND ROSINA M. BECERRA, DEFINING

undertaken to respond to the general problem of child maltreatment, foster care, and adoption. It was during the 1960s that Children's Bureau, a division of the then U.S. Department of Health, Education, & Welfare, proposed the Model Child Abuse Mandatory Reporting Act.[54] It recommended the Act to the states as a model for a new law, which would put aside traditional concepts of family privacy and professional confidentiality and require certain people to report evidence of abuse or neglect. Within only a decade, all jurisdictions enacted some kind of mandatory child abuse and neglect reporting statute.[55] To provide funding for child abuse programs for states, which had enacted child abuse reporting legislation, the U.S. Congress enacted the Child Abuse Prevention and Treatment Act of 1974.

Perhaps not contemplated by policy-makers was the effect widespread reporting would have on state foster care systems. By intervening in the family and removing children who were either abused or neglected and placing them in foster care, the state was placing a burden on an already taxed system not only in financial but human terms. During the six-year period from 1964 to 1970, the number of children in foster care rose from 192,300 to 326,700.[56]

By 1975 a child welfare crisis had developed, and the federal government focused on reducing the number of children in foster care as its next major initiative. To this end, policy-makers concentrated on twin goals: programs designed to rehabilitate parents so that they could be reunited with their children or if that was not possible, to terminate their parental rights in a procedure that was fair to all the parties, and place the children for adoption. Thus, the Model Act to Free Children for Permanent Placement was drafted and recommended to the states for enactment in one form or another.[57] That Act implemented the concept of permanency planning, which the Children's Bureau had developed.

Like so many other human endeavors, solving one problem sometimes creates others. In this instance, it was found that a generation of orphans would be created if adoptive homes could not be found for the children of parents whose parental rights had been terminated. One of the major barriers to adoption was financial. Foster parents who were ready, willing, and able to adopt children in their care learned that adoption would cut off federally funded

---

CHILD ABUSE (1979); SANFORD N. KATZ, WHEN PARENTS FAIL (1971). An important article that described a new syndrome was C. Henry Kempe, Frederic N. Silverman, Brandt F. Steele, William Droege-Mueller & Henry K. Silver, *The Battered Child Syndrome*, 181 J.A.M.A. 4 (1962). For a discussion of the syndrome see page 40.

[54] For the major provisions of the Act, see Katz, *supra* note 53, at 45 n. 13.

[55] *See* 42 U.S.C.A. § 5106a(b) (West 1995).

[56] *See* DAVID FANSHEL & EUGENE B. SHINN, CHILDREN IN FOSTER CARE 29 (1978).

[57] The Act is reproduced in Sanford N. Katz, *Freeing Children for Permanent Placement through a Model Act*, 12 FAM. L.Q. 203 (1978). For a discussion of the development of the Act and the policy underlying it, see Ruth-Arlene W. Howe, *Development of a Model Act to Free Children for Permanent Placement: A Case Study in Law and Social Planning*, 13 FAM. L.Q. 257 (1979). The Act is discussed in Chapter 4.

monthly foster care payments, making adoption unaffordable. The solution to that problem was to create federally funded subsidies that would be attached to foster children who, for whatever reason, were difficult to place for adoption. Thus, the concept of subsidized adoption was born, and the Model Subsidized Adoption Act was recommended to the states.[58] To financially assist states that established subsidy programs, the U.S. Congress passed the Adoption Assistance and Child Welfare Act of 1980.[59] That Act authorized the use of federal funds to support subsidized adoption for 'hard to place children'. In addition, to combat 'foster care drift' (children placed in one foster care facility after another without any planning for the child's permanent home), the Act required states to develop programs to prevent placements outside of the natural family. If a placement in foster care was necessary, the state was mandated to use 'reasonable efforts' to effectuate the child's return to his or her natural family.

During the 1980s and 1990s, the tension that has historically existed between the preservation of parental rights and termination of those rights for purposes of adoptive placement was played out in federal legislation.[60] In the Adoption and Safe Families Act of 1997,[61] the federal government reaffirmed its policy toward protecting parental rights by mandating that state agencies use 'reasonable efforts' to reunite families after an initial intervention has occurred resulting in a child being placed in foster care. In order to further the goal of family preservation, the federal government provides funds to states whose termination of parental rights laws conform to federal requirements. These include severing parental ties because of a parent's serious criminal conduct or in cases in which the child has been in the state foster care system for fifteen of the most recent twenty-two months. The Act lists three exceptions to the time-frame limitation: if the child is placed with a relative (kinship placement), if termination would not be in the child's best interests, or if the state agency has not fulfilled its responsibility of using reasonable efforts to reunite the child with his or her natural family. These three exceptions, the second and third of which being essentially vague,[62] suggest that there may be a reluctance of the federal government to promote adoption over termination even though the Act's stated intent is: 'To promote the adoption of children in foster care'.

[58] The Model Subsidized Adoption Act and Regulations is reproduced in Sanford N. Katz, *Subsidized Adoption in America*, 10 FAM. L.Q. 3 (1976). The Act is discussed in Chapter 4.

[59] Adoption Assistance and Child Welfare Act of 1980, Pub. L. No. 96-272, 94 Stat. 501, 42 U.S.C.A. §§ 620–28, 670–79a (West 1994).

[60] This tension is discussed in ELIZABETH BARTHOLET, NOBODY'S CHILDREN: ABUSE AND NEGLECT, FOSTER DRIFT, AND THE ADOPTION ALTERNATIVE (1999).

[61] Adoption and Safe Families Act of 1997, Pub. L. 105–89, November 19, 1997, 111 Stat. 2115, 42 U.S.C.A. 1305. (West Supp. 1998).

[62] Indeed, in *Suter v. Artist M.*, 503 U.S. 347 (1992), the U.S. Supreme Court held that the phrase 'reasonable efforts' did not 'unambiguously confer an enforceable right upon the Act's beneficiaries' to confer an enforceable private right under 42 U.S.C. § 1983.

Placement

The federal government's involvement in adoption placement factors is only relevant in so far as they relate to programs funded by the government. In 1994 Congress enacted the Multiethnic Placement Act of 1994,[63] which permitted a state agency to consider race as a placement factor if, in conjunction with other factors, it was in the best interests of the child. The Act also required state agencies to actively recruit ethnically diverse foster and adoptive parents. The life of the Multiethnic Placement Act was short. Two years after its enactment, it was replaced with provisions in the Small Business and Job Protection Act of 1996.[64] The provision of that law that deals with adoption prohibits any agency or individual involved in adoption or foster care placement who receives federal funds to deny a child's adoptive or foster care placement on the basis of race, color, or national origin.[65]

Transracial adoption is a very relevant issue in the involuntary system of adoption. The reason is that many children in foster care are African American, and they are in the adoption pool.[66] Proponents of transracial adoption claim that African American children must be placed with parents of a different race because of the lack of suitable adoptive parents who share their race. They make the point that if a rigid race-matching requirement were enforced, African American children would have to remain in some kind of foster care setting beyond the federal mandated time-frame.

The argument that African American families are unavailable to adopt children of their own race is difficult to understand in light of the fact that traditionally African Americans have had a deep rooted tradition of caring for members of their own and extended family as well as friends and neighbors.[67]

---

[63] *See* 42 U.S.C.A. § 5115a (West 1994).

[64] *See* Pub. L. 104–188, Title 1 Sub. tit. H, § 1808, 110 Stat. 1755, 1903 (1996) (amending the Social Security Act). The provisions were designed to 'Remove Barriers to Interethnic Adoption'. An interesting aspect to the federal law is that in addition to providing that an agency will lose federal funds if it does not conform to the requirements of the law, it also gives an aggrieved individual a right to sue in the federal court against a state or agency that is in violation of the Act.

[65] Native Americans are exempt from this provision. The adoption of Native American children is governed by the Indian Child Welfare Act of 1978, which limits placement to the child's family, members of the tribe or other Native American families. *See* 25 U.S.C. §§ 1901–63.

[66] Jane Waldfogel wrote, 'In 1980, 9.5 of every 1,000 African-American children were in placement, as opposed to 3.1 per 1,000 Caucasians. Ten years later, data from the five states [California, Illinois, Michigan, New York, and Texas] with the largest foster-care population indicated that African-Americans continue to be disproportionately likely to be placed.' JANE WALDFOGEL, THE FUTURE OF CHILD PROTECTION: HOW TO BREAK THE CYCLE OF ABUSE AND NEGLECT 11 (1998).

[67] *See* BILLINGSLEY, *supra* note 38, at 15–26; *see also* generally ROBERT B. HILL ET AL., RESEARCH ON THE AFRICAN-AMERICAN FAMILY: A HOLISTIC PERSPECTIVE (1993).

Indeed, many of the African Americans who migrated from the south to the north lived with relatives or friends. Some have suggested that if major efforts as well as incentives were in place to recruit African American families, the results would be positive.[68]

Because of the need for foster and adoptive families for children in the child welfare system, agencies have chosen individuals and couples to care for these children who may offer different styles of family organizations. Single women and men, couples beyond child-bearing years, and same-sex couples can qualify as foster or adoptive parents of children who are hard to place because they may have a physical disability or emotional problems, may be part of a sibling group, or who are above the age of 5.

Open Adoption

Unless an infant has been removed from her mother at birth, for example, because of the mother's drug addiction, children in the involuntary system of adoption may have lived with their parents before their placement in the child welfare system. Thus, the identity of their parents is not an issue. Children may remember their parents and may in fact have had contact with them during their foster care placement.[69] Whereas post-adoption visitation may be the consideration for relinquishing an infant under the voluntary system, it occurs most common at a different stage in the process under the involuntary adoption system. Lawyers for social service agencies or for birth parents use it as a strategy for facilitating a settlement of a termination of parental rights case either before trial or at appeal. Regardless of the adoption system, post-adoption visitation agreements need statutory authority and judicial approval based on the best interests of the child standard.

In approving the enforceability of a post-adoption visitation agreement (if it was in the child's best interests) in an involuntary adoption case, Chief Justice Ellen Peters of the Supreme Court of Connecticut linked the new model of adoption—open adoption—with the new family of the late twentieth century:

Case law in other jurisdictions does not persuade us that we should strike down the visitation agreement in this case. To a significant extent, the cases turn on legislative determinations that vary from state to state. We note nonetheless that [a New York case] concluded, as do we, that the statutory creation of an adoptive family does not automatically require complete severance of the child from all further contact with former relatives. Similarly, [a Maryland case] concluded, as do we, that as long as the

[68] Professor Howe has presented a forceful argument based on current data supporting her position that if agencies made concerted efforts to recruit African American families for children in need of an adoptive home, they would find success. *See* Howe, *Transracial Adoption, supra* note 39, at 427–46.

[69] Parental visitation has been regarded as important for a successful foster care placement. *See* FANSHEL & SHINN, *supra* note 49, at 110–11.

best interests of the child is the determinative criterion, public policy does not forbid an agreement about visitation rights between a genetic parent and adoptive parents. . . .

Traditional models of the nuclear family have come, in recent years, to be replaced by various configurations of parents, stepparents, adoptive parents and grandparents. . . . We are not prepared to assume that the welfare of children is best served by a narrow definition of those whom we permit to continue to manifest their deep concern for a child's grown and development.[70]

It remains to be seen whether judicial recognition of this new family will change other aspects of the involuntary model of adoption.

THE FUTURE OF ADOPTION

During the last half of the twentieth century, the institution of adoption has undergone major changes making it fundamentally different from what it was at the beginning of the century. Throughout the century, but more during the last half, there has been a certain amount of ambivalence about adoption. This attitude may be the result of the common law tradition of using blood ties as determining family membership and ownership of property. In addition, at the beginning of the century, the illegitimate child, the usual subject of adoption, received little protection from the law and was considered a social outcast. The father of the illegitimate child was similarly the object of discrimination. The whole adoption process excluded the father. Illegitimacy with all its negative implications for the mother, father, and child was a status to be concealed. It is little wonder, then, that adoption was clothed in secrecy, and an adopted child's past was hidden from everyone even the child herself. Adoption was in many ways a state imposed legal fiction.

The constitutionalization of family law with its emphasis on the protection of individual rights that began in the 1960s and continued into the 1970s had a direct impact on adoption. During that period, putative fathers who showed some interest in their illegitimate children were successful in pressing their claim for recognition and for due process and equal protection rights. Adult adopted children used these same constitutional arguments in their attempt to gain access to their sealed adoption records. At the same time, maintaining that opening adoption records would violate their constitutional right of privacy, birth parents attempted to keep the records closed. Courts seem to be favoring adult adopted children in this constitutional struggle. The wave of the future is in more openness in adoption.

Open adoption with post-adoption visitation presents a paradox. By the end of the twentieth century, in the vast number of states, for purposes of inheritance adopted children no longer are members of their birth families, but have been fully integrated into their adopted families. Yet post-adoption visitation by

[70] Michaud v. Wawruck, 551 A.2d 738, 741–42 (Conn. 1988).

birth parents continues the relationship that had been legally terminated. If more and more states enact legislation allowing such visitation, two models of adoption will be firmly established in the American adoption laws. One will be open adoption, which will allow post-adoption visitation; the other will be closed adoption.

The central issue at the beginning of a twenty-first century is whether adoption as we have known it, even with the new openness, will continue as the principal alternative to raising one's biological children. If birth and fertility rates drop, and if mothers decide to keep their children and raise them themselves, the voluntary system of adoption may lose its importance. The future of adoption in the involuntary system will be based on the foster care population and the extent to which federal legislation requirements shorten the time children may stay under state supervision. Much depends on the incidence of child abuse and neglect, the major causes for removal of children from their birth parents and their placement in state foster care.

The independent versus agency adoption controversy has raised important issues about state regulation and personal autonomy that are relevant to resolving problems presented by assisted reproduction and surrogacy, perhaps the alternative to traditional adoption in this century. We have seen the abuses that can occur in adoption without regulation: children can become a commodity that can be sold. This is a major concern in surrogacy, and as we have seen, states, alerted to this possibility, have taken legislative steps to prevent it by invalidating surrogacy agreements, or by punishing offenders who broker babies. In the area of reproductive technology, science may be ahead of the public's understanding and the law's reponse to its advancement. Legislatures are the conventional forum in which issues of such social importance are normally resolved. If legislatures fail to act because of lack of will or political consensus, courts will have to respond on a case by case basis. Whether the forum for the resolution of these issues is the legislatures or the courts, the century and a half of the legal history of adoption will be an indispensable guide to the future.

Appendix

Uniform Marriage and Divorce Act
Uniform Pre-Marital Agreement Act
Uniform Parentage Act
Uniform Putative and Unknown Fathers Act
Uniform Child Custody Jurisdiction Act
Uniform Child Custody Jurisdiction and Enforcement Act
Parental Kidnapping Prevention Act

Uniform Marriage and Divorce Act

PART I

GENERAL PROVISIONS

SECTION 101. [SHORT TITLE]. This Act may be cited as the "Uniform Marriage and Divorce Act."

SECTION 102. [PURPOSES: RULES OF CONSTRUCTION]. This Act shall be liberally construed and applied to promote its underlying purposes, which are to:

provide adequate procedures for the solemnization and registration of marriage;

(1) strengthen and preserve the integrity of marriage and safeguard family relationships;

(2) promote the amicable settlement of disputes that have arisen between parties to a marriage;

(3) mitigate the potential harm to the spouses and their children caused by the process of legal dissolution of marriage;

(4) make reasonable provision for spouse and minor children during and after litigation; and

(5) make the law of legal dissolution of marriage effective for dealing with the realities of matrimonial experience by making irretrievable breakdown of the marriage relationship the sole basis for its dissolution.

SECTION 103. [UNIFORMITY OF APPLICATION AND CONSTRUCTION]. This Act shall be so applied and construed as to effectuate its general purpose to make uniform the law with respect to the subject of this Act among those states which enact it.

PART II

MARRIAGE

SECTION 201. [FORMALITIES]. Marriage is a personal relationship between a man and a woman arising out of a civil contract to which the consent of the parties is essential. A marriage licensed, solemnized, and registered as provided in this Act is valid in this State. A marriage may be contracted, maintained, invalidated, or dissolved only as provided by law.

SECTION 202. [MARRIAGE LICENSE AND MARRIAGE CERTIFICATE].

(a) The [Secretary of State, Commissioner of Public Health] shall prescribe the form for an application for a marriage license, which shall include the following information:

   (1) name, sex, occupation, address, social security number, date and place of birth of each party to the proposed marriage;

   (2) if either party was previously married, his name, and the date, place, and court in which the marriage was dissolved or declared invalid or the date and place of death of the former spouse;

   (3) name and address of the parents or guardian of each party; and

   (4) whether the parties are related to each other and, if so, their relationship.

   (5) the name and date of birth of any child of which both parties are parents; born before the making of the application, unless their parental rights and the parent and child relationship with respect to the child have been terminated.

(b) The [Secretary of State, Commissioner of Public Health] shall prescribe the forms for the marriage license, the marriage certificate, and the consent to marriage.

SECTION 203. [LICENSE TO MARRY]. When a marriage application has been completed and signed by both parties to a prospective marriage and at least one party has appeared before the [marriage license] clerk and paid the marriage license fee of [$–], the [marriage license] clerk shall issue a license to marry and a marriage certificate form upon being furnished:

   (1) satisfactory proof that each party to the marriage will have attained the age of 18 years at the time the marriage license is effective, or will have attained the age of 16 years and has either the consent to the marriage of both parents or his guardian, or judicial approval; [or, if under the age of 16 years, has both the consent of both parents or his guardian and judicial approval;] and

   (2) satisfactory proof that the marriage is not prohibited; [and]

   (3) [a certificate of the results of any medical examination required by the laws of this State].

SECTION 204. [LICENSE, EFFECTIVE DATE]. A license to marry becomes effective throughout this state 3 days after the date of issuance, unless the [ ] court orders that the license is effective when issued, and expires 180 days after it becomes effective.

Section 205. [Judicial Approval].

(a) The [ ] court, after a reasonable effort has been made to notify the parents or guardian of each underaged party, may order the [marriage license] clerk to issue a marriage license and a marriage certificate form:

[(1)] to a party aged 16 or 17 years who has no parent capable of consenting to his marriage, or whose parent or guardian has not consented to his marriage; [or

(2) to a party under the age of 16 years who has the consent of both parents to his marriage, if capable of giving consent, or his guardian].

(b) A marriage license and a marriage certificate form may be issued under this section only if the court finds that the underaged party is capable of assuming the responsibilities of marriage and the marriage will serve his best interest. Pregnancy alone does not establish that the best interest of the party will be served.

(c) The [ ] court shall authorize performance of a marriage by proxy upon the showing required by the provisions on solemnization.

SECTION 206. [SOLEMNIZATION AND REGISTRATION].

(a) A marriage may be solemnized by a judge of a court of record, by a public official whose powers include solemnization of marriages, or in accordance with any mode of solemnization recognized by any religious denomination, Indian Nation or Tribe, or Native Group. Either the person solemnizing the marriage, or, if no individual acting alone solemnized the marriage, a party to the marriage, shall complete the marriage certificate form and forward it to the [marriage license] clerk.

(b) If a party to a marriage is unable to be present at the solemnization, he may authorize in writing a third person to act as his proxy. If the person solemnizing the marriage is satisfied that the absent party is unable to be present and has consented to the marriage, he may solemnize the marriage by proxy. If he is not satisfied, the parties may petition the [ ] court for an order permitting the marriage to be solemnized by proxy.

(c) Upon receipt of the marriage certificate, the [marriage license] clerk shall register the marriage.

(d) The solemnization of the marriage is not invalidated by the fact that the person solemnizing the marriage was not legally qualified to solemnize it, if either party to the marriage believed him to be so qualified.

SECTION 207. [PROHIBITED MARRIAGES].

(a) The following marriages are prohibited:

(1) a marriage entered into prior to the dissolution of an earlier marriage of one of the parties;

    (2) a marriage between an ancestor and a descendant, or between a
brother and a sister, whether the relationship is by the half or the
whole blood, or by adoption;

    (3) a marriage between an uncle and a niece or between an aunt and a
nephew, whether the relationship is by the half or the whole blood,
except as to marriages permitted by the established customs of abo-
riginal cultures.

  (b) Parties to a marriage prohibited under this section who cohabit after
removal of the impediment are lawfully married as of the date of the removal
of the impediment.

  (c) Children born of a prohibited marriage are legitimate.

SECTION 208. [DECLARATION OF INVALIDITY].

  (a) The [ ] court shall enter its decree declaring the invalidity of a marriage
entered into under the following circumstances:

    (1) a party lacked capacity to consent to the marriage at the time the mar-
riage was solemnized, either because of mental incapacity or infirmity
or because of the influence of alcohol, drugs, or other incapacitating
substances, or a party was induced to enter into a marriage by force
or duress, or by fraud involving the essentials of marriage;

    (2) a party lacks the physical capacity to consummate the marriage by
sexual intercourse, and at the time the marriage was solemnized the
other party did not know of the incapacity;

    (3) a party [was under the age of 16 years and did not have the consent
of his parents or guardian and judicial approval or] was aged 16 or
17 years and did not have the consent of his parents or guardian
or judicial approval; or

    (4) the marriage is prohibited.

  (b) A declaration of invalidity under subsection (a) (1) through (3) may be
sought by any of the following persons and must be commenced within the
times specified, but in no event may a declaration of invalidity be sought after
the death of either party to the marriage:

    (1) for a reason set forth in subsection (a) (1), by either party or by the
legal representative of the party who lacked capacity to consent, no
later than 90 days after the petitioner obtained knowledge of the
described condition;

    (2) for the reason set forth in subsection (a) (2), by either party, no later
than one year after the petitioner obtained knowledge of the described
condition;

    (3) for the reason set forth in subsection (a) (3), by the underaged party, his
parent or guardian, prior to the time the underaged party reaches the

age at which he could have married without satisfying the omitted requirement.

ALTERNATIVE A

[(c) A declaration of invalidity for the reason set forth in subsection (a) (4) may be sought by either party, the legal spouse in case of a bigamous marriage, the [appropriate state official], or a child of either party, at any time prior to the death of one of the parties.]

ALTERNATIVE B

[(c) A declaration of invalidity for the reason set forth in subsection (a) (4) may be sought by either party, the legal spouse in case of a bigamous marriage, the [appropriate state official] or a child of either party, at any time, not to exceed 5 years following the death of either party.]

(d) Children born of a marriage declared invalid are legitimate.

(e) Unless the court finds, after a consideration of all relevant circumstances, including the effect of a retroactive decree on third parties, that the interests of justice would be served by making the decree not retroactive, it shall declare the marriage invalid as of the date of the marriage. The provisions of this Act relating to property rights of the spouses, maintenance, support, and custody of children on dissolution of marriage are applicable to non-retroactive decrees of invalidity.

SECTION 209. [PUTATIVE SPOUSE]. Any person who has cohabited with another to whom he is not legally married in the good faith belief that he was married to that person is a putative spouse until knowledge of the fact that he is not legally married terminates his status and prevents acquisition of further rights. A putative spouse acquires the rights conferred upon a legal spouse, including the right to maintenance following termination of his status, whether or not the marriage is prohibited (Section 207) or declared invalid (Section 208). If there is a legal spouse or other putative spouses, rights acquired by a putative spouse do not supersede the rights of the legal spouse or those acquired by other putative spouses, but the court shall apportion property, maintenance, and support rights among the claimants as appropriate in the circumstances and in the interests of justice.

SECTION 210. [APPLICATION]. All marriages contracted within this State prior to the effective date of this Act, or outside this State, that were valid at the time of the contract or subsequently validated by the laws of the place in which they were contracted or by the domicile of the parties, are valid in this State.

[SECTION 211. [VALIDITY OF COMMON LAW MARRIAGE]
[ALTERNATIVE A].
Common law marriages are not invalidated by this Act.]

[SECTION 211. [INVALIDITY OF COMMON LAW MARRIAGE]
[ALTERNATIVE B].
Common law marriages contracted in this State after the effective date of this
Act are invalid.]

PART III

DISSOLUTION

SECTION 301. [APPLICATION OF [RULES OF CIVIL PRACTICE] TO PROCEEDINGS UNDER THIS ACT].

(a) The [Rules of Civil Practice] apply to all proceedings under this Act,
except as otherwise provided in this Act.

(b) A proceeding for dissolution of marriage, legal separation, or declaration
of invalidity of marriage shall be entitled "In re the Marriage of——
and——." A custody or support proceeding shall be entitled "In re the
(Custody) (Support) of——."

(c) The initial pleading in all proceedings under this Act shall be denominated a
petition. A responsive pleading shall be denominated a response. Other pleadings,
and all pleadings in other matters under this Act, shall be denominated as provided
in the [Rules of Civil Practice].

(d) In this Act, "decree" includes "judgment."

(e) A decree of dissolution or of legal separation, if made, shall not be awarded
to one of the parties, but shall provide that it affects the status previously existing
between the parties in the manner decreed.

SECTION 302. [DISSOLUTION OF MARRIAGE; LEGAL SEPARATION].

(a) The [ ] court shall enter a decree of dissolution of marriage if:

    (1) the court finds that one of the parties, at the time the action was
commenced, was domiciled in this State, or was stationed in this State
while a member of the armed services, and that the domicil or military
presence has been maintained for 90 days next preceding the making
of the findings;

    (2) the court finds that the marriage is irretrievably broken, if the finding is
supported by evidence that (i) the parties have lived separate and apart
for a period of more than 180 days next preceding the commencement
of the proceeding, or (ii) there is serious marital discord adversely
affecting the attitude of one or both of the parties toward the marriage;

    (3) the court finds that the conciliation provisions of Section 305 either
do not apply or have been met;

(4) to the extent it has jurisdiction to do so, the court has considered, approved, or provided for child custody, the support of any child entitled to support, the maintenance of either spouse, and the disposition of property; or has provided for a separate, later hearing to complete these matters.

(b) If a party requests a decree of legal separation rather than a decree of dissolution of marriage, the court shall grant the decree in that form unless the other party objects.

SECTION 303. [PROCEDURE; COMMENCEMENT; PLEADINGS; ABOLITION OF EXISTING DEFENSES].

(a) All proceedings under this Act shall be commenced as provided by the [Rules of Civil Practice].

(b) The verified petition in a proceeding for dissolution of marriage or legal separation shall allege that the marriage is irretrievably broken and shall set forth:

(1) the age, occupation, and length of residence in this state of each party;

(2) the date of the marriage and the place at which it was registered;

(3) that the jurisdictional requirements of Section 302 exist and the marriage is irretrievably broken in that either (i) the parties have lived separate and apart for a period of more than 180 days next preceding the commencement of the proceeding or (ii) there is serious marital discord adversely affecting the attitude of one or both of the parties toward the marriage, and there is no reasonable prospect of reconciliation;

(4) the names, ages, and addresses of all living children of the marriage, and whether the wife is pregnant;

(5) any arrangements as to support, custody, and visitation of the children and maintenance of a spouse; and

(6) the relief sought.

(c) Either or both parties to the marriage may initiate the proceeding.

(d) If a proceeding is commenced by one of the parties, the other party shall be served in the manner provided by the [Rules of Civil Practice] and may within [30] days after the date of service may file a verified response.

(e) Previously existing defenses to divorce and legal separation, including but not limited to condonation, connivance, collusion, recrimination, insanity, and lapse of time, are abolished.

(f) The court may join additional parties proper for the exercise of its authority to implement this Act.

SECTION 304. [TEMPORARY ORDER OR TEMPORARY INJUNCTION].

(a) In a proceeding for dissolution of marriage or for legal separation, or in a proceeding for disposition of property or for maintenance or support following dissolution of the marriage by a court which lacked personal jurisdiction over the absent spouse, either party may move for temporary maintenance or temporary support of a child of the marriage entitled to support. The motion shall be accompanied by an affidavit setting forth the factual basis for the motion and the amounts requested.

(b) As a part of a motion for temporary maintenance or support or by independent motion accompanied by affidavit, either party may request the court to issue a temporary injunction for any of the following relief:

(1) restraining any person from transferring, encumbering, concealing, or otherwise disposing of any property except in the usual course of business or for the necessities of life, and, if so restrained, requiring him to notify the moving party of any proposed extraordinary expenditures made after the order is issued;

(2) enjoining a party from molesting or disturbing the peace of the other party or of any child;

(3) excluding a party from the family home or from the home of the other party upon a showing that physical or emotional harm would otherwise result;

(4) enjoining a party from removing a child from the jurisdiction of the court; and

(5) providing other injunctive relief proper in the circumstances.

(c) The court may issue a temporary restraining order without requiring notice to the other party only if it finds on the basis of the moving affidavit or other evidence that irreparable injury will result to the moving party if no order is issued until the time for responding has elapsed.

(d) A response may be filed within [20] days after service of notice of motion or at the time specified in the temporary restraining order.

(e) On the basis of the showing made and in conformity with Sections 308 and 309, the court may issue a temporary injunction and an order for temporary maintenance or support in amounts and on terms just and proper in the circumstance.

(f) A temporary order or temporary injunction:

(1) does not prejudice the rights of the parties or the child which are to be adjudicated at subsequent hearings in the proceeding;

(2) may be revoked or modified before final decree on a showing by affidavit of the facts necessary to revocation or modification of a final decree under Section 316; and

(3) terminates when the final decree is entered or when the petition for dissolution or legal separation is voluntarily dismissed.

SECTION 305. [IRRETRIEVABLE BREAKDOWN].

(a) If both of the parties by petition or otherwise have stated under oath or affirmation that the marriage is irretrievably broken, or one of the parties has so stated and the other has not denied it, the court, after hearing, shall make a finding whether the marriage is irretrievably broken.

(b) If one of the parties has denied under oath or affirmation that the marriage is irretrievably broken, the court shall consider all relevant factors, including the circumstances that gave rise to filing the petition and the prospect of reconciliation, and shall:

(1) make a finding whether the marriage is irretrievably broken; or

(2) continue the matter for further hearing not fewer than 30 nor more than 60 days later, or as soon thereafter as the matter may be reached on the court's calendar, and may suggest to the parties that they seek counseling. The court, at the request of either party shall, or on its own motion may, order a conciliation conference. At the adjourned hearing the court shall make a finding whether the marriage is irretrievably broken.

(c) A finding of irretrievable breakdown is a determination that there is no reasonable prospect of reconciliation.

SECTION 306. [SEPARATION AGREEMENT].

(a) To promote amicable settlement of disputes between parties to a marriage attendant upon their separation or the dissolution of their marriage, the parties may enter into a written separation agreement containing provisions for disposition of any property owned by either of them, maintenance of either of them, and support, custody, and visitation of their children.

(b) In a proceeding for dissolution of marriage or for legal separation, the terms of the separation agreement, except those providing for the support, custody, and visitation of children, are binding upon the court unless it finds, after considering the economic circumstances of the parties and any other relevant evidence produced by the parties, on their own motion or on request of the court, that the separation agreement is unconscionable.

(c) If the court finds the separation agreement unconscionable, it may request the parties to submit a revised separation agreement or may make orders for the disposition of property, maintenance, and support.

(d) If the court finds that the separation agreement is not unconscionable as to disposition of property or maintenance, and not unsatisfactory as to support:

(1) unless the separation agreement provides to the contrary, its terms shall be set forth in the decree of dissolution or legal separation and the parties shall be ordered to perform them,

(2) if the separation agreement provides that its terms shall not be set forth in the decree, the decree shall identify the separation agreement and state that the court has found the terms not unconscionable.

(e) Terms of the agreement set forth in the decree are enforceable by all remedies available for enforcement of a judgment, including contempt, and are enforceable as contract terms.

(f) Except for terms concerning the support, custody, or visitation of children, the decree may expressly preclude or limit modification of terms set forth in the decree if the separation agreement so provides. Otherwise, terms of a separation agreement set forth in the decree are automatically modified by modification of the decree.

SECTION 307. [DISPOSITION OF PROPERTY] [ALTERNATIVE A].

(a) In a proceeding for dissolution of a marriage, legal separation, or disposition of property following a decree of dissolution of marriage or legal separation by a court which lacked personal jurisdiction over the absent spouse or lacked jurisdiction to dispose of the property, the court, without regard to marital misconduct, shall, and in a proceeding for legal separation may, finally equitably apportion between the parties the property and assets belonging to either or both however and whenever acquired, and whether the title there to is in the name of the husband or wife or both. In making apportionment the court shall consider the duration of the marriage, any prior marriage of either party, antenuptial agreement of the parties, the age, health, station, occupation, amount and sources of income, vocational skills, employability, estate, liabilities, and needs of each of the parties, custodial provisions, whether the apportionment is in lieu of or in addition to maintenance, and the opportunity of each for future acquisition of capital assets and income. The court shall also consider the contribution or dissipation of each party in the acquisition, preservation, depreciation, or appreciation in value of the respective estates, and the contribution of a spouse as a homemaker or to the family unit.

(b) In the proceeding, the court may protect and promote the best interests of the children by setting aside a portion of the jointly and separately held estates of the parties in a separate fund or trust for the support, maintenance, education, and general welfare of any minor, dependent, or incompetent children of the parties.

SECTION 307. [DISPOSITION OF PROPERTY] [ALTERNATIVE B].
In a proceeding for dissolution of the marriage, legal separation, or disposition of property following a decree of dissolution of the marriage or legal separation by a court which lacked personal jurisdiction over the absent spouse or lacked jurisdiction to dispose of the property, the court shall assign each spouse's separate property to that spouse. It also shall divide community property, without regard to marital misconduct, in just proportions after considering all

relevant factors including:

(1) contribution of each spouse to acquisition of the marital property, including contribution of a spouse as homemaker;

(2) value of the property set apart to each spouse;

(3) duration of the marriage; and

(4) economic circumstances of each spouse when the division of property is to become effective, including the desirability of awarding the family home or the right to live therein for a reasonable period to the spouse having custody of any children.

SECTION 308. [MAINTENANCE].

(a) In a proceeding for dissolution of marriage, legal separation, or maintenance following a decree of dissolution of the marriage by a court which lacked personal jurisdiction over the absent spouse, the court may grant a maintenance order for either spouse only if it finds that the spouse seeking maintenance:

(1) lacks sufficient property to provide for his reasonable needs; and

(2) is unable to support himself through appropriate employment or is the custodian of a child whose condition or circumstances make it appropriate that the custodian not be required to seek employment outside the home.

(b) The maintenance order shall be in amounts and for periods of time the court deems just, without regard to marital misconduct, and after considering all relevant factors including:

(1) the financial resources of the party seeking maintenance, including marital property apportioned to him, his ability to meet his needs independently, and the extent to which a provision for support of a child living with the party includes a sum for that party as custodian;

(2) the time necessary to acquire sufficient education or training to enable the party seeking maintenance to find appropriate employment;

(3) the standard of living established during the marriage;

(4) the duration of the marriage;

(5) the age and the physical and emotional condition of the spouse seeking maintenance; and

(6) the ability of the spouse from whom maintenance is sought to meet his needs while meeting those of the spouse seeking maintenance.

SECTION 309. [CHILD SUPPORT].
In a proceeding for dissolution of marriage, legal separation, maintenance, or child support, the court may order either or both parents owing a duty of support to a child to pay an amount reasonable or necessary for his support, without regard to marital misconduct,

after considering all relevant factors including:

(1) the financial resources of the child;

(2) the financial resources of the custodial parent;

(3) the standard of living the child would have enjoyed had the marriage not been dissolved;

(4) the physical and emotional condition of the child and his educational needs; and

(5) the financial resources and needs of the noncustodial parent.

SECTION 310. [REPRESENTATION OF CHILD]. The court may appoint an attorney to represent the interests of a minor or dependent child with respect to his support, custody, and visitation. The court shall enter an order for costs, fees, and disbursements in favor of the child's attorney. The order shall be made against either or both parents, except that, if the responsible party is indigent, the costs, fees, and disbursements shall be borne by the [appropriate agency].

SECTION 311. [PAYMENT OF MAINTENANCE OR SUPPORT TO COURT].

(a) Upon its own motion or upon motion of either party, the court may order at any time that maintenance or support payments be made to the [clerk of court, court trustee, probation officer] as trustee for remittance to the person entitled to receive the payments.

(b) The [clerk of court, court trustee, probation officer] shall maintain records listing the amount of payments, the date payments are required to be made, and the names and addresses of the parties affected by the order.

(c) The parties affected by the order shall inform the [clerk of court, court trustee, probation officer] of any change of address or of other condition that may affect the administration of the order.

(d) If a party fails to make a required payment, the [clerk of court, court trustee, probation officer] shall send by registered or certified mail notice of the arrearage to the obligor. If payment of the sum due is not made to the [clerk of court, court trustee, probation officer] within 10 days after sending notice, the [clerk of court, court trustee, probation officer] shall certify the amount due to the [prosecuting attorney]. The [prosecuting attorney] shall promptly initiate contempt proceedings against the obligator.

(e) The [prosecuting attorney] shall assist the court on behalf of a person entitled to receive maintenance or support in all proceedings initiated under this section to enforce compliance with the order. The person to whom maintenance or support is awarded may also initiate action to collect arrearages.

(f) If the person obligated to pay support has left or is beyond the jurisdiction of the court, the [prosecuting attorney] may institute any other proceeding available under the laws of this State for enforcement of the duties of support and maintenance.

SECTION 312. [ASSIGNMENTS]. The court may order the person obligated to pay support or maintenance to make an assignment of a part of his periodic earnings or trust income to the person entitled to receive the payments. The assignment is binding on the employer, trustee, or other payor of the funds 2 weeks after service upon him of notice that it has been made. The payor shall withhold from the earnings or trust income payable to the person obligated to support the amount specified in the assignment and shall transmit the payments to the person specified in the order. The payor may deduct from each payment a sum not exceeding [$1.00] as reimbursement for costs. An employer shall not discharge or otherwise discipline an employee as a result of a wage or salary assignment authorized by this section.

SECTION 313. [ATTORNEY'S FEES]. The court from time to time after considering the financial resources of both parties may order a party to pay a reasonable amount for the cost to the other party of maintaining or defending any proceeding under this Act and for attorney's fees, including sums for legal services rendered and costs incurred prior to the commencement of the proceeding or after entry of judgment. The court may order that the amount be paid directly to the attorney, who may enforce the order in his name.

SECTION 314. [DECREE].

(a) A decree of dissolution of marriage or of legal separation is final when entered, subject to the right of appeal. An appeal from the decree of dissolution that does not challenge the finding that the marriage is irretrievably broken does not delay the finality of that provision of the decree which dissolves the marriage beyond the time for appealing from that provision, and either of the parties may remarry pending appeal.

(b) No earlier than 6 months after entry of a decree of legal separation, the court on motion of either party shall convert the decree to a decree of dissolution of marriage.

(c) The Clerk of Court shall give notice of the entry of a decree of dissolution or legal separation:

(1) if the marriage is registered in this State, to the [marriage license] clerk of the [county, judicial district] where the marriage is registered who shall enter the fact of dissolution or separation in the [Registry of Marriage]; or

(2) if the marriage is registered in another jurisdiction, to the appropriate official of that jurisdiction, with the request that he enter the fact of dissolution in the appropriate record.

(d) Upon request by a wife whose marriage is dissolved or declared invalid, the court may, and if there are no children of the parties shall, order her maiden name or a former name restored.

SECTION 315. [INDEPENDENCE OF PROVISIONS OF DECREE OR TEMPORARY ORDER]. If a party fails to comply with a provision of a decree or temporary order or injunction, the obligation of the other party to make payments for support or maintenance or to permit visitation is not suspended; but he may move the court to grant an appropriate order.

SECTION 316. [MODIFICATION AND TERMINATION OF PROVISIONS FOR MAINTENANCE, SUPPORT AND PROPERTY DISPOSITION].

(a) Except as otherwise provided in subsection (f) of Section 306, the provisions of any decree respecting maintenance or support may be modified only as to installments accruing subsequent to the motion for modification and only upon a showing of changed circumstances so substantial and continuing as to make the terms unconscionable. The provisions as to property disposition may not be revoked or modified, unless the court finds the existence of conditions that justify the reopening of a judgment under the laws of this state.

(b) Unless otherwise agreed in writing or expressly provided in the decree, the obligation to pay future maintenance is terminated upon the death of either party or the remarriage of the party receiving maintenance.

(c) Unless otherwise agreed in writing or expressly provided in the decree, provisions for the support of a child are terminated by emancipation of the child but not by the death of a parent obligated to support the child. When a parent obligated to pay support dies, the amount of support may be modified, revoked, or commuted to a lump sum payment, to the extent just and appropriate in the circumstances.

PART IV

CUSTODY

SECTION 401. [JURISDICTION; COMMENCEMENT OF PROCEEDING].

(a) A court of this State competent to decide child custody matters has jurisdiction to make a child custody determination by initial or modification decree if

(1) this State (i) is the home state of the child at the time of commencement of the proceeding, or (ii) had been the child's home state within 6 months before commencement of the proceeding and the child is absent from this State because of his removal or retention by a person claiming his custody or for other reason, and a parent or person acting as parent continues to live in this State; or

(2) it is in the best interest of the child that a court of this State assume jurisdiction because (i) the child and his parents, or the child and at least one contestant, have a significant connection with this State, and (ii) there is

available in this State substantial evidence concerning the child's present or future care, protection, training, and personal relationships; or

(3) the child is physically present in this State and (i) has been abandoned or (ii) it is necessary in an emergency to protect him because he has been subjected to or threatened with mistreatment or abuse or is neglected or dependent; or

(4) (i) no other state has jurisdiction under prerequisites substantially in accordance with paragraphs (1), (2) or (3), or another state has declined to exercise jurisdiction on the ground that this State is the more appropriate forum to determine custody of the child, and (ii) it is in his best interest that the court assume jurisdiction.

(b) Except under paragraphs (3) and (4) of subsection (a), physical presence in this State of the child, or of the child and one of the contestants, is not alone sufficient to confer jurisdiction on a court of this State to make a child custody determination.

(c) Physical presence of the child, while desirable, is not a prerequisite for jurisdiction to determine his custody.

(d) A child custody proceeding is commenced in the [ ] court:

(1) by a parent, by filing a petition (i) for dissolution or legal separation; or

    (ii) for custody of the child in the [county, judicial district] in which he is permanently resident or found; or

(2) by a person other than a parent, by filing a petition for custody of the child in the [county, judicial district] in which he is permanently resident or found, but only if he is not in the physical custody of one of his parents.

(e) Notice of a child custody proceeding shall be given to the child's parent, guardian, and custodian, who may appear, be heard, and file a responsive pleading. The court, upon a showing of good cause, may permit intervention of other interested parties.

SECTION 402. [BEST INTEREST OF CHILD]. The court shall determine custody in accordance with the best interest of the child. The court shall consider all relevant factors including:

(1) the wishes of the child's parent or parents as to his custody;

(2) the wishes of the child as to his custodian;

(3) the interaction and interrelationship of the child with his parent or parents, his siblings, and any other person who may significantly affect the child's best interest;

(4) the child's adjustment to his home, school, and community; and

(5) the mental and physical health of all individuals involved.

The court shall not consider conduct of a proposed custodian that does not affect his relationship to the child.

SECTION 403. [TEMPORARY ORDERS].

(a) A party to a custody proceeding may move for a temporary custody order. The motion must be supported by an affidavit as provided in Section 410. The court may award temporary custody under the standards of Section 402 after a hearing, or, if there is no objection, solely on the basis of the affidavits.

(b) If a proceeding for dissolution of marriage or legal separation is dismissed, any temporary custody order is vacated unless a parent or the child's custodian moves that the proceeding continue as a custody proceeding and the court finds, after a hearing, that the circumstances of the parents and the best interest of the child requires that a custody decree be issued.

(c) If a custody proceeding commenced in the absence of a petition for dissolution of marriage or legal separation under subsection (1)(ii) or (2) of Section 401 is dismissed, any temporary custody order is vacated.

SECTION 404. [INTERVIEWS].

(a) The court may interview the child in chambers to ascertain the child's wishes as to his custodian and as to visitation. The court may permit counsel to be present at the interview. The court shall cause a record of the interview to be made and to be part of the record in the case.

(b) The court may seek the advice of professional personnel, whether or not employed by the court on a regular basis. The advice given shall be in writing and made available by the court to counsel upon request. Counsel may examine as a witness any professional personnel consulted by the court.

SECTION 405. [INVESTIGATIONS AND REPORTS].

(a) In contested custody proceedings, and in other custody proceedings if a parent or the child's custodian so requests, the court may order an investigation and report concerning custodial arrangements for the child. The investigation and report may be made by [the court social service agency, the staff of the juvenile court, the local probation or welfare department, or a private agency employed by the court for the purpose].

(b) In preparing his report concerning a child, the investigator may consult any person who may have information about the child and his potential custodial arrangements. Upon order of the court, the investigator may refer the child to professional personnel for diagnosis. The investigator may consult with and obtain information from medical, psychiatric, or other expert persons who have served the child in the past without obtaining the consent of the parent or the child's custodian; but the child's consent must be obtained if he has reached the age of 16, unless the court finds that he lacks mental capacity to consent. If the requirements of subsection (c) are fulfilled, the investigator's report may be received in evidence at the hearing.

Uniform Pre-Marital Agreement Act

SECTION 1. DEFINITIONS. As used in this Act:

(1) "Premarital agreement" means an agreement between prospective spouses made in contemplation of marriage and to be effective upon marriage.

(2) "Property" means an interest, present or future, legal or equitable, vested or contingent, in real or personal property, including income and earnings.

SECTION 2. FORMALITIES. A premarital agreement must be in writing and signed by both parties. It is enforceable without consideration.

SECTION 3. CONTENT.

(a) Parties to a premarital agreement may contract with respect to:

(1) the rights and obligations of each of the parties in any of the property of either or both of them whenever and wherever acquired or located;

(2) the right to buy, sell, use, transfer, exchange, abandon, lease, consume, expend, assign, create a security interest in, mortgage, encumber, dispose of, or otherwise manage and control property;

(3) the disposition of property upon separation, marital dissolution, death, or the occurrence or nonoccurrence of any other event;

(4) the modification or elimination of spousal support;

(5) the making of a will, trust, or other arrangement to carry out the provisions of the agreement;

(6) the ownership rights in and disposition of the death benefit from a life insurance policy;

(7) the choice of law governing the construction of the agreement; and

(8) any other matter, including their personal rights and obligations, not in violation of public policy or a statute imposing a criminal penalty.

(b) The right of a child to support may not be adversely affected by a premarital agreement.

SECTION 4. EFFECT OF MARRIAGE. A premarital agreement becomes effective upon marriage.

SECTION 5. AMENDMENT, REVOCATION. After marriage, a premarital agreement may be amended or revoked only by a written agreement signed by the parties. The amended agreement or the revocation is enforceable without consideration.

SECTION 6. ENFORCEMENT.

(a) A premarital agreement is not enforceable if the party against whom enforcement is sought proves that:

(1) that party did not execute the agreement voluntarily; or

(2) the agreement was unconscionable when it was executed and, before execution of the agreement, that party:

(i) was not provided a fair and reasonable disclosure of the property or financial obligations of the other party;

(ii) did not voluntarily and expressly waive, in writing, any right to disclosure of the property or financial obligations of the other party beyond the disclosure provided; and

(iii) did not have, or reasonably could not have had, an adequate knowledge of the property or financial obligations of the other party.

(b) If a provision of a premarital agreement modifies or eliminates spousal support and that modification or elimination causes one party to the agreement to be eligible for support under a program of public assistance at the time of separation or marital dissolution, a court, notwithstanding the terms of the agreement, may require the other party to provide support to the extent necessary to avoid that eligibility.

(c) An issue of unconscionability of a premarital agreement shall be decided by the court as a matter of law.

SECTION 7. ENFORCEMENT: VOID MARRIAGE. If a marriage is determined to be void, an agreement that would otherwise have been a premarital agreement is enforceable only to the extent necessary to avoid an inequitable result.

SECTION 8. LIMITATION OF ACTIONS. Any statute of limitations applicable to an action asserting a claim for relief under a premarital agreement is tolled during the marriage of the parties to the agreement. However, equitable defenses limiting the time for enforcement, including laches and estoppel, are available to either party.

SECTION 9. APPLICATION AND CONSTRUCTION. This [Act] shall be applied and construed to effectuate its general purpose to make uniform the law with respect to the subject of this [Act] among states enacting it.

SECTION 10. SHORT TITLE. This [Act] may be cited as the Uniform Premarital Agreement Act.

SECTION 11. SEVERABILITY. If any provision of this [Act] or its application to any person or circumstance is held invalid, the invalidity does not affect other provisions or applications of this [Act] which can be given effect without the invalid provision or application, and to this end the provisions of this [Act] are severable.

Uniform Parentage Act

. . .

SECTION 102. DEFINITIONS. In this [Act]:

(1) "Acknowledged father" means a man who has established a father–child relationship under [Article] 3.

(2) "Adjudicated father" means a man who has been adjudicated by a court of competent jurisdiction to be the father of a child.

(3) "Alleged father" means a man who alleges himself to be, or is alleged to be, the genetic father or a possible genetic father of a child, but whose paternity has not been determined. The term does not include:

(A) a presumed father;

(B) a man whose parental rights have been terminated or declared not to exist; or

(C) a male donor.

. . .

(5) "Child" means an individual of any age whose parentage may be determined under this [Act].

. . .

(7) "Determination of parentage" means the establishment of the parent–child relationship by the signing of a valid acknowledgment of paternity under [Article] 3 or adjudication by the court.

. . .

(12) "Man" means a male individual of any age.

(13) "Parent" means an individual who has established a parent–child relationship under Section 201.

(14) "Parent–child relationship" means the legal relationship between a child and a parent of the child. The term includes the mother–child relationship and the father–child relationship.

. . .

ARTICLE 2

PARENT–CHILD RELATIONSHIP

SECTION 201. ESTABLISHMENT OF PARENT–CHILD RELATIONSHIP.

(a) The mother–child relationship is established between a woman and a child by:

(1) the woman's having given birth to the child, [except as otherwise provided in [Article] 8];

(2) an adjudication of the woman's maternity; [or]

(3) adoption of the child by the woman; [or

(4) an adjudication confirming the woman as a parent of a child born to a gestational mother if the agreement was validated under [Article] 8 or is enforceable under other law].

(b) The father–child relationship is established between a man and a child by:

(1) an unrebutted presumption of the man's paternity of the child under Section 204;

(2) an effective acknowledgment of paternity by the man under [Article] 3, unless the acknowledgment has been rescinded or successfully challenged;

(3) an adjudication of the man's paternity;

(4) adoption of the child by the man; [or]

(5) the man's having consented to assisted reproduction by a woman under [Article] 7 which resulted in the birth of the child; [or

(6) an adjudication confirming the man as a parent of a child born to a gestational mother if the agreement was validated under [Article] 8 or is enforceable under other law].

SECTION 202. NO DISCRIMINATION BASED ON MARITAL STATUS.

A child born to parents who are not married to each other has the same rights under the law as a child born to parents who are married to each other.

. . .

SECTION 204. PRESUMPTION OF PATERNITY.

(a) A man is presumed to be the father of a child if:

(1) he and the mother of the child are married to each other and the child is born during the marriage;

(2) he and the mother of the child were married to each other and the child is born within 300 days after the marriage is terminated by death, annulment, declaration of invalidity, or divorce, [or after a decree of separation];

(3) before the birth of the child, he and the mother of the child married each other in apparent compliance with law, even if the attempted marriage is or could be declared invalid, and the child is born during the invalid marriage or within 300 days after its termination by death, annulment, declaration of invalidity, or divorce [, or after a decree of separation];

(4) after the birth of the child, he and the mother of the child married each other in apparent compliance with law, whether or not the marriage is or could be declared invalid, and he voluntarily asserted his paternity of the child, and:

(A) the assertion is in a record filed with [state agency maintaining birth records];

(B) he agreed to be and is named as the child's father on the child's birth certificate; or

(C) he promised in a record to support the child as his own; or

(5) for the first two years of the child's life, he resided in the same household with the child and openly held out the child as his own.

(b) A presumption of paternity established under this section may be rebutted only by an adjudication under [Article] 6.

ARTICLE 3

VOLUNTARY ACKNOWLEDGMENT OF PATERNITY

SECTION 301. ACKNOWLEDGMENT OF PATERNITY. The mother of a child and a man claiming to be the genetic father of the child may sign an acknowledgment of paternity with intent to establish the man's paternity.

SECTION 302. EXECUTION OF ACKNOWLEDGMENT OF PATERNITY.

(a) An acknowledgment of paternity must:

(1) be in a record;

(2) be signed, or otherwise authenticated, under penalty of perjury by the mother and by the man seeking to establish his paternity;

(3) state that the child whose paternity is being acknowledged:

(A) does not have a presumed father, or has a presumed father whose full name is stated; and

(B) does not have another acknowledged or adjudicated father;

(4) state whether there has been genetic testing and, if so, that the acknowledging man's claim of paternity is consistent with the results of the testing; and

(5) state that the signatories understand that the acknowledgment is the equivalent of a judicial adjudication of paternity of the child and that a challenge to the acknowledgment is permitted only under limited circumstances and is barred after two years.

(b) An acknowledgment of paternity is void if it:

(1) states that another man is a presumed father, unless a denial of paternity signed or otherwise authenticated by the presumed father is filed with the [agency maintaining birth records];

(2) states that another man is an acknowledged or adjudicated father; or

(3) falsely denies the existence of a presumed, acknowledged, or adjudicated father of the child.

(c) A presumed father may sign or otherwise authenticate an acknowledgment of paternity.

SECTION 303. DENIAL OF PATERNITY. A presumed father may sign a denial of his paternity. The denial is valid only if:

(1) an acknowledgment of paternity signed, or otherwise authenticated, by another man is filed pursuant to Section 305;

(2) the denial is in a record, and is signed, or otherwise authenticated, under penalty of perjury; and

(3) the presumed father has not previously:

(A) acknowledged his paternity, unless the previous acknowledgment has been rescinded pursuant to Section 307 or successfully challenged pursuant to Section 308; or

(B) been adjudicated to be the father of the child.

SECTION 304. RULES FOR ACKNOWLEDGMENT AND DENIAL OF PATERNITY.

(a) An acknowledgment of paternity and a denial of paternity may be contained in a single document or may be signed in counterparts, and may be filed separately or simultaneously. If the acknowledgement and denial are both necessary, neither is valid until both are filed.

(b) An acknowledgment of paternity or a denial of paternity may be signed before the birth of the child.

(c) Subject to subsection (a), an acknowledgment of paternity or denial of paternity takes effect on the birth of the child or the filing of the document with the [agency maintaining birth records], whichever occurs later.

(d) An acknowledgment of paternity or denial of paternity signed by a minor is valid if it is otherwise in compliance with this [Act].

SECTION 305. EFFECT OF ACKNOWLEDGMENT OR DENIAL OF PATERNITY.

(a) Except as otherwise provided in Sections 307 and 308, a valid acknowledgment of paternity filed with the [agency maintaining birth records] is equivalent to an adjudication of paternity of a child and confers upon the acknowledged father all of the rights and duties of a parent.

(b) Except as otherwise provided in Sections 307 and 308, a valid denial of paternity by a presumed father filed with the [agency maintaining birth records] in conjunction with a valid acknowledgment of paternity is equivalent to an adjudication of the nonpaternity of the presumed father and discharges the presumed father from all rights and duties of a parent.

. . .

SECTION 307. PROCEEDING FOR RESCISSION. A signatory may rescind an acknowledgment of paternity or denial of paternity by commencing a proceeding to rescind before the earlier of:

(1) 60 days after the effective date of the acknowledgment or denial, as provided in Section 304; or

(2) the date of the first hearing, in a proceeding to which the signatory is a party, before a court to adjudicate an issue relating to the child, including a proceeding that establishes support.

SECTION 308. CHALLENGE AFTER EXPIRATION OF PERIOD FOR RESCISSION.

(a) After the period for rescission under Section 307 has expired, a signatory of an acknowledgment of paternity or denial of paternity may commence a proceeding to challenge the acknowledgment or denial only:

(1) on the basis of fraud, duress, or material mistake of fact; and

(2) within two years after the acknowledgment or denial is filed with the [agency maintaining birth records].

(b) A party challenging an acknowledgment of paternity or denial of paternity has the burden of proof.

SECTION 309. PROCEDURE FOR RESCISSION OR CHALLENGE.

(a) Every signatory to an acknowledgment of paternity and any related denial of paternity must be made a party to a proceeding to rescind or challenge the acknowledgment or denial.

(b) For the purpose of rescission of, or challenge to, an acknowledgment of paternity or denial of paternity, a signatory submits to personal jurisdiction of this State by signing the acknowledgment or denial, effective upon the filing of the document with the [agency maintaining birth records].

(c) Except for good cause shown, during the pendency of a proceeding to rescind or challenge an acknowledgment of paternity or denial of paternity, the court may not suspend the legal responsibilities of a signatory arising from the acknowledgment, including the duty to pay child support.

(d) A proceeding to rescind or to challenge an acknowledgment of paternity or denial of paternity must be conducted in the same manner as a proceeding to adjudicate parentage under [Article] 6.

(e) At the conclusion of a proceeding to rescind or challenge an acknowledgment of paternity or denial of paternity, the court shall order the [agency maintaining birth records] to amend the birth record of the child, if appropriate.

SECTION 310. RATIFICATION BARRED. A court or administrative agency conducting a judicial or administrative proceeding is not required or permitted to ratify an unchallenged acknowledgment of paternity.

SECTION 311. FULL FAITH AND CREDIT. A court of this State shall give full faith and credit to an acknowledgment of paternity or denial of paternity effective in another State if the acknowledgment or denial has been signed and is otherwise in compliance with the law of the other State.

. . .

ARTICLE 4

REGISTRY OF PATERNITY

Part 1

General Provisions

SECTION 401. ESTABLISHMENT OF REGISTRY. A registry of paternity is established in the [agency maintaining the registry].

SECTION 402. REGISTRATION FOR NOTIFICATION.

(a) Except as otherwise provided in subsection (b) or Section 405, a man who desires to be notified of a proceeding for adoption of, or termination of parental rights regarding, a child that he may have fathered must register in the registry of paternity before the birth of the child or within 30 days after the birth.

(b) A man is not required to register if:

[(1)] a father–child relationship between the man and the child has been established under this [Act] or other law; [or

(2) the man commences a proceeding to adjudicate his paternity before the court has terminated his parental rights].

(c) A registrant shall promptly notify the registry in a record of any change in the information registered. The [agency maintaining the registry] shall incorporate all new information received into its records but need not affirmatively seek to obtain current information for incorporation in the registry.

SECTION 403. NOTICE OF PROCEEDING. Notice of a proceeding for the adoption of, or termination of parental rights regarding, a child must be given to a registrant who has timely registered. Notice must be given in a manner prescribed for service of process in a civil action.

SECTION 404. TERMINATION OF PARENTAL RIGHTS: CHILD UNDER ONE YEAR OF AGE. The parental rights of a man who may be the father of a child may be terminated without notice if:

(1) the child has not attained one year of age at the time of the termination of parental rights;

(2) the man did not register timely with the [agency maintaining the registry]; and

(3) the man is not exempt from registration under Section 402.

SECTION 405. TERMINATION OF PARENTAL RIGHTS: CHILD AT LEAST ONE YEAR OF AGE.

(a) If a child has attained one year of age, notice of a proceeding for adoption of, or termination of parental rights regarding, the child must be given to every alleged father of the child, whether or not he has registered with the [agency maintaining the registry].

(b) Notice must be given in a manner prescribed for service of process in a civil action.

Part 2

Operation of Registry

SECTION 411. REQUIRED FORM. The [agency maintaining the registry] shall prepare a form for registering with the agency. The form must require the signature of the registrant. The form must state that the form is signed under penalty of perjury. The form must also state that:

(1) a timely registration entitles the registrant to notice of a proceeding for adoption of the child or termination of the registrant's parental rights;

(2) a timely registration does not commence a proceeding to establish paternity;

(3) the information disclosed on the form may be used against the registrant to establish paternity;

(4) services to assist in establishing paternity are available to the registrant through the support-enforcement agency;

(5) the registrant should also register in another State if conception or birth of the child occurred in the other State;

(6) information on registries of other States is available from [appropriate state agency or agencies]; and

(7) procedures exist to rescind the registration of a claim of paternity.

SECTION 412. FURNISHING OF INFORMATION; CONFIDENTIALITY.

(a) The [agency maintaining the registry] need not seek to locate the mother of a child who is the subject of a registration, but the [agency maintaining the registry] shall send a copy of the notice of registration to a mother if she has provided an address.

(b) Information contained in the registry is confidential and may be released on request only to:

(1) a court or a person designated by the court;

(2) the mother of the child who is the subject of the registration;

(3) an agency authorized by other law to receive the information;

(4) a licensed child-placing agency;

(5) a support-enforcement agency;

(6) a party or the party's attorney of record in a proceeding under this [Act] or in a proceeding for adoption of, or for termination of parental rights regarding, a child who is the subject of the registration; and

(7) the registry of paternity in another State.

. . .

SECTION 414. RESCISSION OF REGISTRATION. A registrant may rescind his registration at any time by sending to the registry a rescission in a record signed or otherwise authenticated by him, and witnessed or notarized.

SECTION 415. UNTIMELY REGISTRATION. If a man registers more than 30 days after the birth of the child, the [agency] shall notify the registrant that on its face his registration was not filed timely.

. . .

Part 3

Search of Registries

SECTION 421. SEARCH OF APPROPRIATE REGISTRY.

(a) If a father–child relationship has not been established under this [Act] for a child under one year of age, a [petitioner] for adoption of, or termination of parental rights regarding, the child, must obtain a certificate of search of the registry of paternity.

(b) If a [petitioner] for adoption of, or termination of parental rights regarding, a child has reason to believe that the conception or birth of the child may have occurred in another State, the [petitioner] must also obtain a certificate of search from the registry of paternity, if any, in that State.

SECTION 422. CERTIFICATE OF SEARCH OF REGISTRY.

(a) The [agency maintaining the registry] shall furnish to the requester a certificate of search of the registry on request of an individual, court, or agency identified in Section 412.

(b) A certificate provided by the [agency maintaining the registry] must be signed on behalf of the [agency] and state that:

(1) a search has been made of the registry; and

(2) a registration containing the information required to identify the registrant:

(A) has been found and is attached to the certificate of search; or

(B) has not been found.

(c) A [petitioner] must file the certificate of search with the court before a proceeding for adoption of, or termination of parental rights regarding, a child may be concluded.

SECTION 423. ADMISSIBILITY OF REGISTERED INFORMATION.
A certificate of search of the registry of paternity in this or another State is admissible in a proceeding for adoption of, or termination of parental rights regarding, a child and, if relevant, in other legal proceedings.

. . .

ARTICLE 6

PROCEEDING TO ADJUDICATE PARENTAGE

Part 1

Nature of Proceeding

SECTION 601. PROCEEDING AUTHORIZED. A civil proceeding may be maintained to adjudicate the parentage of a child. The proceeding is governed by the [rules of civil procedure].

SECTION 602. STANDING TO MAINTAIN PROCEEDING. Subject to [Article] 3 and Sections 607 and 609, a proceeding to adjudicate parentage may be maintained by:

(1) the child;

(2) the mother of the child;

(3) a man whose paternity of the child is to be adjudicated;

(4) the support-enforcement agency [or other governmental agency authorized by other law];

(5) an authorized adoption agency or licensed child-placing agency; [or]

(6) a representative authorized by law to act for an individual who would otherwise be entitled to maintain a proceeding but who is deceased, incapacitated, or a minor [; or

(7) an intended parent under [Article] 8].

SECTION 603. PARTIES TO PROCEEDING. The following individuals must be joined as parties in a proceeding to adjudicate parentage:

(1) the mother of the child; and

(2) a man whose paternity of the child is to be adjudicated.

SECTION 604. PERSONAL JURISDICTION.

(a) An individual may not be adjudicated to be a parent unless the court has personal jurisdiction over the individual.

(b) A court of this State having jurisdiction to adjudicate parentage may exercise personal jurisdiction over a nonresident individual, or the guardian or conservator of the individual, if the conditions prescribed in [Section 201 of the Uniform Interstate Family Support Act] are fulfilled.

(c) Lack of jurisdiction over one individual does not preclude the court from making an adjudication of parentage binding on another individual over whom the court has personal jurisdiction.

SECTION 605. VENUE. Venue for a proceeding to adjudicate parentage is in the [county] of this State in which:

(1) the child resides or is found;

(2) the [respondent] resides or is found if the child does not reside in this State; or

(3) a proceeding for probate or administration of the presumed or alleged father's estate has been commenced.

SECTION 606. NO LIMITATION: CHILD HAVING NO PRESUMED, ACKNOWLEDGED, OR ADJUDICATED FATHER. A proceeding to adjudicate the parentage of a child having no presumed, acknowledged, or adjudicated father may be commenced at any time, even after:

(1) the child becomes an adult, but only if the child initiates the proceeding; or

(2) an earlier proceeding to adjudicate paternity has been dismissed based on the application of a statute of limitation then in effect.

. . .

SECTION 608. AUTHORITY TO DENY MOTION FOR GENETIC TESTING.

(a) In a proceeding to adjudicate the parentage of a child having a presumed father or to challenge the paternity of a child having an acknowledged father, the court may deny a motion seeking an order for genetic testing of the mother, the child, and the presumed or acknowledged father if the court determines that:

(1) the conduct of the mother or the presumed or acknowledged father estops that party from denying parentage; and

(2) it would be inequitable to disprove the father–child relationship between the child and the presumed or acknowledged father.

(b) In determining whether to deny a motion seeking an order for genetic testing under this section, the court shall consider the best interest of the child, including the following factors:

(1) the length of time between the proceeding to adjudicate parentage and the time that the presumed or acknowledged father was placed on notice that he might not be the genetic father;

(2) the length of time during which the presumed or acknowledged father has assumed the role of father of the child;

(3) the facts surrounding the presumed or acknowledged father's discovery of his possible nonpaternity;

(4) the nature of the relationship between the child and the presumed or acknowledged father;

(5) the age of the child;

(6) the harm that may result to the child if presumed or acknowledged paternity is successfully disproved;

(7) the nature of the relationship between the child and any alleged father;

(8) the extent to which the passage of time reduces the chances of establishing the paternity of another man and a child-support obligation in favor of the child; and

(9) other factors that may affect the equities arising from the disruption of the father–child relationship between the child and the presumed or acknowledged father or the chance of other harm to the child.

(c) In a proceeding involving the application of this section, a minor or incapacitated child must be represented by a guardian ad litem.

(d) Denial of a motion seeking an order for genetic testing must be based on clear and convincing evidence.

(e) If the court denies a motion seeking an order for genetic testing, it shall issue an order adjudicating the presumed or acknowledged father to be the father of the child.

SECTION 609. LIMITATION: CHILD HAVING ACKNOWLEDGED OR ADJUDICATED FATHER.

(a) If a child has an acknowledged father, a signatory to the acknowledgment of paternity or denial of paternity may commence a proceeding seeking to rescind the acknowledgement or denial or challenge the paternity of the child only within the time allowed under Section 307 or 308.

(b) If a child has an acknowledged father or an adjudicated father, an individual, other than the child, who is neither a signatory to the acknowledgment of paternity nor a party to the adjudication and who seeks an adjudication of paternity of the child must commence a proceeding not later than two years after the effective date of the acknowledgment or adjudication.

(c) A proceeding under this section is subject to the application of the principles of estoppel established in Section 608.

SECTION 610. JOINDER OF PROCEEDINGS.

(a) Except as otherwise provided in subsection (b), a proceeding to adjudicate parentage may be joined with a proceeding for adoption, termination of parental rights, child custody or visitation, child support, divorce, annulment, [legal separation or separate maintenance,] probate or administration of an estate, or other appropriate proceeding.

(b) A [respondent] may not join a proceeding described in subsection (a) with a proceeding to adjudicate parentage brought under [the Uniform Interstate Family Support Act].

SECTION 611. PROCEEDING BEFORE BIRTH.
A proceeding to determine parentage may be commenced before the birth of the child, but may not be concluded until after the birth of the child. The following actions may be taken before the birth of the child:

(1) service of process;

(2) discovery; and

(3) except as prohibited by Section 502, collection of specimens for genetic testing.

SECTION 612. CHILD AS PARTY; REPRESENTATION.

(a) A minor child is a permissible party, but is not a necessary party to a proceeding under this [article].

(b) The court shall appoint an [attorney ad litem] to represent a minor or incapacitated child if the child is a party or the court finds that the interests of the child are not adequately represented.

Part 2

Special Rules for Proceeding to Adjudicate Parentage

SECTION 621. ADMISSIBILITY OF RESULTS OF GENETIC TESTING; EXPENSES.

(a) Except as otherwise provided in subsection (c), a record of a genetic-testing expert is admissible as evidence of the truth of the facts asserted in the report unless a party objects to its admission within [14] days after its receipt by the objecting party and cites specific grounds for exclusion. The admissibility of the report is not affected by whether the testing was performed:

(1) voluntarily or pursuant to an order of the court or a support-enforcement agency; or

(2) before or after the commencement of the proceeding.

(b) A party objecting to the results of genetic testing may call one or more genetic-testing experts to testify in person or by telephone, videoconference, deposition, or another method approved by the court. Unless otherwise ordered by the court, the party offering the testimony bears the expense for the expert testifying.

(c) If a child has a presumed, acknowledged, or adjudicated father, the results of genetic testing are inadmissible to adjudicate parentage unless performed:

(1) with the consent of both the mother and the presumed, acknowledged, or adjudicated father; or

(2) pursuant to an order of the court under Section 502.

(d) Copies of bills for genetic testing and for prenatal and postnatal health care for the mother and child which are furnished to the adverse party not less than 10 days before the date of a hearing are admissible to establish:

(1) the amount of the charges billed; and

(2) that the charges were reasonable, necessary, and customary.

SECTION 622. CONSEQUENCES OF DECLINING GENETIC TESTING.

(a) An order for genetic testing is enforceable by contempt.

(b) If an individual whose paternity is being determined declines to submit to genetic testing ordered by the court, the court for that reason may adjudicate parentage contrary to the position of that individual.

(c) Genetic testing of the mother of a child is not a condition precedent to testing the child and a man whose paternity is being determined. If the mother is unavailable or declines to submit to genetic testing, the court may order the testing of the child and every man whose paternity is being adjudicated.

SECTION 623. ADMISSION OF PATERNITY AUTHORIZED.

(a) A [respondent] in a proceeding to adjudicate parentage may admit to the paternity of a child by filing a pleading to that effect or by admitting paternity under penalty of perjury when making an appearance or during a hearing.

(b) If the court finds that the admission of paternity satisfies the requirements of this section and finds that there is no reason to question the admission, the court shall issue an order adjudicating the child to be the child of the man admitting paternity.

SECTION 624. TEMPORARY ORDER.

(a) In a proceeding under this [article], the court shall issue a temporary order for support of a child if the order is appropriate and the individual ordered to pay support is:

(1) a presumed father of the child;

(2) petitioning to have his paternity adjudicated;

(3) identified as the father through genetic testing under Section 505;

(4) an alleged father who has declined to submit to genetic testing;

(5) shown by clear and convincing evidence to be the father of the child; or

(6) the mother of the child.

(b) A temporary order may include provisions for custody and visitation as provided by other law of this State.

Part 3

Hearings and Adjudication

SECTION 631. RULES FOR ADJUDICATION OF PATERNITY. The court shall apply the following rules to adjudicate the paternity of a child:

(1) The paternity of a child having a presumed, acknowledged, or adjudicated father may be disproved only by admissible results of genetic testing excluding that man as the father of the child or identifying another man as the father of the child.

(2) Unless the results of genetic testing are admitted to rebut other results of genetic testing, a man identified as the father of a child under Section 505 must be adjudicated the father of the child.

(3) If the court finds that genetic testing under Section 505 neither identifies nor excludes a man as the father of a child, the court may not dismiss the proceeding. In that event, the results of genetic testing, and other evidence, are admissible to adjudicate the issue of paternity.

(4) Unless the results of genetic testing are admitted to rebut other results of genetic testing, a man excluded as the father of a child by genetic testing must be adjudicated not to be the father of the child.

SECTION 632. JURY PROHIBITED. The court, without a jury, shall adjudicate paternity of a child.

SECTION 633. HEARINGS; INSPECTION OF RECORDS.

(a) On request of a party and for good cause shown, the court may close a proceeding under this [article].

(b) A final order in a proceeding under this [article] is available for public inspection. Other papers and records are available only with the consent of the parties or on order of the court for good cause.

SECTION 634. ORDER ON DEFAULT. The court shall issue an order adjudicating the paternity of a man who:

(1) after service of process, is in default; and

(2) is found by the court to be the father of a child.

SECTION 635. DISMISSAL FOR WANT OF PROSECUTION. The court may issue an order dismissing a proceeding commenced under this [Act] for want of prosecution only without prejudice. An order of dismissal for want of prosecution purportedly with prejudice is void and has only the effect of a dismissal without prejudice.

SECTION 636. ORDER ADJUDICATING PARENTAGE.

(a) The court shall issue an order adjudicating whether a man alleged or claiming to be the father is the parent of the child.

(b) An order adjudicating parentage must identify the child by name and date of birth.

(c) Except as otherwise provided in subsection (d), the court may assess filing fees, reasonable attorney's fees, fees for genetic testing, other costs, and necessary travel and other reasonable expenses incurred in a proceeding under this [article]. The court may award attorney's fees, which may be paid directly to the attorney, who may enforce the order in the attorney's own name.

(d) The court may not assess fees, costs, or expenses against the support-enforcement agency of this State or another State, except as provided by other law.

(e) On request of a party and for good cause shown, the court may order that the name of the child be changed.

(f) If the order of the court is at variance with the child's birth certificate, the court shall order [agency maintaining birth records] to issue an amended birth registration.

SECTION 637. BINDING EFFECT OF DETERMINATION OF PARENTAGE.

(a) Except as otherwise provided in subsection (b), a determination of parentage is binding on:

(1) all signatories to an acknowledgement or denial of paternity as provided in [Article] 3; and

(2) all parties to an adjudication by a court acting under circumstances that satisfy the jurisdictional requirements of [Section 201 of the Uniform Interstate Family Support Act].

(b) A child is not bound by a determination of parentage under this [Act] unless:

(1) the determination was based on an unrescinded acknowledgment of paternity and the acknowledgement is consistent with the results of genetic testing;

(2) the adjudication of parentage was based on a finding consistent with the results of genetic testing and the consistency is declared in the determination or is otherwise shown; or

(3) the child was a party or was represented in the proceeding determining parentage by an [attorney ad litem].

(c) In a proceeding to dissolve a marriage, the court is deemed to have made an adjudication of the parentage of a child if the court acts under circumstances that satisfy the jurisdictional requirements of [Section 201 of the Uniform Interstate Family Support Act], and the final order:

(1) expressly identifies a child as a "child of the marriage," "issue of the marriage," or similar words indicating that the husband is the father of the child; or

(2) provides for support of the child by the husband unless paternity is specifically disclaimed in the order.

(d) Except as otherwise provided in subsection (b), a determination of parentage may be a defense in a subsequent proceeding seeking to adjudicate parentage by an individual who was not a party to the earlier proceeding.

(e) A party to an adjudication of paternity may challenge the adjudication only under law of this State relating to appeal, vacation of judgments, or other judicial review.

ARTICLE 7

CHILD OF ASSISTED REPRODUCTION

SECTION 701. SCOPE OF ARTICLE. This [article] does not apply to the birth of a child conceived by means of sexual intercourse, [or as the result of a gestational agreement as provided in [Article] 8].

SECTION 702. PARENTAL STATUS OF DONOR. A donor is not a parent of a child conceived by means of assisted reproduction.

SECTION 703. PATERNITY OF CHILD OF ASSISTED REPRODUCTION. A man who provides sperm for, or consents to, assisted reproduction by a woman as provided in Section 704 with the intent to be the parent of her child, is a parent of the resulting child.

SECTION 704. CONSENT TO ASSISTED REPRODUCTION.

(a) Consent by a woman, and a man who intends to be a parent of a child born to the woman by assisted reproduction must be in a record signed by the woman and the man. This requirement does not apply to a donor.

(b) Failure of a man to sign a consent required by subsection (a), before or after birth of the child, does not preclude a finding of paternity if the woman and the man, during the first two years of the child's life resided together in the same household with the child and openly held out the child as their own.

SECTION 705. LIMITATION ON HUSBAND'S DISPUTE OF PATERNITY.

(a) Except as otherwise provided in subsection (b), the husband of a wife who gives birth to a child by means of assisted reproduction may not challenge his paternity of the child unless:

(1) within two years after learning of the birth of the child he commences a proceeding to adjudicate his paternity; and

(2) the court finds that he did not consent to the assisted reproduction, before or after birth of the child.

(b) A proceeding to adjudicate paternity may be maintained at any time if the court determines that:

(1) the husband did not provide sperm for, or before or after the birth of the child consent to, assisted reproduction by his wife;

(2) the husband and the mother of the child have not cohabited since the probable time of assisted reproduction; and

(3) the husband never openly held out the child as his own.

(c) The limitation provided in this section applies to a marriage declared invalid after assisted reproduction.

SECTION 706. EFFECT OF DISSOLUTION OF MARRIAGE OR WITHDRAWAL OF CONSENT.

(a) If a marriage is dissolved before placement of eggs, sperm, or embryos, the former spouse is not a parent of the resulting child unless the former spouse consented in a record that if assisted reproduction were to occur after a divorce, the former spouse would be a parent of the child.

(b) The consent of a woman or a man to assisted reproduction may be withdrawn by that individual in a record at any time before placement of eggs, sperm, or embryos. An individual who withdraws consent under this section is not a parent of the resulting child.

SECTION 707. PARENTAL STATUS OF DECEASED INDIVIDUAL. If an individual who consented in a record to be a parent by assisted reproduction dies before placement of eggs, sperm, or embryos, the deceased individual is not a parent of the resulting child unless the deceased spouse consented in a record that if assisted reproduction were to occur after death, the deceased individual would be a parent of the child.

. . .

ARTICLE 8

GESTATIONAL AGREEMENT

SECTION 801. GESTATIONAL AGREEMENT AUTHORIZED.

(a) A prospective gestational mother, her husband if she is married, a donor or the donors, and the intended parents may enter into a written agreement providing that:

(1) the prospective gestational mother agrees to pregnancy by means of assisted reproduction;

(2) the prospective gestational mother, her husband if she is married, and the donors relinquish all rights and duties as the parents of a child conceived through assisted reproduction; and

(3) the intended parents become the parents of the child.

(b) The man and the woman who are the intended parents must both be parties to the gestational agreement.

(c) A gestational agreement is enforceable only if validated as provided in Section 803.

(d) A gestational agreement does not apply to the birth of a child conceived by means of sexual intercourse.

(e) A gestational agreement may provide for payment of consideration.

(f) A gestational agreement may not limit the right of the gestational mother to make decisions to safeguard her health or that of the embryos or fetus.

SECTION 802. REQUIREMENTS OF PETITION.

(a) The intended parents and the prospective gestational mother may commence a proceeding in the [appropriate court] to validate a gestational agreement.

(b) A proceeding to validate a gestational agreement may not be maintained unless:

(1) the mother or the intended parents have been residents of this State for at least 90 days;

(2) the prospective gestational mother's husband, if she is married, is joined in the proceeding; and

(3) a copy of the gestational agreement is attached to the [petition].

SECTION 803. HEARING TO VALIDATE GESTATIONAL AGREEMENT.

(a) If the requirements of subsection (b) are satisfied, a court may issue an order validating the gestational agreement and declaring that the intended parents will be the parents of a child born during the term of the of the agreement.

(b) The court may issue an order under subsection (a) only on finding that:

(1) the residence requirements of Section 802 have been satisfied and the parties have submitted to the jurisdiction of the court under the jurisdictional standards of this [Act];

(2) unless waived by the court, the [relevant child-welfare agency] has made a home study of the intended parents and the intended parents meet the standards of suitability applicable to adoptive parents;

(3) all parties have voluntarily entered into the agreement and understand its terms;

(4) adequate provision has been made for all reasonable health-care expense associated with the gestational agreement until the birth of the child, including responsibility for those expenses if the agreement is terminated; and

(5) the consideration, if any, paid to the prospective gestational mother is reasonable.

SECTION 804. INSPECTION OF RECORDS.
The proceedings, records, and identities of the individual parties to a gestational agreement under this [article] are subject to inspection under the standards of confidentiality applicable to adoptions as provided under other law of this State.

SECTION 805. EXCLUSIVE, CONTINUING JURISDICTION.
Subject to the jurisdictional standards of [Section 201 of the Uniform Child Custody Jurisdiction and Enforcement Act], the court conducting a proceeding under this [article] has exclusive, continuing jurisdiction of all matters arising out of the gestational agreement until a child born to the gestational mother during the period governed by the agreement attains the age of 180 days.

SECTION 806. TERMINATION OF GESTATIONAL AGREEMENT.

(a) After issuance of an order under this [article], but before the prospective gestational mother becomes pregnant by means of assisted reproduction, the prospective gestational mother, her husband, or either of the intended parents may terminate the gestational agreement by giving written notice of termination to all other parties.

(b) The court for good cause shown may terminate the gestational agreement.

(c) An individual who terminates a gestational agreement shall file notice of the termination with the court. On receipt of the notice, the court shall vacate the order issued under this [article]. An individual who does not notify the court of the termination of the agreement is subject to appropriate sanctions.

(d) Neither a prospective gestational mother nor her husband, if any, is liable to the intended parents for terminating a gestational agreement pursuant to this section.

SECTION 807. PARENTAGE UNDER VALIDATED GESTATIONAL AGREEMENT.

(a) Upon birth of a child to a gestational mother, the intended parents shall file notice with the court that a child has been born to the gestational mother within 300 days after assisted reproduction. Thereupon, the court shall issue an order:

(1) confirming that the intended parents are the parents of the child;

(2) if necessary, ordering that the child be surrendered to the intended parents; and

(3) directing the [agency maintaining birth records] to issue a birth certificate naming the intended parents as parents of the child.

(b) If the parentage of a child born to a gestational mother is alleged not to be the result of assisted reproduction, the court shall order genetic testing to determine the parentage of the child.

(c) If the intended parents fail to file notice required under subsection (a), the gestational mother or the appropriate State agency may file notice with the court that a child has been born to the gestational mother within 300 days after assisted reproduction. Upon proof of a court order issued pursuant to Section 803 validating the gestational agreement, the court shall order the intended parents are the parents of the child and are financially responsible for the child.

SECTION 808. GESTATIONAL AGREEMENT: EFFECT OF SUBSEQUENT MARRIAGE.

After the issuance of an order under this [article], subsequent marriage of the gestational mother does not affect the validity of a gestational agreement, her husband's consent to the agreement is not required, and her husband is not a presumed father of the resulting child.

SECTION 809. EFFECT OF NONVALIDATED GESTATIONAL AGREEMENT.

(a) A gestational agreement, whether in a record or not, that is not judicially validated is not enforceable.

(b) If a birth results under a gestational agreement that is not judicially validated as provided in this [article], the parent–child relationship is determined as provided in [Article] 2.

(c) Individuals who are parties to a nonvalidated gestational agreement as intended parents may be held liable for support of the resulting child, even if the agreement is otherwise unenforceable. The liability under this subsection includes assessing all expenses and fees as provided in Section 636.

. . .

Uniform Putative and Unknown Fathers Act

SECTION 1. DEFINITIONS. In this [Act]:

(1) "Man" means a male individual of any age.

(2) "Putative father" means a man who claims to be, or is named as, the biological father or a possible biological father of a child, and whose paternity of the child has not been judicially determined, excluding:

(i) a man whose parental rights with respect to the child have been previously judicially terminated or declared not to exist;

(ii) a donor of semen used in artificial insemination or in vitro fertilization whose identity is not known by the mother of the resulting child or whose semen was donated under circumstances indicating that the donor did not anticipate having an interest in the resulting child;

(iii) a man who is or was married to the mother of the child, and the child is born during the marriage [or within 300 days after the marriage was terminated by death, annulment, declaration of invalidity, divorce, or marital dissolution, or after a decree of separation was entered by a court];

(iv) a man who, before the birth of the child, attempted to marry the mother of the child in apparent compliance with law, although the attempted marriage is, or could be declared, invalid, and:

(A) if the attempted marriage could be declared invalid only by a court, the child is born during the attempted marriage [, or within 300 days after its termination by death, annulment, declaration of invalidity, divorce, or marital dissolution]; or

(B) if the attempted marriage is invalid without a court order declaring its invalidity, the child is born during, or within 300 days after the termination of, cohabitation; and

(v) a man who, after the birth of the child, married or attempted to marry the mother of the child in apparent compliance with law, although the attempted marriage is, or could be declared, invalid, and:

(A) has acknowledged his paternity of the child in a writing filed with the [appropriate court or Vital Statistics Bureau];

(B) with his consent, is named as the child's biological father on the child's birth certificate; or

(C) is obligated to support the child under a written promise or by court order.

(3) "Unknown father" means a child's biological father whose identity is unascertained. However, the term does not include a donor of semen used in artificial insemination or in vitro fertilization whose identity is not known to the mother of the resulting child or whose semen was donated under circumstances indicating that the donor did not anticipate having any interest in the resulting child.

SECTION 2. RIGHT TO DETERMINATION OF PATERNITY.

(a) A putative father may bring an action to determine whether he is the biological father of a particular child [, in accordance with [applicable state law],] at any time, unless his paternity or possible parental rights have already been determined or are in issue in pending litigation.

(b) An agreement between a putative father and the mother or between him and the child does not bar an action under this section [, unless the agreement has been judicially approved [under applicable state law]].]

SECTION 3. NOTICE OF JUDICIAL PROCEEDINGS FOR ADOPTION OR TERMINATION OF PARENTAL RIGHTS.

(a) In an adoption or other judicial proceeding that may result in termination of any man's parental rights with respect to a child, the person seeking termination shall give notice to every putative father of the child known to that person.

(b) The notice must be given (i) at a time and place and in a manner appropriate under the [rules of civil procedure for the service of process in a civil action in this State] or (ii) at a time and place and in a manner as the court directs and which provides actual notice.

(c) A putative father may participate as a party in a proceeding described in subsection (a).

(d) If, at any time in the proceeding, it appears to the court that there is a putative father of the child who has not been given notice, the court shall require notice of the proceeding to be given to him in accordance with subsection (b).

(e) If, at any time in the proceeding, it appears to the court that an unknown father may not have been given notice, the court shall determine whether he can be identified. The determination must be based on evidence that includes inquiry of appropriate persons in an effort to identify him for the purpose of providing notice. The inquiry must include:

(1) whether the mother was married at the probable time of conception of the child or at a later time;

(2) whether the mother was cohabiting with a man at the probable time of conception of the child;

(3) whether the mother has received support payments or promises of support, other than from a governmental agency, with respect to the child or because of her pregnancy;

(4) whether the mother has named any man as the biological father in connection with applying for or receiving public assistance; and

(5) whether any man has formally or informally acknowledged or claimed paternity of the child in a jurisdiction in which the mother resided at the time of or since conception of the child or in which the child has resided or resides at the time of the inquiry.

(f) If the inquiry required by subsection (e) identifies any man as the unknown father, the court shall require notice of the proceeding to be given to him pursuant to subsection (b). If the inquiry so identifies a man, but his whereabouts are unknown, the court shall proceed in accordance with subsections (b) and (g).

(g) If, after the inquiry required by subsection (e), it appears to the court that there may be an unknown father of the child, the court shall consider whether publication or public posting of notice of the proceeding is likely to lead to actual notice to him. The court may order publication or public posting of the notice only if, on the basis of all information available, the court determines that the publication or posting is likely to lead to actual notice to him.

SECTION 4. NOTICE OF JUDICIAL PROCEEDINGS REGARDING CUSTODY OR VISITATION.

(a) The petitioner in a judicial proceeding to change or establish legal or physical custody of or visitation rights with respect to a child shall give notice to every putative father of the child known to the petitioner, except a proceeding for annulment, declaration of invalidity, divorce, marital dissolution, legal separation, modification of child custody, or determination of paternity.

(b) The notice must be given (i) at a time and place and in a manner appropriate under the [rules of civil procedure for the service of process in a civil action in this State] or (ii) as the court determines will likely provide actual notice.

(c) If, at any time in the proceeding, it appears to the court that there is a putative father of the child who has not been given notice of the proceeding, the court shall require notice of the proceeding to be given to him pursuant to subsection (b).

(d) If, at any time in the proceeding, it appears to the court that there may be an unknown father who has not been given notice of the proceeding, the court, in the best interest of the child, may attempt to identify him pursuant to Section 3(e) and require notice of the proceeding to be given to him pursuant to Section 3(f) and (g).

(e) A putative father may participate as a party in a proceeding described in subsection (a).

SECTION 5. FACTORS IN DETERMINING PARENTAL RIGHTS OF FATHER. In determining whether to preserve or terminate the parental rights of a putative father in a proceeding governed by Section 3 or 4, the court shall consider all of the following factors that are pertinent:

(1) the age of the child;

(2) the nature and quality of any relationship between the man and the child;

(3) the reasons for any lack of a relationship between the man and the child;

(4) whether a parent and child relationship has been established between the child and another man;

(5) whether the child has been abused or neglected;

(6) whether the man has a history of substance abuse or of abuse of the mother or the child;

(7) any proposed plan for the child;

(8) whether the man seeks custody and is able to provide the child with emotional or financial support and a home, whether or not he has had opportunity to establish a parent and child relationship with the child;

(9) whether the man visits the child, has shown any interest in visitation, or, desiring visitation, has been effectively denied an opportunity to visit the child;

(10) whether the man is providing financial support for the child according to his means;

(11) whether the man provided emotional or financial support for the mother during prenatal, natal, and postnatal care;

(12) the circumstances of the child's conception, including whether the child was conceived as a result of incest or forcible rape;

(13) whether the man has formally or informally acknowledged or declared his possible paternity of the child; and

(14) other factors the court considers relevant to the standards for making an order, as stated in Section 6(d) and (g).

SECTION 6. COURT DETERMINATIONS AND ORDERS.

(a) If a man appears in a proceeding described in Section 3, other than as a petitioner or prospective adoptive parent, the court may:

(1) [in accordance with [applicable state law],] determine whether the man is the biological father of the child and, if the court determines that he is, enter an order in accordance with subsection (d); or

(2) without determining paternity, and consistent with the standards in subsection (d), enter an order, after considering the factors in Section 5, terminating any parental rights he may have, or declaring that he has no parental rights, with respect to the child.

(b) If the court makes an order under subsection (a), the court may also make an order (i) terminating the parental rights of any other man given notice who does not appear, or (ii) declaring that no man has any parental rights with respect to the child.

(c) If a man who appears in a proceeding described in Section 3 is determined by the court to be the father, the court, after considering evidence of the factors in Section 5, shall determine (i) whether a familial bond between the father and the child has been established; or (ii) whether the failure to establish a familial bond is justified, and the father has the desire and potential to establish the bond.

(d) If the court makes an affirmative determination under subsection (c), the court may terminate the parental rights of the father [, in accordance with [applicable state law],] only if failure to do so would be detrimental to the child. If the court does not make an affirmative determination, it may terminate the parental rights of the father if doing so is in the best interest of the child.

(e) If no man appears in a proceeding described in Section 3, the court may enter an order:

(1) terminating with respect to the child the parental rights of any man given notice; or

(2) declaring that no putative father or unknown father has any parental rights with respect to the child.

(f) If the court does not require notice under Section 3, it shall enter an order declaring that no putative father or unknown father has any parental rights with respect to the child.

(g) If a man appears in a proceeding described in Section 4 and requests custody or visitation based on a claim of paternity, the court shall either determine [, in accordance with [applicable state law],] whether he is the biological father of the child or, after considering the factors in Section 5, deny him the custody of or visitation with the child. If the court determines that he is the biological father, the court shall determine, after considering evidence of the factors listed in Section 5, whether or not to grant him custody or visitation and shall make such other orders as are appropriate. All orders issued under this subsection must be in the child's best interest.

(h) A court order under subsection (a)(2), (b), (d), or (e) terminating the parental rights of a man, or declaring that no man has parental rights, with respect to the child, is not a determination that the man is or is not the biological father of the child.

(i) [Six months] after the date of issuance of an order under this section terminating parental rights or declaring that no man has parental rights, no person may directly or collaterally challenge the order upon any ground, including fraud, misrepresentation, failure to give a required notice, or lack of jurisdiction over the parties or of the subject matter. The running of this period of limitation may not be extended for any reason.

. . .

Uniform Child Custody Jurisdiction Act

SECTION 1. [PURPOSES OF ACT; CONSTRUCTION OF PROVISIONS.]

(a) The general purposes of this Act are to:

(1) void jurisdictional competition and conflict with courts of other states in matters of child custody which have in the past resulted in the shifting of children from state to state with harmful effects on their well-being;

(2) promote cooperation with the courts of other states to the end that a custody decree is rendered in that state which can best decide the case in the interest of the child;

(3) assure that litigation concerning the custody of a child take place ordinarily in the state with which the child and his family have the closest connection and where significant evidence concerning his care, protection, training, and personal relationships is most readily available, and that courts of this state decline the exercise of jurisdiction when the child and his family have a closer connection with another state;

(4) discourage continuing controversies over child custody in the interest of greater stability of home environment and of secure family relationships for the child;

(5) deter abductions and other unilateral removals of children undertaken to obtain custody awards;

(6) avoid re-litigation of custody decisions of other states in this state insofar as feasible;

(7) facilitate the enforcement of custody decrees of other states;

(8) promote and expand the exchange of information and other forms of mutual assistance between the courts of this state and those of other states concerned with the same child; and

(9) make uniform the law of those states which enact it.

(b) This Act shall be construed to promote the general purposes stated in this section.

SECTION 2. [DEFINITIONS.] As used in this Act:

(1) "contestant" means a person, including a parent, who claims a right to custody or visitation rights with respect to a child;

(2) "custody determination" means a court decision and court orders and instructions providing for the custody of a child, including visitation rights; it does not include a decision relating to child support or any other monetary obligation of any person;

(3) "custody proceeding" includes proceedings in which a custody determination is one of several issues, such as an action for divorce or separation, and includes child neglect and dependency proceedings;

(4) "decree" or "custody decree" means a custody determination contained in a judicial decree or order made in a custody proceeding, and includes an initial decree and a modification decree;

(5) "home state" means the state in which the child immediately preceding the time involved lived with his parents, a parent, or a person acting as parent, for at least 6 consecutive months, and in the case of a child less than 6 months old the state in which the child lived from birth with any of the persons mentioned. Periods of temporary absence of any of the named persons are counted as part of the 6-month or other period;

(6) "initial decree" means the first custody decree concerning a particular child;

(7) "modification decree" means a custody decree which modifies or replaces a prior decree, whether made by the court which rendered the prior decree or by another court;

(8) "physical custody" means actual possession and control of a child;

(9) "person acting as parent" means a person, other than a parent, who has physical custody of a child and who has either been awarded custody by a court or claims a right to custody; and

(10) "state" means any state, territory, or possession of the United States, the Commonwealth of Puerto Rico, and the District of Columbia.

SECTION 3. [*JURISDICTION.*]

(a) A court of this State which is competent to decide child custody matters has jurisdiction to make a child custody determination by initial or modification decree if:

(1) this State (i) is the home state of the child at the time of commencement of the proceeding, or (ii) had been the child's home state within 6 months before commencement of the proceeding and the child is absent from this State because of his removal or retention by a person claiming his custody or for other reasons, and a parent or person acting as parent continues to live in this State; or

(2) it is in the best interest of the child that a court of this State assume jurisdiction because (i) the child and his parents, or the child and at least one contestant, have a significant connection with this State, and (ii) there is

available in this State substantial evidence concerning the child's present or future care, protection, training, and personal relationships; or

(3) the child is physically present in this State and (i) the child has been abandoned or (ii) it is necessary in an emergency to protect the child because he has been subjected to or threatened with mistreatment or abuse or is otherwise neglected [or dependent]; or

(4)(i) it appears that no other state would have jurisdiction under prerequisites substantially in accordance with paragraphs (1), (2), or (3), or another state has declined to exercise jurisdiction on the ground that this State is the more appropriate forum to determine the custody of the child, and (ii) it is in the best interest of the child that this court assume jurisdiction.

(b) Except under paragraphs (3) and (4) of subsection (a), physical presence in this State of the child, or of the child and one of the contestants, is not alone sufficient to confer jurisdiction on a court of this State to make a child custody determination.

(c) Physical presence of the child, while desirable, is not a prerequisite for jurisdiction to determine his custody.

SECTION 4. [*NOTICE AND OPPORTUNITY TO BE HEARD.*] Before making a decree under this Act, reasonable notice and opportunity to be heard shall be given to the contestants, any parent whose parental rights have not been previously terminated, and any person who has physical custody of the child. If any of these persons is outside this State, notice and opportunity to be heard shall be given pursuant to section 5.

SECTION 5. [*NOTICE TO PERSONS OUTSIDE THIS STATE; SUBMISSION TO JURISDICTION.*]

(a) Notice required for the exercise of jurisdiction over a person outside this State shall be given in a manner reasonably calculated to give actual notice, and may be:

(1) by personal delivery outside this State in the manner prescribed for service of process within this State;

(2) in the manner prescribed by the law of the place in which the service is made for service of process in that place in an action in any of its courts of general jurisdiction;

(3) by any form of mail addressed to the person to be served and requesting a receipt; or

(4) as directed by the court [including publication, if other means of notification are ineffective].

(b) Notice under this section shall be served, mailed, or delivered, [or last published] at least [10, 20] days before any hearing in this State.

(c) Proof of service outside this State may be made by affidavit of the individual who made the service, or in the manner prescribed by the law of this State, the order pursuant to which the service is made, or the law of the place in which the service is made. If service is made by mail, proof may be a receipt signed by the addressee or other evidence of delivery to the addressee.

(d) Notice is not required if a person submits to the jurisdiction of the court.

SECTION 6. [*SIMULTANEOUS PROCEEDINGS IN OTHER STATES.*]

(a) A court of this State shall not exercise its jurisdiction under this Act if at the time of filing the petition a proceeding concerning the custody of the child was pending in a court of another state exercising jurisdiction substantially in conformity with this Act, unless the proceeding is stayed by the court of the other state because this State is a more appropriate forum or for other reasons.

(b) Before hearing the petition in a custody proceeding the court shall examine the pleadings and other information supplied by the parties under section 9 and shall consult the child custody registry established under section 16 concerning the pendency of proceedings with respect to the child in other states. If the court has reason to believe that proceedings may be pending in another state it shall direct an inquiry to the state court administrator or other appropriate official of the other state.

(c) If the court is informed during the course of the proceeding that a proceeding concerning the custody of the child was pending in another state before the court assumed jurisdiction it shall stay the proceeding and communicate with the court in which the other proceeding is pending to the end that the issue may be litigated in the more appropriate forum and that information be exchanged in accordance with sections 19 through 22. If a court of this State has made a custody decree before being informed of a pending proceeding in a court of another state it shall immediately inform that court of the fact. If the court is informed that a proceeding was commenced in another state after it assumed jurisdiction it shall likewise inform the other court to the end that the issues may be litigated in the more appropriate forum.

SECTION 7. [*INCONVENIENT FORUM.*]

(a) A court which has jurisdiction under this Act to make an initial or modification decree may decline to exercise its jurisdiction any time before making a decree if it finds that it is an inconvenient forum to make a custody determination under the circumstances of the case and that a court of another state is a more appropriate forum.

(b) A finding of inconvenient forum may be made upon the court's own motion or upon motion of a party or a guardian ad litem or other representative of the child.

(c) In determining if it is an inconvenient forum, the court shall consider if it is in the interest of the child that another state assume jurisdiction. For this purpose it may take into account the following factors, among others:

(1) if another state is or recently was the child's home state;

(2) if another state has a closer connection with the child and his family or with the child and one or more of the contestants;

(3) if substantial evidence concerning the child's present or future care, protection, training, and personal relationships is more readily available in another state;

(4) if the parties have agreed on another forum which is no less appropriate; and

(5) if the exercise of jurisdiction by a court of this state would contravene any of the purposes stated in section 1.

(d) Before determining whether to decline or retain jurisdiction the court may communicate with a court of another state and exchange information pertinent to the assumption of jurisdiction by either court with a view to assuring that jurisdiction will be exercised by the more appropriate court and that a forum will be available to the parties.

(e) If the court finds that it is an inconvenient forum and that a court of another state is a more appropriate forum, it may dismiss the proceedings, or it may stay the proceedings upon condition that a custody proceeding be promptly commenced in another named state or upon any other conditions which may be just and proper, including the condition that a moving party stipulate his consent and submission to the jurisdiction of the other forum.

(f) The court may decline to exercise its jurisdiction under this Act if a custody determination is incidental to an action for divorce or another proceeding while retaining jurisdiction over the divorce or other proceeding.

(g) If it appears to the court that it is clearly an inappropriate forum it may require the party who commenced the proceedings to pay, in addition to the costs of the proceedings in this State, necessary travel and other expenses, including attorneys' fees, incurred by other parties or their witnesses. Payment is to be made to the clerk of the court for remittance to the proper party.

(h) Upon dismissal or stay of proceedings under this section the court shall inform the court found to be the more appropriate forum of this fact or, if the court which would have jurisdiction in the other state is not certainly known, shall transmit the information to the court administrator or other appropriate official for forwarding to the appropriate court.

(i) Any communication received from another state informing this State of a finding of inconvenient forum because a court of this State is the more appropriate forum shall be filed in the custody registry of the appropriate court. Upon assuming jurisdiction the court of this State shall inform the original court of this fact.

SECTION 8. [*JURISDICTION DECLINED BY REASON OF CONDUCT.*]

(a) If the petitioner for an initial decree has wrongfully taken the child from another state or has engaged in similar reprehensible conduct the court may decline to exercise jurisdiction if this is just and proper under the circumstances.

(b) Unless required in the interest of the child, the court shall not exercise its jurisdiction to modify a custody decree of another state if the petitioner, without consent of the person entitled to custody, has improperly removed the child from the physical custody of the person entitled to custody or has improperly retained the child after a visit or other temporary relinquishment of physical custody. If the petitioner has violated any other provision of a custody decree of another state the court may decline to exercise its jurisdiction if this is just and proper under the circumstances.

(c) In appropriate cases a court dismissing a petition under this section may charge the petitioner with necessary travel and other expenses, including attorneys' fees, incurred by other parties or their witnesses.

SECTION 9. [*INFORMATION UNDER OATH TO BE SUBMITTED TO THE COURT.*]

(a) Every party in a custody proceeding in his first pleading or in an affidavit attached to that pleading shall give information under oath as to the child's present address, the places where the child has lived within the last 5 years, and the names and present addresses of the persons with whom the child has lived during that period. In this pleading or affidavit every party shall further declare under oath whether:

(1) he has participated (as a party, witness, or in any other capacity) in any other litigation concerning the custody of the same child in this or any other state;

(2) he has information of any custody proceeding concerning the child pending in a court of this or any other state; and

(3) he knows of any person not a party to the proceedings who has physical custody of the child or claims to have custody or visitation rights with respect to the child.

(b) If the declaration as to any of the above items is in the affirmative the declarant shall give additional information under oath as required by the court. The court may examine the parties under oath as to details of the information furnished and as to other matters pertinent to the court's jurisdiction and the disposition of the case.

(c) Each party has a continuing duty to inform the court of any custody proceeding concerning the child in this or any other state of which he obtained information during this proceeding.

SECTION 10. [*ADDITIONAL PARTIES.*] If the court learns from information furnished by the parties pursuant to section 9 or from other sources that a person not a party to the custody proceeding has physical custody of the child or claims to have custody or visitation rights with respect to the child, it shall order that person to be joined as a party and to be duly notified of the pendency of the proceeding and of his joinder as a party. If the person joined as a party is outside this State he shall be served with process or otherwise notified in accordance with section 5.

SECTION 11. [*APPEARANCE OF PARTIES AND THE CHILD.*]

[(a) The court may order any party to the proceeding who is in this State to appear personally before the court. If that party has physical custody of the child the court may order that he appear personally with the child.]

(b) If a party to the proceeding whose presence is desired by the court is outside this State with or without the child the court may order that the notice given under section 5 include a statement directing that party to appear personally with or without the child and declaring that failure to appear may result in a decision adverse to that party.

(c) If a party to the proceeding who is outside this State is directed to appear under subsection (b) or desires to appear personally before the court with or without the child, the court may require another party to pay to the clerk of the court travel and other necessary expenses of the party so appearing and of the child if this is just and proper under the circumstances.

SECTION 12. [*BINDING FORCE AND RES JUDICATA EFFECT OF CUSTODY DECREE.*] A custody decree rendered by a court of this State which had jurisdiction under section 3 binds all parties who have been served in this State or notified in accordance with section 5 or who have submitted to the jurisdiction of the court, and who have been given an opportunity to be heard. As to these parties the custody decree is conclusive as to all issues of law and fact decided and as to the custody determination made unless and until that determination is modified pursuant to law, including the provisions of this Act.

SECTION 13. [*RECOGNITION OF OUT-OF-STATE CUSTODY DECREES.*] The courts of this State shall recognize and enforce an initial or modification decree of a court of another state which had assumed jurisdiction under statutory provisions substantially in accordance with this Act or which was made under factual circumstances meeting the jurisdictional standards of the Act, so long as this decree has not been modified in accordance with jurisdictional standards substantially similar to those of this Act.

SECTION 14. [*MODIFICATION OF CUSTODY DECREE OF ANOTHER STATE.*]

(a) If a court of another state has made a custody decree, a court of this State shall not modify that decree unless (1) it appears to the court of this State that the court which rendered the decree does not now have jurisdiction under jurisdictional prerequisites substantially in accordance with this Act or has declined to assume jurisdiction to modify the decree and (2) the court of this State has jurisdiction.

(b) If a court of this State is authorized under subsection (a) and section 8 to modify a custody decree of another state it shall give due consideration to the transcript of the record and other documents of all previous proceedings submitted to it in accordance with section 22.

SECTION 15. [*FILING AND ENFORCEMENT OF CUSTODY DECREE OF ANOTHER STATE.*]

(a) A certified copy of a custody decree of another state may be filed in the office of the clerk of any [District Court, Family Court] of this State. The clerk shall treat the decree in the same manner as a custody decree of the [District Court, Family Court] of this State. A custody decree so filed has the same effect and shall be enforced in like manner as a custody decree rendered by a court of this State.

(b) A person violating a custody decree of another state which makes it necessary to enforce the decree in this State may be required to pay necessary travel and other expenses, including attorneys' fees, incurred by the party entitled to the custody or his witnesses.

SECTION 16. [*REGISTRY OF OUT-OF-STATE CUSTODY DECREES AND PROCEEDINGS.*] The clerk of each [District Court, Family Court] shall maintain a registry in which he shall enter the following:

(1) certified copies of custody decrees of other states received for filing;

(2) communications as to the pendency of custody proceedings in other states;

(3) communications concerning a finding of inconvenient forum by a court of another state; and

(4) other communications or documents concerning custody proceedings in another state which may affect the jurisdiction of a court of this State or the disposition to be made by it in a custody proceeding.

SECTION 17. [*CERTIFIED COPIES OF CUSTODY DECREE.*] The Clerk of the [District Court, Family Court] of this State, at the request of the court of another state or at the request of any person who is affected by or has a legitimate interest in a custody decree, shall certify and forward a copy of the decree to that court or person.

SECTION 18. [*TAKING TESTIMONY IN ANOTHER STATE.*] In addition to other procedural devices available to a party, any party to the proceeding or a

guardian ad litem or other representative of the child may adduce testimony of witnesses, including parties and the child, by deposition or otherwise, in another state. The court on its own motion may direct that the testimony of a person be taken in another state and may prescribe the manner in which and the terms upon which the testimony shall be taken.

SECTION 19. [*HEARINGS AND STUDIES IN ANOTHER STATE; ORDERS TO APPEAR.*]

(a) A court of this State may request the appropriate court of another state to hold a hearing to adduce evidence, to order a party to produce or give evidence under other procedures of that state, or to have social studies made with respect to the custody of a child involved in proceedings pending in the court of this State; and to forward to the court of this State certified copies of the transcript of the record of the hearing, the evidence otherwise adduced, or any social studies prepared in compliance with the request. The cost of the services may be assessed against the parties or, if necessary, ordered paid by the [County, State].

(b) A court of this State may request the appropriate court of another state to order a party to custody proceedings pending in the court of this State to appear in the proceedings, and if that party has physical custody of the child, to appear with the child. The request may state that travel and other necessary expenses of the party and of the child whose appearance is desired will be assessed against another party or will otherwise be paid.

SECTION 20. [*ASSISTANCE TO COURTS OF OTHER STATES.*]

(a) Upon request of the court of another state the courts of this State which are competent to hear custody matters may order a person in this State to appear at a hearing to adduce evidence or to produce or give evidence under other procedures available in this State [or may order social studies to be made for use in a custody proceeding in another state]. A certified copy of the transcript of the record of the hearing or the evidence otherwise adduced [and any social studies prepared] shall be forwarded by the clerk of the court to the requesting court.

(b) A person within this State may voluntarily give his testimony or statement in this State for use in a custody proceeding outside this State.

(c) Upon request of the court of another state a competent court of this State may order a person in this State to appear alone or with the child in a custody proceeding in another state. The court may condition compliance with the request upon assurance by the other state that state travel and other necessary expenses will be advanced or reimbursed.

SECTION 21. [*PRESERVATION OF DOCUMENTS FOR USE IN OTHER STATES.*] In any custody proceeding in this State the court shall preserve the

pleadings, orders and decrees, any record that has been made of its hearings, social studies, and other pertinent documents until the child reaches [18, 21] years of age. Upon appropriate request of the court of another state the court shall forward to the other court certified copies of any or all of such documents.

SECTION 22. [*REQUEST FOR COURT RECORDS OF ANOTHER STATE.*] If a custody decree has been rendered in another state concerning a child involved in a custody proceeding pending in a court of this State, the court of this State upon taking jurisdiction of the case shall request of the court of the other state a certified copy of the transcript of any court record and other documents mentioned in section 21.

SECTION 23. [*INTERNATIONAL APPLICATION.*] The general policies of this Act extend to the international area. The provisions of this Act relating to the recognition and enforcement of custody decrees of other states apply to custody decrees and decrees involving legal institutions similar in nature to custody institutions rendered by appropriate authorities of other nations if reasonable notice and opportunity to be heard were given to all affected persons.

SECTION 24. [*PRIORITY.*] Upon the request of a party to a custody proceeding which raises a question of existence or exercise of jurisdiction under this Act the case shall be given calendar priority and handled expeditiously.]

SECTION 25. [*SEVERABILITY.*] If any provision of this Act or the application thereof to any person or circumstance is held invalid, its invalidity does not affect other provisions or applications of the Act which can be given effect without the invalid provision or application, and to this end the provisions of this Act are severable.

. . .

SECTION 28. [*TIME OF TAKING EFFECT.*] This Act shall take effect . . .

Uniform Child Custody Jurisdiction and Enforcement Act (1997)

[ARTICLE] 1

GENERAL PROVISIONS

. . .

SECTION 102. DEFINITIONS. In this [Act]:

(1) "Abandoned" means left without provision for reasonable and necessary care or supervision.

(2) "Child" means an individual who has not attained 18 years of age.

(3) "Child-custody determination" means a judgment, decree, or other order of a court providing for the legal custody, physical custody, or visitation with respect to a child. The term includes a permanent, temporary, initial, and modification order. The term does not include an order relating to child support or other monetary obligation of an individual.

(4) "Child-custody proceeding" means a proceeding in which legal custody, physical custody, or visitation with respect to a child is an issue. The term includes a proceeding for divorce, separation, neglect, abuse, dependency, guardianship, paternity, termination of parental rights, and protection from domestic violence, in which the issue may appear. The term does not include a proceeding involving juvenile delinquency, contractual emancipation, or enforcement under [Article] 3.

(5) "Commencement" means the filing of the first pleading in a proceeding.

(6) "Court" means an entity authorized under the law of a State to establish, enforce, or modify a child-custody determination.

(7) "Home State" means the State in which a child lived with a parent or a person acting as a parent for at least six consecutive months immediately before the commencement of a child-custody proceeding. In the case of a child less than six months of age, the term means the State in which the child lived from birth with any of the persons mentioned. A period of temporary absence of any of the mentioned persons is part of the period.

(8) "Initial determination" means the first child-custody determination concerning a particular child.

(9) "Issuing court" means the court that makes a child-custody determination for which enforcement is sought under this [Act].

(10) "Issuing State" means the State in which a child-custody determination is made.

(11) "Modification" means a child-custody determination that changes, replaces, supersedes, or is otherwise made after a previous determination concerning the same child, whether or not it is made by the court that made the previous determination.

(12) "Person" means an individual, corporation, business trust, estate, trust, partnership, limited liability company, association, joint venture, government; governmental subdivision, agency, or instrumentality; public corporation; or any other legal or commercial entity.

(13) "Person acting as a parent" means a person, other than a parent, who:

(A) has physical custody of the child or has had physical custody for a period of six consecutive months, including any temporary absence, within one year immediately before the commencement of a child-custody proceeding; and

(B) has been awarded legal custody by a court or claims a right to legal custody under the law of this State.

(14) "Physical custody" means the physical care and supervision of a child.

(15) "State" means a State of the United States, the District of Columbia, Puerto Rico, the United States Virgin Islands, or any territory or insular possession subject to the jurisdiction of the United States.

[(16) "Tribe" means an Indian tribe or band, or Alaskan Native village, which is recognized by federal law or formally acknowledged by a State.]

(17) "Warrant" means an order issued by a court authorizing law enforcement officers to take physical custody of a child.

SECTION 103. PROCEEDINGS GOVERNED BY OTHER LAW. This [Act] does not govern an adoption proceeding or a proceeding pertaining to the authorization of emergency medical care for a child.

SECTION 104. APPLICATION TO INDIAN TRIBES.

(a) A child-custody proceeding that pertains to an Indian child as defined in the Indian Child Welfare Act, 25 U.S.C. § 1901 et seq., is not subject to this [Act] to the extent that it is governed by the Indian Child Welfare Act.

[(b) A court of this State shall treat a tribe as if it were a State of the United States for the purpose of applying [Articles] 1 and 2.]

[(c) A child-custody determination made by a tribe under factual circumstances in substantial conformity with the jurisdictional standards of this [Act] must be recognized and enforced under [Article] 3.]

SECTION 105. INTERNATIONAL APPLICATION OF [ACT].

(a) A court of this State shall treat a foreign country as if it were a State of the United States for the purpose of applying [Articles] 1 and 2.

(b) Except as otherwise provided in subsection (c), a child-custody determination made in a foreign country under factual circumstances in substantial conformity with the jurisdictional standards of this [Act] must be recognized and enforced under [Article] 3.

(c) A court of this State need not apply this [Act] if the child custody law of a foreign country violates fundamental principles of human rights.

SECTION 106. EFFECT OF CHILD-CUSTODY DETERMINATION. A child-custody determination made by a court of this State that had jurisdiction under this [Act] binds all persons who have been served in accordance with the laws of this State or notified in accordance with Section 108 or who have submitted to the jurisdiction of the court, and who have been given an opportunity to be heard. As to those persons, the determination is conclusive as to all decided issues of law and fact except to the extent the determination is modified.

. . .

SECTION 108. NOTICE TO PERSONS OUTSIDE STATE.

(a) Notice required for the exercise of jurisdiction when a person is outside this State may be given in a manner prescribed by the law of this State for service of process or by the law of the State in which the service is made. Notice must be given in a manner reasonably calculated to give actual notice but may be by publication if other means are not effective.

(b) Proof of service may be made in the manner prescribed by the law of this State or by the law of the State in which the service is made.

(c) Notice is not required for the exercise of jurisdiction with respect to a person who submits to the jurisdiction of the court.

SECTION 109. APPEARANCE AND LIMITED IMMUNITY.

(a) A party to a child-custody proceeding, including a modification proceeding, or a petitioner or respondent in a proceeding to enforce or register a child-custody determination, is not subject to personal jurisdiction in this State for another proceeding or purpose solely by reason of having participated, or of having been physically present for the purpose of participating, in the proceeding.

(b) A person who is subject to personal jurisdiction in this State on a basis other than physical presence is not immune from service of process in this State. A party present in this State who is subject to the jurisdiction of another State is not immune from service of process allowable under the laws of that State.

(c) The immunity granted by subsection (a) does not extend to civil litigation based on acts unrelated to the participation in a proceeding under this [Act] committed by an individual while present in this State.

SECTION 110. COMMUNICATION BETWEEN COURTS.

(a) A court of this State may communicate with a court in another State concerning a proceeding arising under this [Act].

(b) The court may allow the parties to participate in the communication. If the parties are not able to participate in the communication, they must be given the opportunity to present facts and legal arguments before a decision on jurisdiction is made.

(c) Communication between courts on schedules, calendars, court records, and similar matters may occur without informing the parties. A record need not be made of the communication.

(d) Except as otherwise provided in subsection (c), a record must be made of a communication under this section. The parties must be informed promptly of the communication and granted access to the record.

(e) For the purposes of this section, "record" means information that is inscribed on a tangible medium or that is stored in an electronic or other medium and is retrievable in perceivable form.

SECTION 111. TAKING TESTIMONY IN ANOTHER STATE.

(a) In addition to other procedures available to a party, a party to a child-custody proceeding may offer testimony of witnesses who are located in another State, including testimony of the parties and the child, by deposition or other means allowable in this State for testimony taken in another State. The court on its own motion may order that the testimony of a person be taken in another State and may prescribe the manner in which and the terms upon which the testimony is taken.

(b) A court of this State may permit an individual residing in another State to be deposed or to testify by telephone, audiovisual means, or other electronic means before a designated court or at another location in that State. A court of this State shall cooperate with courts of other States in designating an appropriate location for the deposition or testimony.

SECTION 112. COOPERATION BETWEEN COURTS;
PRESERVATION OF RECORDS.

(a) A court of this State may request the appropriate court of another State to:

(1) hold an evidentiary hearing;

(2) order a person to produce or give evidence pursuant to procedures of that State;

(3) order that an evaluation be made with respect to the custody of a child involved in a pending proceeding;

(4) forward to the court of this State a certified copy of the transcript of the record of the hearing, the evidence otherwise presented, and any evaluation prepared in compliance with the request; and

(5) order a party to a child-custody proceeding or any person having physical custody of the child to appear in the proceeding with or without the child.

(b) Upon request of a court of another State, a court of this State may hold a hearing or enter an order described in subsection (a).

(c) Travel and other necessary and reasonable expenses incurred under subsections (a) and (b) may be assessed against the parties according to the law of this State.

(d) A court of this State shall preserve the pleadings, orders, decrees, records of hearings, evaluations, and other pertinent records with respect to a child-custody proceeding until the child attains 18 years of age. Upon appropriate request by a court or law enforcement official of another State, the court shall forward a certified copy of those records.

[ARTICLE] 2

JURISDICTION

SECTION 201. INITIAL CHILD-CUSTODY JURISDICTION.

(a) Except as otherwise provided in Section 204, a court of this State has jurisdiction to make an initial child-custody determination only if:

(1) this State is the home State of the child on the date of the commencement of the proceeding, or was the home State of the child within six months before the commencement of the proceeding and the child is absent from this State but a parent or person acting as a parent continues to live in this State;

(2) a court of another State does not have jurisdiction under paragraph (1), or a court of the home State of the child has declined to exercise jurisdiction on the ground that this State is the more appropriate forum under Section 207 or 208, and:

(A) the child and the child's parents, or the child and at least one parent or a person acting as a parent, have a significant connection with this State other than mere physical presence; and

(B) substantial evidence is available in this State concerning the child's care, protection, training, and personal relationships;

(3) all courts having jurisdiction under paragraph (1) or (2) have declined to exercise jurisdiction on the ground that a court of this State is the more appropriate forum to determine the custody of the child under Section 207 or 208; or

(4) no court of any other State would have jurisdiction under the criteria specified in paragraph (1), (2), or (3).

(b) Subsection (a) is the exclusive jurisdictional basis for making a child-custody determination by a court of this State.

(c) Physical presence of, or personal jurisdiction over, a party or a child is not necessary or sufficient to make a child-custody determination.

SECTION 202. EXCLUSIVE, CONTINUING JURISDICTION.

(a) Except as otherwise provided in Section 204, a court of this State which has made a child-custody determination consistent with Section 201 or 203 has exclusive, continuing jurisdiction over the determination until:

(1) a court of this State determines that neither the child, nor the child and one parent, nor the child and a person acting as a parent have a significant connection with this State and that substantial evidence is no longer available in this State concerning the child's care, protection, training, and personal relationships; or

(2) a court of this State or a court of another State determines that the child, the child's parents, and any person acting as a parent do not presently reside in this State.

(b) A court of this State which has made a child-custody determination and does not have exclusive, continuing jurisdiction under this section may modify that determination only if it has jurisdiction to make an initial determination under Section 201.

SECTION 203. JURISDICTION TO MODIFY DETERMINATION. Except as otherwise provided in Section 204, a court of this State may not modify a child-custody determination made by a court of another State unless a court of this State has jurisdiction to make an initial determination under Section 201(a)(1) or (2) and:

(1) the court of the other State determines it no longer has exclusive, continuing jurisdiction under Section 202 or that a court of this State would be a more convenient forum under Section 207; or

(2) a court of this State or a court of the other State determines that the child, the child's parents, and any person acting as a parent do not presently reside in the other State.

SECTION 204. TEMPORARY EMERGENCY JURISDICTION.

(a) A court of this State has temporary emergency jurisdiction if the child is present in this State and the child has been abandoned or it is necessary in an emergency to protect the child because the child, or a sibling or parent of the child, is subjected to or threatened with mistreatment or abuse.

(b) If there is no previous child-custody determination that is entitled to be enforced under this [Act] and a child-custody proceeding has not been commenced in a court of a State having jurisdiction under Sections 201 through 203, a child-custody determination made under this section remains in effect until an order is obtained from a court of a State having jurisdiction under Sections 201 through 203. If a child-custody proceeding has not been or is not commenced in a court of a State having jurisdiction under Sections 201 through 203, a child-custody determination made under this section becomes a final determination, if it so provides and this State becomes the home State of the child.

(c) If there is a previous child-custody determination that is entitled to be enforced under this [Act], or a child-custody proceeding has been commenced in a court of a State having jurisdiction under Sections 201 through 203, any order issued by a court of this State under this section must specify in the order a period that the court considers adequate to allow the person seeking an order to obtain an order from the State having jurisdiction under Sections 201 through 203. The order issued in this State remains in effect until an order is obtained from the other State within the period specified or the period expires.

(d) A court of this State which has been asked to make a child-custody determination under this section, upon being informed that a child-custody proceeding has been commenced in, or a child-custody determination has been made by, a court of a State having jurisdiction under Sections 201 through 203, shall immediately communicate with the other court. A court of this State which is exercising jurisdiction pursuant to Sections 201 through 203, upon being informed that a child-custody proceeding has been commenced in, or a child-custody determination has been made by, a court of another State under a statute similar to this section shall immediately communicate with the court of that State to resolve the emergency, protect the safety of the parties and the child, and determine a period for the duration of the temporary order.

SECTION 205. NOTICE; OPPORTUNITY TO BE HEARD; JOINDER.

(a) Before a child-custody determination is made under this [Act], notice and an opportunity to be heard in accordance with the standards of Section 108 must be given to all persons entitled to notice under the law of this State as in child-custody proceedings between residents of this State, any parent whose parental rights have not been previously terminated, and any person having physical custody of the child.

(b) This [Act] does not govern the enforceability of a child-custody determination made without notice or an opportunity to be heard.

(c) The obligation to join a party and the right to intervene as a party in a child-custody proceeding under this [Act] are governed by the law of this State as in child-custody proceedings between residents of this State.

SECTION 206. SIMULTANEOUS PROCEEDINGS.

(a) Except as otherwise provided in Section 204, a court of this State may not exercise its jurisdiction under this [article] if, at the time of the commencement of the proceeding, a proceeding concerning the custody of the child has been commenced in a court of another State having jurisdiction substantially in conformity with this [Act], unless the proceeding has been terminated or is stayed by the court of the other State because a court of this State is a more convenient forum under Section 207.

(b) Except as otherwise provided in Section 204, a court of this State, before hearing a child-custody proceeding, shall examine the court documents and other information supplied by the parties pursuant to Section 209. If the court determines that a child-custody proceeding has been commenced in a court in another State having jurisdiction substantially in accordance with this [Act], the court of this State shall stay its proceeding and communicate with the court of the other State. If the court of the State having jurisdiction substantially in accordance with this [Act] does not determine that the court of this State is a more appropriate forum, the court of this State shall dismiss the proceeding.

(c) In a proceeding to modify a child-custody determination, a court of this State shall determine whether a proceeding to enforce the determination has been commenced in another State. If a proceeding to enforce a child-custody determination has been commenced in another State, the court may:

(1) stay the proceeding for modification pending the entry of an order of a court of the other State enforcing, staying, denying, or dismissing the proceeding for enforcement;

(2) enjoin the parties from continuing with the proceeding for enforcement; or

(3) proceed with the modification under conditions it considers appropriate.

SECTION 207. INCONVENIENT FORUM.

(a) A court of this State which has jurisdiction under this [Act] to make a child-custody determination may decline to exercise its jurisdiction at any time if it determines that it is an inconvenient forum under the circumstances and that a court of another State is a more appropriate forum. The issue of inconvenient forum may be raised upon motion of a party, the court's own motion, or request of another court.

(b) Before determining whether it is an inconvenient forum, a court of this State shall consider whether it is appropriate for a court of another State to exercise jurisdiction. For this purpose, the court shall allow the parties to submit information and shall consider all relevant factors, including:

(1) whether domestic violence has occurred and is likely to continue in the future and which State could best protect the parties and the child;

(2) the length of time the child has resided outside this State;

(3) the distance between the court in this State and the court in the State that would assume jurisdiction;

(4) the relative financial circumstances of the parties;

(5) any agreement of the parties as to which State should assume jurisdiction;

(6) the nature and location of the evidence required to resolve the pending litigation, including testimony of the child;

(7) the ability of the court of each State to decide the issue expeditiously and the procedures necessary to present the evidence; and

(8) the familiarity of the court of each State with the facts and issues in the pending litigation.

(c) If a court of this State determines that it is an inconvenient forum and that a court of another State is a more appropriate forum, it shall stay the proceedings upon condition that a child-custody proceeding be promptly commenced in another designated State and may impose any other condition the court considers just and proper.

(d) A court of this State may decline to exercise its jurisdiction under this [Act] if a child-custody determination is incidental to an action for divorce or another proceeding while still retaining jurisdiction over the divorce or other proceeding.

SECTION 208. JURISDICTION DECLINED BY REASON OF CONDUCT.

(a) Except as otherwise provided in Section 204 [or by other law of this State], if a court of this State has jurisdiction under this [Act] because a person seeking to invoke its jurisdiction has engaged in unjustifiable conduct, the court shall decline to exercise its jurisdiction unless:

(1) the parents and all persons acting as parents have acquiesced in the exercise of jurisdiction;

(2) a court of the State otherwise having jurisdiction under Sections 201 through 203 determines that this State is a more appropriate forum under Section 207; or

(3) no court of any other State would have jurisdiction under the criteria specified in Sections 201 through 203.

(b) If a court of this State declines to exercise its jurisdiction pursuant to subsection (a), it may fashion an appropriate remedy to ensure the safety of the child and prevent a repetition of the unjustifiable conduct, including staying the proceeding until a child-custody proceeding is commenced in a court having jurisdiction under Sections 201 through 203.

(c) If a court dismisses a petition or stays a proceeding because it declines to exercise its jurisdiction pursuant to subsection (a), it shall assess against the party seeking to invoke its jurisdiction necessary and reasonable expenses including costs, communication expenses, attorney's fees, investigative fees, expenses for witnesses, travel expenses, and child care during the course of the proceedings, unless the party from whom fees are sought establishes that the assessment would be clearly inappropriate. The court may not assess fees, costs, or expenses against this State unless authorized by law other than this [Act].

SECTION 209. INFORMATION TO BE SUBMITTED TO COURT.

(a) [Subject to [local law providing for the confidentiality of procedures, addresses, and other identifying information], in] [In] a child-custody proceeding, each party, in its first pleading or in an attached affidavit, shall give information, if reasonably ascertainable, under oath as to the child's present address or whereabouts, the places where the child has lived during the last five years, and the names and present addresses of the persons with whom the child has lived during that period. The pleading or affidavit must state whether the party:

(1) has participated, as a party or witness or in any other capacity, in any other proceeding concerning the custody of or visitation with the child and, if so, identify the court, the case number, and the date of the child-custody determination, if any;

(2) knows of any proceeding that could affect the current proceeding, including proceedings for enforcement and proceedings relating to domestic violence, protective orders, termination of parental rights, and adoptions and, if so, identify the court, the case number, and the nature of the proceeding; and

(3) knows the names and addresses of any person not a party to the proceeding who has physical custody of the child or claims rights of legal custody or physical custody of, or visitation with, the child and, if so, the names and addresses of those persons.

(b) If the information required by subsection (a) is not furnished, the court, upon motion of a party or its own motion, may stay the proceeding until the information is furnished.

(c) If the declaration as to any of the items described in subsection (a)(1) through (3) is in the affirmative, the declarant shall give additional information under oath as required by the court. The court may examine the parties under oath as to details of the information furnished and other matters pertinent to the court's jurisdiction and the disposition of the case.

(d) Each party has a continuing duty to inform the court of any proceeding in this or any other State that could affect the current proceeding.

[(e) If a party alleges in an affidavit or a pleading under oath that the health, safety, or liberty of a party or child would be jeopardized by disclosure of identifying information, the information must be sealed and may not be disclosed to the other party or the public unless the court orders the disclosure to be made after a hearing in which the court takes into consideration the health, safety, or liberty of the party or child and determines that the disclosure is in the interest of justice.]

SECTION 210. APPEARANCE OF PARTIES AND CHILD.

(a) In a child-custody proceeding in this State, the court may order a party to the proceeding who is in this State to appear before the court in person with or without the child. The court may order any person who is in this State and who has physical custody or control of the child to appear in person with the child.

(b) If a party to a child-custody proceeding whose presence is desired by the court is outside this State, the court may order that a notice given pursuant to Section 108 include a statement directing the party to appear in person with or without the child and informing the party that failure to appear may result in a decision adverse to the party.

(c) The court may enter any orders necessary to ensure the safety of the child and of any person ordered to appear under this section.

(d) If a party to a child-custody proceeding who is outside this State is directed to appear under subsection (b) or desires to appear personally before the court with or without the child, the court may require another party to pay reasonable and necessary travel and other expenses of the party so appearing and of the child.

[ARTICLE] 3

ENFORCEMENT

SECTION 301. DEFINITIONS. In this [article]:

(1) "Petitioner" means a person who seeks enforcement of an order for return of a child under the Hague Convention on the Civil Aspects of International Child Abduction or enforcement of a child-custody determination.

(2) "Respondent" means a person against whom a proceeding has been commenced for enforcement of an order for return of a child under the Hague Convention on the Civil Aspects of International Child Abduction or enforcement of a child-custody determination.

SECTION 302. ENFORCEMENT UNDER HAGUE CONVENTION.

Under this [article] a court of this State may enforce an order for the return of the child made under the Hague Convention on the Civil Aspects of International Child Abduction as if it were a child-custody determination.

SECTION 303. DUTY TO ENFORCE.

(a) A court of this State shall recognize and enforce a child-custody determination of a court of another State if the latter court exercised jurisdiction in substantial conformity with this [Act] or the determination was made under factual circumstances meeting the jurisdictional standards of this [Act] and the determination has not been modified in accordance with this [Act].

(b) A court of this State may utilize any remedy available under other law of this State to enforce a child-custody determination made by a court of another State. The remedies provided in this [article] are cumulative and do not affect the availability of other remedies to enforce a child-custody determination.

SECTION 304. TEMPORARY VISITATION.

(a) A court of this State which does not have jurisdiction to modify a child-custody determination, may issue a temporary order enforcing:

(1) a visitation schedule made by a court of another State; or

(2) the visitation provisions of a child-custody determination of another State that does not provide for a specific visitation schedule.

(b) If a court of this State makes an order under subsection (a)(2), it shall specify in the order a period that it considers adequate to allow the petitioner to obtain an order from a court having jurisdiction under the criteria specified in [Article] 2. The order remains in effect until an order is obtained from the other court or the period expires.

SECTION 305. REGISTRATION OF CHILD-CUSTODY DETERMINATION.

(a) A child-custody determination issued by a court of another State may be registered in this State, with or without a simultaneous request for enforcement, by sending to [the appropriate court] in this State:

(1) a letter or other document requesting registration;

(2) two copies, including one certified copy, of the determination sought to be registered, and a statement under penalty of perjury that to the best of the knowledge and belief of the person seeking registration the order has not been modified; and

(3) except as otherwise provided in Section 209, the name and address of the person seeking registration and any parent or person acting as a parent who has been awarded custody or visitation in the child-custody determination sought to be registered.

(b) On receipt of the documents required by subsection (a), the registering court shall:

(1) cause the determination to be filed as a foreign judgment, together with one copy of any accompanying documents and information, regardless of their form; and

(2) serve notice upon the persons named pursuant to subsection (a)(3) and provide them with an opportunity to contest the registration in accordance with this section.

(c) The notice required by subsection (b)(2) must state that:

(1) a registered determination is enforceable as of the date of the registration in the same manner as a determination issued by a court of this State;

(2) a hearing to contest the validity of the registered determination must be requested within 20 days after service of notice; and

(3) failure to contest the registration will result in confirmation of the child-custody determination and preclude further contest of that determination with respect to any matter that could have been asserted.

(d) A person seeking to contest the validity of a registered order must request a hearing within 20 days after service of the notice. At that hearing, the court shall confirm the registered order unless the person contesting registration establishes that:

(1) the issuing court did not have jurisdiction under [Article] 2;

(2) the child-custody determination sought to be registered has been vacated, stayed, or modified by a court having jurisdiction to do so under [Article] 2; or

(3) the person contesting registration was entitled to notice, but notice was not given in accordance with the standards of Section 108, in the proceedings before the court that issued the order for which registration is sought.

(e) If a timely request for a hearing to contest the validity of the registration is not made, the registration is confirmed as a matter of law and the person requesting registration and all persons served must be notified of the confirmation.

(f) Confirmation of a registered order, whether by operation of law or after notice and hearing, precludes further contest of the order with respect to any matter that could have been asserted at the time of registration.

SECTION 306. ENFORCEMENT OF REGISTERED DETERMINATION.

(a) A court of this State may grant any relief normally available under the law of this State to enforce a registered child-custody determination made by a court of another State.

(b) A court of this State shall recognize and enforce, but may not modify, except in accordance with [Article] 2, a registered child-custody determination of a court of another State.

SECTION 307. SIMULTANEOUS PROCEEDINGS. If a proceeding for enforcement under this [article] is commenced in a court of this State and the court determines that a proceeding to modify the determination is pending in a court of another State having jurisdiction to modify the determination under [Article] 2, the enforcing court shall immediately communicate with the modifying court. The proceeding for enforcement continues unless the enforcing court, after consultation with the modifying court, stays or dismisses the proceeding.

SECTION 308. EXPEDITED ENFORCEMENT OF CHILD-CUSTODY DETERMINATION.

(a) A petition under this [article] must be verified. Certified copies of all orders sought to be enforced and of any order confirming registration must be attached to the petition. A copy of a certified copy of an order may be attached instead of the original.

(b) A petition for enforcement of a child-custody determination must state:

(1) whether the court that issued the determination identified the jurisdictional basis it relied upon in exercising jurisdiction and, if so, what the basis was;

(2) whether the determination for which enforcement is sought has been vacated, stayed, or modified by a court whose decision must be enforced under this [Act] and, if so, identify the court, the case number, and the nature of the proceeding;

(3) whether any proceeding has been commenced that could affect the current proceeding, including proceedings relating to domestic violence, protective orders, termination of parental rights, and adoptions and, if so, identify the court, the case number, and the nature of the proceeding;

(4) the present physical address of the child and the respondent, if known;

(5) whether relief in addition to the immediate physical custody of the child and attorney's fees is sought, including a request for assistance from [law enforcement officials] and, if so, the relief sought; and

(6) if the child-custody determination has been registered and confirmed under Section 305, the date and place of registration.

(c) Upon the filing of a petition, the court shall issue an order directing the respondent to appear in person with or without the child at a hearing and may enter any order necessary to ensure the safety of the parties and the child. The hearing must be held on the next judicial day after service of the order unless that date is impossible. In that event, the court shall hold the hearing on the first judicial day possible. The court may extend the date of hearing at the request of the petitioner.

(d) An order issued under subsection (c) must state the time and place of the hearing and advise the respondent that at the hearing the court will order that the petitioner may take immediate physical custody of the child and the payment of fees, costs, and expenses under Section 312, and may schedule a hearing to determine whether further relief is appropriate, unless the respondent appears and establishes that:

(1) the child-custody determination has not been registered and confirmed under Section 305 and that:

(A) the issuing court did not have jurisdiction under [Article] 2;

(B) the child-custody determination for which enforcement is sought has been vacated, stayed, or modified by a court having jurisdiction to do so under [Article] 2; or

(C) the respondent was entitled to notice, but notice was not given in accordance with the standards of Section 108, in the proceedings before the court that issued the order for which enforcement is sought; or

(2) the child-custody determination for which enforcement is sought was registered and confirmed under Section 304, but has been vacated, stayed, or modified by a court of a State having jurisdiction to do so under [Article] 2.

SECTION 309. SERVICE OF PETITION AND ORDER. Except as otherwise provided in Section 311, the petition and order must be served, by any method authorized [by the law of this State], upon respondent and any person who has physical custody of the child.

SECTION 310. HEARING AND ORDER.

(a) Unless the court issues a temporary emergency order pursuant to Section 204, upon a finding that a petitioner is entitled to immediate physical custody of the child, the court shall order that the petitioner may take immediate physical custody of the child unless the respondent establishes that:

(1) the child-custody determination has not been registered and confirmed under Section 305 and that:

(A) the issuing court did not have jurisdiction under [Article] 2;

(B) the child-custody determination for which enforcement is sought has been vacated, stayed, or modified by a court of a State having jurisdiction to do so under [Article] 2; or

(C) the respondent was entitled to notice, but notice was not given in accordance with the standards of Section 108, in the proceedings before the court that issued the order for which enforcement is sought; or

(2) the child-custody determination for which enforcement is sought was registered and confirmed under Section 305 but has been vacated, stayed, or modified by a court of a State having jurisdiction to do so under [Article] 2.

(b) The court shall award the fees, costs, and expenses authorized under Section 312 and may grant additional relief, including a request for the assistance of [law enforcement officials], and set a further hearing to determine whether additional relief is appropriate.

(c) If a party called to testify refuses to answer on the ground that the testimony may be self-incriminating, the court may draw an adverse inference from the refusal.

(d) A privilege against disclosure of communications between spouses and a defense of immunity based on the relationship of husband and wife or parent and child may not be invoked in a proceeding under this [article].

SECTION 311. WARRANT TO TAKE PHYSICAL CUSTODY OF CHILD.

(a) Upon the filing of a petition seeking enforcement of a child-custody determination, the petitioner may file a verified application for the issuance of a warrant to take physical custody of the child if the child is immediately likely to suffer serious physical harm or be removed from this State.

(b) If the court, upon the testimony of the petitioner or other witness, finds that the child is imminently likely to suffer serious physical harm or be removed from this State, it may issue a warrant to take physical custody of the child. The petition must be heard on the next judicial day after the warrant is executed unless that date is impossible. In that event, the court shall hold the hearing on the first judicial day possible. The application for the warrant must include the statements required by Section 308(b).

(c) A warrant to take physical custody of a child must:

(1) recite the facts upon which a conclusion of imminent serious physical harm or removal from the jurisdiction is based;

(2) direct law enforcement officers to take physical custody of the child immediately; and

(3) provide for the placement of the child pending final relief.

(d) The respondent must be served with the petition, warrant, and order immediately after the child is taken into physical custody.

(e) A warrant to take physical custody of a child is enforceable throughout this State. If the court finds on the basis of the testimony of the petitioner or other witness that a less intrusive remedy is not effective, it may authorize law enforcement officers to enter private property to take physical custody of the child. If required by exigent circumstances of the case, the court may author-ize law enforcement officers to make a forcible entry at any hour.

(f) The court may impose conditions upon placement of a child to ensure the appearance of the child and the child's custodian.

SECTION 312. COSTS, FEES, AND EXPENSES.

(a) The court shall award the prevailing party, including a State, necessary and reasonable expenses incurred by or on behalf of the party, including costs, communication expenses, attorney's fees, investigative fees, expenses for witnesses, travel expenses, and child care during the course of the proceedings, unless the party from whom fees or expenses are sought establishes that the award would be clearly inappropriate.

(b) The court may not assess fees, costs, or expenses against a State unless authorized by law other than this [Act].

SECTION 313. RECOGNITION AND ENFORCEMENT. A court of this State shall accord full faith and credit to an order issued by another State and consistent with this [Act] which enforces a child-custody determination by a court of another State unless the order has been vacated, stayed, or modified by a court having jurisdiction to do so under [Article] 2.

SECTION 314. APPEALS. An appeal may be taken from a final order in a proceeding under this [article] in accordance with [expedited appellate proce-dures in other civil cases]. Unless the court enters a temporary emergency order under Section 204, the enforcing court may not stay an order enforcing a child-custody determination pending appeal.

SECTION 315. ROLE OF [PROSECUTOR OR PUBLIC OFFICIAL].

(a) In a case arising under this [Act] or involving the Hague Convention on the Civil Aspects of International Child Abduction, the [prosecutor or other appropriate public official] may take any lawful action, including resort to a proceeding under this [article] or any other available civil proceeding to locate a child, obtain the return of a child, or enforce a child-custody determination if there is:

(1) an existing child-custody determination;

(2) a request to do so from a court in a pending child-custody proceeding;

(3) a reasonable belief that a criminal statute has been violated; or

(4) a reasonable belief that the child has been wrongfully removed or retained in violation of the Hague Convention on the Civil Aspects of International Child Abduction.

(b) A [prosecutor or appropriate public official] acting under this section acts on behalf of the court and may not represent any party.

SECTION 316. ROLE OF [LAW ENFORCEMENT]. At the request of a [prosecutor or other appropriate public official] acting under Section 315, a [law enforcement officer] may take any lawful action reasonably necessary to locate a child or a party and assist [a prosecutor or appropriate public official] with responsibilities under Section 315.

SECTION 317. COSTS AND EXPENSES. If the respondent is not the prevailing party, the court may assess against the respondent all direct expenses and costs incurred by the [prosecutor or other appropriate public official] and [law enforcement officers] under Section 315 or 316.

Parental Kidnapping Prevention Act 28 U.S.C. 1738A (1982)

SECTION 1738A. Full faith and credit given to child custody determinations

(a) The appropriate authorities of every State shall enforce according to its terms, and shall not modify except as provided in subsection (f) of this section, any child custody determination made consistently with the provisions of this section by a court of another State.

(b) As used in this section, the term

(1) "child" means a person under the age of eighteen;

(2) "contestant" means a person, including a parent, who claims a right to custody or visitation of a child;

(3) "custody determination" means a judgment, decree, or other order of a court providing for the custody or visitation of a child, and includes permanent and temporary orders, and initial orders and modifications;

(4) "home State" means the State in which, immediately preceding the time involved, the child lived with his parents, a parent, or a person acting as parent, for at least six consecutive months, and in the case of a child less than six months old, the State in which the child lived from birth with any of such persons. Periods of temporary absence of any of such persons are counted as part of the six-month or other period;

(5) "modification" and "modify" refer to a custody determination which modifies, replaces, supersedes, or otherwise is made subsequent to, a prior custody determination concerning the same child, whether made by the same court or not;

(6) "person acting as a parent" means a person, other than a parent, who has physical custody of a child and who has either been awarded custody by a court or claims a right to custody;

(7) "physical custody" means actual possession and control of a child; and

(8) "State" means a State of the United States, the District of Columbia, the Commonwealth of Puerto Rico, or a territory or possession of the United States.

(c) A child custody determination made by a court of a State is consistent with the provisions of this section only if-

(1) such court has jurisdiction under the law of such State; and

(2) one of the following conditions is met:

(A) such State (i) is the home State of the child on the date of the commencement of the proceeding, or (ii) had been the child's home State within six months before the date of the commencement of the proceeding and the child is absent from such State because of his removal or retention by a contestant or for other reasons, and a contestant continues to live in such State;

(B) (i) it appears that no other State would have jurisdiction under subparagraph (A), and (ii) it is in the best interest of the child that a court of such State assume jurisdiction because (I) the child and his parents, or the child and at least one contestant, have a significant connection with such State other than mere physical presence in such State, and (11) there is available in such State substantial evidence concerning the child's present or future care, protection, training, and personal relationships;

(C) the child is physically present in such State and (i) the child has been abandoned, or (ii) it is necessary in an emergency to protect the child because he has been subjected to or threatened with mistreatment or abuse;

(D) (1) it appears that no other State would have jurisdiction under subparagraph (A), (B), (C), or (E), or another State has declined to exercise jurisdiction on the ground that the State whose jurisdiction is in issue is the more appropriate forum to determine the custody of the child, and (ii) it is in the best interest of the child that such court assume jurisdiction; or (E) the court has continuing jurisdiction pursuant to subsection (d) of this section.

(d) The jurisdiction of a court of a State which has made a child custody determination consistently with the provisions of this section continues as long as the requirement of subsection (c) (1) of this section continues to be met and such State remains the residence of the child or of any contestant.

(e) Before a child custody determination is made, reasonable notice and opportunity to be heard shall be given to the contestants, any parent whose parental rights have not been previously terminated and any person who has physical custody of a child.

(f) A court of a State may modify a determination of the custody of the same child made by a court of another State, if

(1) it has jurisdiction to make such a child custody determination; and

(2) the court of the other State no longer has jurisdiction, or it has declined to exercise such jurisdiction to modify such determination.

(g) A court of a State shall not exercise jurisdiction in any proceeding for a custody determination commenced during the pendency of a proceeding in a court of another State where such court of that other State is exercising jurisdiction consistently with the provisions of this section to make a custody determination.

Index

Abortion
  American law 70–2
  Constitutional issues 69–72
  Criminalization 70
  Marital privacy 70
  Parental notice 71
  Role of physician 71
  Spousal notice 70–1
  Use of public funds 71
  Trimester framework 71
  Undue burden standard 71
  Women's right to privacy 72
American Bar Association
  Establishment of the Family
    Law Section 2
Adoption
  Generally 153–7
  Adopters, choice of, by parents 168
  Agency adoptions
    generally 158, 160–1, 182
    baby selling 159–60, 182
    consent of mother 158
    disclosure requirements 161
    fees 159–60
    states that restrict adoption agency
      adoptions 158
  Birth records, access to 168
  Confidentiality 155, 169
  Fathers
    Constitutional issues 154
    Rights to notice 153–4
    Unwed 153, 166; Putative Father
      Registry 153; Uniform Putative
      and Unknown Fathers Act 154
  Foster care and 179, 180, 182
  Genetic information disclosures 161
  Incest and 49, 51–2
  Independent or private placement
    Generally 158–9
    As a business 159
    Investigations 160
    Reasons for 159
  Inheritance rights of adopted children
    167
  Inheritance rights of birth parents 167
  Involuntary 176–81, contrasted with
    voluntary 155–7

Multiethnic Placement Act of 1994 179
Native American children and the Indian
    Child Welfare Act of 1978 179
Open (visitation by birth parents) 8,
    167–71, 180–2
Parental rights, termination of 7, 178
Placement, criteria for 171, 179–80
Qualifications of adopters
  adult adoptions 169
  best interest standard 155
  Massachusetts statute 15
  unmarried persons 174
Racial matching 5, 7, 171–2, 174
Reasonable efforts to promote 171
Religious matching 7, 171
Revocation of consent 166
Same-sex adoptive parents 17, 174, 175,
    180
Sealing of records 8, 169
Secrecy in 8, 155, 168, 181
Social class 155
Step-parents, by 174–6
Subsidized 5, 143–4, 148, 178
Trading in children 159
Transracial 39, 172–3, 179
Voluntary 157–76, contrasted with
    involuntary 155–7
Wrongful adoption, tort of 160–1
Adoption Assistance and Child Welfare Act
    (1980) 145–6, 178
Best interests standard 178
Reasonable efforts to preserve families
    145–6, 178
Adoption and Safe Families Act (1997)
Generally 146–7, 178
Adultery
  As grounds for divorce 2, 78–9
Alimony
  ALI approach 94
  Alimony/property distinction 9
  Appellate review 95
  As economic link to spouse 95
  As maintenance 97
  Civil contempt as a remedy for
    violation 98
  Cohabitation clause terminating
    alimony 97

Alimony (*cont.*)
  Contract aspects 98
  Control of post-divorce conduct through
      conditions 97
  Duration of 95–6
  Earning capacity of husband 85
  Effect of cohabitation on award 98
  Effect of remarriage 95, 97
  Fault as a basis 80
  For husbands 94
  Factors in award of 93–4, 97
  Judicial discretion in 94, 96
  Lump sum 95
  Merged in the decree 98
  Mitigation of damages 96
  Modification of decree 94, 97, 98
  Non-cohabitation clause 97
  Periodically paid 95
  Permanent or life-time 95, 96
  Rehabilitative alimony 96–7
  Reimbursement alimony 91
  Remarriage 95, 97
  Remedy 98
  Severance pay 95
  Substitute for social security 95
  Uniform Marriage and Divorce
      Act 94
American Law Institute (ALI) Principles
  Alimony 83, 94
  Child custody 8, 94, 110, 116
  Child support 8, 102
  Contract cohabitation 8
  Domestic partnership 8, 19
  Pre-marital agreements 31
Annulment
  As alternative to divorce 43
  Consequences 42–5
  Duty to disclose information 43
  Essentials of marriage 44
  Fraud as a basis for 42–5
  Grounds 43
  Material facts 43
  Mental competence 47–8
  Misrepresentation 44
  Reynolds v. Reynolds 43
  Underage marriages 45–6
  Void and voidable marriages 42–3
Antenuptial Agreements
  see Pre-Nuptial Agreements
Antimiscegenation statutes
  see Marriage
Attorney Fees
  In divorce 124

Battered Child Syndrome
  see Child Abuse and Neglect
Best Interests of the Child
  see Child Custody
Beyond the Best Interests of the Child
  see Goldstein, Freud, and Solnit
Bigamy
  Marriage validity 40, 58–60

Child Abuse and Neglect
  Generally 131, 137–9
  Battered child syndrome 140, 177
  Child Abuse Prevention and Treatment Act
      of 1974 144–5
  Colonial Massachusetts 131
  *DeShaney v. Winnebago County
      Department of Social Services* 132,
      149–52
  Giovannoni and Becerra study 137–8
  Overview of court systems 132
  Parens patriae doctrine 132, 152
  Parens patriae state responsibilities,
      development of 139–40
  Punishment as 133–5
  Reporting Laws
    Confidentiality conflicts 4, 140–1
    Failure to report 141
    Foundation for family violence laws 5
    History of 4–5
    Immunity 141
    Mandated reporters and reports 4–5,
        141
    Model Mandatory Child Abuse
        Reporting Act 4 140–1
    Priest penance exception 142–3
  Reasonable efforts requirements in
      termination proceedings 146–7
  Sexual abuse by priests 142
Child Custody
  Abuse of discretion as basis for
      appeal 104
  ALI Principles 110, 116
  Appellate review 104
  Best interests of the child defined
      1, 3, 102–3, 106–8
  Changed circumstances 113
  Child development principles 6
  Child's preference or wishes as a factor 3,
      103, 106, 110
  Consideration of child's attachment with
      others 107, 113
  Constitutional issues 119–22
  Continuity of care principle 6, 118

De facto parents, rights of 118–19
Evaluation by psychologist or social
    worker 108
Father's rights 153–4, 181
Federal Parental Kidnapping Prevention
    Act 117–18
Financial consideration 108
Full faith and credit to decrees 117
Grandparent visitation 118–23
Guardian ad litem 108–9
Hague Convention on the Civil Aspects of
    International Child Abduction 118
Joint or shared custody 111–12
Judicial discretion 3, 102–3
Lawyer's role in child custody matters
    108, 111
Maternal preference rule 103
Modification of custody decrees 107
Parental alienation 107
Presumptions 103, 106, 109, 110, 111
Primary caretaker preference and
    presumption 104–6
Psychological parent 6
Race as a factor 109, 110
Religion as a factor 109
Relocation 113–16
Role of lawyer for the child 108
Tender years presumption 103, 105
Uniform Child Custody Jurisdiction Act
    117
Uniform Child Custody Jurisdiction and
    Enforcement Act 117
Uniform Marriage and Divorce Act 3, 103
Vagueness of standard 3
Visitation rights 111–12, 115–16, 118–22
Written opinion 104
Child Protection System
    Adoption Assistance and Child Welfare
        Act 145–6
    Child protection process 147–9
    Intervention limits 147
    Liabilities of protection system 151–2
    Liability for harm to child 151–2
    Prosecutorial and social service roles 146
    Reasonable efforts requirements 146–7
    Reunification 146
Child Support
    Agreements regarding 99–102
    College expenses 101
    Deviation from guidelines 101
    Discretionary standards 101
    Empirical data on child support 100
    Enforcement 101–2

Equality for females and males 45
    Guideline provisions 100
    Illegitimate children 17
    Modification 100
    Serial marriages 101
    Step parent obligation 101, 118
    Wage withholding orders 100
Child Support Enforcement
    Amendments 1
    Defenses 100–1
    Federal act 100
Civil Rights Movement
    Impact on family law 2
Civil unions
    see Domestic Partnership
Cohabitation
    Agreements 11–17
    Clauses in property settlements 98–9
    Consortium rights 16
    Contract cohabitation defined 11
    Custody and visitation claims 13, 16–17
    Domestic partnerships 17–23
    Effect on common law marriage 13–14
    Equitable remedies 14–15
    Hawaii laws 20–2
    Immorality and 13
    Inheritance rights of cohabitants 16
    Legal status of children 16–17
    Marvin v. Marvin, importance of 13–15
    Mutual support 19
    Rights of cohabitants 15–16
    Second parent adoption 17
    Statistics on 11–12, 17
    Statutes regulating 16, 19
    Validity of contracts 12–13
    Vermont Civil Union Act 21–2
    Worker's compensation 16, 27
    Wrongful death 16, 20, 23, 25
Common Law or Informal Marriage
    Abolition of 26, 28
    Basis for putative marriage 23
    Choice of law 23–4
    Criticism of 26
    Definition of 23
    Elements 23–7
    Evidentiary standards for proving the
        status 25
    Historical background 23–4
    Impediment to, removal of 24–6
    Legitimacy of children 24
    Misunderstandings about 26
    Number and names of states allowing the
        status 24

Common Law or Informal Marriage (*cont.*)
  Proof of Agreement 24–6
  Relationship to cohabitation 13–14
Conflict of Laws and Recognition
  Civil unions 22–3
  Equitable distribution 87–8
  Marriage 50–2, 64
  Restatement of Conflict of Laws 50
Consortium
  Cohabitant's claim 16
Constructive Trust
  Cohabitation claims 14
Contempt
  Civil and criminal contempt 98
  Interference with visitation 98
Contract Cohabitation
  see under Cohabitation
Corporal Punishment
  Generally 133
  Cultural understanding of 136–7
  Parental immunity doctrine 133
  Parental rights 133
  Reasonableness 136
  Religious aspects 135–6
  Spare the rod quotation 133
Criminal Conversation
  Abolition of 72
  Definition of 72
Cruelty
  As grounds for divorce 78–9

Defense of Marriage Act
  Criticism of 38
  Mini-Defense of Marriage Act 23
  Same-sex marriage 38
Dissolution of Marriage
  see Divorce
Divorce
  Adversarial method 129
  By registration 124, 128
  Common law divorce 78
  Defenses in fault system 78
    collusion
    condonation
    connivance
    recrimination and comparative rectitude
  Equity powers of judges 119
  Fault based 78–80, 85
  Grounds 78–80
  Historical background 76–8
  Impact on men 85
  Impact on women 86
  Jurisdiction 80–2

Marriage breakdown 128
Mediation 76, 125–8
Migratory 81
Negotiation by lawyers 77
New programs to assist litigants 129
New York law 2, 81
No-fault 82–6, 128
Procedure 76–86
Pro se 129
Rates 84
Religious divorce ('get') 99
Reno divorce 81
Residency 80–2
Separation agreements 116
Summary process or simplified 124–5,
    128
Uniform Marriage and Divorce Act 3, 29,
    82, 93
Domestic Partnership
  California's law 19–20
  Compared with contract
      cohabitation 17–18
  District of Columbia law 20
  Formal requirements 18
  Hawaii's Reciprocal Beneficiary Law
      20–1
  Local government and 18–19
  Mutual support obligations 19
  Purpose of 18
  Recognition of 22–3
  Registration requirements 17–18
  Vermont Civil Union Act 21–2
Domestic Violence (Involving Adults)
  In divorce as physical or mental cruelty
      48, 68
  In marriage 67–8
  Stalking of women 69
  Violence Against Women Act 67
Domicile
  Basis for divorce jurisdiction 81–2
Due Process Clause
  Custody proceedings 219–20
  Family members 70
  Father's rights 153–4, 181
  Stanley v. Illinois 153

Economic Aspects of Divorce
  see Marital Property
Equal Protection Clause
  Alimony 94
  Distribution of contraceptives 72
  Domestic partnerships 20
  Family members 70

Father's rights 153, 181
  Marital age 45
  Race and marriage 39–40
  Relocation cases 114
  Same-sex marriages 54
Equal Rights of Husbands and Fathers
  Alimony for husbands 94
  Custody for fathers 103
  Equal Rights Amendment 63
Equitable Distribution of Property
  see Marital Property
Estoppel
  Marriage by 29–30
  Validity of divorce 101
  Validity of marriage 29–30

Family Courts
  As community-based institution 129
  Bar's attitude toward 4
Family Law
  As discretionary law 1
  Defined 8, 10
  Early casebooks and textbooks 1
  In the twentieth century 1–2
  Marginalization in law schools 1
Family Law Practice
  Low status 1
Family Privacy
  Parental rights 4
Federal Government
  Role in child support enforcement 100
  Role in child welfare generally 4–5,
    139–47, 176
Feminist Analyses
  Pre-nuptial agreements 33
  Reproductive rights 165
  Surrogacy contracts 163–5
Foster Care
  Generally 143
  Contrasted with adoption 168
  Federal funding assistance 143
  Group homes 148
  Kinship care 148
  Long term 146, 148
  Orphanages 148
  Permanency hearings 5, 147
  Reasonable efforts standard 146–7
  Statistics on 143
Friendship
  Defined period 10
  Romantic 10
Full Faith and Credit Clause
  Custody decrees 118

Defense of Marriage Act 38
Divorce decrees 82

Gay Rights
  Advancement of 7, 75
Goldstein, Freud, and Solnit
  Beyond the Best Interests of the Child 6,
    105, 108
Grandparents
  Visitation rights of 118–22
Guardian Ad Litem
  Child custody cases 109
  Contrasted with counsel for the child 109
  Professional responsibilities 109
Guardianship of Children
  Appointment of guardian 108–9
  Contrasted with adoption 17, 168
  In cohabitation arrangement 17
  Obligations of guardian 108–9

Home State
  Federal Parental Kidnapping Prevention
    Act of 1980 258
  Uniform Child Custody Jurisdiction Act
    231, 234
  Uniform Child Custody Jurisdiction and
    Enforcement Act (1997) 240, 244
Homemaker Services
  see Marital Property

Illegitimacy of Children
  Child's name 65
  Child support 100
  In cohabitation arrangements 17
  Inheritance rights of illegitimate children
    153–4
  Relationship with birth father 154
  Social status 181
Incest
  Freudian explanation 48
  Marriage restrictions 48–52
  Relationship by adoption 49–50
In Loco Parentis
  Child support 101
Income Tax
  Child support 100
Inconvenient Forum
  Uniform Child Custody Jurisdiction Act
    233, 247
Indian Child Welfare Act of 1978
  see under Adoption
Informal Marriage
  see Common Law Marriage

Insurance Fraud
  see under Marital Torts
Interracial Marriage
  see Marriage
Interspousal Immunity
  see under Marital Torts

Jewish Law
  Uncle and niece marriage allowed 51
  see also Divorce, Religious divorce
Jurisdiction
  Federal Jurisdiction over divorce and
    custody 80–2
  In personam jurisdiction for financial
    claims 82
  Kidnapping of children 117–18
  Residency requirements 80–2

Marital Agreements
  see Postnuptial Agreements; Prenuptial
    Agreements
Marital Misconduct
  Factor in equitable distribution of property
    82
  Fault grounds for divorce 78
Marital Property
  Alimony/property distinction 94
  Celebrity status, reputation and career
    89–90
  Commingling 88
  Common law property system 87
  Community Property 87–90
  Contribution as important factor in
    equitable distribution 88–9, 95
  Debts, division of 90–1
  Deferred compensation 89
  Dissipation of assets 91
  Educational degree and professional
    license 90
  Equitable distribution 87–8, 92–3
  Freedom of testation 61
  Gifts 90
  Goodwill of a business 89
  Homemaker's contributions 92
  Inheritance 88, 90
  Judicial discretion 3, 93
  Lawyer's role and malpractice
    86–7
  Long term 96
  Marital home 101
  Married Woman's Property Acts 62–3,
    194
  Pensions 89

Personal injury claim and disability
    benefits 89–90
  Presumption that property is marital 88
  Professional degrees and licenses 90–1
  Separate versus marital property 88–90
  Statutory factors 92–3
  Stock options 89, 92
  Timing of valuation 90
  Title theory of property 3, 87–8
  Tracing 88
  Treatment of women in 69
  Transmutation 88
  Uniform Marriage and Divorce Act 3, 92,
    93, 94
  Valuation 86
Marital Rape
  Model Penal Code provision 69
  see also Domestic Violence
Marital Torts
  Battery 66–7
  Fraud generally 67
  Insurance fraud 66
  Interspousal immunity 65–7
  Procedural Issues 65
Marriage
  Age of Majority Act of 1929 45
  Age requirements 45–6
  Aids testing for licensing 41
  Annulment 42–5
  As contract 36
  As egalitarian relationship 37
  As obligation 61
  As partnership 37, 88
  As status and as contract 35–6
  Between adoptive siblings 49–50
  Bigamy 58–60
  Capacity 47–8
  Choice of law 45, 49–52
  Common law marriage 23–7
  Conflict of laws 51
  Consanguinity and affinity 48–9
  Consent requirement for 45–6
  Contraceptives 72–5
  Dependency of wife 66, 69, 75
  Distribution of wealth 61
  Engagement period 10
  Essentials of marriage 44
  Equality in 60–2, 75
  Evidence rules 61
  Foundation of family 75
  Fundamental right 39–40
  Historical background 35–7
  Incestuous marriage 48–52

Individual rights in 75
Judeo-Christian tradition 58
Legitimacy of children 24, 166
Licensing and solemnization 40–2, 44
Marital privacy 69–72
Marriage by estoppel 29
Mental disability 40–2, 47–8
Miscegenation (prohibition against
        interracial marriage) 38–9
Name in 63–4
Personal autonomy in 37, 60–70
Polygamous marriage 59
Preservation of 75
Prisoner's marriage 46–7
Procedural marriage 27–9
Procreation as a purpose 57
Procreative rights of wife 70
Proof of marriage 24–6
Putative marriage 29–30
Restriction on re-marriage 40
Right of privacy in 72
Right to marry 39–40, 46, 49
Roman marriage 58
Same-sex marriage 20–1, 53–8
Transsexuals 52–3
Uniform Marriage and Divorce Act 3, 51
Uniform Marriage Evasion Act 51
Unity theory 37, 62, 63, 65
Validation 40–60
Void and Voidable distinction 42–3
Married Women's Property Acts
    History of 62–3, 194
Mediation and Alternative Dispute
        Settlement Methods
    Use in negotiations for divorce settlements
        3, 4, 125–7, 130
Model Acts
    Act to Free Children for Permanent
        Placement 5, 140, 143–4, 177
    Mandatory Child Abuse Reporting Act 4,
        140–2, 177
    Subsidized Adoption Act 5, 140, 143–4
Mormons
    see Bigamy
Multiethnic Placement Act of 1994
    see under Adoption

Names
    Children's 65
    Married women 7, 64–5
No-fault Divorce
    California's first act 2, 80
    Criticism of 83–6

Future of 128
Historical background 78–80
Incompatibility 83
Impact on women 85
Irretrievable breakdown 83
Statistics on 84

Orphan Trains
    History of 131

Parens Patriae
    see under Child Abuse and Neglect
Polygamy
    Definition and practice of 59
Postnuptial Agreements
    Generally 65–7
Prenuptial Agreements
    Generally 30–4
    ALI requirements 32
    Concerning raising and educating children
        34
    Contractual aspects 31
    Duty to disclose assets 31–2
    Effect on divorce 30
    Entering into 10, 30–4
    Evaluation of fairness, time of 31
    Fair process 31
    Feminist approach 33
    Formalities 31
    History of 30
    Inheritance and 30
    Non-financial provisions 33–4
    Presumption of non-disclosure 32
    Regulation of personal relations 33–4
    Religious agreements 34
    Specific performance 34
    Unconscionability 32–3
    Timing of signing 31
    Uniform Pre-Marital Act 32–3
    Validity 31–4
Presumptions
    In support of marriage 27
    Validity of later marriage 27
Pre-trial conference
    As part of divorce procedure 127
Prison Inmates
    Right to marry 46–7
Professional Degree and License
    see under Marital Property
Property Settlement and Custody Agreement
    Independent status 98
    Merged into divorce decree 98
    Remedies for enforcement 98

Punishment
    see Corporal Punishment
Putative Father Registry
    see Adoption, Fathers
Putative Father Rights
    Generally 153–4
Putative Marriage
    see under Marriage

Registered Domestic Partnership
    see under Domestic Partnership
Rehabilitative Alimony
    see under Alimony
Reimbursement Alimony
    see under Alimony
Religious Rights
    Child labor laws 131
    Priest penance exception to reporting child
        abuse 142–3
    Roman Catholic Church and sexual
        abuse 142
Relocation of Children
    see under Child Custody
Reproductive Technologies
    Adoption 182
    Assisted Reproduction 219–22
    Impact on family law 7
    In defining male and female 8
    Surrogacy 161–7
    Uniform Status of Children of Assisted
        Conception Act 162
Restraining Orders
    see under Spousal Abuse

Same-Sex Couples
    As adoptive parents 167
    Cohabitation agreements 11–17
    Custody and visitation disputes 13, 16–17
    Domestic Partnership 17–23
    Marriage and 53–8
Same-Sex Marriage
    Generally 53–8
    Baehr v. Lewin 20, 53–5
    Baker v. State of Vermont 20, 55–6
    Litigation involving state and federal
        constitutional law 21, 57
    Validity of 53–8
Sodomy

Constitutional right to practice 73–5
Specific Performance
    As a remedy in family law matters 98
Spousal Abuse
    As physical or mental cruelty in divorce
        48, 68
    Battered Woman Syndrome 67–9
    Defense to criminal charge 69
    Rape by husband 68–9
    Restraining orders 69
    Violence Against Women Act 67
Spousal Support
    see Alimony
Stalking
    see under Domestic Violence
Surrogacy
    Generally 161–7
    Adoption 182
    Feminist views 165
    In re Baby M 161, 165–7
    Uniform Status of Children of Assisted
        Conception Act 162

Termination of Parental Rights
    Court fees, inability to pay 39
    Evidentiary standard 148
    Federally mandated termination 146
    Hearings 147
    Model Act to Free Children for Permanent
        Placement 5, 143–4, 177
    Poverty as factor 147
    Proof standard 147
    Social class considerations 147
Transsexualism
    see under Marriage

Uniform Acts
    Parental Kidnapping Prevention Act
        258
    Uniform Child Custody Jurisdiction Act
        230
    Uniform Child Custody Jurisdiction and
        Enforcement Act 240
    Uniform Marriage and Divorce Act 185
    Uniform Parentage Act 204
    Uniform Pre-Marital Agreement Act 201
    Uniform Putative and Unknown Fathers
        Act 225